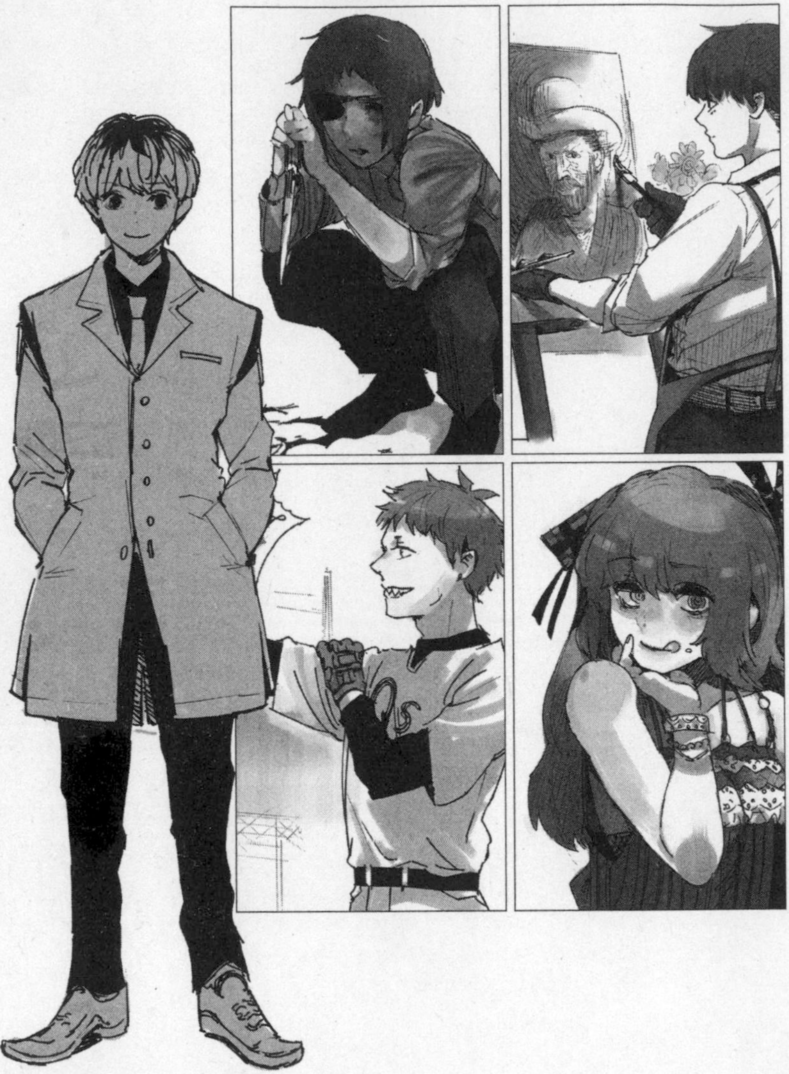

TOKYO GHOUL:re 5
東京喰種

SUI ISHIDA

TOKYO GHOUL:re 5
東 京 喰 種

CONTENTS

- 42: Retort   5
- 43: Region   23
- 44: #   41
- 45: Plant   61
- 46: °C   81
- 47: Rematch   99
- 48: N.T.   117
- 49: Repulse   135
- 50: Hand   153
- 51: Resolution   171
- 52: Eve   189

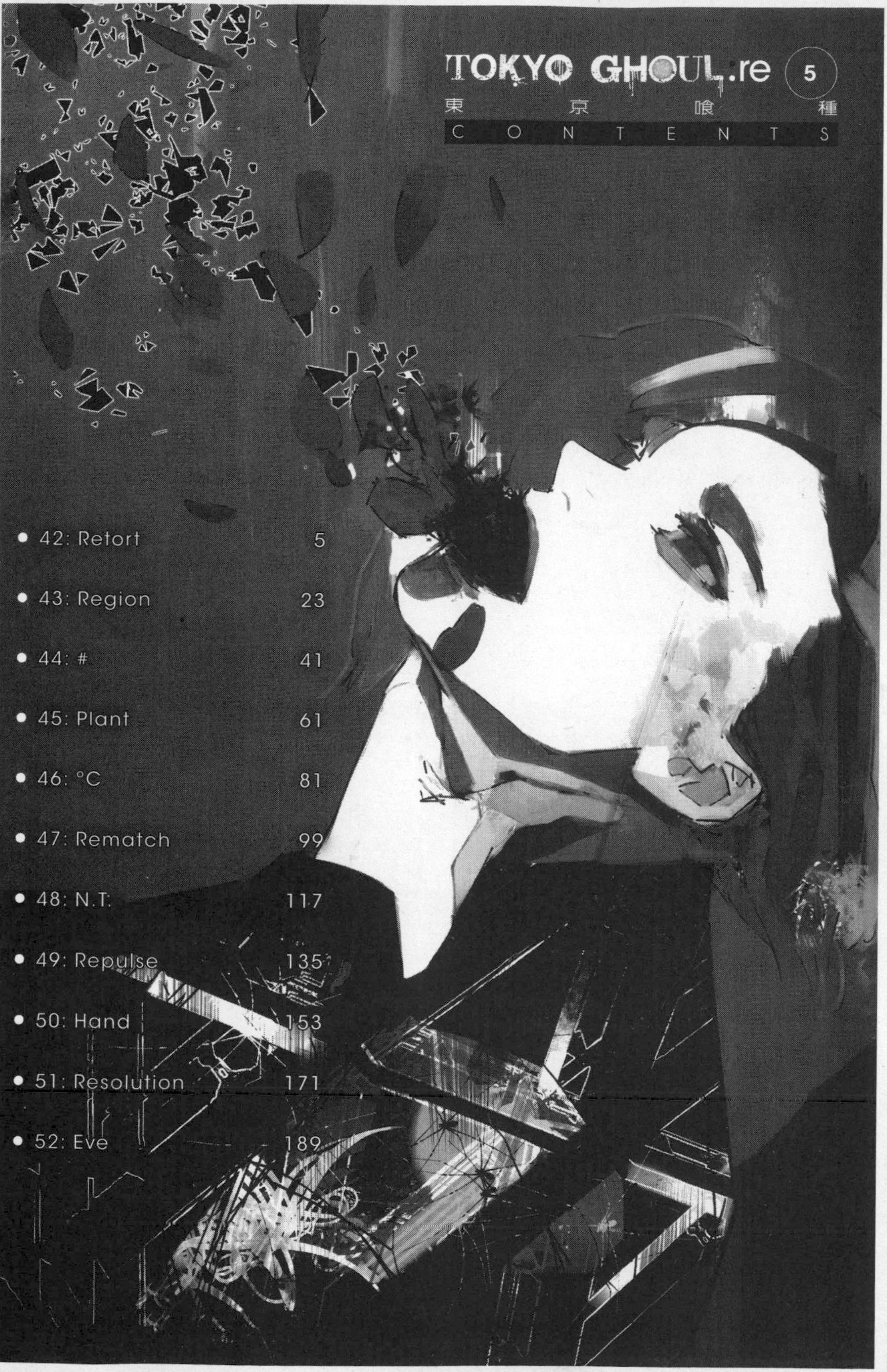

CCG Ghoul Investigators

Tokyo Ghoul :re

The CCG is the only organization in the world that investigates and solves Ghoul-related crimes. Founded by the Washu family, the CCG developed and evolved Quinques, a type of weapon derived from Ghouls' Kagune. Quinx, an advanced, next-generation technology in which humans are implanted with Quinques, is currently under development.

Mado Squad

Qs (Quinx)
● Investigators implanted with Quinque. They all live together
● in a house called the **Chateau** with Investigator Sasaki.

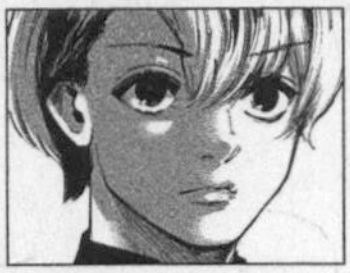

● Haise Sasaki
佐々木琲世
Rank 1 Investigator
Mentor to the Quinx Squad. Despite being half-Ghoul, he is passionate about guiding the Quinxes. He has no memory of his past. And whose voice sometimes echoes in his head...?!

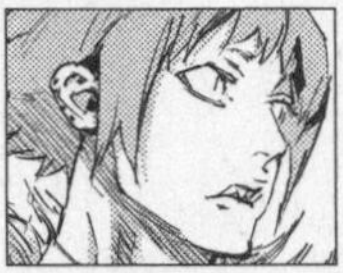

● Ginshi Shirazu
不知吟士
Rank 3 Investigator
Current Quinx squad leader. He agreed to the Quinx procedure for mainly financial reasons. Despite his thuggish appearance, he has a very caring side. Struggling to master his Quinque.

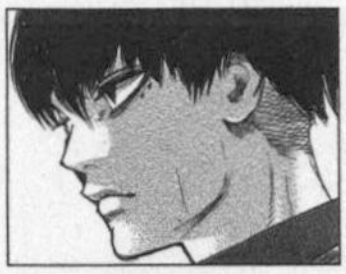

● Kuki Urie
瓜江久生
Rank 2 Investigator
Former Quinx squad leader. The squad's most talented fighter. His father, a special investigator, was killed by a Ghoul. Urie seeks to avenge his death. Has a strong sense of rivalry towards Takeomi Kuroiwa.

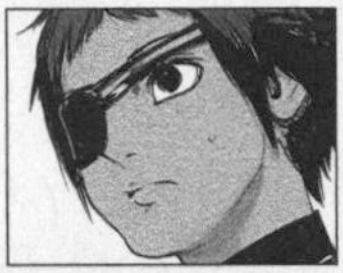

● Toru Mutsuki
六月 透
Rank 3 Investigator
He decided to become a Ghoul investigator after his parents were killed by a Ghoul. Assigned female at birth, he decided to transition after undergoing the Quinx procedure. Promoted two ranks for his achievements during Operation Auction Sweep.

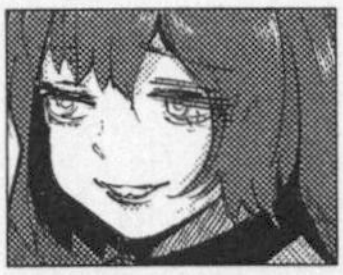

● Saiko Yonebayashi
米林才子
Rank 3 Investigator
Has little aptitude as an investigator, but was by far the most suitable candidate for the Quinx procedure. Very bad with time management. A sucker for games and snacks. Self-proclaimed "fairy of the Chateau."

S1 Squad

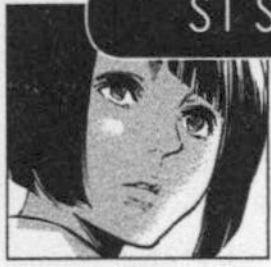

● Kori Ui
宇井 郡
Senior Investigator
Formerly assigned to the Arima Squad. Became a Special Investigator at a young age. Has a stubborn side. Considers Haise to be a threat.

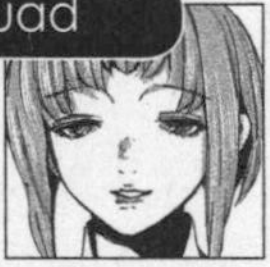

● Hairu Ihei
伊丙 入
Senior Investigator
A young investigator from the Hakubi Garden who ruthlessly hunts Ghouls. Once worked alongside Arima.

Shimoguchi Squad

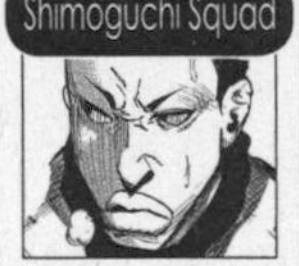

● Nobu Shimoguchi
下口 房
Senior Investigator
Lost many men to the Aogiri Tree during the Torso investigation. Now commands two investigators who lost their squad leader. Has a foul mouth.

Fura Squad

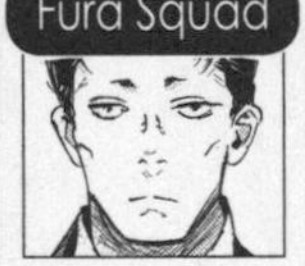

● Taishi Fura
富良太志
Senior Investigator
A veteran investigator who has known Ui for a long time. He is disappointed with the treatment of smokers. A loving husband.

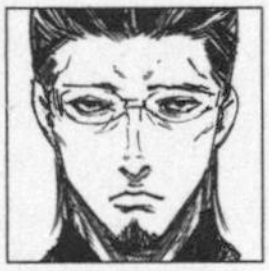

● Matsuri Washu
和修 政
Senior Investigator
Yoshitoki's son. A Washu supremacist who takes pride in his lineage. Is skeptical of Quinxes. Brought down the Rosewald family in Germany.

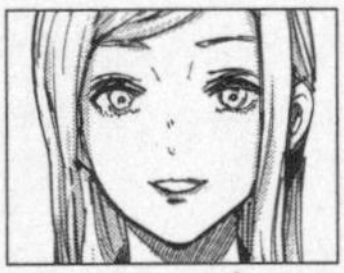

● Akira Mado
真戸 暁
Senior Investigator
Mentor to Haise. Takes after her father and is determined to eradicate Ghouls. She is investigating the Aogiri Tree and is concerned about Fueguchi.

Kijima Squad

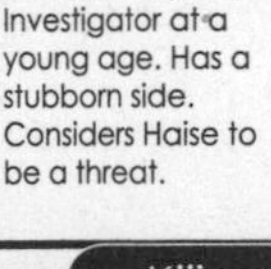

● Shiki Kijima
キジマ 式
Assistant Special Investigator
He tracks down Ghouls using unique and brutal methods.

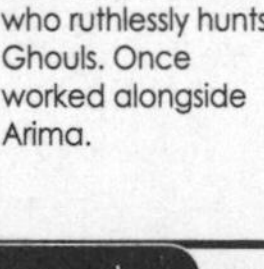

● Furuta
旧多
Rank 1 Investigator
Shiki Kijima's subordinate.

Ito Squad

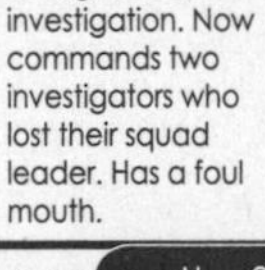

● Kuramoto Ito
伊東倉元
Senior Investigator
Took over as leader of Hirako Squad. In high spirits, but feeling some pressure.

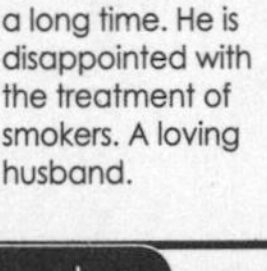

● Takeomi Kuroiwa
黒磐武臣
Rank 1 Investigator
Has a strong sense of justice and has restrained Ghouls with his bare hands.

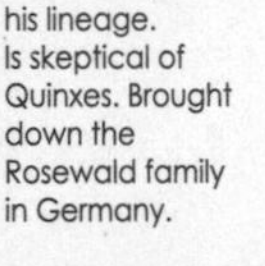

● Kisho Arima
有馬貴将
Special Investigator
An undefeated investigator respected by many at the CCG.

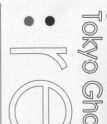

Tokyo Ghoul :re

T ● K Y ● G H ● U L

Tokyo Ghoul :re ● Ghouls

They appear human, but have a unique predation organ called Kagune and can only survive by feeding on human flesh. They are the nemesis of humanity. Besides human flesh, the only other thing they can ingest is coffee. Ghouls can only be wounded by Kagune or a Quinque made from a Kagune. One of the most prominent Ghoul factions is the Aogiri Tree, a hostile organization that is increasing its strength.

Rosewald Family Faction

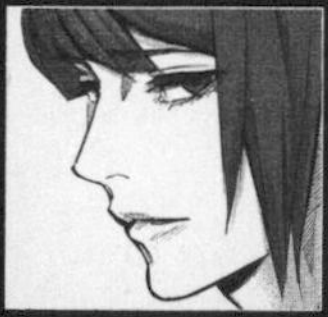

● Shu Tsukiyama
月山 習

A Ghoul who has an interest in the gourmet. He has fed poorly since the disappearance of Ken Kaneki, but when he sees Kaneki's shadow in Haise, he begins to take action.

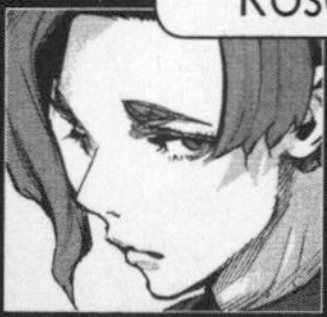

● Kanae von Rosewald
カナエ＝フォン・ロゼヴァルト

Tsukiyama family retainer. Procures gourmet meals for Shu Tsukiyama.

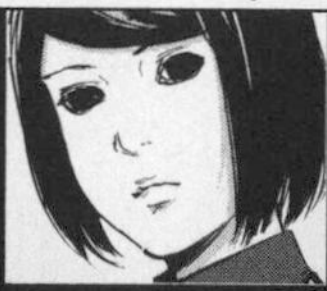

● Matsumae
松前

A fiercly loyal Tsukiyama family retainer. Uses a detachable Kagune.

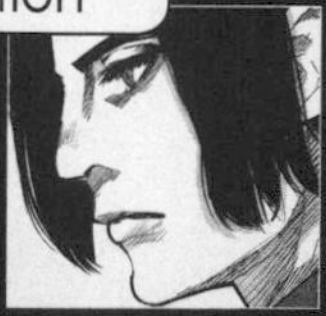

● Milo
マイロ

Tsukiyama family retainer.

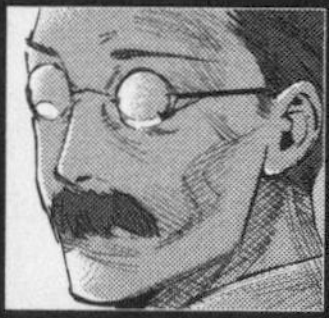

● Mirumo Tsukiyama
月山観母

Shu's father and head of the Tsukiyama family.

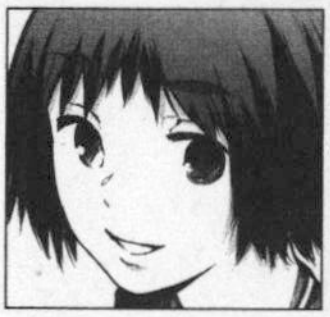

● Chie Hori
掘 ちえ

She is a freelance photographer who sells information. She has interactions with the Tsukiyama family and provides Kanae with useful information.

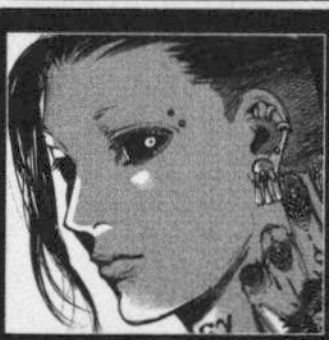

● Uta
ウタ

Owner of HySy Art Mask Studio. Making masks for Haise's new operation.

Aogiri Tree

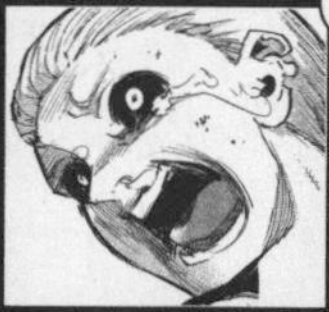

● Naki
ナキ

Member of the Aogiri Tree. Rate S, but frequently flips out of control. Grieving the deaths of Gaki and Guge in Operation Auction Sweep.

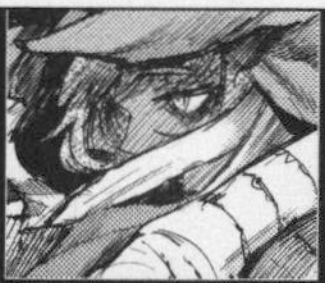

● Eto
エト

Member of the Aogiri Tree.

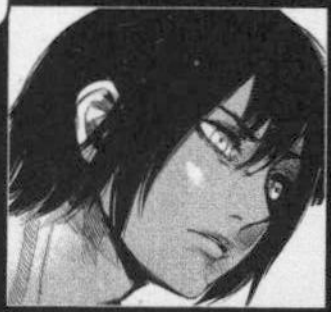

● Ayato
アヤト

A leading member of the Aogiri Tree. Rate SS Ghoul the Rabbit.

Café:re

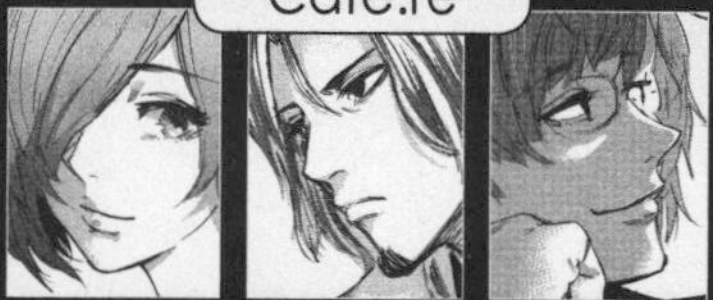

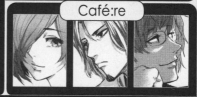

So far in :re

T ● K Y ● G H ● U L

The Quinx Project was implemented to develop investigators to surpass Kisho Arima in order to combat the growing strength of Ghoul organizations. Some in the CCG view these unusual investigators who fight with Ghoul abilities with suspicion. However, the four Qs investigators and their mentor Haise Sasaki have all received promotions for their achievements during Operation Auction Sweep. They are now working the Rosé case. But as the case progresses, the voice in Haise's head rings louder. Kanae incessantly pursues Haise and the Qs for his master Shu, but the focus of the investigation is rapidly narrowing in on the Tsukiyama family!

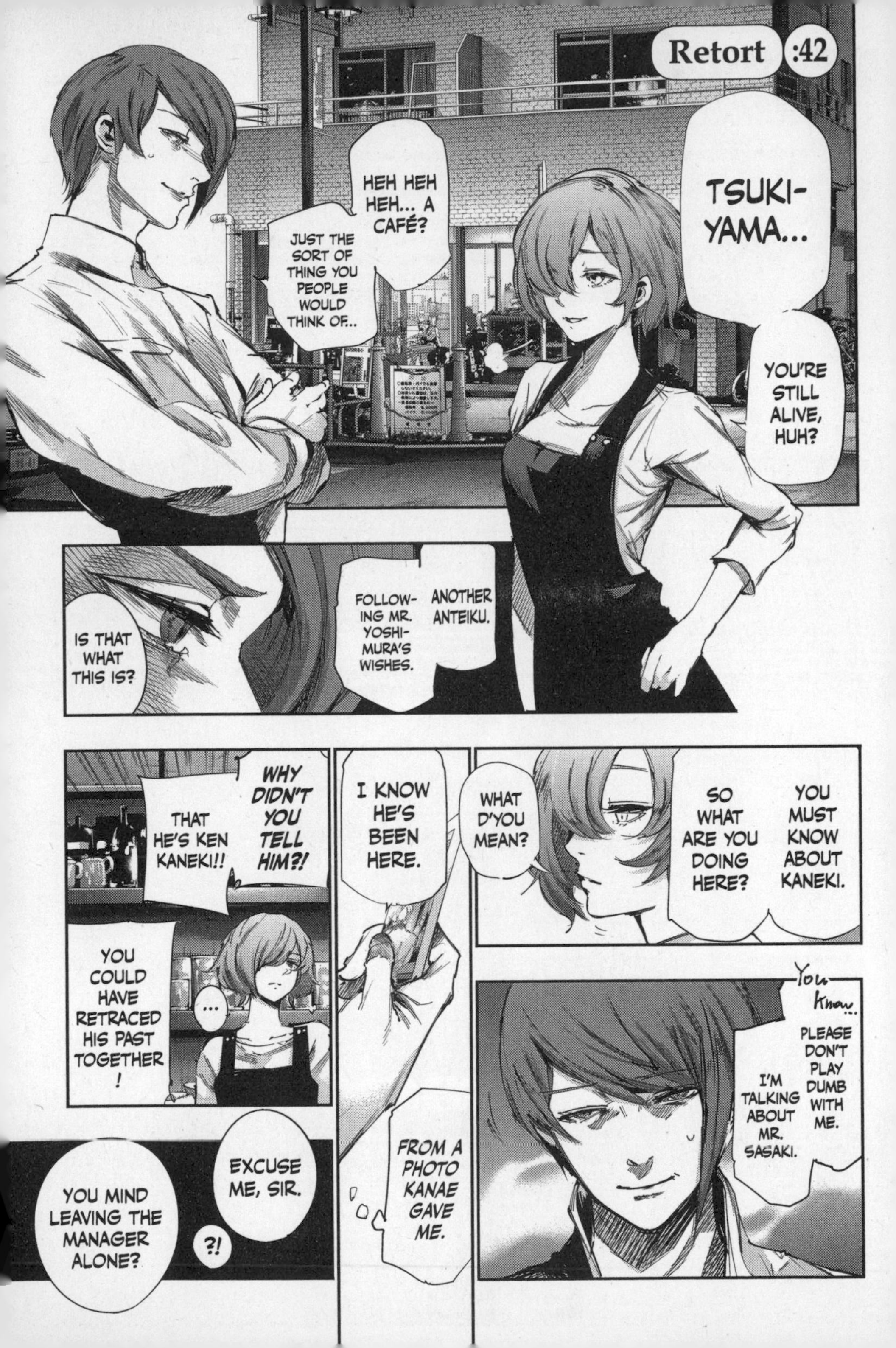
Retort :42
TSUKI-YAMA...
YOU'RE STILL ALIVE, HUH?
HEH HEH HEH... A CAFÉ?
JUST THE SORT OF THING YOU PEOPLE WOULD THINK OF...
ANOTHER ANTEIKU.
FOLLOW-ING MR. YOSHI-MURA'S WISHES.
IS THAT WHAT THIS IS?
YOU MUST KNOW ABOUT KANEKI.
SO WHAT ARE YOU DOING HERE?
WHAT D'YOU MEAN?
You know...
PLEASE DON'T PLAY DUMB WITH ME.
I'M TALKING ABOUT MR. SASAKI.
I KNOW HE'S BEEN HERE.
FROM A PHOTO KANAE GAVE ME.
WHY DIDN'T YOU TELL HIM?!
THAT HE'S KEN KANEKI!!
YOU COULD HAVE RETRACED HIS PAST TOGETHER!
...
EXCUSE ME, SIR.
?!
YOU MIND LEAVING THE MANAGER ALONE?

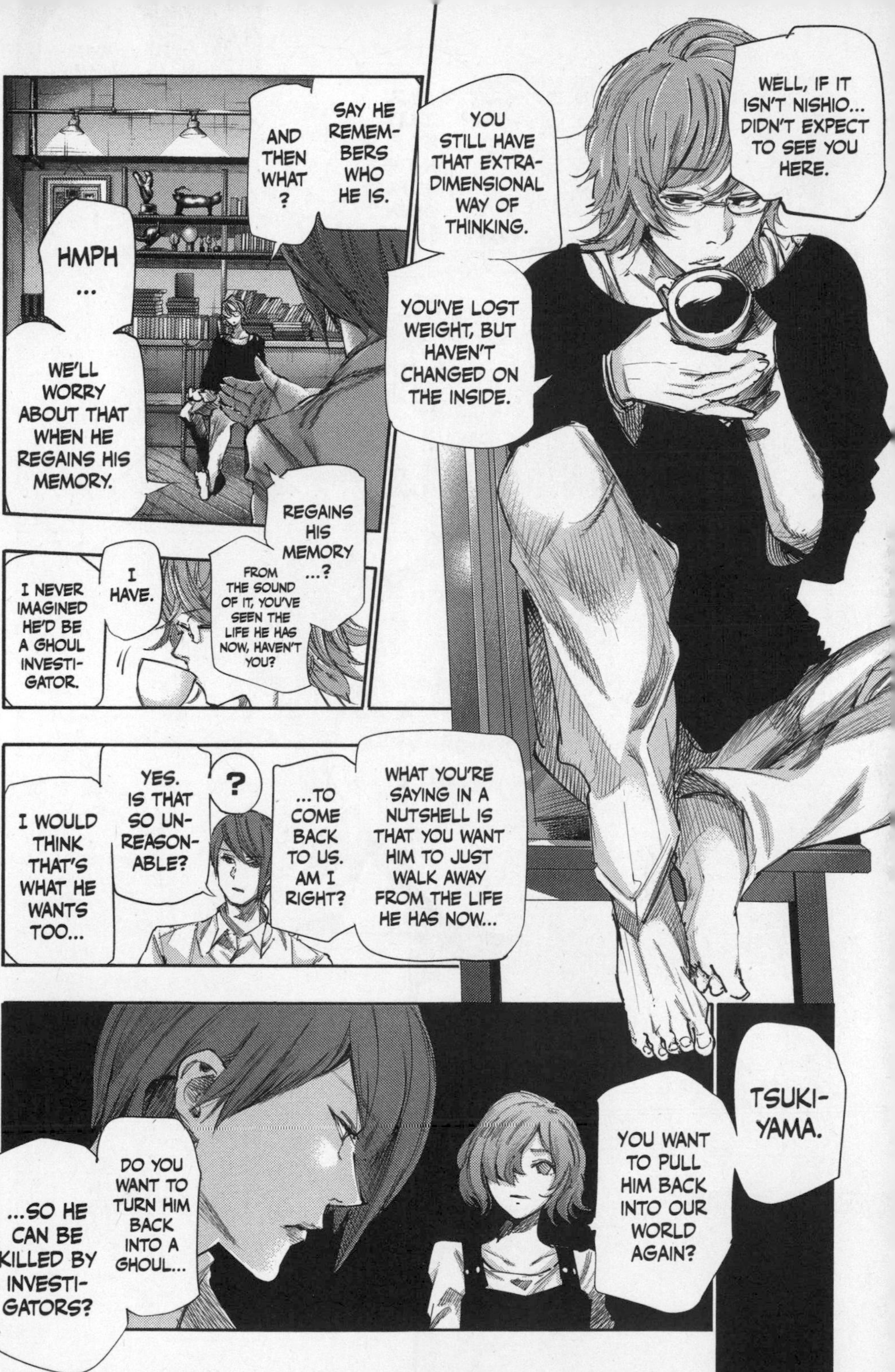
WELL, IF IT ISN'T NISHIO... DIDN'T EXPECT TO SEE YOU HERE.
YOU STILL HAVE THAT EXTRA-DIMENSIONAL WAY OF THINKING.
YOU'VE LOST WEIGHT, BUT HAVEN'T CHANGED ON THE INSIDE.
SAY HE REMEMBERS WHO HE IS.
AND THEN WHAT?
HMPH...
WE'LL WORRY ABOUT THAT WHEN HE REGAINS HIS MEMORY.
REGAINS HIS MEMORY...?
FROM THE SOUND OF IT, YOU'VE SEEN THE LIFE HE HAS NOW, HAVEN'T YOU?
I HAVE.
I NEVER IMAGINED HE'D BE A GHOUL INVESTIGATOR.
WHAT YOU'RE SAYING IN A NUTSHELL IS THAT YOU WANT HIM TO JUST WALK AWAY FROM THE LIFE HE HAS NOW...
...TO COME BACK TO US. AM I RIGHT?
?
YES. IS THAT SO UNREASONABLE?
I WOULD THINK THAT'S WHAT HE WANTS TOO...
TSUKIYAMA.
YOU WANT TO PULL HIM BACK INTO OUR WORLD AGAIN?
DO YOU WANT TO TURN HIM BACK INTO A GHOUL...
...SO HE CAN BE KILLED BY INVESTIGATORS?

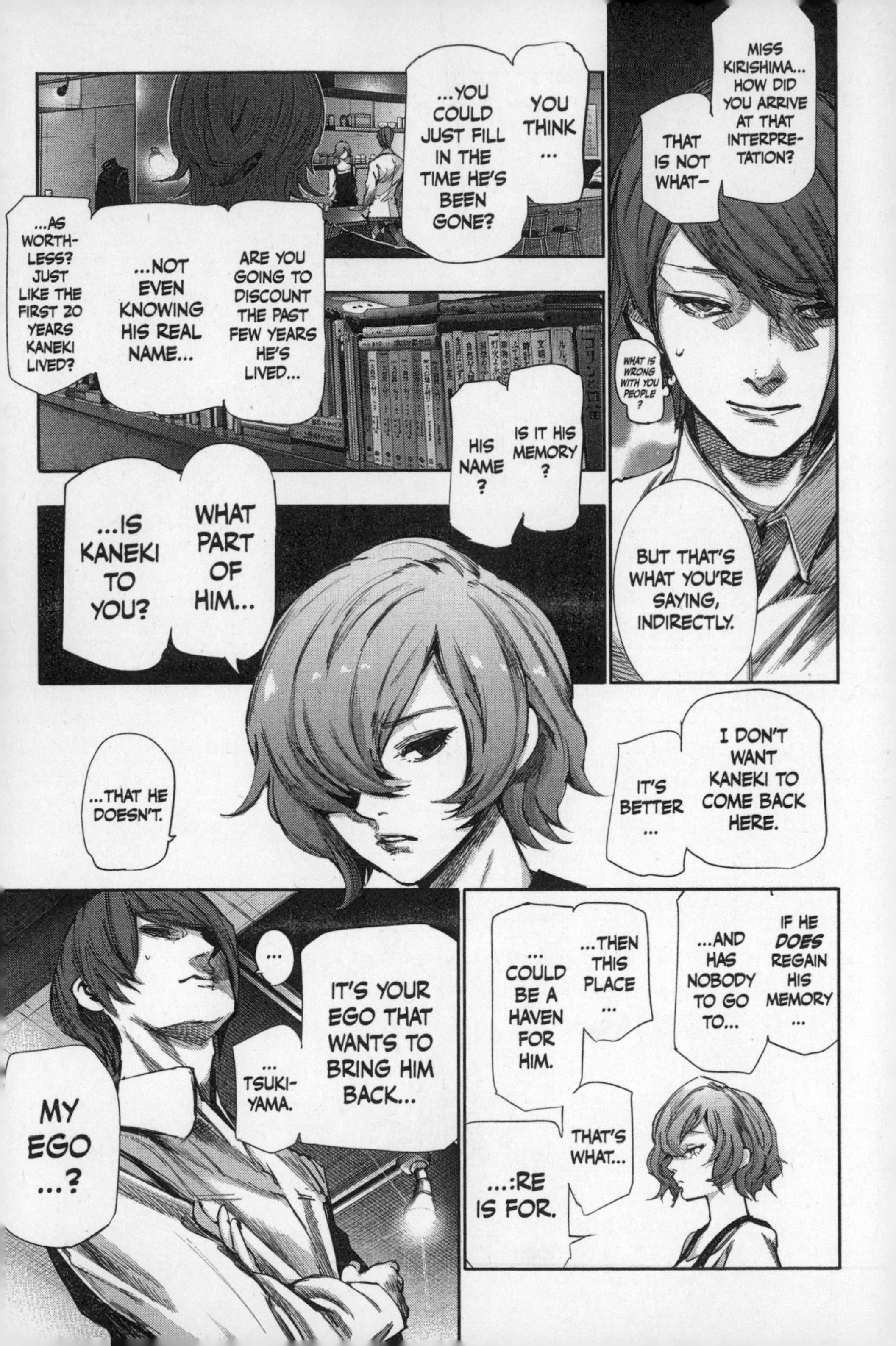
MISS KIRISHIMA... HOW DID YOU ARRIVE AT THAT INTERPRETATION?
THAT IS NOT WHAT—
WHAT IS WRONG WITH YOU PEOPLE?
BUT THAT'S WHAT YOU'RE SAYING, INDIRECTLY.
YOU THINK...
...YOU COULD JUST FILL IN THE TIME HE'S BEEN GONE?
ARE YOU GOING TO DISCOUNT THE PAST FEW YEARS HE'S LIVED...
...NOT EVEN KNOWING HIS REAL NAME...
...AS WORTHLESS? JUST LIKE THE FIRST 20 YEARS KANEKI LIVED?
IS IT HIS MEMORY?
HIS NAME?
WHAT PART OF HIM...
...IS KANEKI TO YOU?
I DON'T WANT KANEKI TO COME BACK HERE.
IT'S BETTER...
...THAT HE DOESN'T.
IF HE *DOES* REGAIN HIS MEMORY...
...AND HAS NOBODY TO GO TO...
...THEN THIS PLACE...
...COULD BE A HAVEN FOR HIM.
THAT'S WHAT...
...:RE IS FOR.
...
IT'S YOUR EGO THAT WANTS TO BRING HIM BACK...
...TSUKIYAMA.
MY EGO...?

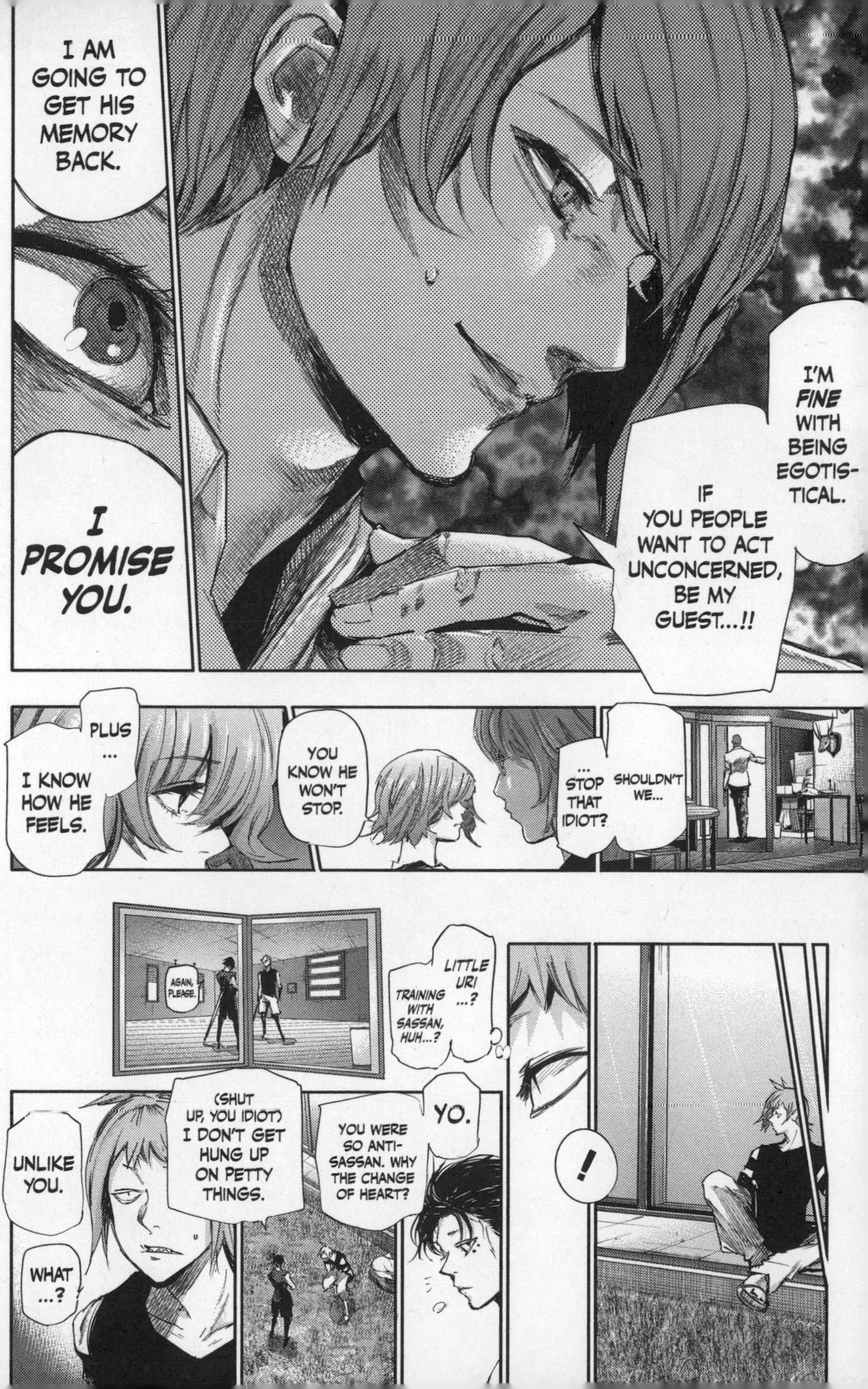
I'M *FINE* WITH BEING EGOTISTICAL.
IF YOU PEOPLE WANT TO ACT UNCONCERNED, BE MY GUEST...!!
I AM GOING TO GET HIS MEMORY BACK.
I PROMISE YOU.
SHOULDN'T WE...
...STOP THAT IDIOT?
YOU KNOW HE WON'T STOP.
PLUS...
I KNOW HOW HE FEELS.
!
LITTLE URI ...?
TRAINING WITH SASSAN, HUH...?
AGAIN, PLEASE.
YO.
YOU WERE SO ANTI-SASSAN. WHY THE CHANGE OF HEART?
(SHUT UP, YOU IDIOT) I DON'T GET HUNG UP ON PETTY THINGS.
UNLIKE YOU.
WHAT ...?

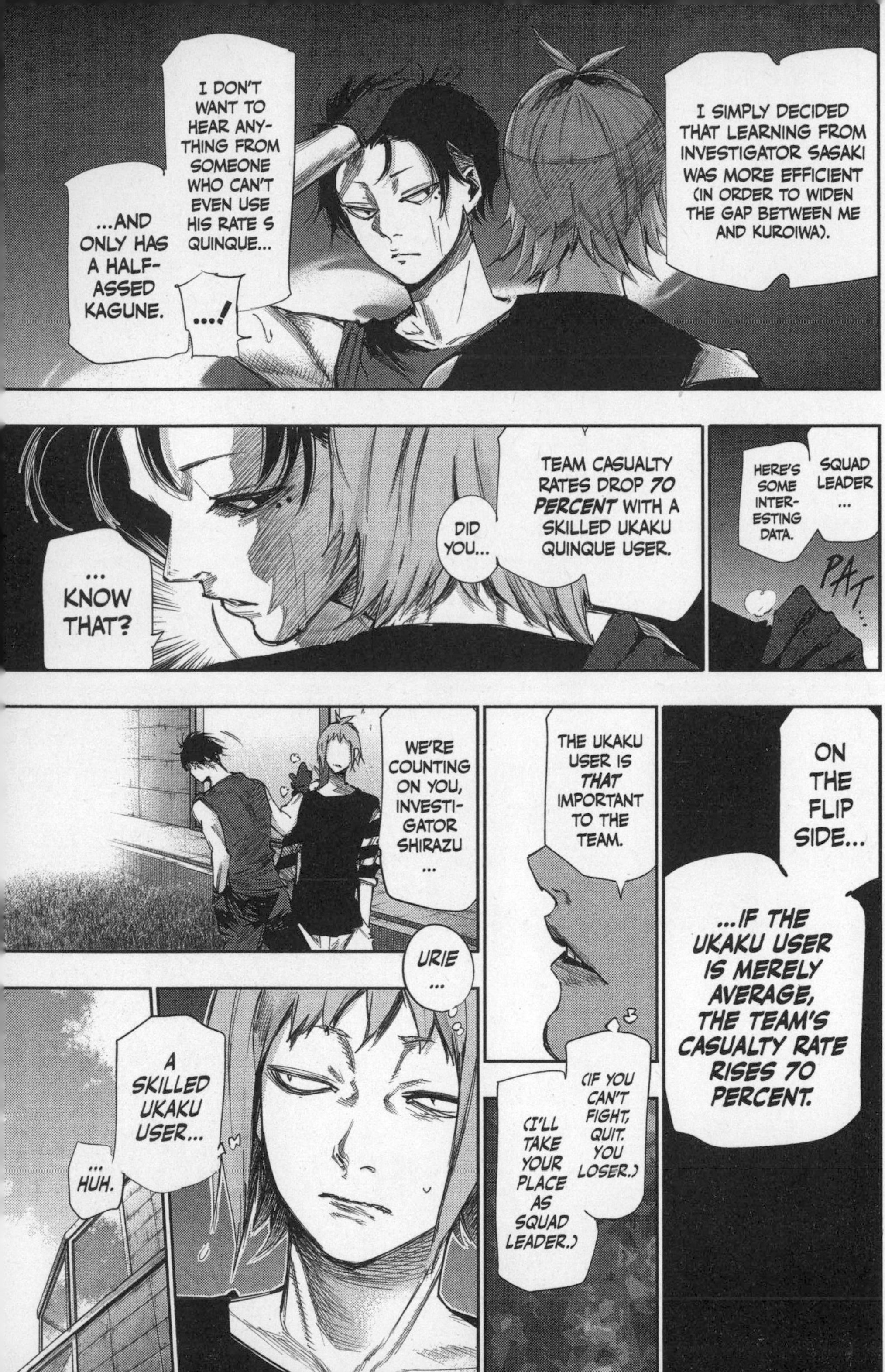
I SIMPLY DECIDED THAT LEARNING FROM INVESTIGATOR SASAKI WAS MORE EFFICIENT (IN ORDER TO WIDEN THE GAP BETWEEN ME AND KUROIWA).
I DON'T WANT TO HEAR ANY-THING FROM SOMEONE WHO CAN'T EVEN USE HIS RATE S QUINQUE...
...AND ONLY HAS A HALF-ASSED KAGUNE.
...!
SQUAD LEADER...
HERE'S SOME INTER-ESTING DATA.
PAT...
TEAM CASUALTY RATES DROP 70 PERCENT WITH A SKILLED UKAKU QUINQUE USER.
DID YOU...
...KNOW THAT?
ON THE FLIP SIDE...
...IF THE UKAKU USER IS MERELY AVERAGE, THE TEAM'S CASUALTY RATE RISES 70 PERCENT.
THE UKAKU USER IS THAT IMPORTANT TO THE TEAM.
(IF YOU CAN'T FIGHT, QUIT. YOU LOSER.)
(I'LL TAKE YOUR PLACE AS SQUAD LEADER.)
WE'RE COUNTING ON YOU, INVESTI-GATOR SHIRAZU...
URIE...
A SKILLED UKAKU USER...
...HUH.

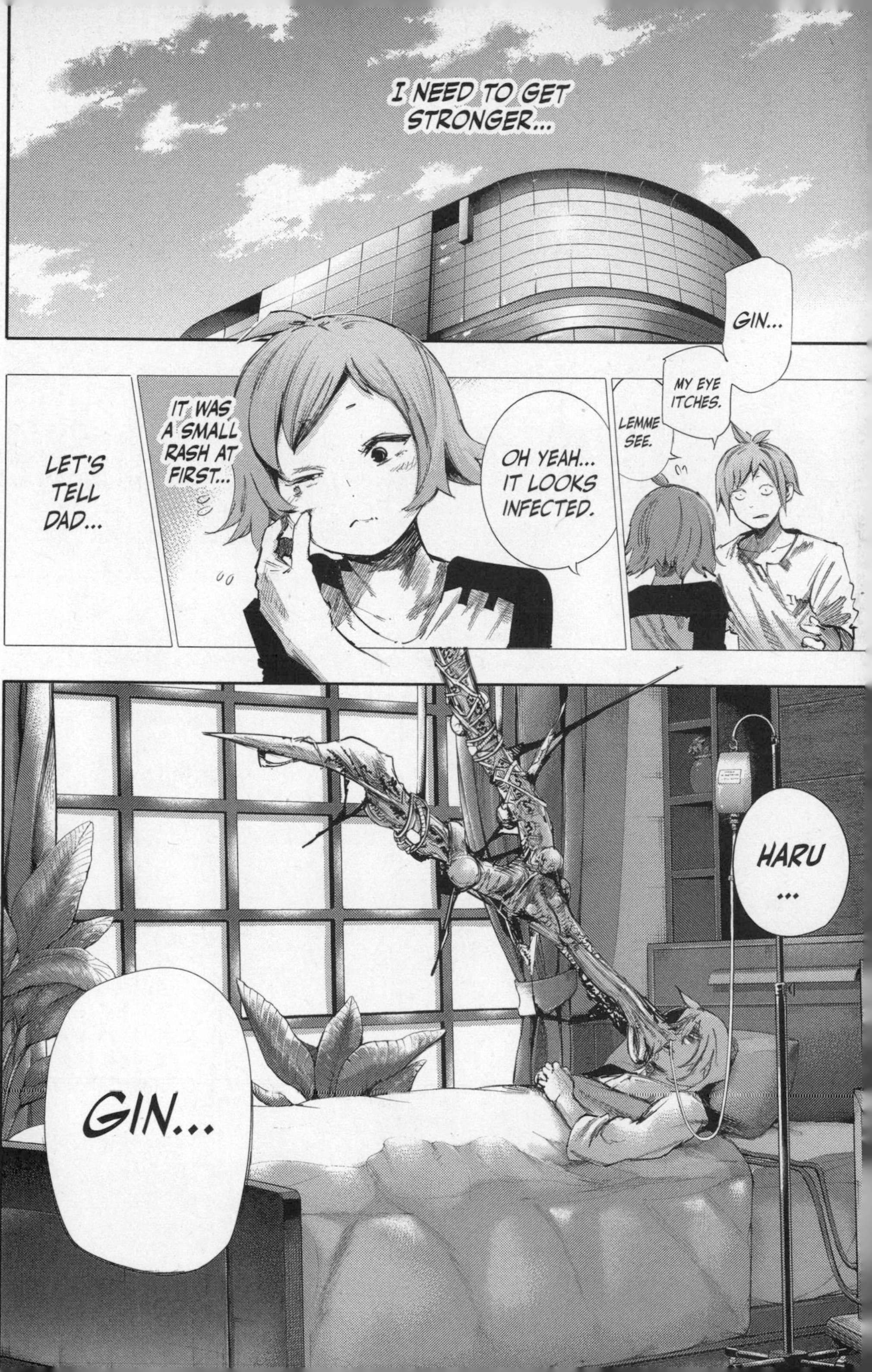

I NEED TO GET STRONGER...
GIN...
MY EYE ITCHES.
LEMME SEE.
OH YEAH... IT LOOKS INFECTED.
IT WAS A SMALL RASH AT FIRST...
LET'S TELL DAD...
HARU...
GIN...

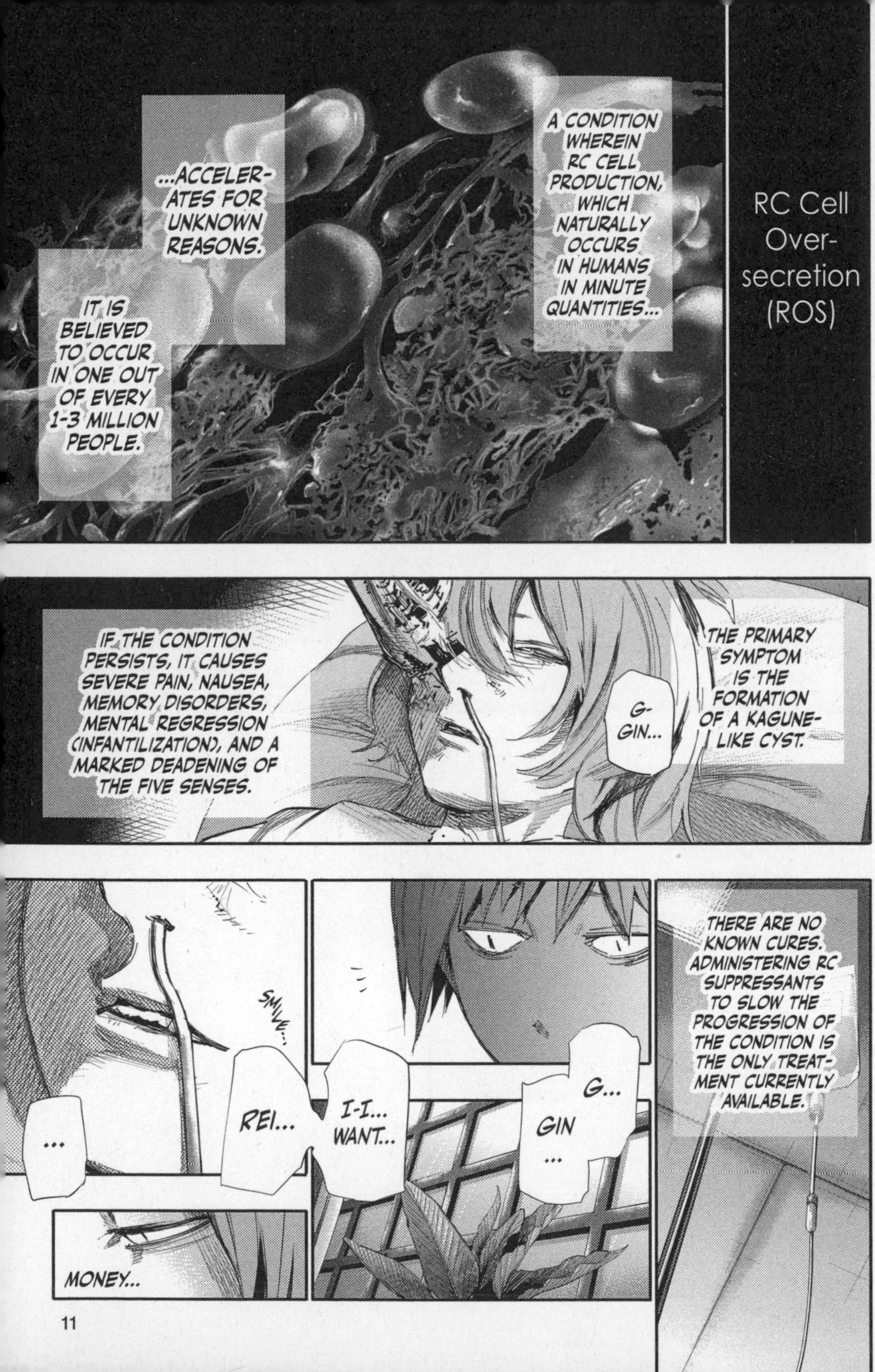
RC Cell Over-secretion (ROS)
A CONDITION WHEREIN RC CELL PRODUCTION, WHICH NATURALLY OCCURS IN HUMANS IN MINUTE QUANTITIES...
...ACCELERATES FOR UNKNOWN REASONS.
IT IS BELIEVED TO OCCUR IN ONE OUT OF EVERY 1-3 MILLION PEOPLE.
THE PRIMARY SYMPTOM IS THE FORMATION OF A KAGUNE-LIKE CYST.
G-GIN...
IF THE CONDITION PERSISTS, IT CAUSES SEVERE PAIN, NAUSEA, MEMORY DISORDERS, MENTAL REGRESSION (INFANTILIZATION), AND A MARKED DEADENING OF THE FIVE SENSES.
THERE ARE NO KNOWN CURES. ADMINISTERING RC SUPPRESSANTS TO SLOW THE PROGRESSION OF THE CONDITION IS THE ONLY TREATMENT CURRENTLY AVAILABLE.
G... GIN ...
SMILE...
I-I... WANT...
REI...
...
MONEY...

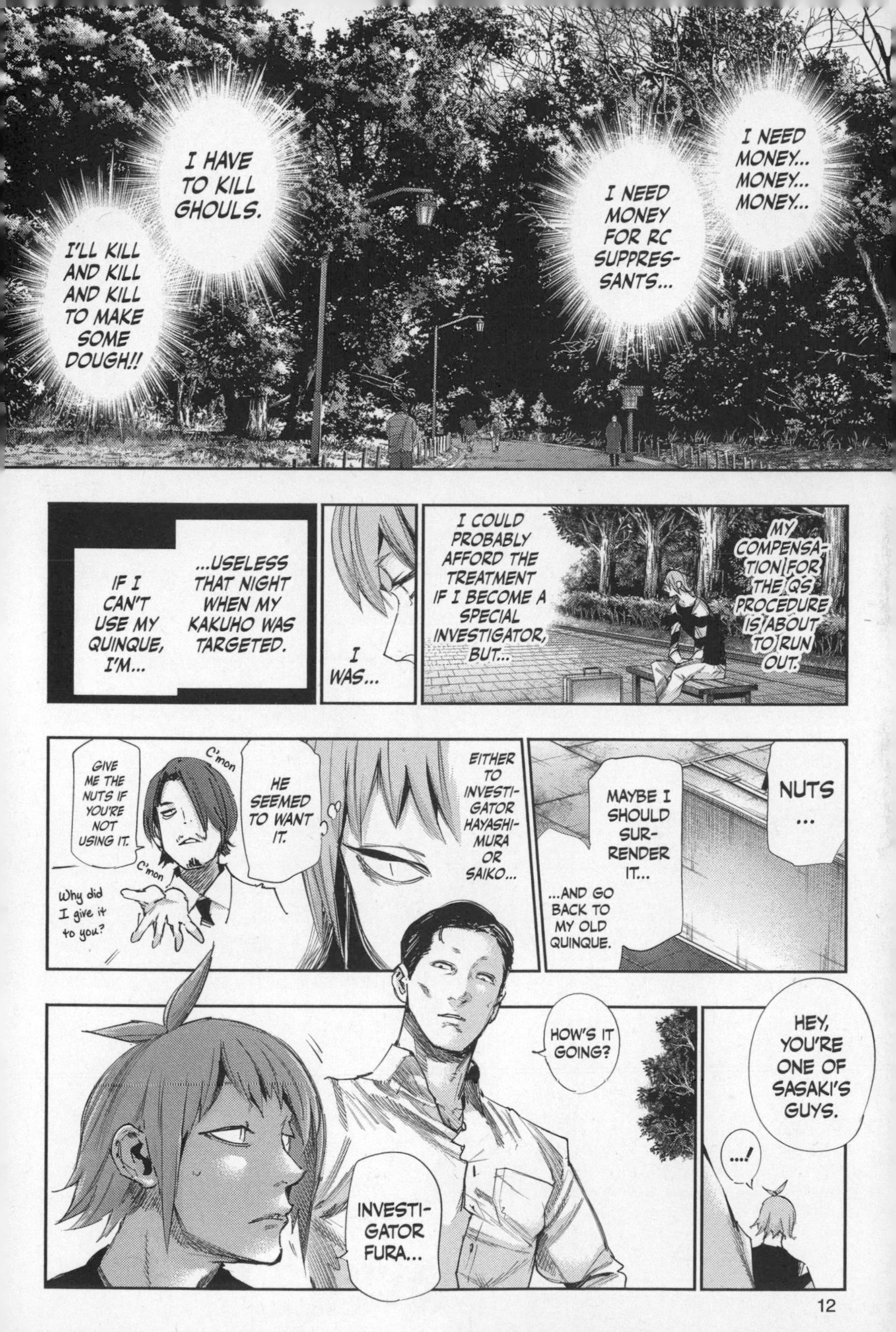
I NEED MONEY... MONEY... MONEY...
I NEED MONEY FOR RC SUPPRESSANTS...
I HAVE TO KILL GHOULS.
I'LL KILL AND KILL AND KILL TO MAKE SOME DOUGH!!
MY COMPENSATION FOR THE QS PROCEDURE IS ABOUT TO RUN OUT.
I COULD PROBABLY AFFORD THE TREATMENT IF I BECOME A SPECIAL INVESTIGATOR, BUT...
I WAS...
...USELESS THAT NIGHT WHEN MY KAKUHO WAS TARGETED.
IF I CAN'T USE MY QUINQUE, I'M...
NUTS ...
MAYBE I SHOULD SURRENDER IT...
...AND GO BACK TO MY OLD QUINQUE.
EITHER TO INVESTIGATOR HAYASHIMURA OR SAIKO...
HE SEEMED TO WANT IT.
C'mon
GIVE ME THE NUTS IF YOU'RE NOT USING IT.
C'mon
Why did I give it to you?
HEY, YOU'RE ONE OF SASAKI'S GUYS.
...!
HOW'S IT GOING?
INVESTIGATOR FURA...

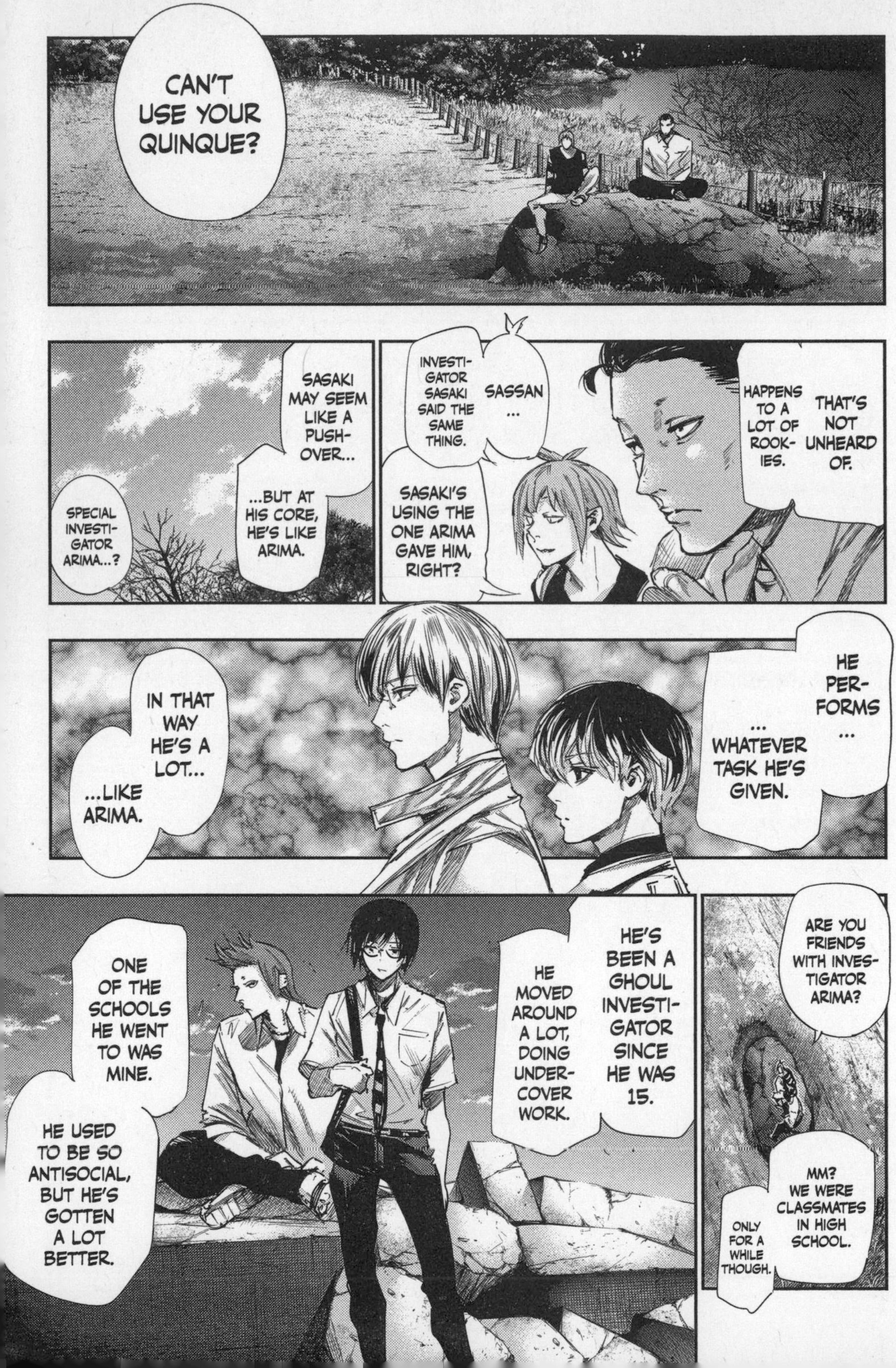
CAN'T USE YOUR QUINQUE?
THAT'S NOT UNHEARD OF.
HAPPENS TO A LOT OF ROOKIES.
SASSAN ...
INVESTIGATOR SASAKI SAID THE SAME THING.
SASAKI'S USING THE ONE ARIMA GAVE HIM, RIGHT?
SASAKI MAY SEEM LIKE A PUSHOVER...
...BUT AT HIS CORE, HE'S LIKE ARIMA.
SPECIAL INVESTIGATOR ARIMA...?
HE PERFORMS ...
... WHATEVER TASK HE'S GIVEN.
IN THAT WAY HE'S A LOT...
...LIKE ARIMA.
ARE YOU FRIENDS WITH INVESTIGATOR ARIMA?
MM? WE WERE CLASSMATES IN HIGH SCHOOL.
ONLY FOR A WHILE THOUGH.
HE'S BEEN A GHOUL INVESTIGATOR SINCE HE WAS 15.
HE MOVED AROUND A LOT, DOING UNDERCOVER WORK.
ONE OF THE SCHOOLS HE WENT TO WAS MINE.
HE USED TO BE SO ANTISOCIAL, BUT HE'S GOTTEN A LOT BETTER.

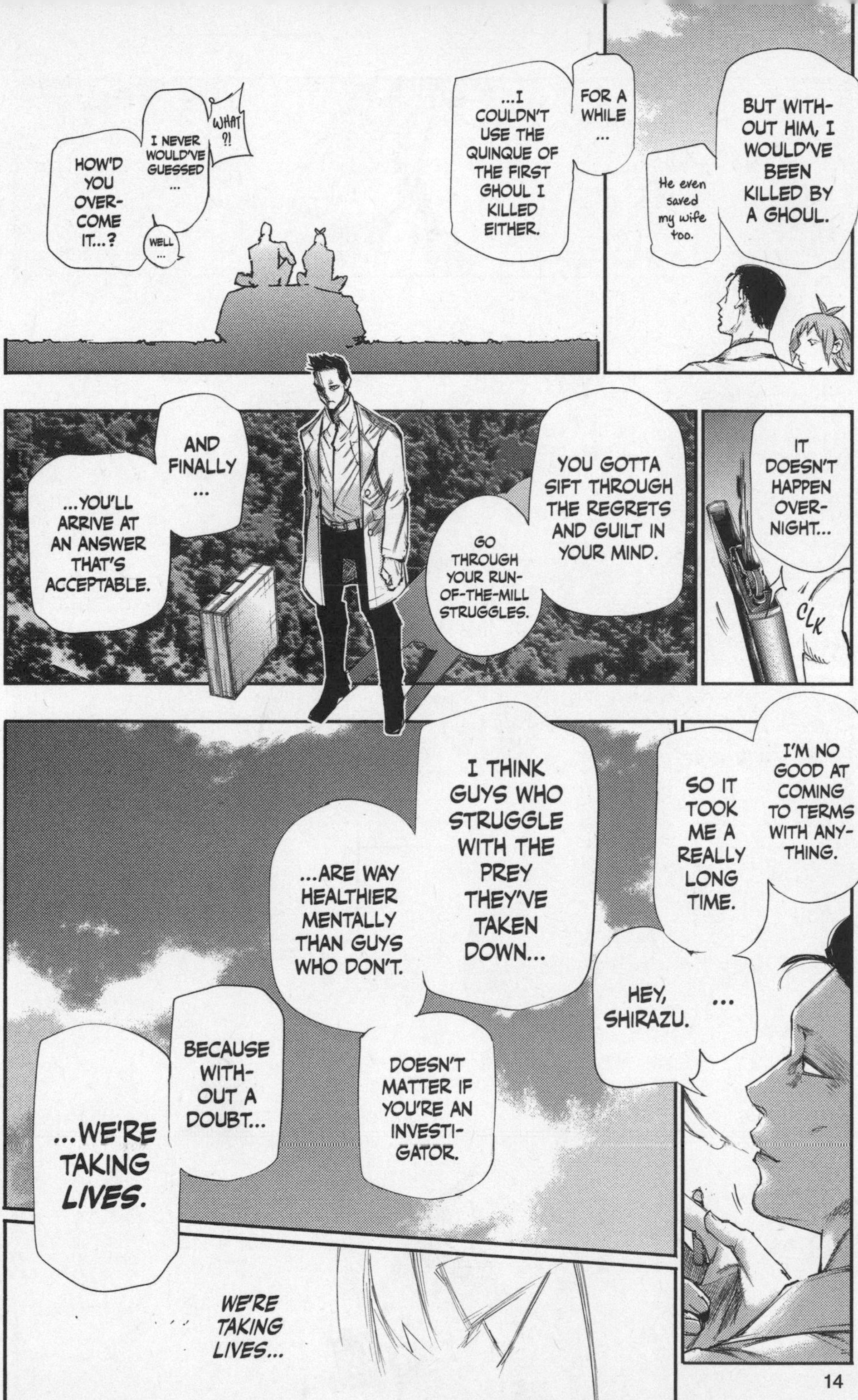
BUT WITHOUT HIM, I WOULD'VE BEEN KILLED BY A GHOUL.
He even saved my wife too.
FOR A WHILE...
...I COULDN'T USE THE QUINQUE OF THE FIRST GHOUL I KILLED EITHER.
WHAT?!
I NEVER WOULD'VE GUESSED...
HOW'D YOU OVERCOME IT...?
WELL...
IT DOESN'T HAPPEN OVERNIGHT...
CLK
YOU GOTTA SIFT THROUGH THE REGRETS AND GUILT IN YOUR MIND.
GO THROUGH YOUR RUN-OF-THE-MILL STRUGGLES.
AND FINALLY...
...YOU'LL ARRIVE AT AN ANSWER THAT'S ACCEPTABLE.
I'M NO GOOD AT COMING TO TERMS WITH ANYTHING.
SO IT TOOK ME A REALLY LONG TIME.
...
HEY, SHIRAZU.
I THINK GUYS WHO STRUGGLE WITH THE PREY THEY'VE TAKEN DOWN...
...ARE WAY HEALTHIER MENTALLY THAN GUYS WHO DON'T.
DOESN'T MATTER IF YOU'RE AN INVESTIGATOR.
BECAUSE WITHOUT A DOUBT...
...WE'RE TAKING *LIVES*.
WE'RE TAKING LIVES...

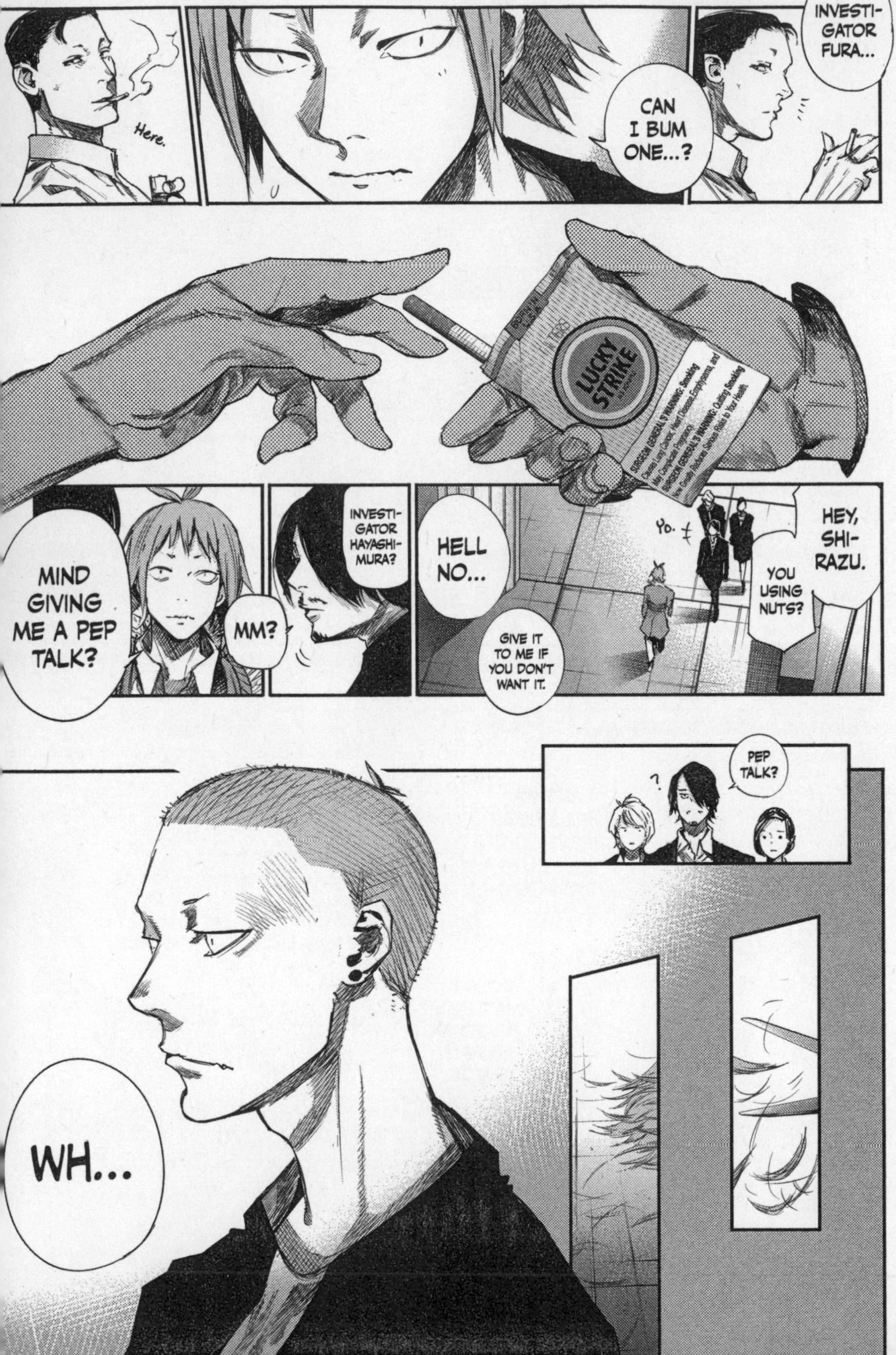
INVESTI-GATOR FURA...
CAN I BUM ONE...?
Here.
LUCKY STRIKE
HEY, SHI-RAZU.
YOU USING NUTS?
Yo.
HELL NO...
GIVE IT TO ME IF YOU DON'T WANT IT.
INVESTI-GATOR HAYASHI-MURA?
MM?
MIND GIVING ME A PEP TALK?
PEP TALK?
WH...

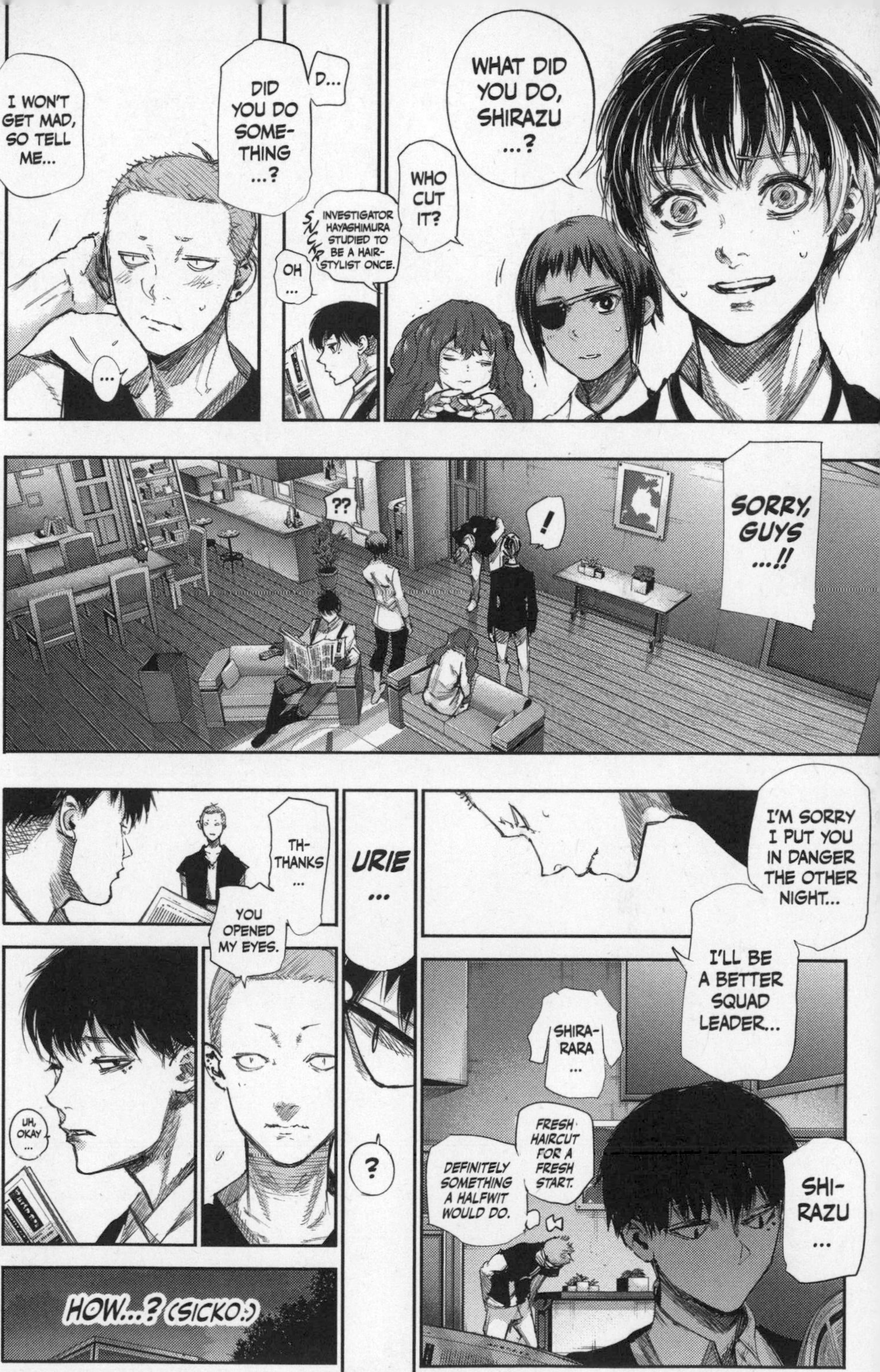
WHAT DID YOU DO, SHIRAZU ...?
WHO CUT IT?
D...
DID YOU DO SOME-THING ...?
INVESTIGATOR HAYASHIMURA STUDIED TO BE A HAIR-STYLIST ONCE.
SNCKR
OH ...
I WON'T GET MAD, SO TELL ME...
...
SORRY, GUYS ...!!
!
??
I'M SORRY I PUT YOU IN DANGER THE OTHER NIGHT...
URIE ...
TH-THANKS ...
YOU OPENED MY EYES.
I'LL BE A BETTER SQUAD LEADER...
SHIRA-RARA ...
SHI-RAZU ...
FRESH HAIRCUT FOR A FRESH START.
DEFINITELY SOMETHING A HALFWIT WOULD DO.
?
UH, OKAY ...
HOW...? (SICKO:)

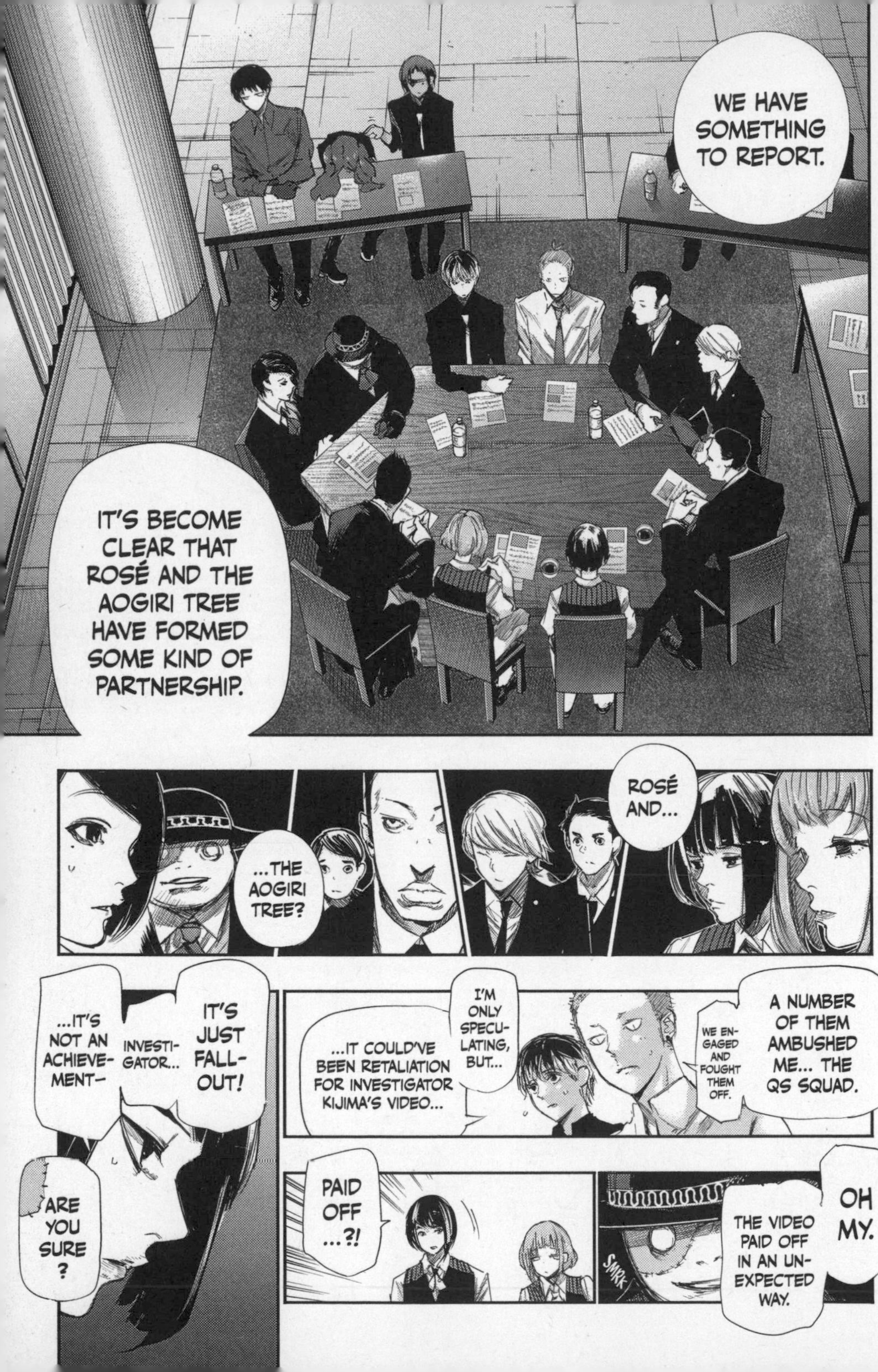
WE HAVE SOMETHING TO REPORT.
IT'S BECOME CLEAR THAT ROSÉ AND THE AOGIRI TREE HAVE FORMED SOME KIND OF PARTNERSHIP.
ROSÉ AND...
...THE AOGIRI TREE?
A NUMBER OF THEM AMBUSHED ME... THE QS SQUAD.
WE ENGAGED AND FOUGHT THEM OFF.
I'M ONLY SPECULATING, BUT...
...IT COULD'VE BEEN RETALIATION FOR INVESTIGATOR KIJIMA'S VIDEO...
OH MY.
THE VIDEO PAID OFF IN AN UNEXPECTED WAY.
SMRK
PAID OFF ...?!
IT'S JUST FALL-OUT!
INVESTIGATOR...
...IT'S NOT AN ACHIEVEMENT–
ARE YOU SURE?

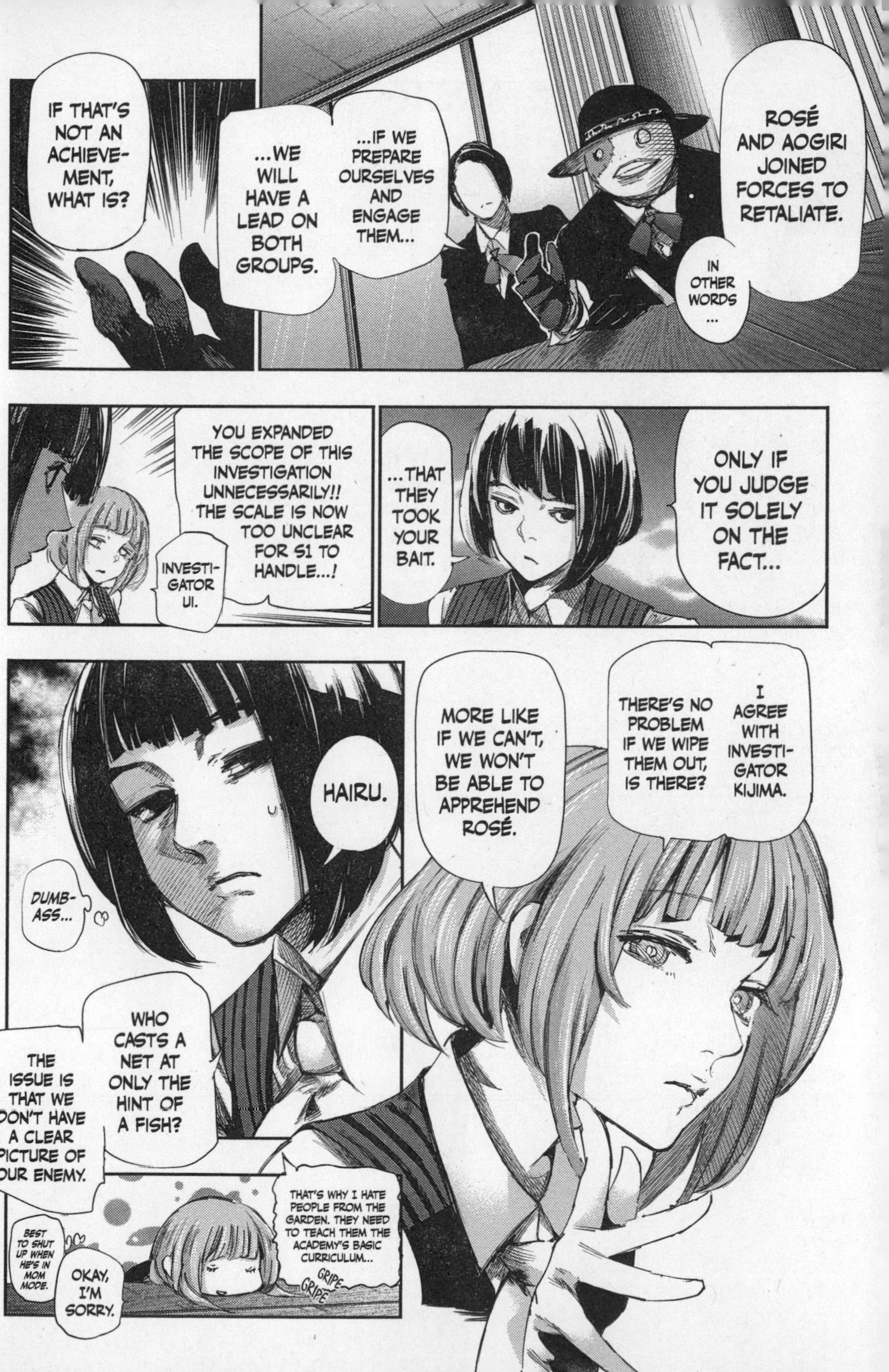
ROSÉ AND AOGIRI JOINED FORCES TO RETALIATE.
IN OTHER WORDS...
...IF WE PREPARE OURSELVES AND ENGAGE THEM...
...WE WILL HAVE A LEAD ON BOTH GROUPS.
IF THAT'S NOT AN ACHIEVEMENT, WHAT IS?
ONLY IF YOU JUDGE IT SOLELY ON THE FACT...
...THAT THEY TOOK YOUR BAIT.
YOU EXPANDED THE SCOPE OF THIS INVESTIGATION UNNECESSARILY!! THE SCALE IS NOW TOO UNCLEAR FOR S1 TO HANDLE...!
INVESTIGATOR UI.
I AGREE WITH INVESTIGATOR KIJIMA.
THERE'S NO PROBLEM IF WE WIPE THEM OUT, IS THERE?
MORE LIKE IF WE CAN'T, WE WON'T BE ABLE TO APPREHEND ROSÉ.
HAIRU.
DUMBASS...
WHO CASTS A NET AT ONLY THE HINT OF A FISH?
THE ISSUE IS THAT WE DON'T HAVE A CLEAR PICTURE OF OUR ENEMY.
THAT'S WHY I HATE PEOPLE FROM THE GARDEN. THEY NEED TO TEACH THEM THE ACADEMY'S BASIC CURRICULUM...
GRIPE GRIPE
OKAY, I'M SORRY.
BEST TO SHUT UP WHEN HE'S IN MOM MODE.

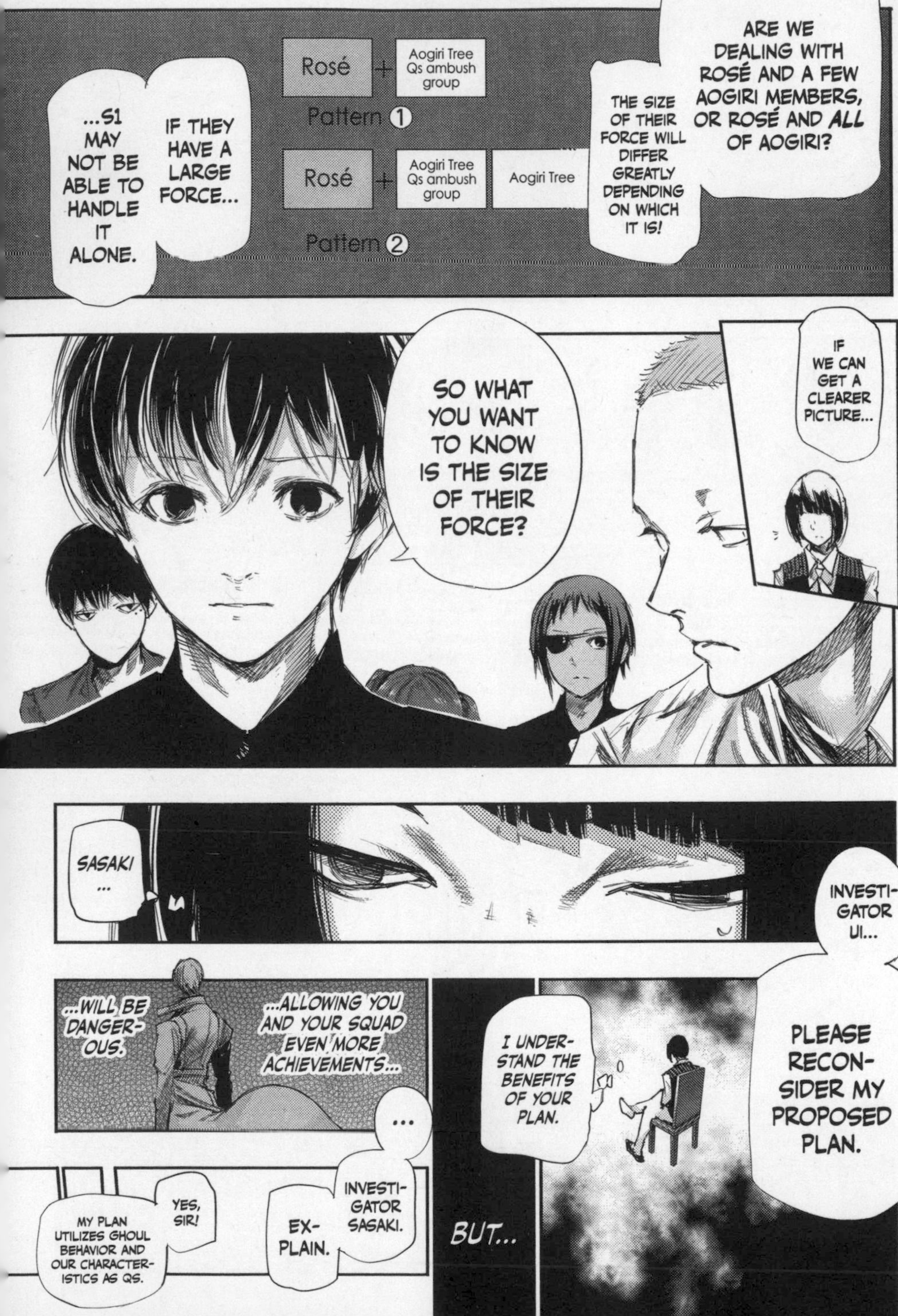

ARE WE DEALING WITH ROSÉ AND A FEW AOGIRI MEMBERS, OR ROSÉ AND *ALL* OF AOGIRI?
THE SIZE OF THEIR FORCE WILL DIFFER GREATLY DEPENDING ON WHICH IT IS!
Rosé + Aogiri Tree Qs ambush group
Pattern ①
Rosé + Aogiri Tree Qs ambush group + Aogiri Tree
Pattern ②
IF THEY HAVE A LARGE FORCE...
...S1 MAY NOT BE ABLE TO HANDLE IT ALONE.
IF WE CAN GET A CLEARER PICTURE...
SO WHAT YOU WANT TO KNOW IS THE SIZE OF THEIR FORCE?
SASAKI ...
INVESTI-GATOR UI...
PLEASE RECON-SIDER MY PROPOSED PLAN.
I UNDER-STAND THE BENEFITS OF YOUR PLAN.
BUT...
...ALLOWING YOU AND YOUR SQUAD EVEN MORE ACHIEVEMENTS...
...WILL BE DANGER-OUS.
...
INVESTI-GATOR SASAKI.
EX-PLAIN.
YES, SIR!
MY PLAN UTILIZES GHOUL BEHAVIOR AND OUR CHARACTER-ISTICS AS QS.

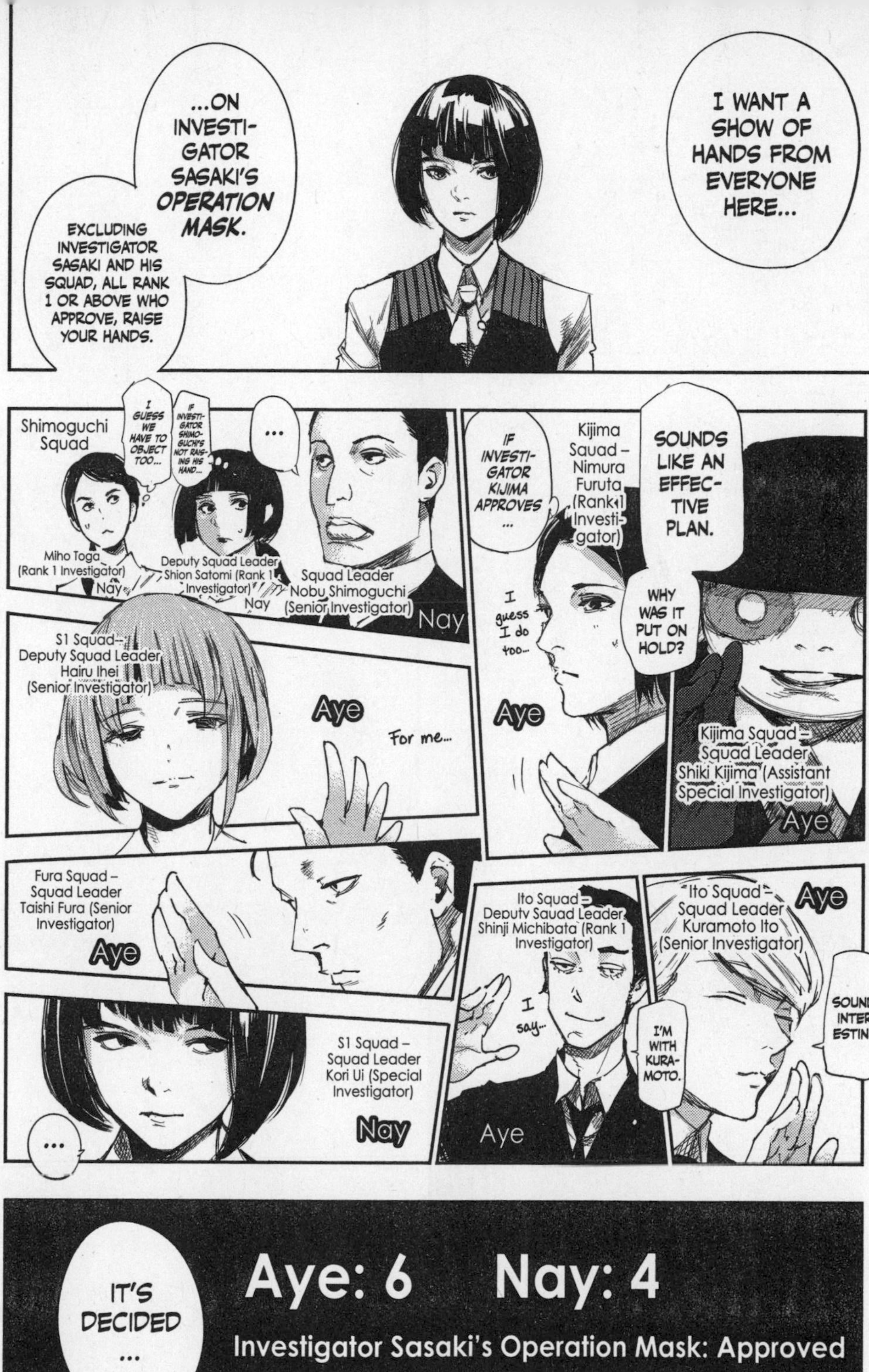
I WANT A SHOW OF HANDS FROM EVERYONE HERE...
...ON INVESTIGATOR SASAKI'S OPERATION MASK.
EXCLUDING INVESTIGATOR SASAKI AND HIS SQUAD, ALL RANK 1 OR ABOVE WHO APPROVE, RAISE YOUR HANDS.
SOUNDS LIKE AN EFFECTIVE PLAN.
WHY WAS IT PUT ON HOLD?
Kijima Squad – Squad Leader Shiki Kijima (Assistant Special Investigator)
Aye
Kijima Squad – Nimura Furuta (Rank 1 Investigator)
IF INVESTIGATOR KIJIMA APPROVES ...
I guess I do too...
Aye
Shimoguchi Squad
...
Squad Leader Nobu Shimoguchi (Senior Investigator)
Nay
IF INVESTIGATOR SHIMOGUCHI'S NOT RAISING HIS HAND...
Deputy Squad Leader Shion Satomi (Rank 1 Investigator)
Nay
I GUESS WE HAVE TO OBJECT TOO...
Miho Toga (Rank 1 Investigator)
Nay
S1 Squad – Deputy Squad Leader Hairu Ihei (Senior Investigator)
Aye
For me...
Ito Squad – Squad Leader Kuramoto Ito (Senior Investigator)
Aye
SOUNDS INTERESTING.
Ito Squad – Deputy Squad Leader Shinji Michibata (Rank 1 Investigator)
I'M WITH KURAMOTO.
I say...
Aye
Fura Squad – Squad Leader Taishi Fura (Senior Investigator)
Aye
S1 Squad – Squad Leader Kori Ui (Special Investigator)
Nay
...
Aye: 6 Nay: 4
IT'S DECIDED ...
Investigator Sasaki's Operation Mask: Approved

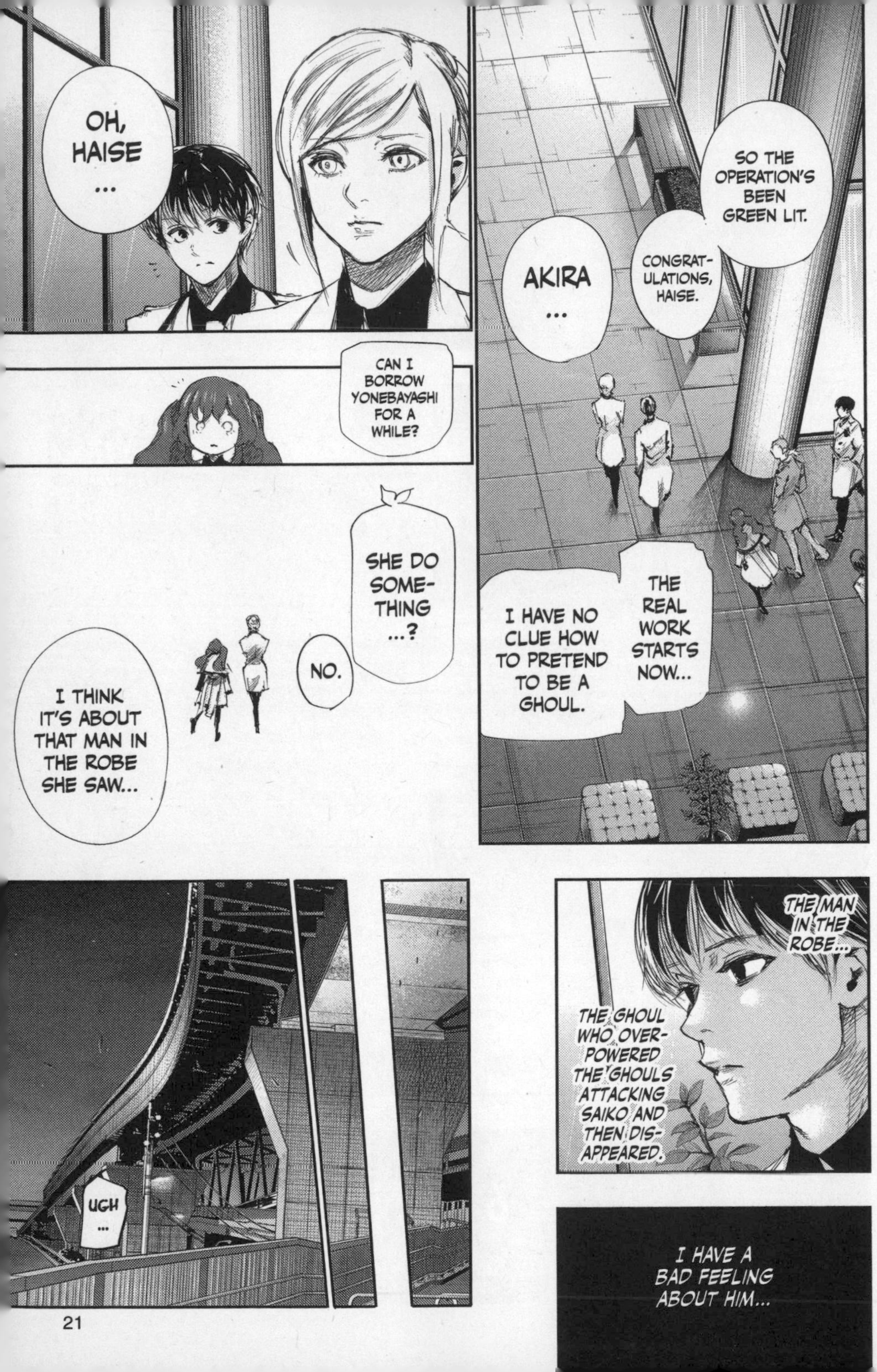
SO THE OPERATION'S BEEN GREEN LIT.
CONGRAT-ULATIONS, HAISE.
AKIRA ...
THE REAL WORK STARTS NOW...
I HAVE NO CLUE HOW TO PRETEND TO BE A GHOUL.
OH, HAISE ...
CAN I BORROW YONEBAYASHI FOR A WHILE?
SHE DO SOME-THING ...?
NO.
I THINK IT'S ABOUT THAT MAN IN THE ROBE SHE SAW...
THE MAN IN THE ROBE...
THE GHOUL WHO OVER-POWERED THE GHOULS ATTACKING SAIKO AND THEN DIS-APPEARED.
I HAVE A BAD FEELING ABOUT HIM...
UGH ...

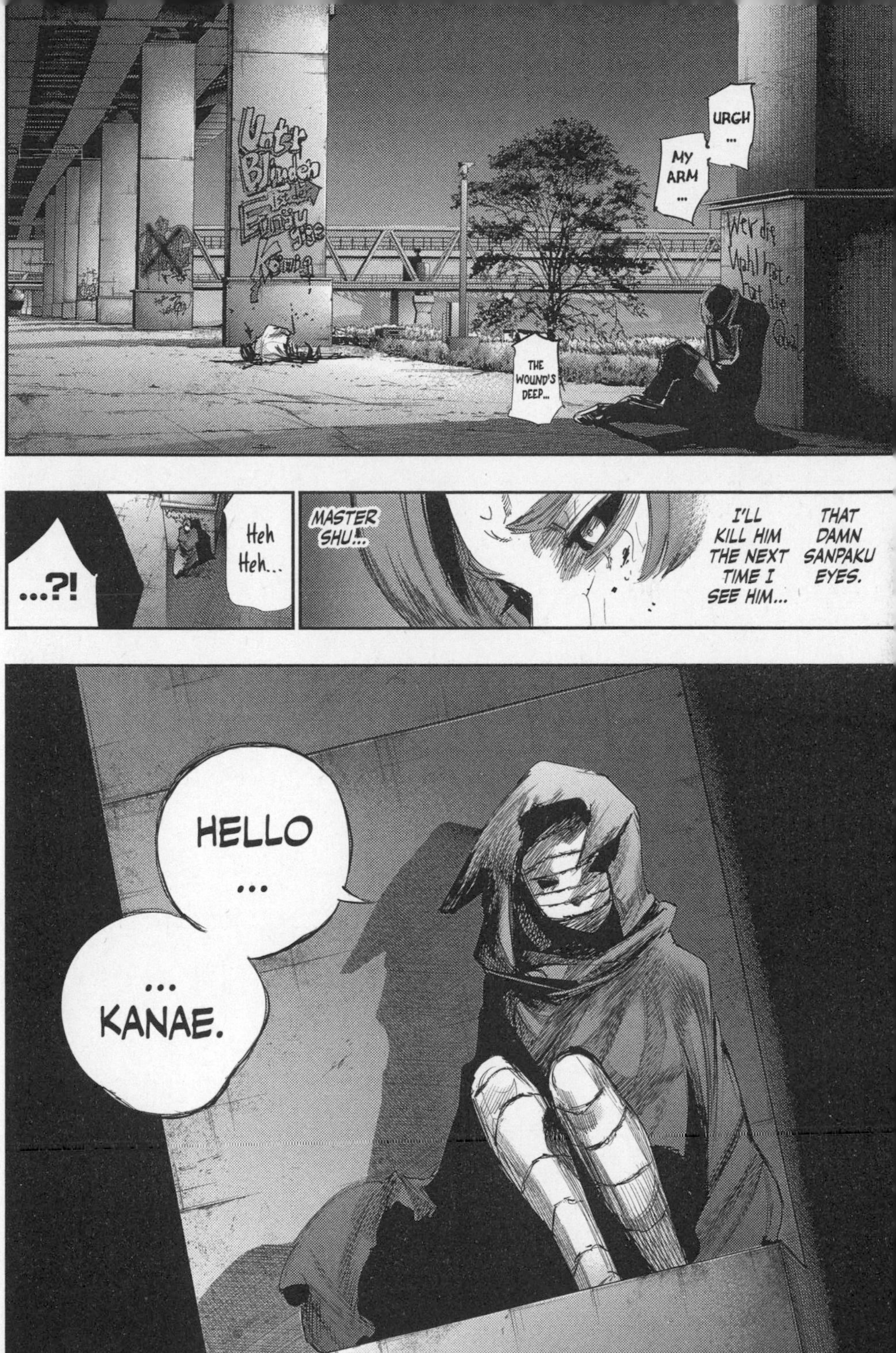
URGH ...
MY ARM ...
THE WOUND'S DEEP...
THAT DAMN SANPAKU EYES.
I'LL KILL HIM THE NEXT TIME I SEE HIM...
MASTER SHU...
Heh Heh...
...?!
HELLO ...
... KANAE.

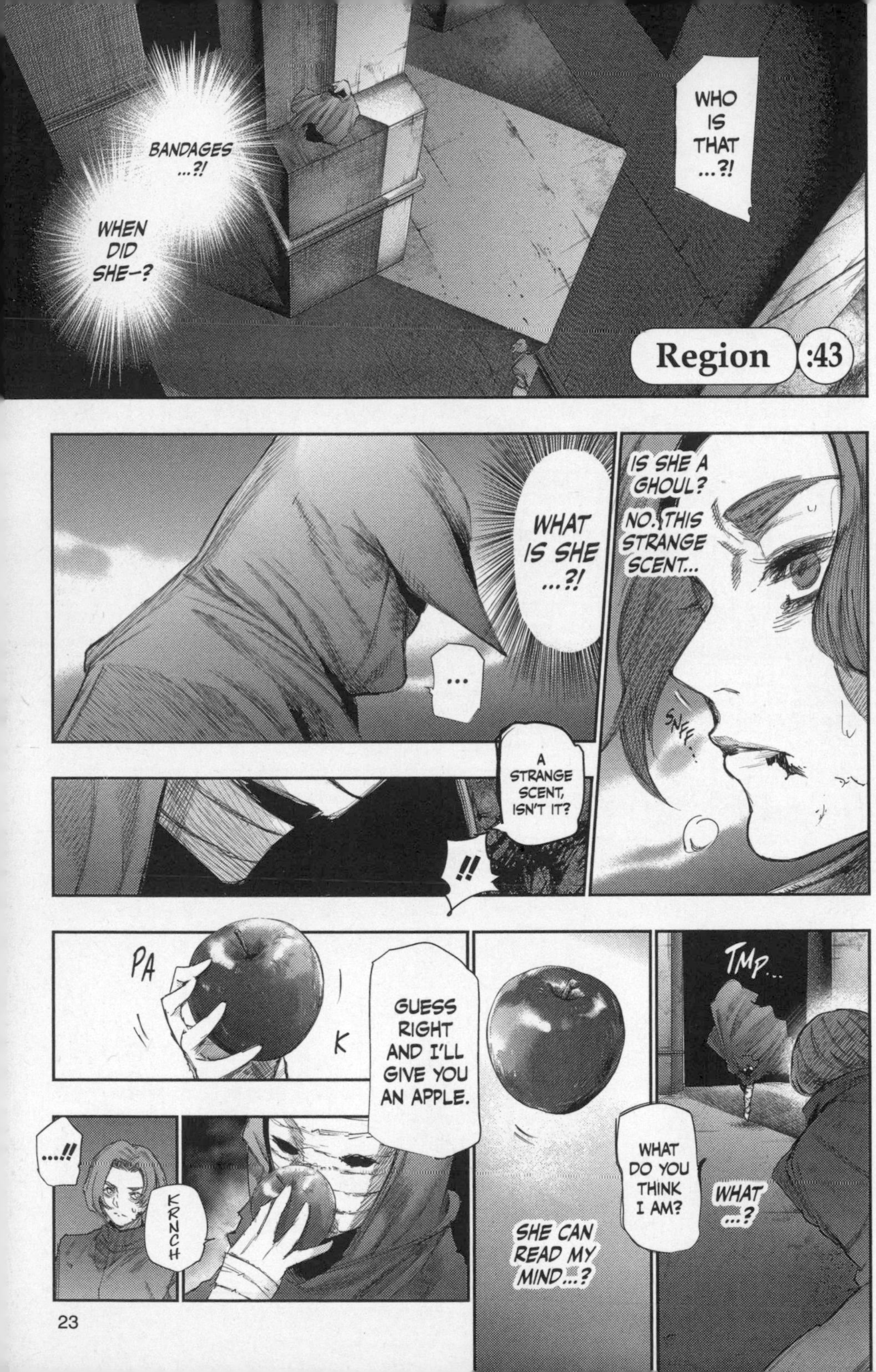

WHO IS THAT ...?!
BANDAGES ...?!
WHEN DID SHE–?
Region :43
IS SHE A GHOUL?
NO. THIS STRANGE SCENT...
SNFF...
WHAT IS SHE ...?!
...
A STRANGE SCENT, ISN'T IT?
!!
TMP...
WHAT ...?
WHAT DO YOU THINK I AM?
GUESS RIGHT AND I'LL GIVE YOU AN APPLE.
PA
K
SHE CAN READ MY MIND...?
KRNCH
...!!

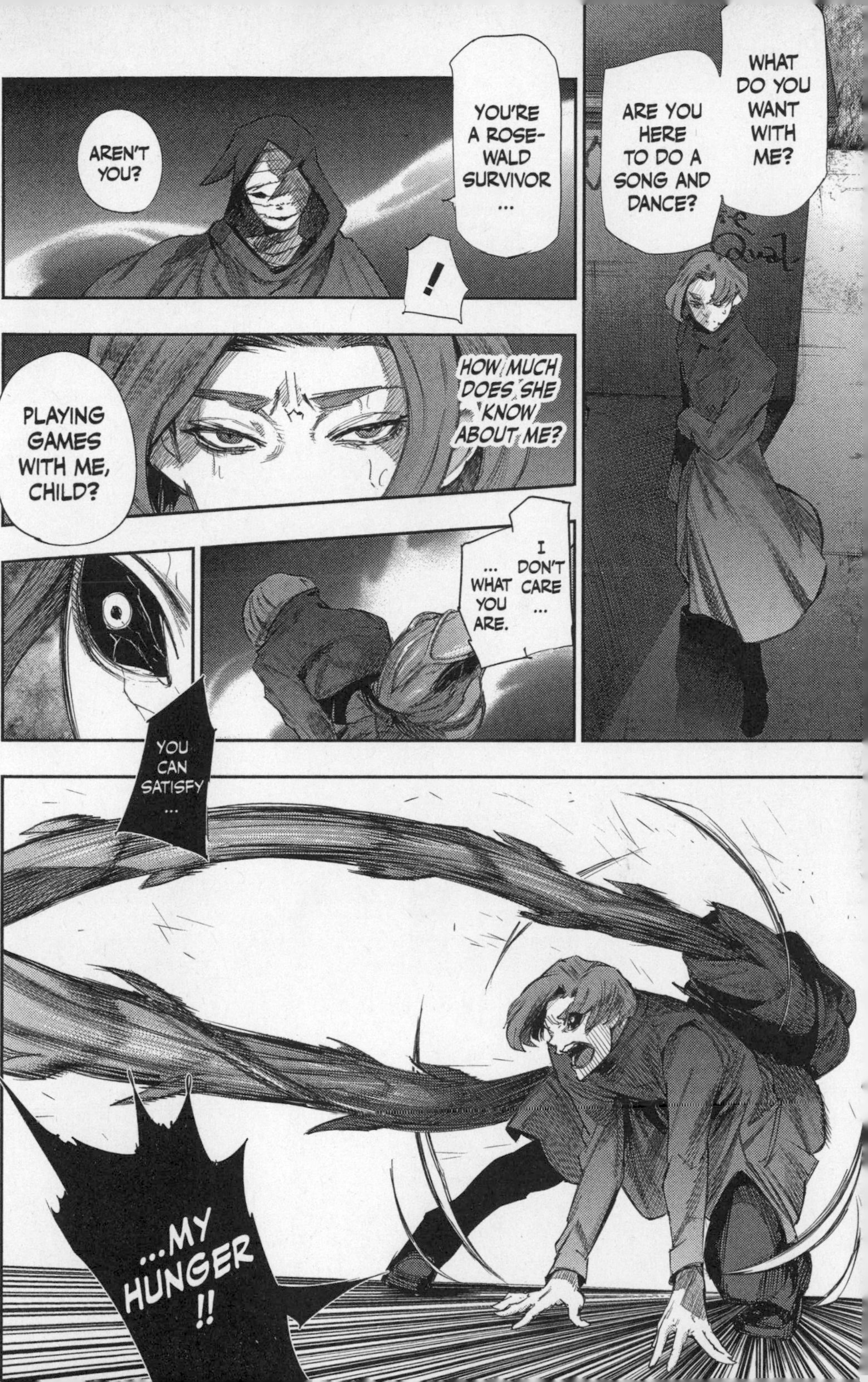
WHAT DO YOU WANT WITH ME?
ARE YOU HERE TO DO A SONG AND DANCE?
YOU'RE A ROSE-WALD SURVIVOR ...
AREN'T YOU?
!
HOW MUCH DOES SHE KNOW ABOUT ME?
PLAYING GAMES WITH ME, CHILD?
I DON'T CARE ...
... WHAT YOU ARE.
YOU CAN SATISFY ...
...MY HUNGER !!

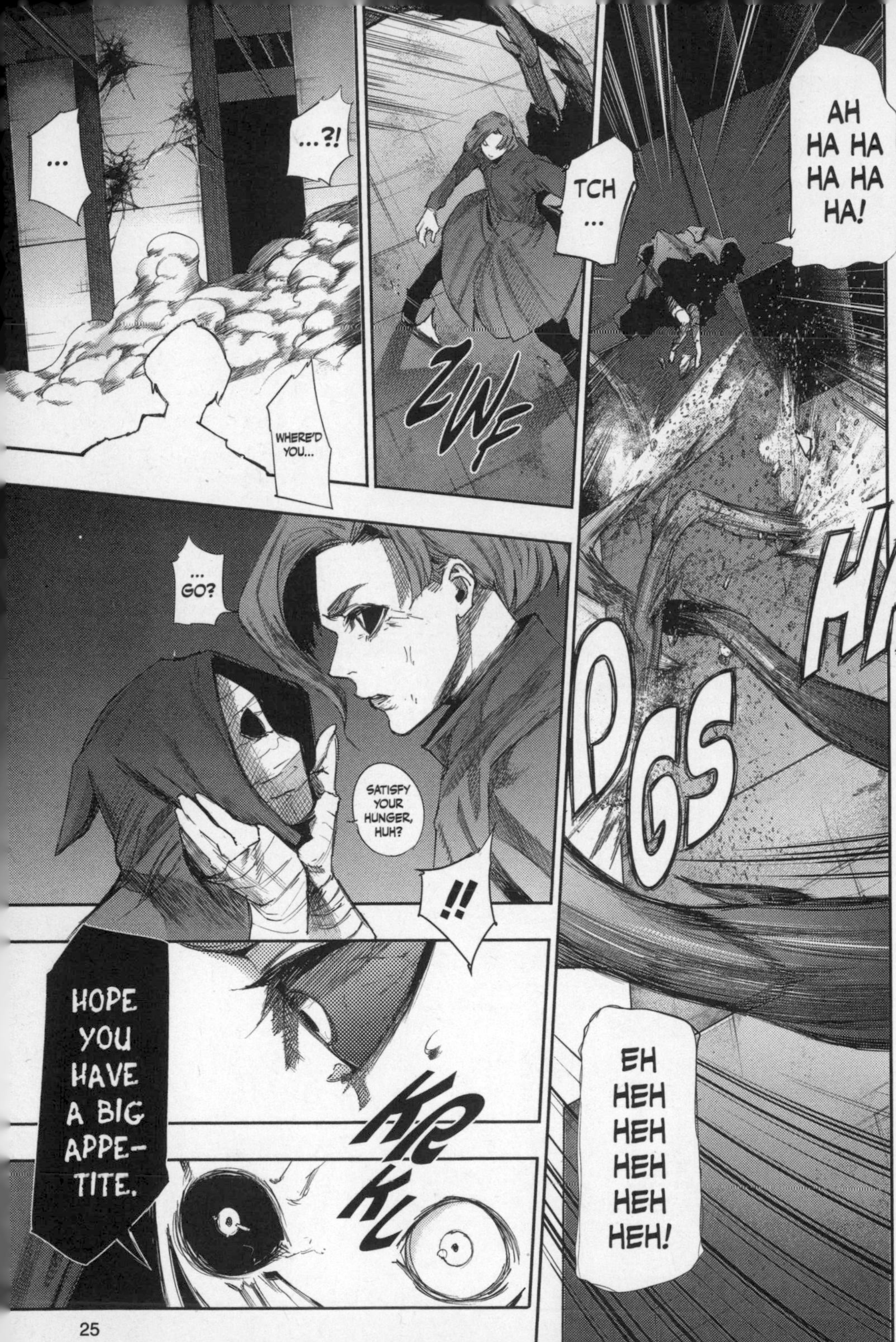
AH HA HA HA HA HA!
EH HEH HEH HEH HEH HEH HEH!
TCH ...
ZWF
...?!
...
WHERE'D YOU...
... GO?
SATISFY YOUR HUNGER, HUH?
!!
HOPE YOU HAVE A BIG APPE-TITE.

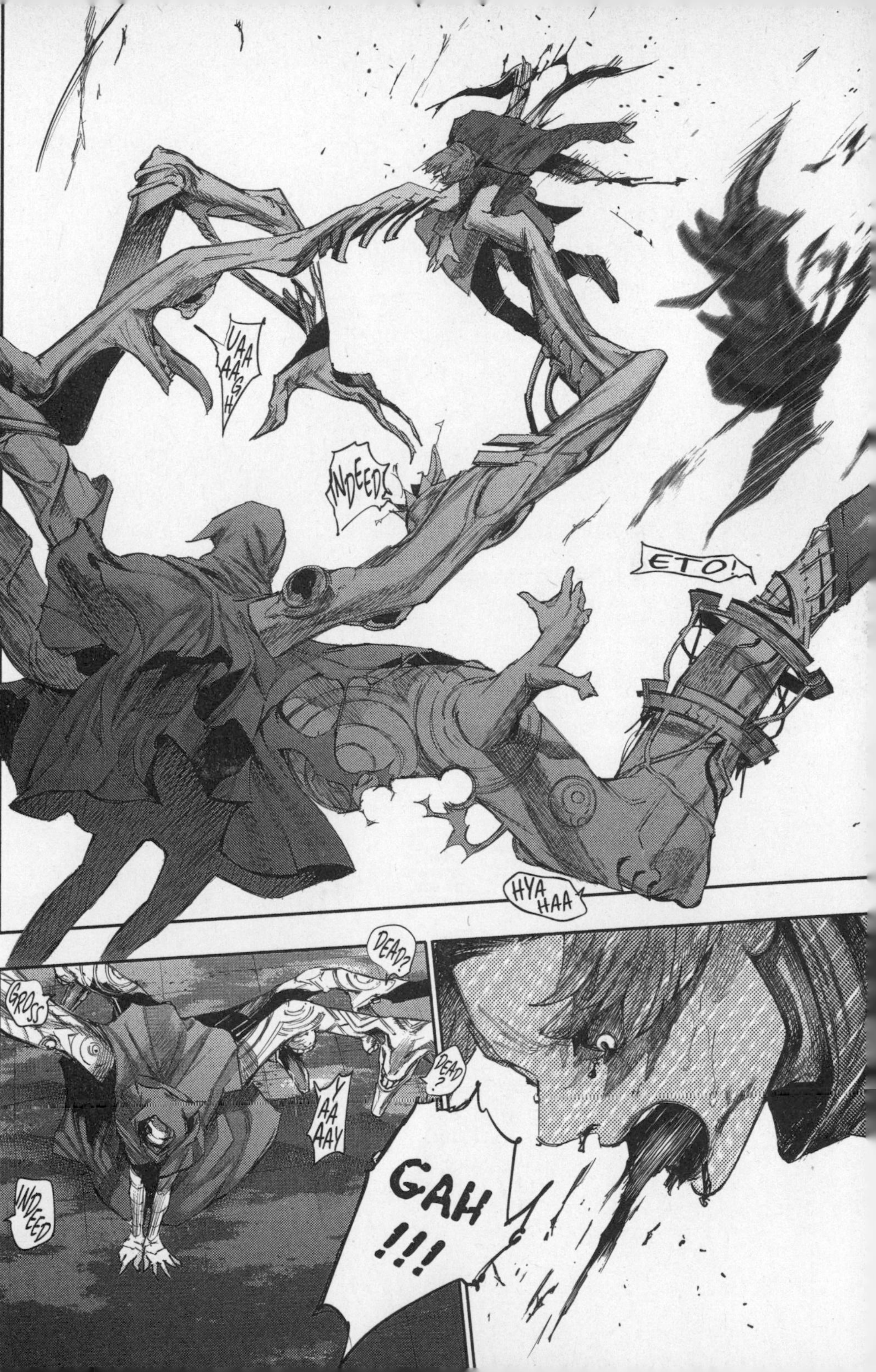
UAAAAAGH
INDEED
ETO!
HYA HAA
GAH!!!
DEAD?
GROSS
DEAD?
YAAAAY
INDEED

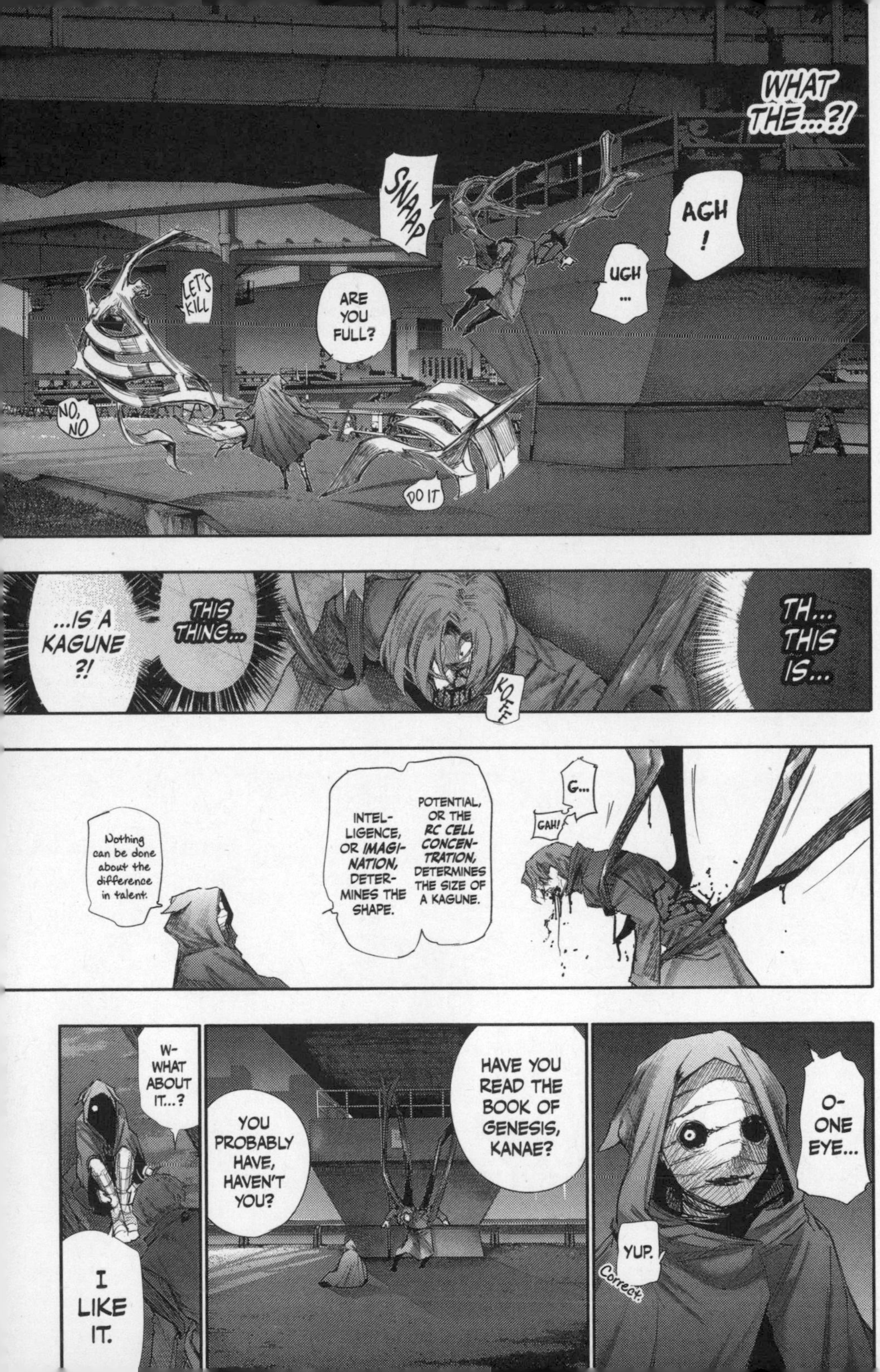
WHAT THE...?!
AGH!
UGH...
SNAAP
ARE YOU FULL?
LET'S KILL
NO, NO
DO IT
TH... THIS IS...
KOFF
THIS THING...
...IS A KAGUNE?!
G...
GAH!
POTENTIAL, OR THE RC CELL CONCENTRATION, DETERMINES THE SIZE OF A KAGUNE.
INTELLIGENCE, OR IMAGINATION, DETERMINES THE SHAPE.
Nothing can be done about the difference in talent.
O- ONE EYE...
YUP.
Correct.
HAVE YOU READ THE BOOK OF GENESIS, KANAE?
YOU PROBABLY HAVE, HAVEN'T YOU?
W- WHAT ABOUT IT...?
I LIKE IT.

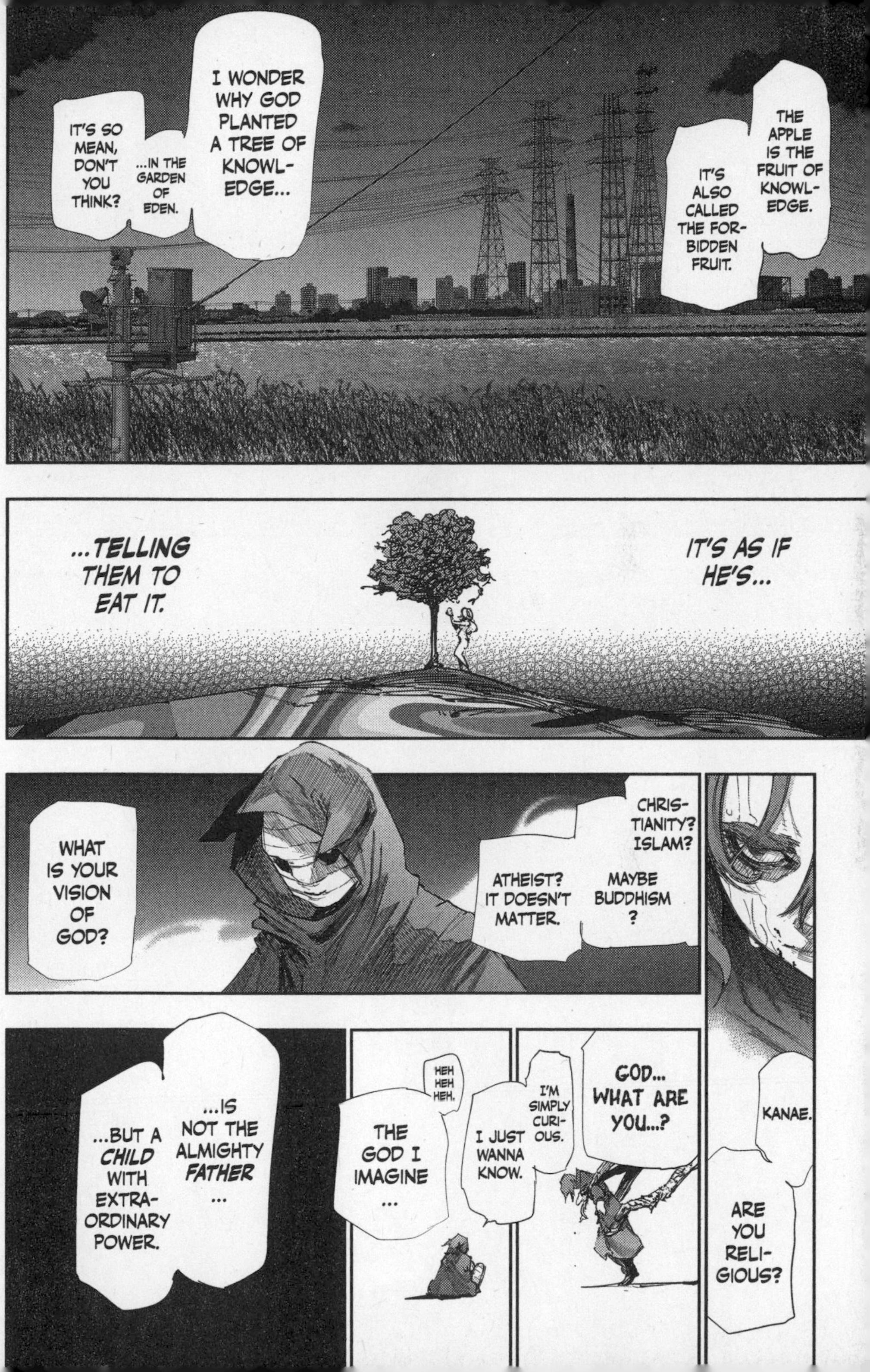
THE APPLE IS THE FRUIT OF KNOWLEDGE.
IT'S ALSO CALLED THE FORBIDDEN FRUIT.
I WONDER WHY GOD PLANTED A TREE OF KNOWLEDGE...
...IN THE GARDEN OF EDEN.
IT'S SO MEAN, DON'T YOU THINK?
IT'S AS IF HE'S...
...TELLING THEM TO EAT IT.
KANAE.
ARE YOU RELIGIOUS?
CHRISTIANITY? ISLAM?
MAYBE BUDDHISM?
ATHEIST? IT DOESN'T MATTER.
WHAT IS YOUR VISION OF GOD?
GOD... WHAT ARE YOU...?
I'M SIMPLY CURIOUS.
I JUST WANNA KNOW.
HEH HEH HEH.
THE GOD I IMAGINE...
...IS NOT THE ALMIGHTY *FATHER*...
...BUT A *CHILD* WITH EXTRAORDINARY POWER.

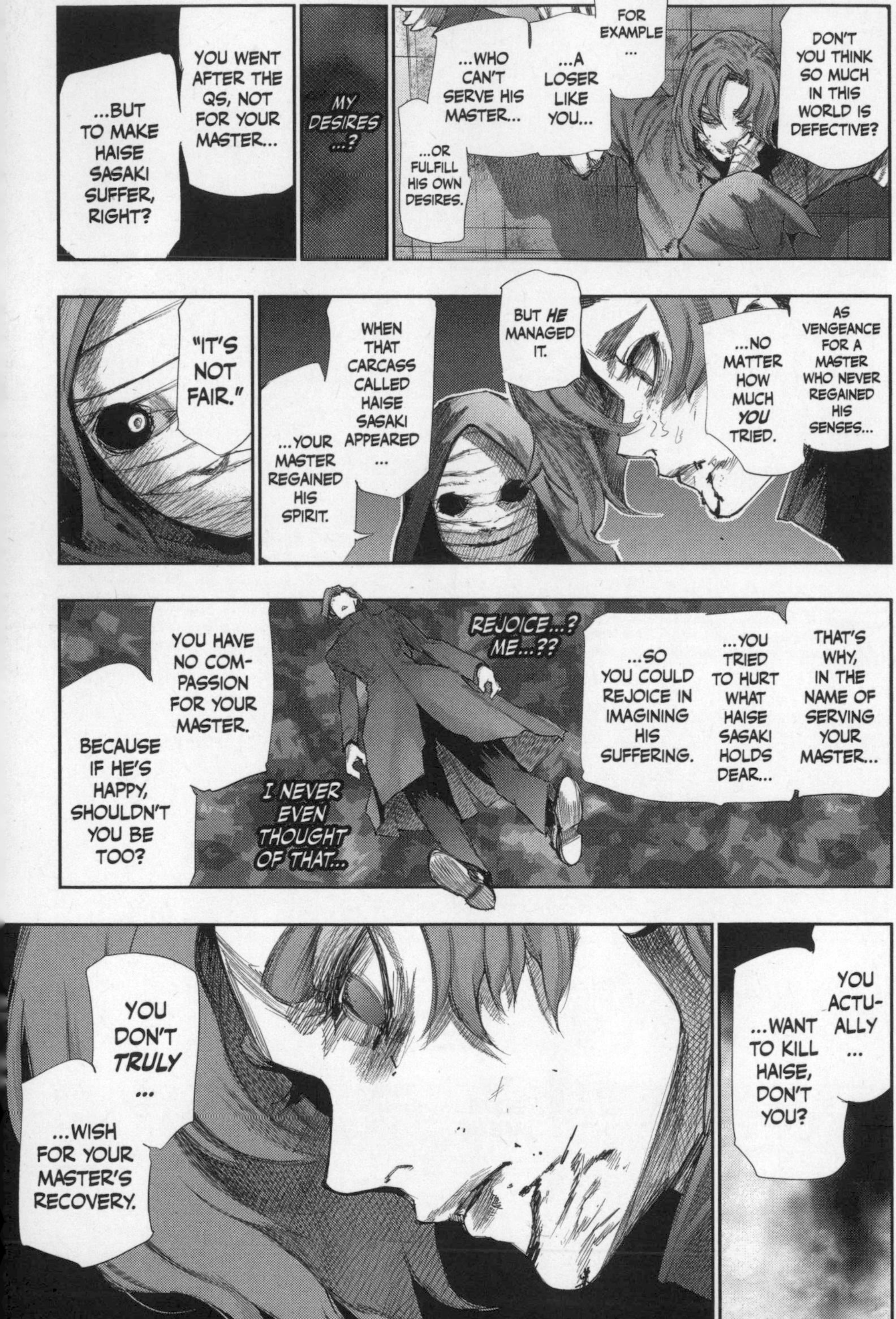

DON'T YOU THINK SO MUCH IN THIS WORLD IS DEFECTIVE?
FOR EXAMPLE...
...A LOSER LIKE YOU...
...WHO CAN'T SERVE HIS MASTER...
...OR FULFILL HIS OWN DESIRES.
MY DESIRES ...?
YOU WENT AFTER THE QS, NOT FOR YOUR MASTER...
...BUT TO MAKE HAISE SASAKI SUFFER, RIGHT?
AS VENGEANCE FOR A MASTER WHO NEVER REGAINED HIS SENSES...
...NO MATTER HOW MUCH *YOU* TRIED.
BUT *HE* MANAGED IT.
WHEN THAT CARCASS CALLED HAISE SASAKI APPEARED...
...YOUR MASTER REGAINED HIS SPIRIT.
"IT'S NOT FAIR."
THAT'S WHY, IN THE NAME OF SERVING YOUR MASTER...
...YOU TRIED TO HURT WHAT HAISE SASAKI HOLDS DEAR...
...SO YOU COULD REJOICE IN IMAGINING HIS SUFFERING.
REJOICE...? ME...??
YOU HAVE NO COMPASSION FOR YOUR MASTER.
BECAUSE IF HE'S HAPPY, SHOULDN'T YOU BE TOO?
I NEVER EVEN THOUGHT OF THAT...
YOU ACTUALLY...
...WANT TO KILL HAISE, DON'T YOU?
YOU DON'T *TRULY* ...
...WISH FOR YOUR MASTER'S RECOVERY.

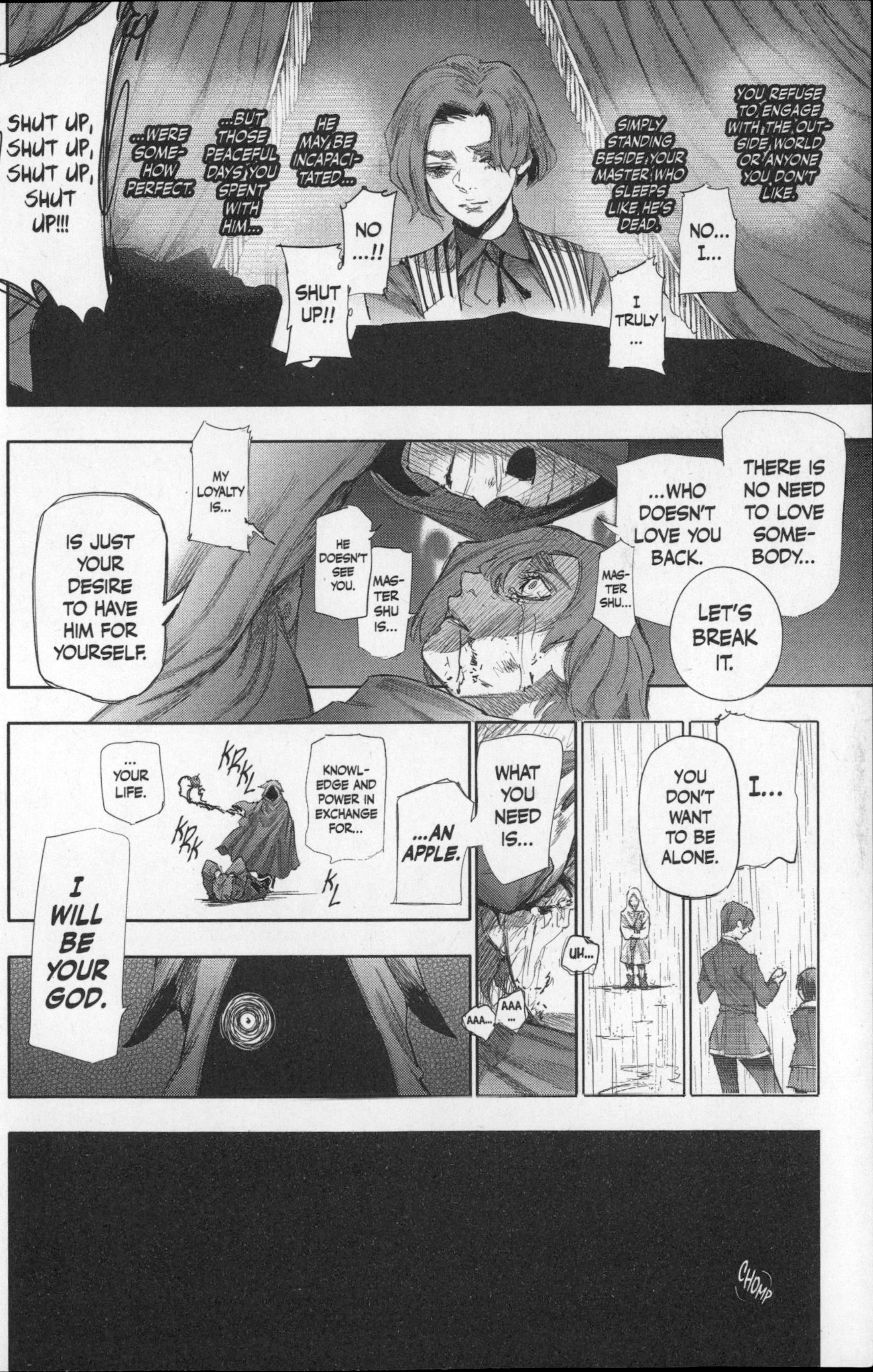
YOU REFUSE TO ENGAGE WITH THE OUTSIDE WORLD OR ANYONE YOU DON'T LIKE.
NO... I...
SIMPLY STANDING BESIDE YOUR MASTER WHO SLEEPS LIKE HE'S DEAD.
I TRULY ...
HE MAY BE INCAPACITATED...
NO ...!!
...BUT THOSE PEACEFUL DAYS YOU SPENT WITH HIM...
SHUT UP!!
...WERE SOMEHOW PERFECT.
SHUT UP, SHUT UP, SHUT UP, SHUT UP!!!
THERE IS NO NEED TO LOVE SOMEBODY...
...WHO DOESN'T LOVE YOU BACK.
LET'S BREAK IT.
MASTER SHU...
MY LOYALTY IS...
MASTER SHU IS...
HE DOESN'T SEE YOU.
IS JUST YOUR DESIRE TO HAVE HIM FOR YOURSELF.
I...
YOU DON'T WANT TO BE ALONE.
UH...
WHAT YOU NEED IS...
...AN APPLE.
AAA...
AAA ...
KNOWLEDGE AND POWER IN EXCHANGE FOR...
KRKL
KRK
KL
... YOUR LIFE.
I WILL BE YOUR GOD.
CHOMP

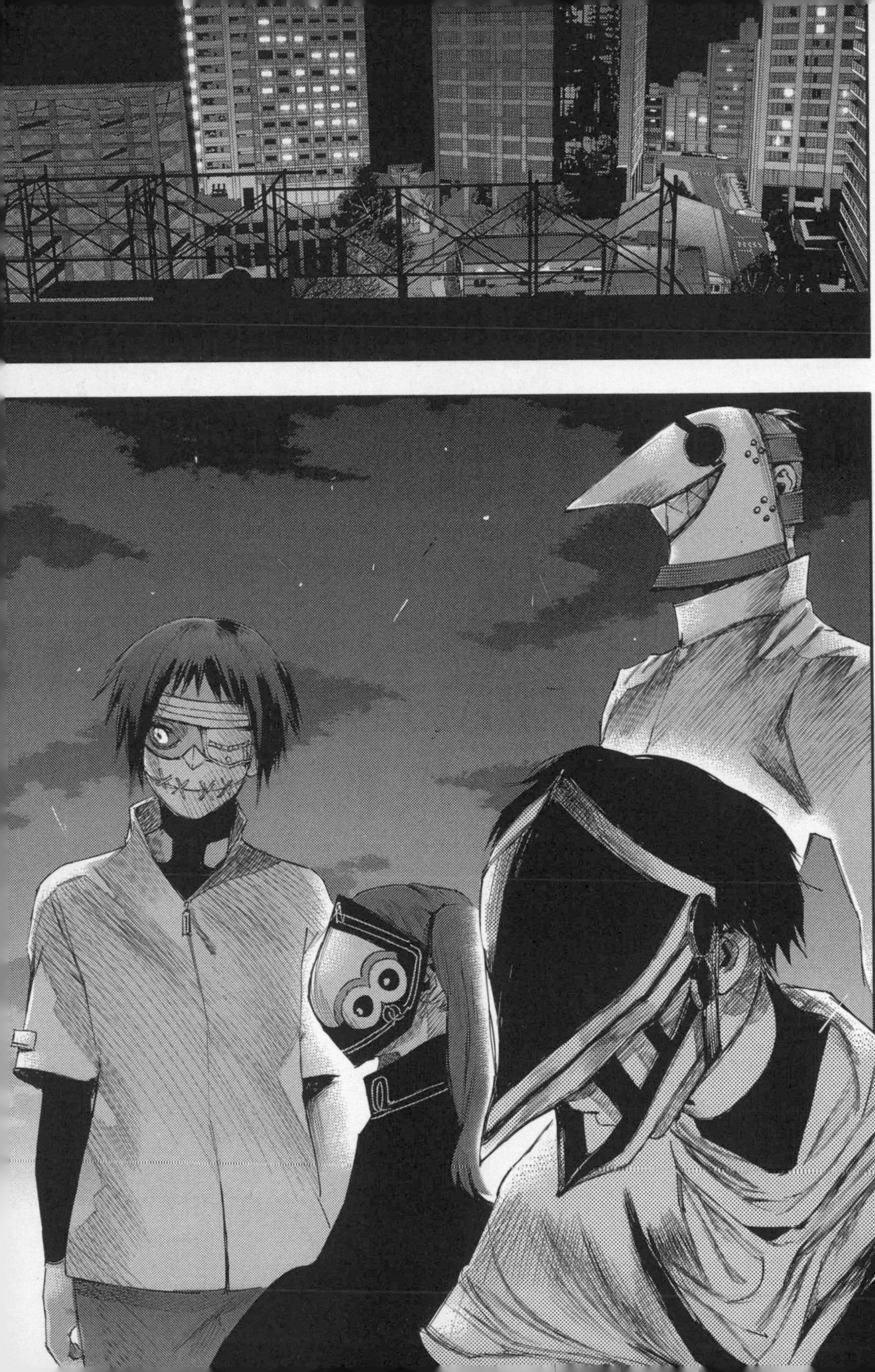

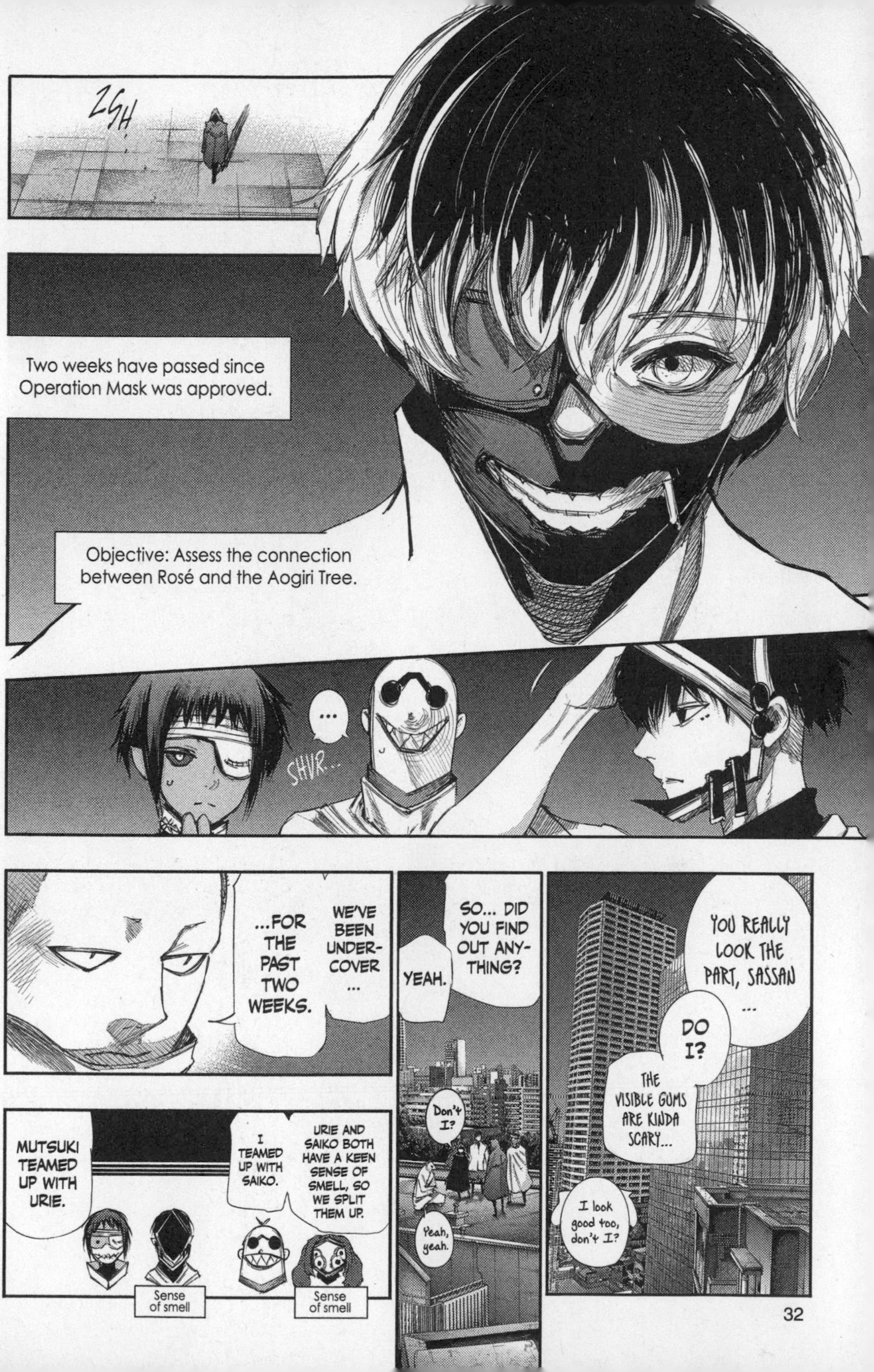
ZSH
Two weeks have passed since Operation Mask was approved.
Objective: Assess the connection between Rosé and the Aogiri Tree.
...
SHVR...
YOU REALLY LOOK THE PART, SASSAN ...
DO I?
THE VISIBLE GUMS ARE KINDA SCARY...
I look good too, don't I?
SO... DID YOU FIND OUT ANYTHING?
YEAH.
Don't I?
Yeah, yeah.
WE'VE BEEN UNDERCOVER ...
...FOR THE PAST TWO WEEKS.
URIE AND SAIKO BOTH HAVE A KEEN SENSE OF SMELL, SO WE SPLIT THEM UP.
I TEAMED UP WITH SAIKO.
MUTSUKI TEAMED UP WITH URIE.
Sense of smell
Sense of smell

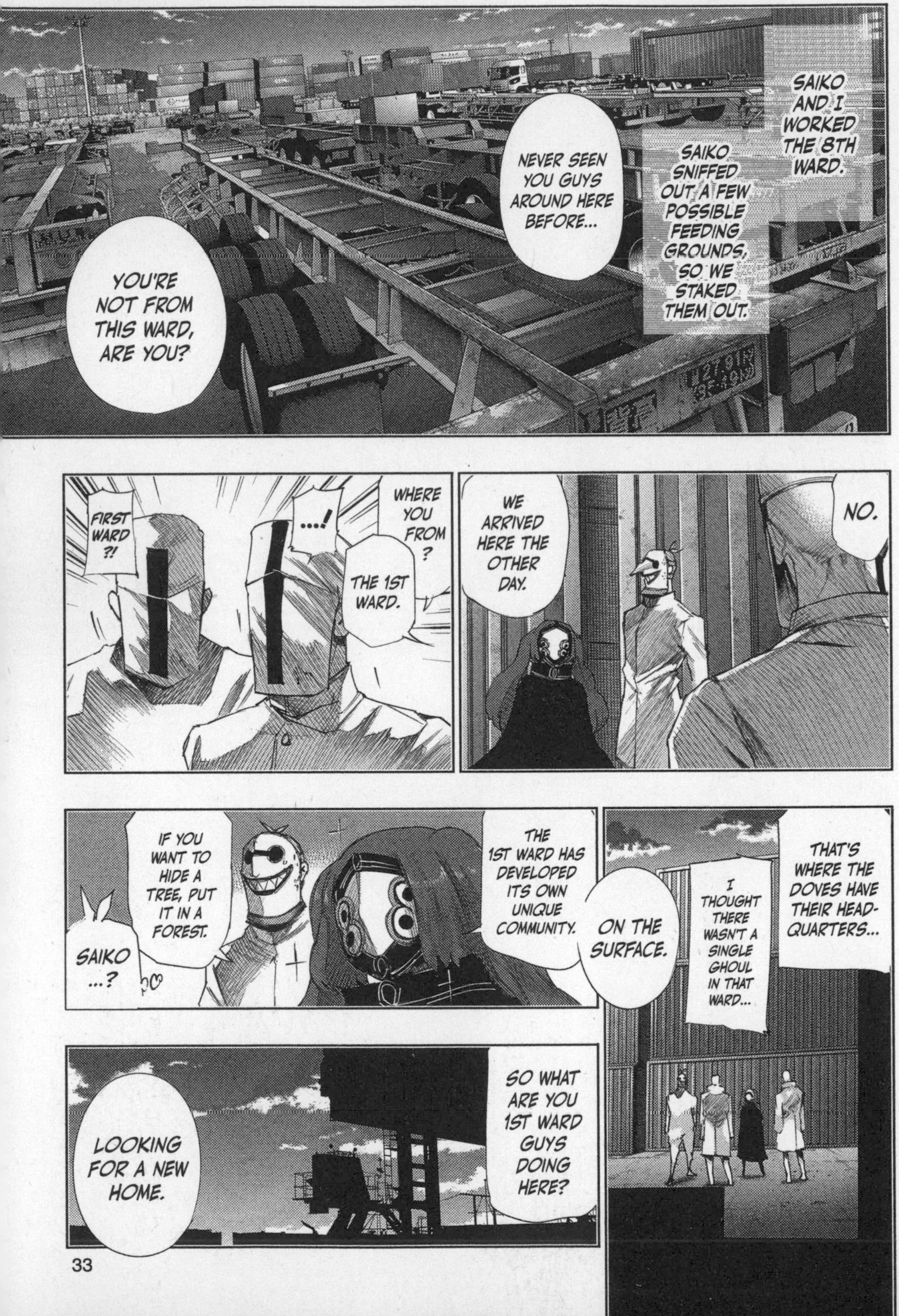
SAIKO AND I WORKED THE 8TH WARD.
SAIKO SNIFFED OUT A FEW POSSIBLE FEEDING GROUNDS, SO WE STAKED THEM OUT.
NEVER SEEN YOU GUYS AROUND HERE BEFORE...
YOU'RE NOT FROM THIS WARD, ARE YOU?
NO.
WE ARRIVED HERE THE OTHER DAY.
WHERE YOU FROM?
THE 1ST WARD.
...!
FIRST WARD?!
THAT'S WHERE THE DOVES HAVE THEIR HEAD-QUARTERS...
I THOUGHT THERE WASN'T A SINGLE GHOUL IN THAT WARD...
ON THE SURFACE.
THE 1ST WARD HAS DEVELOPED ITS OWN UNIQUE COMMUNITY.
IF YOU WANT TO HIDE A TREE, PUT IT IN A FOREST.
SAIKO ...?
SO WHAT ARE YOU 1ST WARD GUYS DOING HERE?
LOOKING FOR A NEW HOME.

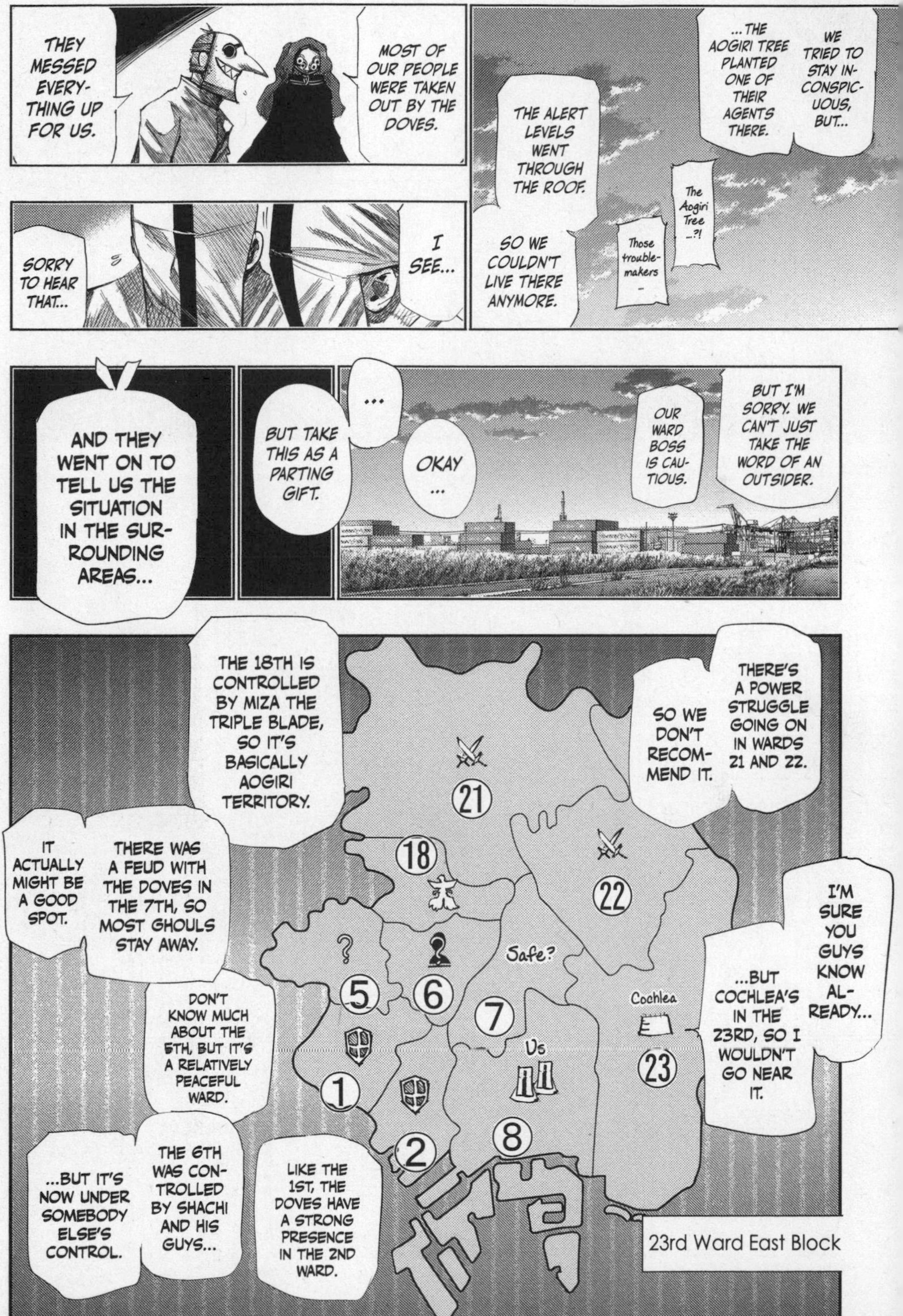
WE TRIED TO STAY INCONSPICUOUS, BUT...
...THE AOGIRI TREE PLANTED ONE OF THEIR AGENTS THERE.
The Aogiri Tree ...?!
Those troublemakers ...
THE ALERT LEVELS WENT THROUGH THE ROOF.
SO WE COULDN'T LIVE THERE ANYMORE.
MOST OF OUR PEOPLE WERE TAKEN OUT BY THE DOVES.
THEY MESSED EVERYTHING UP FOR US.
I SEE...
SORRY TO HEAR THAT...
BUT I'M SORRY. WE CAN'T JUST TAKE THE WORD OF AN OUTSIDER.
OUR WARD BOSS IS CAUTIOUS.
...
OKAY ...
BUT TAKE THIS AS A PARTING GIFT.
AND THEY WENT ON TO TELL US THE SITUATION IN THE SURROUNDING AREAS...
THERE'S A POWER STRUGGLE GOING ON IN WARDS 21 AND 22.
SO WE DON'T RECOMMEND IT.
THE 18TH IS CONTROLLED BY MIZA THE TRIPLE BLADE, SO IT'S BASICALLY AOGIRI TERRITORY.
21
22
18
I'M SURE YOU GUYS KNOW ALREADY...
...BUT COCHLEA'S IN THE 23RD, SO I WOULDN'T GO NEAR IT.
Cochlea
23
THERE WAS A FEUD WITH THE DOVES IN THE 7TH, SO MOST GHOULS STAY AWAY.
IT ACTUALLY MIGHT BE A GOOD SPOT.
Safe?
?
5
6
7
Us
DON'T KNOW MUCH ABOUT THE 5TH, BUT IT'S A RELATIVELY PEACEFUL WARD.
1
2
8
LIKE THE 1ST, THE DOVES HAVE A STRONG PRESENCE IN THE 2ND WARD.
THE 6TH WAS CONTROLLED BY SHACHI AND HIS GUYS...
...BUT IT'S NOW UNDER SOMEBODY ELSE'S CONTROL.
23rd Ward East Block

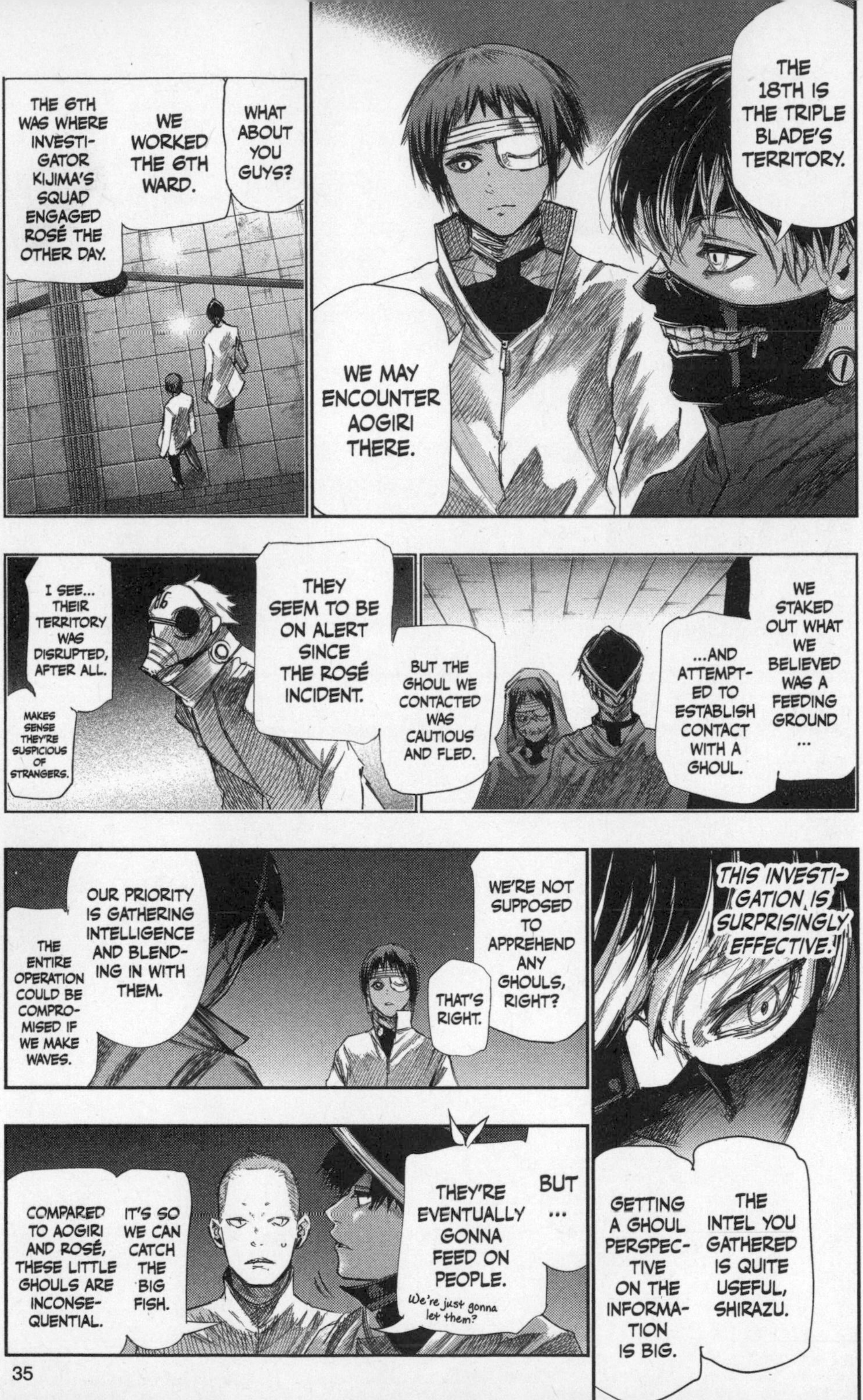
THE 18TH IS THE TRIPLE BLADE'S TERRITORY.
WE MAY ENCOUNTER AOGIRI THERE.
WHAT ABOUT YOU GUYS?
WE WORKED THE 6TH WARD.
THE 6TH WAS WHERE INVESTIGATOR KIJIMA'S SQUAD ENGAGED ROSÉ THE OTHER DAY.
WE STAKED OUT WHAT WE BELIEVED WAS A FEEDING GROUND...
...AND ATTEMPTED TO ESTABLISH CONTACT WITH A GHOUL.
BUT THE GHOUL WE CONTACTED WAS CAUTIOUS AND FLED.
THEY SEEM TO BE ON ALERT SINCE THE ROSÉ INCIDENT.
I SEE... THEIR TERRITORY WAS DISRUPTED, AFTER ALL.
MAKES SENSE THEY'RE SUSPICIOUS OF STRANGERS.
THIS INVESTIGATION IS SURPRISINGLY EFFECTIVE!
THE INTEL YOU GATHERED IS QUITE USEFUL, SHIRAZU.
GETTING A GHOUL PERSPECTIVE ON THE INFORMATION IS BIG.
WE'RE NOT SUPPOSED TO APPREHEND ANY GHOULS, RIGHT?
THAT'S RIGHT.
OUR PRIORITY IS GATHERING INTELLIGENCE AND BLENDING IN WITH THEM.
THE ENTIRE OPERATION COULD BE COMPROMISED IF WE MAKE WAVES.
BUT...
THEY'RE EVENTUALLY GONNA FEED ON PEOPLE.
We're just gonna let them?
IT'S SO WE CAN CATCH THE BIG FISH.
COMPARED TO AOGIRI AND ROSÉ, THESE LITTLE GHOULS ARE INCONSEQUENTIAL.

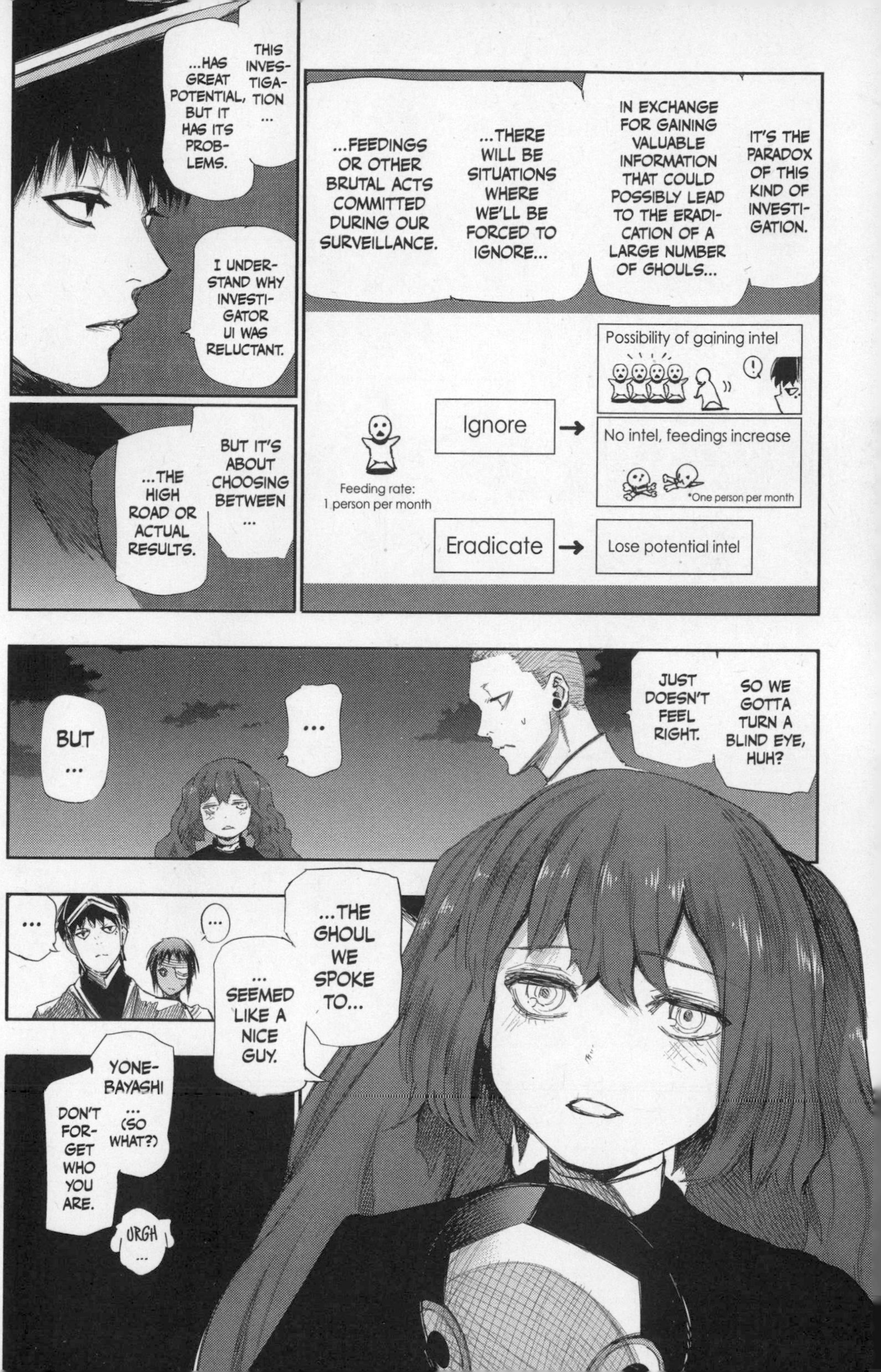
IT'S THE PARADOX OF THIS KIND OF INVESTIGATION.
IN EXCHANGE FOR GAINING VALUABLE INFORMATION THAT COULD POSSIBLY LEAD TO THE ERADICATION OF A LARGE NUMBER OF GHOULS...
...THERE WILL BE SITUATIONS WHERE WE'LL BE FORCED TO IGNORE...
...FEEDINGS OR OTHER BRUTAL ACTS COMMITTED DURING OUR SURVEILLANCE.
Feeding rate: 1 person per month
Ignore
Possibility of gaining intel
No intel, feedings increase
*One person per month
Eradicate
Lose potential intel
THIS INVESTIGATION...
...HAS GREAT POTENTIAL, BUT IT HAS ITS PROBLEMS.
I UNDERSTAND WHY INVESTIGATOR UI WAS RELUCTANT.
BUT IT'S ABOUT CHOOSING BETWEEN...
...THE HIGH ROAD OR ACTUAL RESULTS.
SO WE GOTTA TURN A BLIND EYE, HUH?
JUST DOESN'T FEEL RIGHT.
...
BUT ...
...THE GHOUL WE SPOKE TO...
... SEEMED LIKE A NICE GUY.
...
...
YONE-BAYASHI ... (SO WHAT?)
DON'T FORGET WHO YOU ARE.
URGH ...

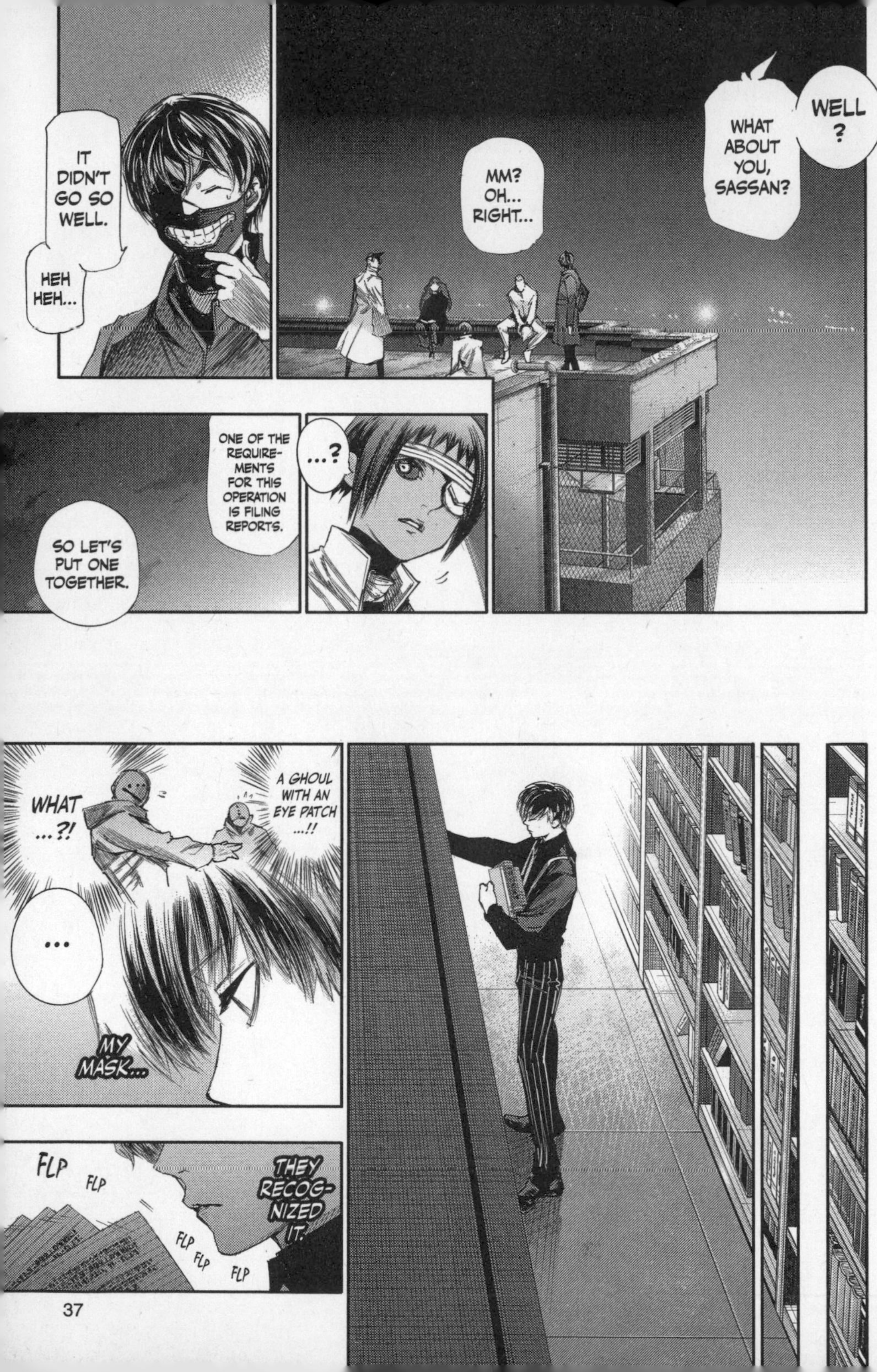
WELL?
WHAT ABOUT YOU, SASSAN?
MM? OH... RIGHT...
IT DIDN'T GO SO WELL.
HEH HEH...
...?
ONE OF THE REQUIRE-MENTS FOR THIS OPERATION IS FILING REPORTS.
SO LET'S PUT ONE TOGETHER.
A GHOUL WITH AN EYE PATCH ...!!
WHAT ...?!
...
MY MASK...
THEY RECOG-NIZED IT.
FLP
FLP
FLP
FLP
FLP

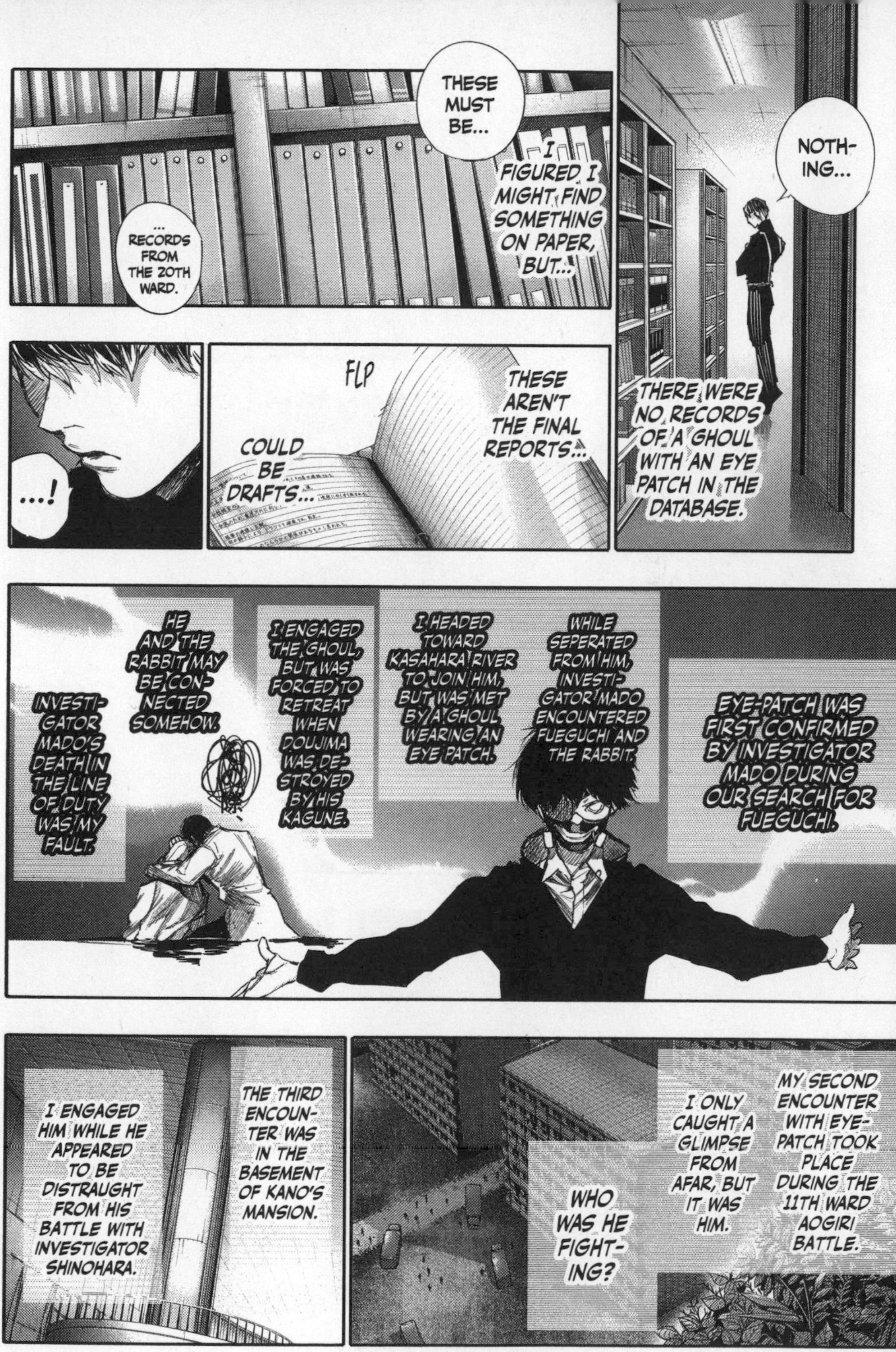
NOTH-ING...
THERE WERE NO RECORDS OF A GHOUL WITH AN EYE PATCH IN THE DATABASE.
THESE MUST BE...
I FIGURED I MIGHT FIND SOMETHING ON PAPER, BUT...
... RECORDS FROM THE 20TH WARD.
THESE AREN'T THE FINAL REPORTS...
FLP
COULD BE DRAFTS...
...!
EYE-PATCH WAS FIRST CONFIRMED BY INVESTIGATOR MADO DURING OUR SEARCH FOR FUEGUCHI.
WHILE SEPERATED FROM HIM, INVESTI-GATOR MADO ENCOUNTERED FUEGUCHI AND THE RABBIT.
I HEADED TOWARD KASAHARA RIVER TO JOIN HIM, BUT WAS MET BY A GHOUL WEARING AN EYE PATCH.
I ENGAGED THE GHOUL, BUT WAS FORCED TO RETREAT WHEN DOUJIMA WAS DE-STROYED BY HIS KAGUNE.
HE AND THE RABBIT MAY BE CON-NECTED SOMEHOW.
INVESTI-GATOR MADO'S DEATH IN THE LINE OF DUTY WAS MY FAULT.
MY SECOND ENCOUNTER WITH EYE-PATCH TOOK PLACE DURING THE 11TH WARD AOGIRI BATTLE.
I ONLY CAUGHT A GLIMPSE FROM AFAR, BUT IT WAS HIM.
WHO WAS HE FIGHT-ING?
THE THIRD ENCOUN-TER WAS IN THE BASEMENT OF KANO'S MANSION.
I ENGAGED HIM WHILE HE APPEARED TO BE DISTRAUGHT FROM HIS BATTLE WITH INVESTIGATOR SHINOHARA.

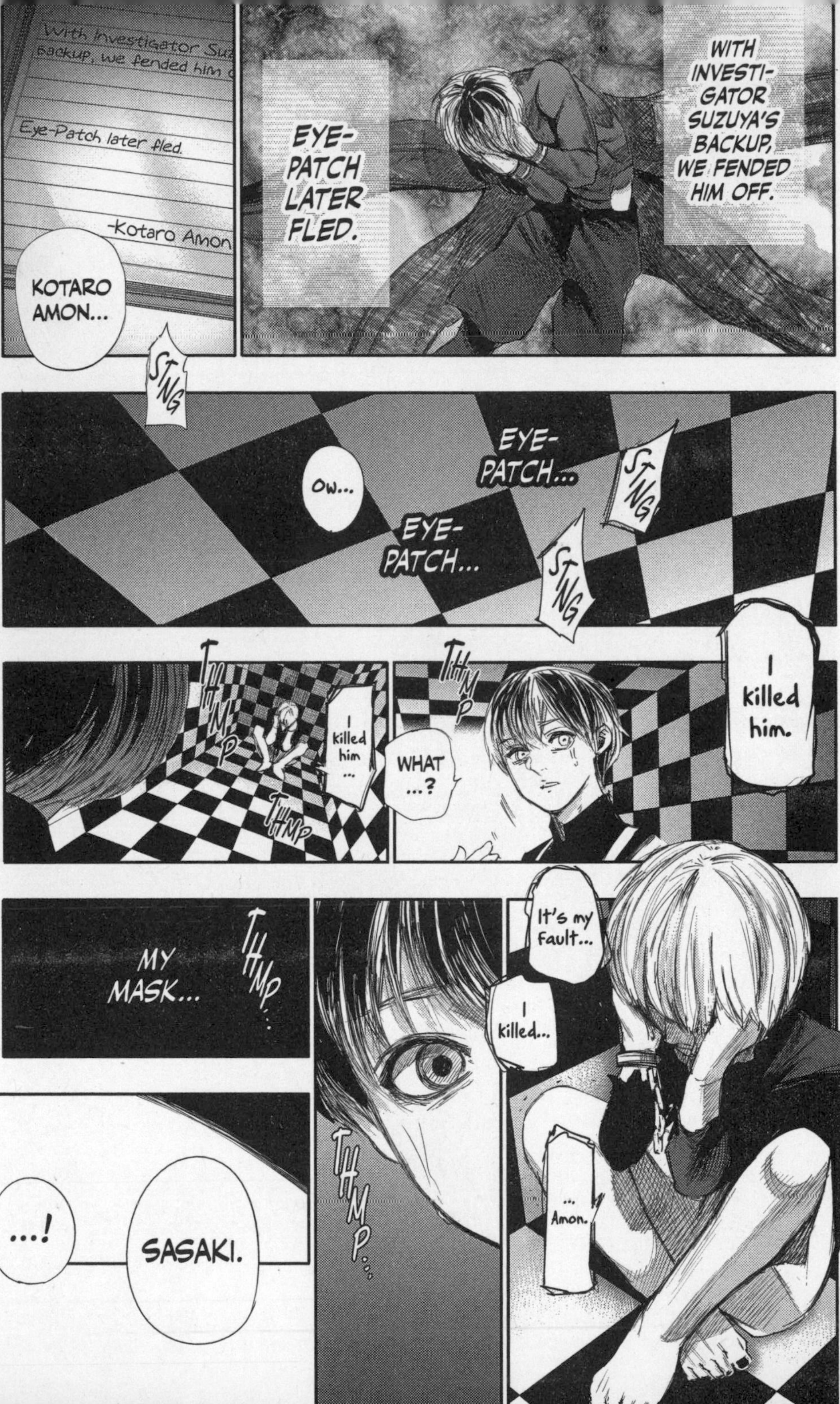
WITH INVESTIGATOR SUZUYA'S BACKUP, WE FENDED HIM OFF.
EYE-PATCH LATER FLED.
Eye-Patch later fled.
-Kotaro Amon
KOTARO AMON...
STING
STING
STING
EYE-PATCH...
EYE-PATCH...
Ow...
I killed him.
THMP
WHAT ...?
THMP
I killed him ...
THMP
It's my fault...
I killed...
... Amon.
THMP...
THMP...
MY MASK...
SASAKI.
...!

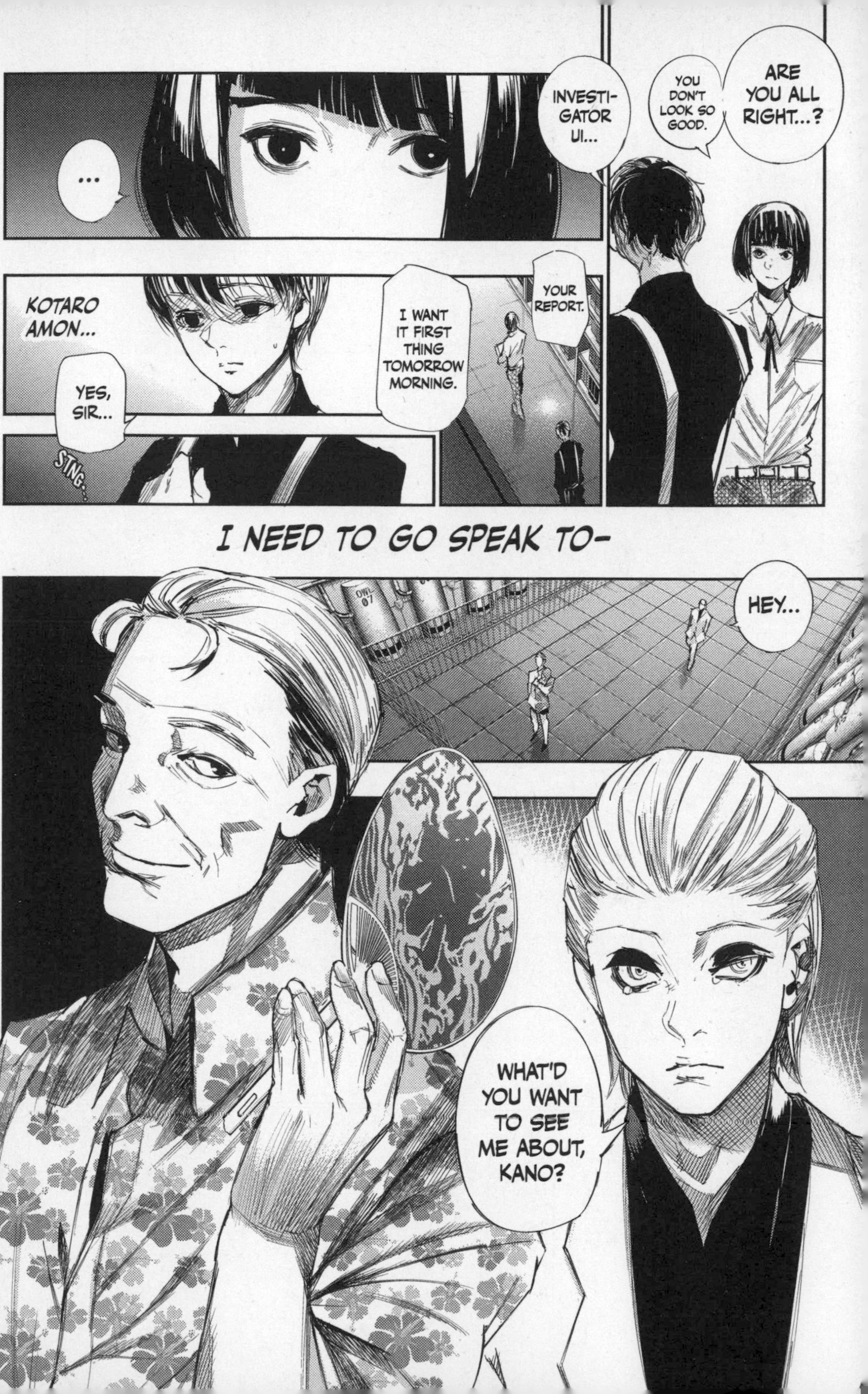
ARE YOU ALL RIGHT...?
YOU DON'T LOOK SO GOOD.
INVESTI-GATOR UI...
...
YOUR REPORT.
I WANT IT FIRST THING TOMORROW MORNING.
KOTARO AMON...
YES, SIR...
STNG...
I NEED TO GO SPEAK TO-
HEY...
WHAT'D YOU WANT TO SEE ME ABOUT, KANO?

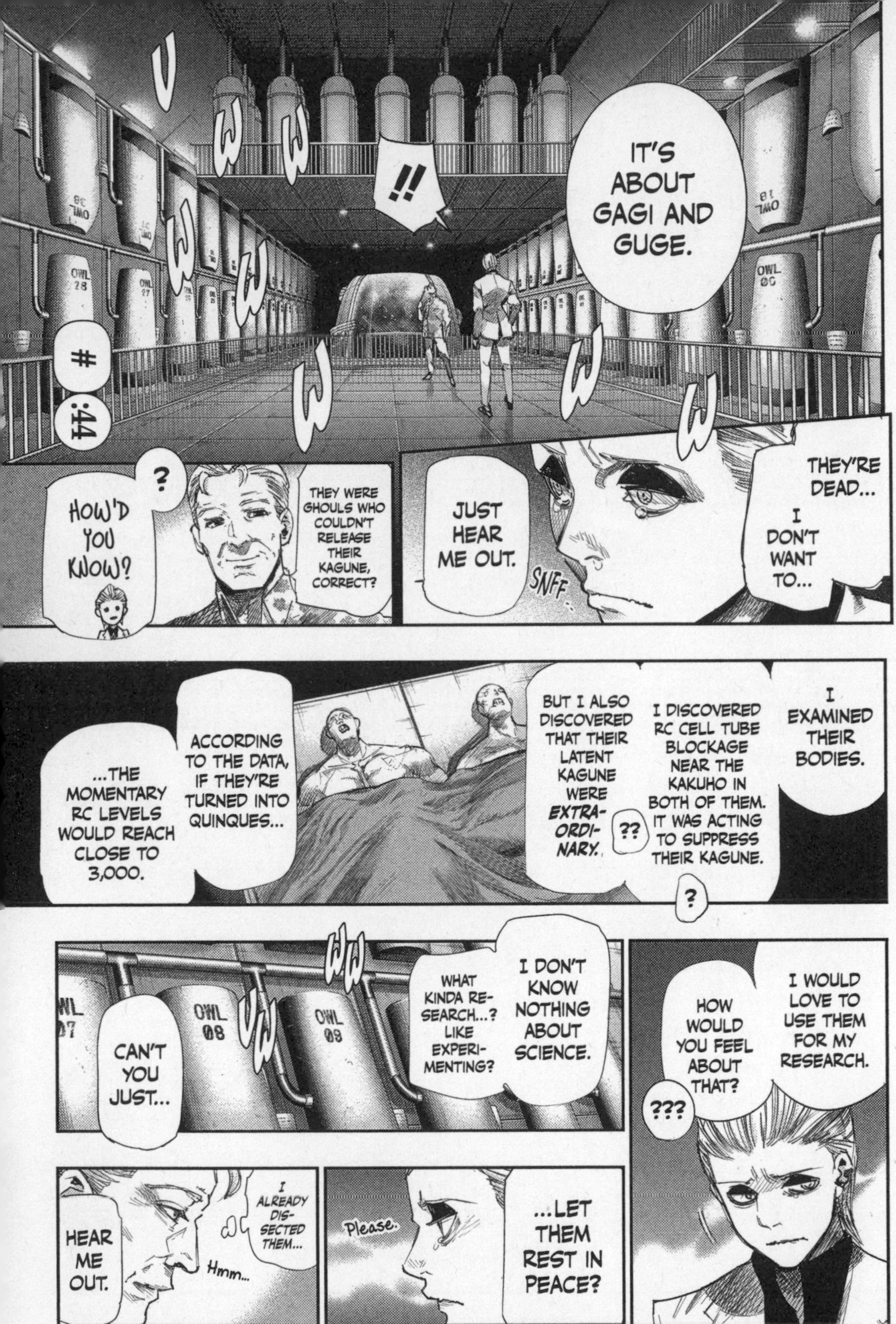
IT'S ABOUT GAGI AND GUGE.
!!
#:44
THEY'RE DEAD... I DON'T WANT TO...
JUST HEAR ME OUT.
SNFF
THEY WERE GHOULS WHO COULDN'T RELEASE THEIR KAGUNE, CORRECT?
?
HOW'D YOU KNOW?
I EXAMINED THEIR BODIES.
I DISCOVERED RC CELL TUBE BLOCKAGE NEAR THE KAKUHO IN BOTH OF THEM. IT WAS ACTING TO SUPPRESS THEIR KAGUNE.
?
BUT I ALSO DISCOVERED THAT THEIR LATENT KAGUNE WERE EXTRAORDINARY.
??
ACCORDING TO THE DATA, IF THEY'RE TURNED INTO QUINQUES...
...THE MOMENTARY RC LEVELS WOULD REACH CLOSE TO 3,000.
I WOULD LOVE TO USE THEM FOR MY RESEARCH.
HOW WOULD YOU FEEL ABOUT THAT?
???
I DON'T KNOW NOTHING ABOUT SCIENCE.
WHAT KINDA RESEARCH...? LIKE EXPERIMENTING?
CAN'T YOU JUST...
OWL 08
OWL 09
...LET THEM REST IN PEACE?
Please.
I ALREADY DISSECTED THEM...
Hmm...
HEAR ME OUT.

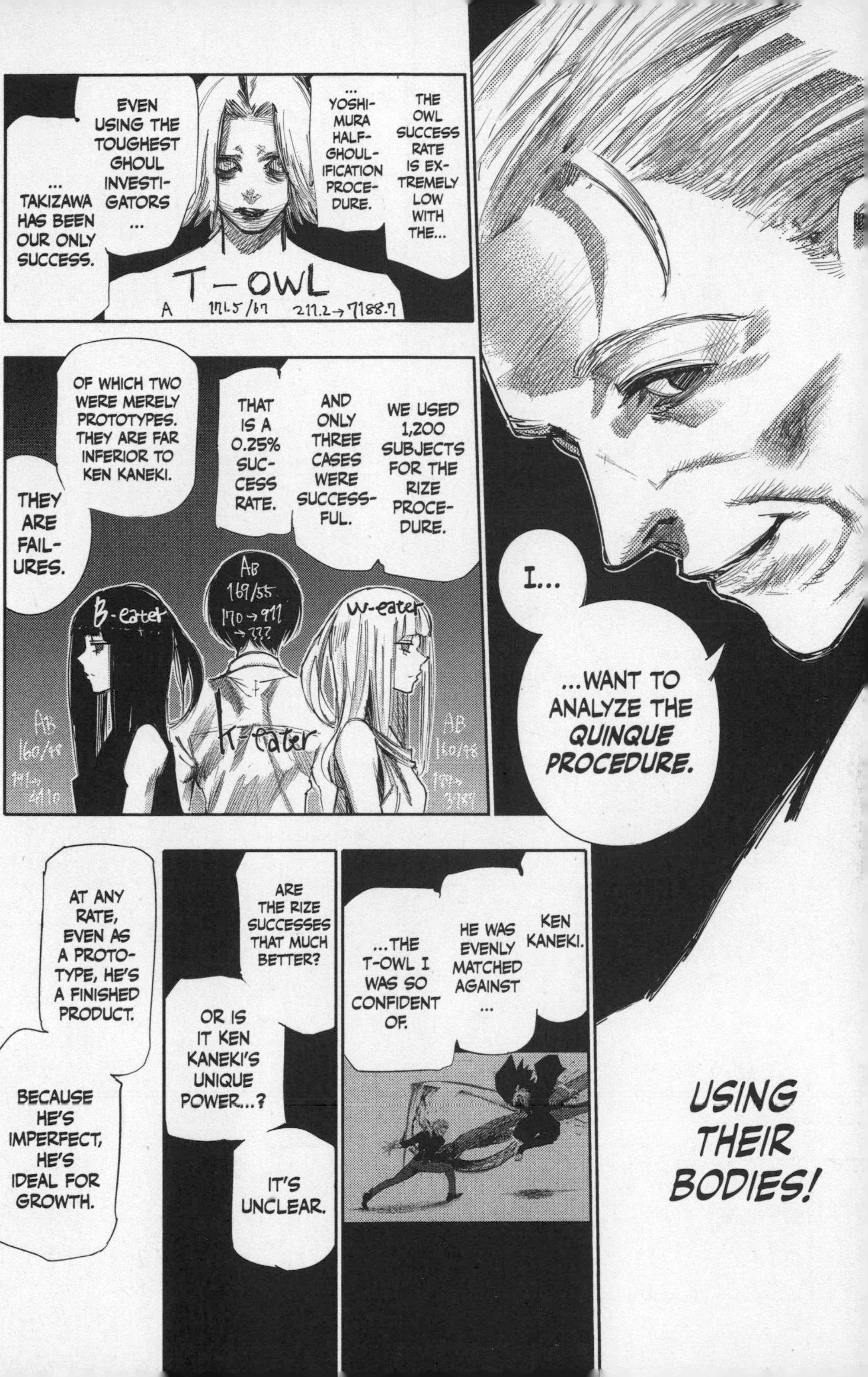
I...
...WANT TO ANALYZE THE *QUINQUE PROCEDURE.*
USING THEIR BODIES!
THE OWL SUCCESS RATE IS EXTREMELY LOW WITH THE...
...YOSHIMURA HALF-GHOULIFICATION PROCEDURE.
EVEN USING THE TOUGHEST GHOUL INVESTIGATORS...
...TAKIZAWA HAS BEEN OUR ONLY SUCCESS.
T-OWL
A 171.5/67 211.2→7188.7
WE USED 1,200 SUBJECTS FOR THE RIZE PROCEDURE.
AND ONLY THREE CASES WERE SUCCESSFUL.
THAT IS A 0.25% SUCCESS RATE.
OF WHICH TWO WERE MERELY PROTOTYPES. THEY ARE FAR INFERIOR TO KEN KANEKI.
THEY ARE FAILURES.
W-eater
AB 169/55 170→911 →???
B-eater
K-eater
KEN KANEKI.
HE WAS EVENLY MATCHED AGAINST...
...THE T-OWL I WAS SO CONFIDENT OF.
ARE THE RIZE SUCCESSES THAT MUCH BETTER?
OR IS IT KEN KANEKI'S UNIQUE POWER...?
IT'S UNCLEAR.
AT ANY RATE, EVEN AS A PROTOTYPE, HE'S A FINISHED PRODUCT.
BECAUSE HE'S IMPERFECT, HE'S IDEAL FOR GROWTH.

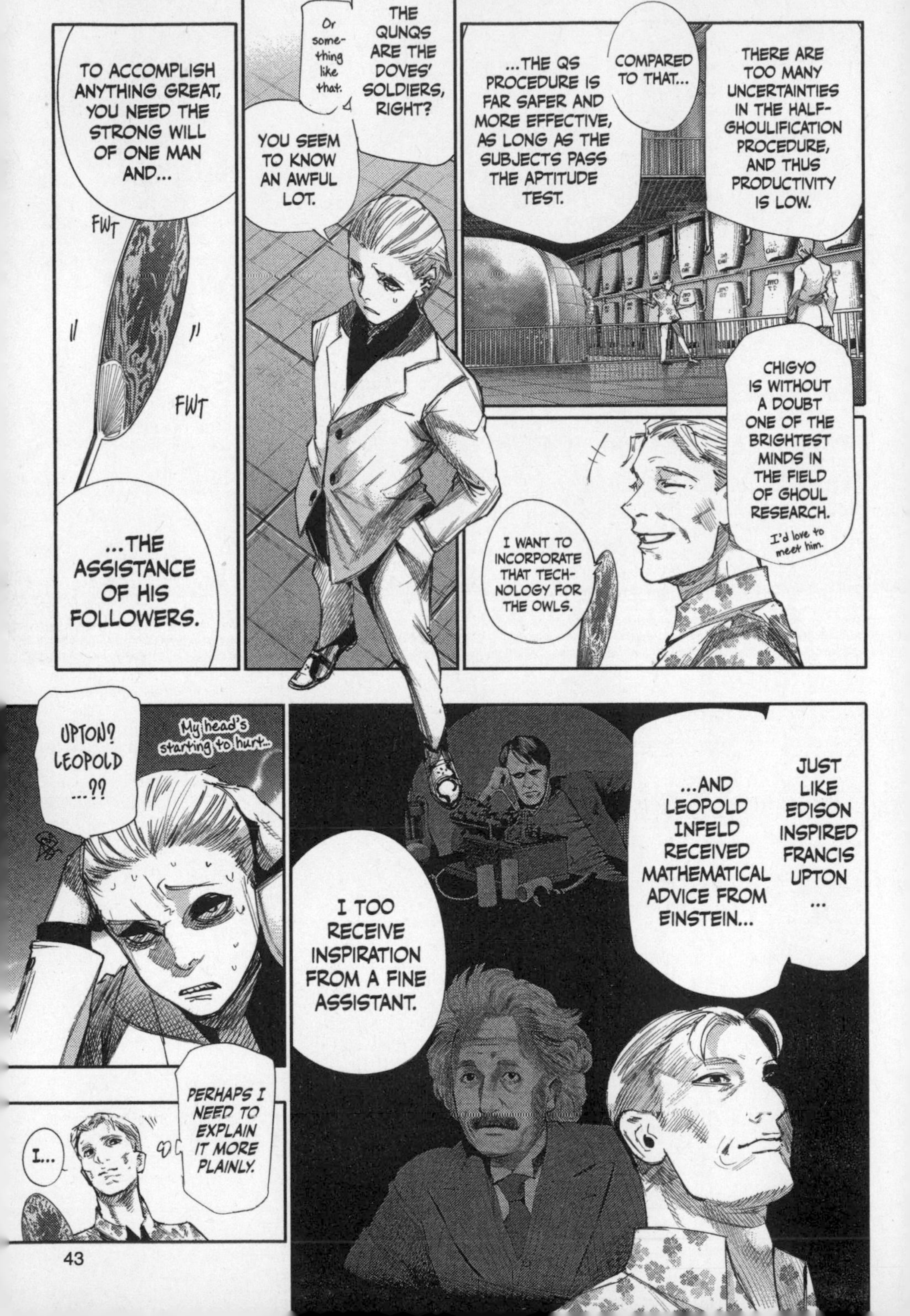
THERE ARE TOO MANY UNCERTAINTIES IN THE HALF-GHOULIFICATION PROCEDURE, AND THUS PRODUCTIVITY IS LOW.
COMPARED TO THAT...
...THE QS PROCEDURE IS FAR SAFER AND MORE EFFECTIVE, AS LONG AS THE SUBJECTS PASS THE APTITUDE TEST.
CHIGYO IS WITHOUT A DOUBT ONE OF THE BRIGHTEST MINDS IN THE FIELD OF GHOUL RESEARCH.
I'd love to meet him.
I WANT TO INCORPORATE THAT TECH-NOLOGY FOR THE OWLS.
THE QUNQS ARE THE DOVES' SOLDIERS, RIGHT?
Or some-thing like that.
YOU SEEM TO KNOW AN AWFUL LOT.
TO ACCOMPLISH ANYTHING GREAT, YOU NEED THE STRONG WILL OF ONE MAN AND...
FWT
FWT
...THE ASSISTANCE OF HIS FOLLOWERS.
JUST LIKE EDISON INSPIRED FRANCIS UPTON...
...AND LEOPOLD INFELD RECEIVED MATHEMATICAL ADVICE FROM EINSTEIN...
I TOO RECEIVE INSPIRATION FROM A FINE ASSISTANT.
UPTON? LEOPOLD ...??
My head's starting to hurt...
PERHAPS I NEED TO EXPLAIN IT MORE PLAINLY.
I...

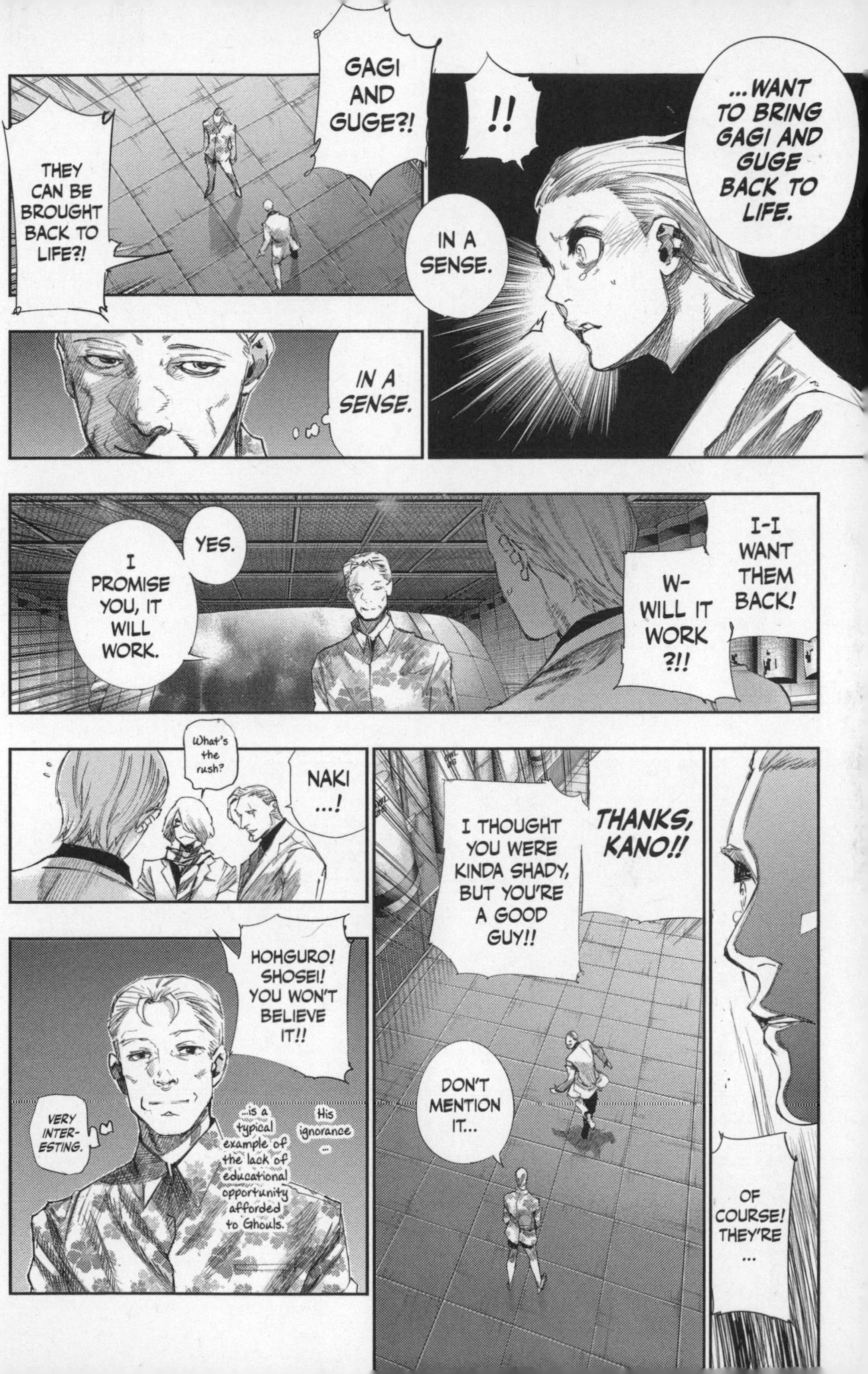
...WANT TO BRING GAGI AND GUGE BACK TO LIFE.
!!
IN A SENSE.
GAGI AND GUGE?!
THEY CAN BE BROUGHT BACK TO LIFE?!
IN A SENSE.
I-I WANT THEM BACK!
W-WILL IT WORK?!!
YES.
I PROMISE YOU, IT WILL WORK.
OF COURSE! THEY'RE ...
THANKS, KANO!!
I THOUGHT YOU WERE KINDA SHADY, BUT YOU'RE A GOOD GUY!!
DON'T MENTION IT...
NAKI ...!
What's the rush?
HOHGURO! SHOSEI! YOU WON'T BELIEVE IT!!
His ignorance ...
...is a typical example of the lack of educational opportunity afforded to Ghouls.
VERY INTERESTING.

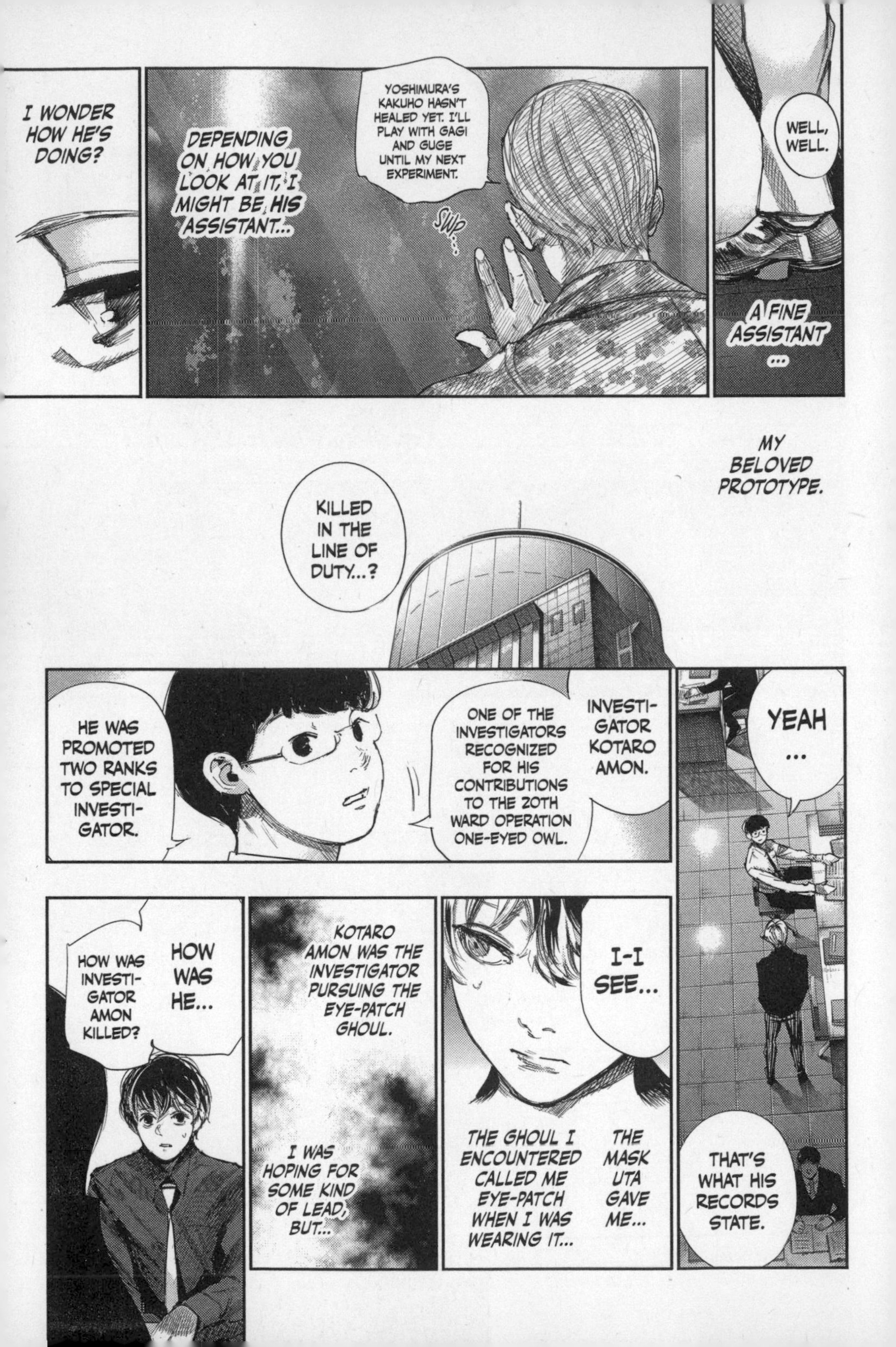
WELL, WELL.
A FINE ASSISTANT ...
YOSHIMURA'S KAKUHO HASN'T HEALED YET. I'LL PLAY WITH GAGI AND GUGE UNTIL MY NEXT EXPERIMENT.
DEPENDING ON HOW YOU LOOK AT IT, I MIGHT BE HIS ASSISTANT...
SWP...
I WONDER HOW HE'S DOING?
MY BELOVED PROTOTYPE.
KILLED IN THE LINE OF DUTY...?
YEAH ...
THAT'S WHAT HIS RECORDS STATE.
INVESTIGATOR KOTARO AMON.
ONE OF THE INVESTIGATORS RECOGNIZED FOR HIS CONTRIBUTIONS TO THE 20TH WARD OPERATION ONE-EYED OWL.
HE WAS PROMOTED TWO RANKS TO SPECIAL INVESTIGATOR.
I-I SEE...
THE MASK UTA GAVE ME...
THE GHOUL I ENCOUNTERED CALLED ME EYE-PATCH WHEN I WAS WEARING IT...
KOTARO AMON WAS THE INVESTIGATOR PURSUING THE EYE-PATCH GHOUL.
I WAS HOPING FOR SOME KIND OF LEAD, BUT...
HOW WAS HE...
HOW WAS INVESTIGATOR AMON KILLED?

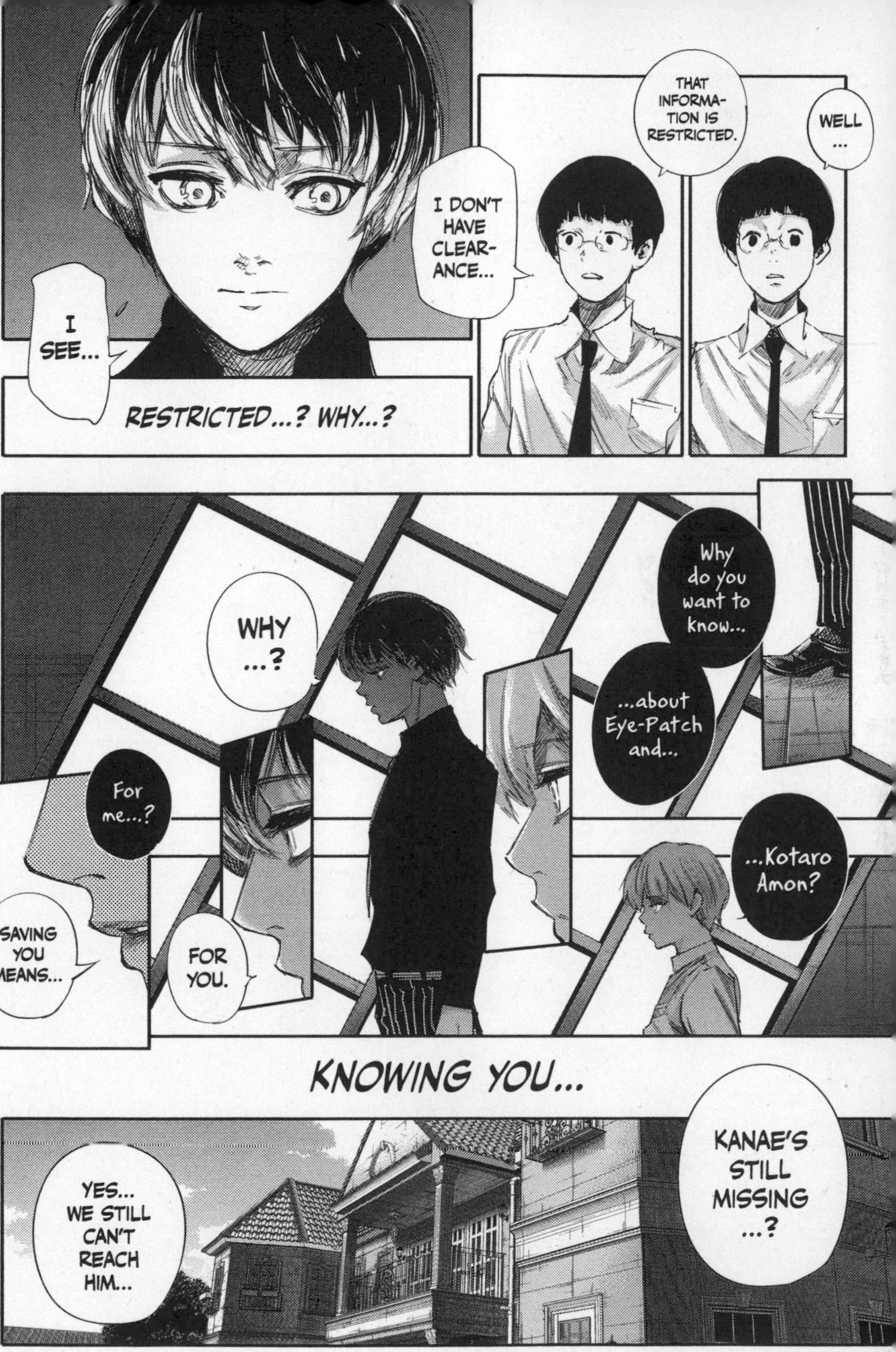

WELL ...
THAT INFORMATION IS RESTRICTED.
I DON'T HAVE CLEARANCE...
I SEE...
RESTRICTED...? WHY...?
Why do you want to know...
...about Eye-Patch and...
...Kotaro Amon?
WHY ...?
For me...?
FOR YOU.
SAVING YOU MEANS...
KNOWING YOU...
KANAE'S STILL MISSING ...?
YES... WE STILL CAN'T REACH HIM...

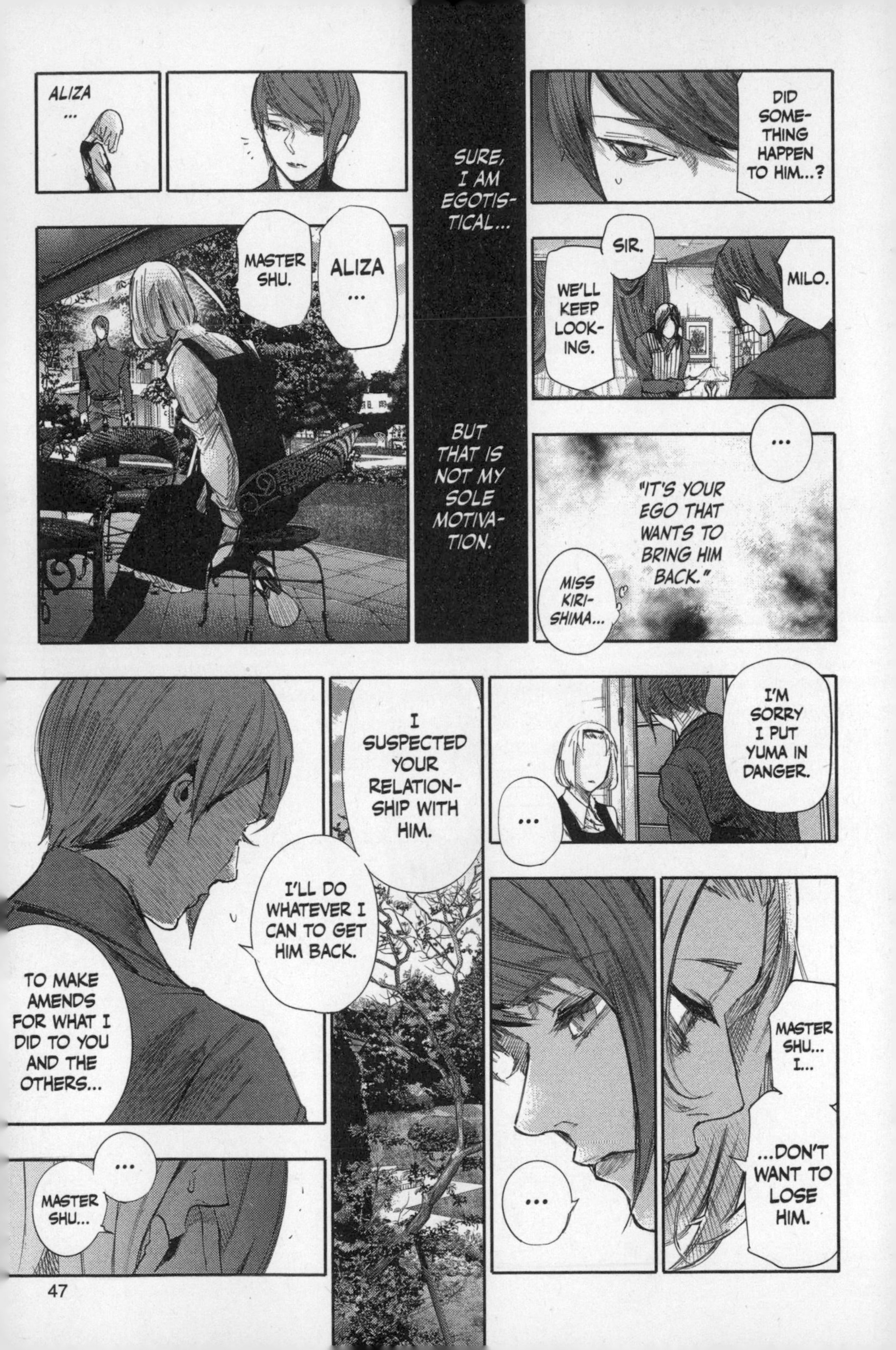
DID SOMETHING HAPPEN TO HIM...?
MILO.
SIR.
WE'LL KEEP LOOKING.
...
"IT'S YOUR EGO THAT WANTS TO BRING HIM BACK."
MISS KIRISHIMA...
SURE, I AM EGOTISTICAL...
BUT THAT IS NOT MY SOLE MOTIVATION.
ALIZA ...
ALIZA ...
MASTER SHU.
I'M SORRY I PUT YUMA IN DANGER.
...
I SUSPECTED YOUR RELATIONSHIP WITH HIM.
I'LL DO WHATEVER I CAN TO GET HIM BACK.
TO MAKE AMENDS FOR WHAT I DID TO YOU AND THE OTHERS...
MASTER SHU... I...
...DON'T WANT TO LOSE HIM.
...
...
MASTER SHU...

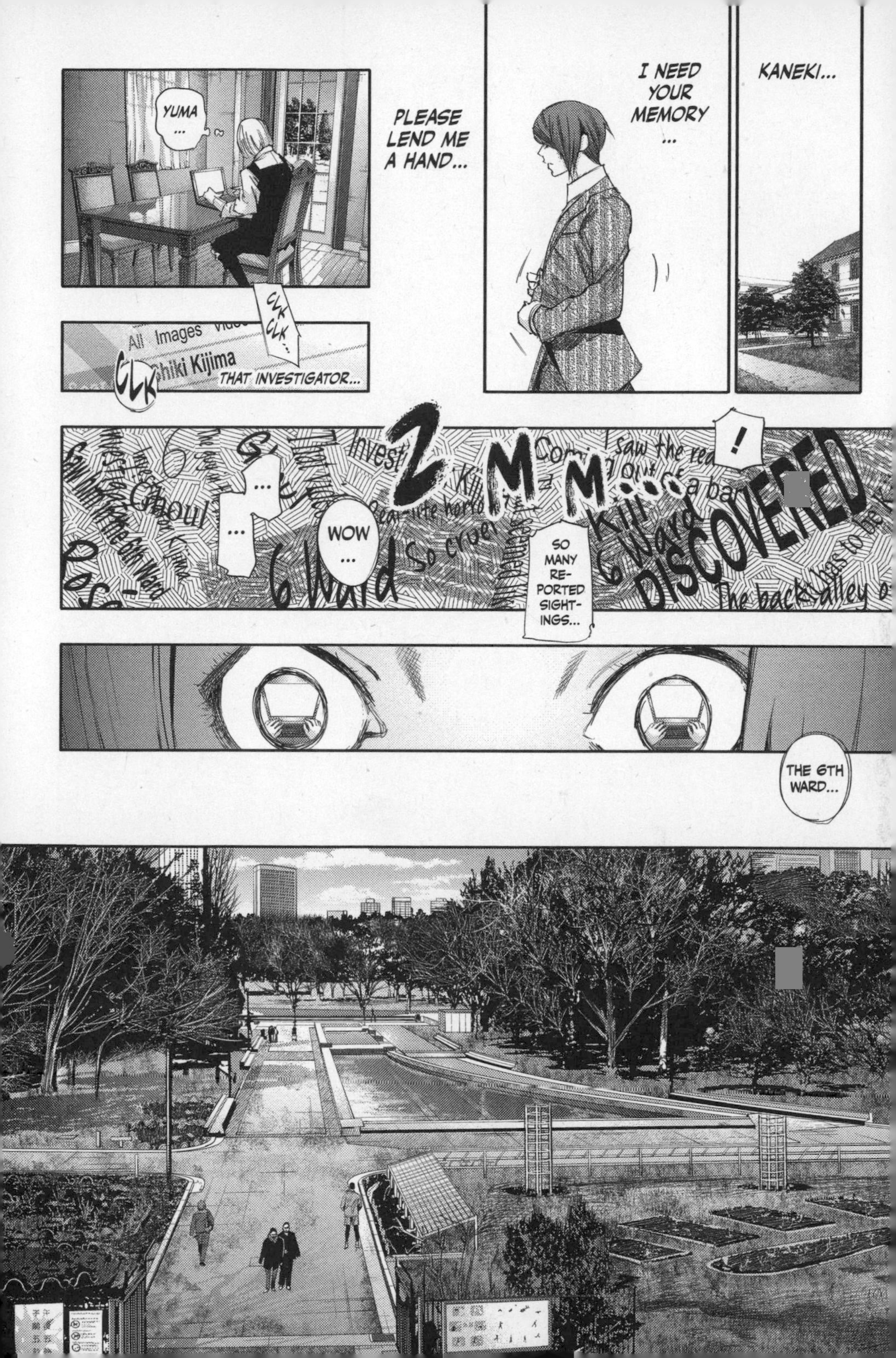
KANEKI...
I NEED YOUR MEMORY...
PLEASE LEND ME A HAND...
YUMA...
CLK CLK...
All Images
Shiki Kijima
CLK
THAT INVESTIGATOR...
!
DISCOVERED
6 Ward
SO MANY RE-PORTED SIGHT-INGS...
ZMM...
WOW...
6 Ward
...
...
Ghoul
THE 6TH WARD...

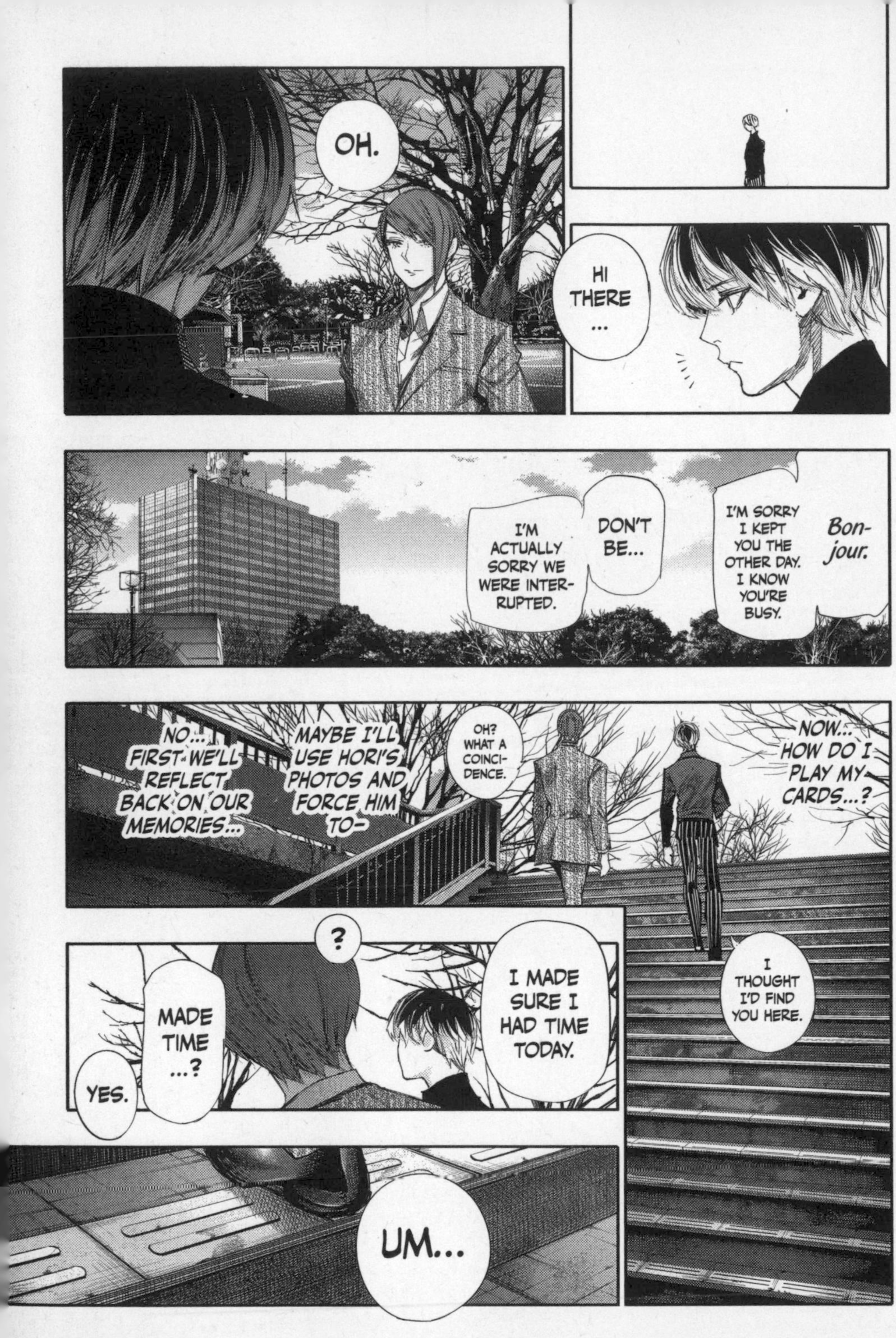
HI THERE ...
OH.
Bon-jour.
I'M SORRY I KEPT YOU THE OTHER DAY. I KNOW YOU'RE BUSY.
DON'T BE...
I'M ACTUALLY SORRY WE WERE INTER-RUPTED.
NOW... HOW DO I PLAY MY CARDS...?
OH? WHAT A COINCI-DENCE.
MAYBE I'LL USE HORI'S PHOTOS AND FORCE HIM TO-
NO... FIRST WE'LL REFLECT BACK ON OUR MEMORIES...
I THOUGHT I'D FIND YOU HERE.
?
I MADE SURE I HAD TIME TODAY.
MADE TIME ...?
YES.
UM...

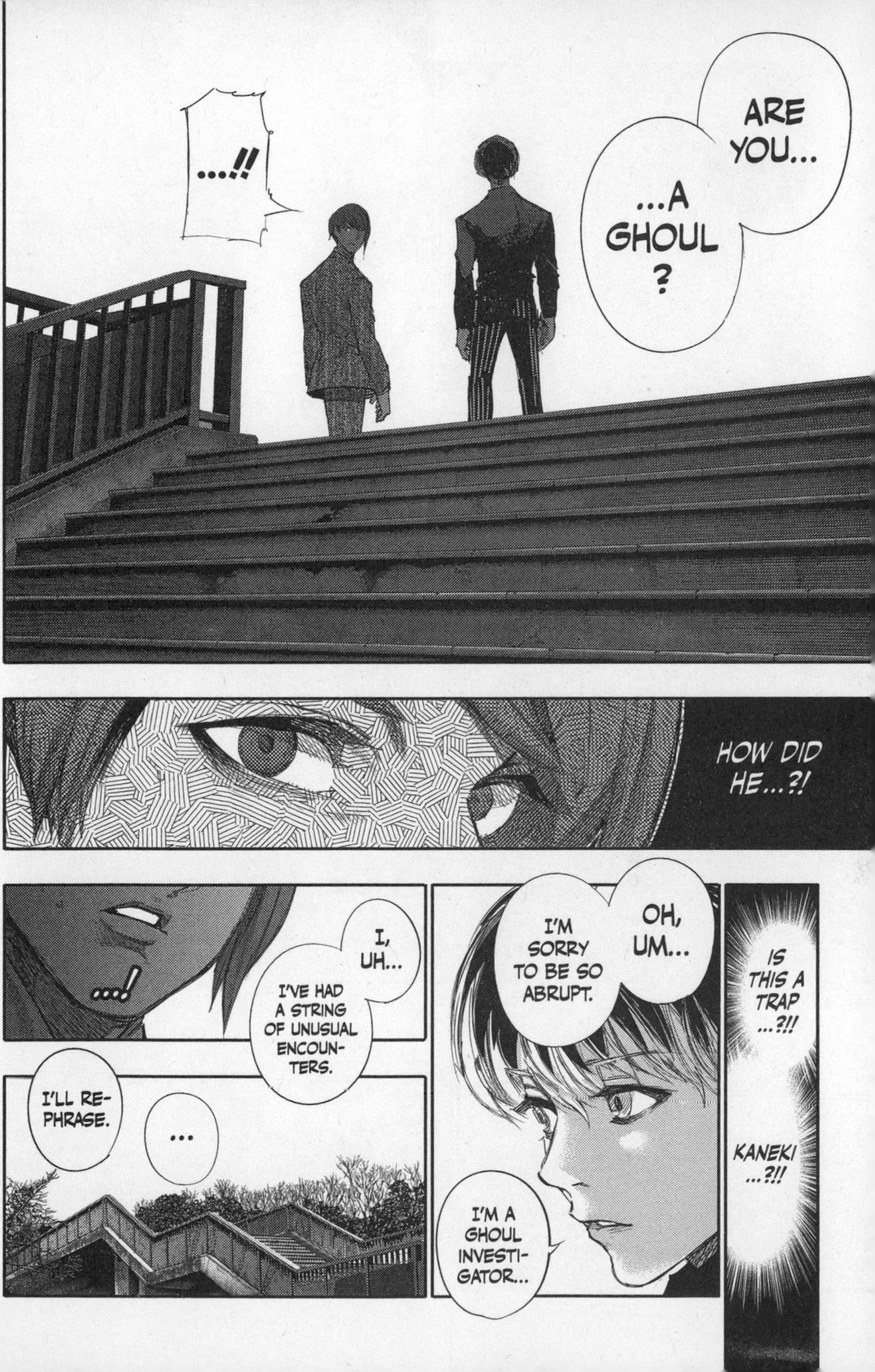
ARE YOU...
...A GHOUL ?
...!!
HOW DID HE...?!
IS THIS A TRAP ...?!!
KANEKI ...?!!
OH, UM...
I'M SORRY TO BE SO ABRUPT.
I'VE HAD A STRING OF UNUSUAL ENCOUNTERS.
I'M A GHOUL INVESTIGATOR...
...!
I, UH...
...
I'LL RE-PHRASE.

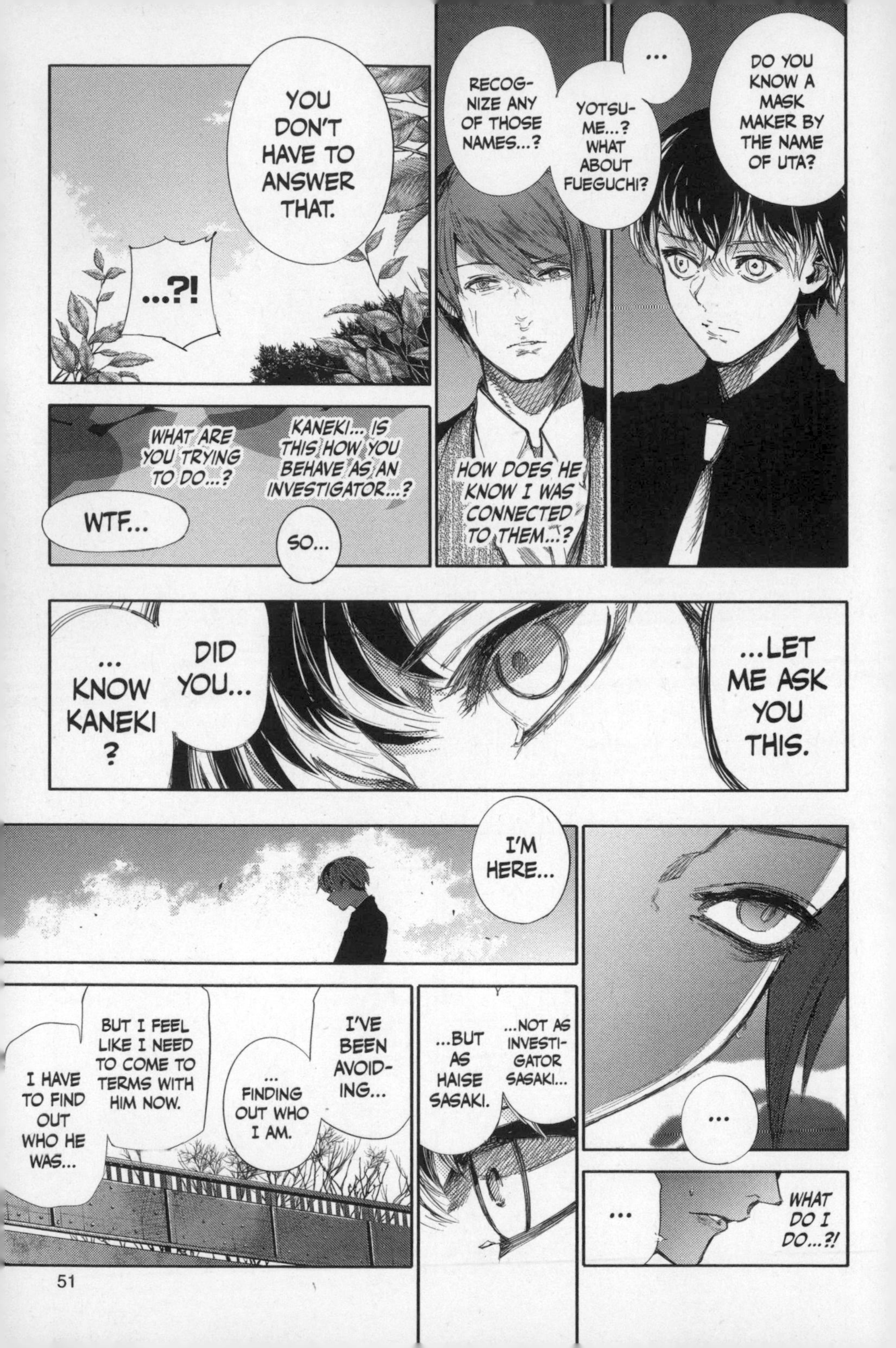
DO YOU KNOW A MASK MAKER BY THE NAME OF UTA?
...
YOTSUME...? WHAT ABOUT FUEGUCHI?
RECOGNIZE ANY OF THOSE NAMES...?
HOW DOES HE KNOW I WAS CONNECTED TO THEM...?
YOU DON'T HAVE TO ANSWER THAT.
...?!
KANEKI... IS THIS HOW YOU BEHAVE AS AN INVESTIGATOR...?
SO...
WHAT ARE YOU TRYING TO DO...?
WTF...
...LET ME ASK YOU THIS.
DID YOU...
... KNOW KANEKI?
...
...
WHAT DO I DO...?!
I'M HERE...
...NOT AS INVESTIGATOR SASAKI...
...BUT AS HAISE SASAKI.
I'VE BEEN AVOIDING...
... FINDING OUT WHO I AM.
BUT I FEEL LIKE I NEED TO COME TO TERMS WITH HIM NOW.
I HAVE TO FIND OUT WHO HE WAS...

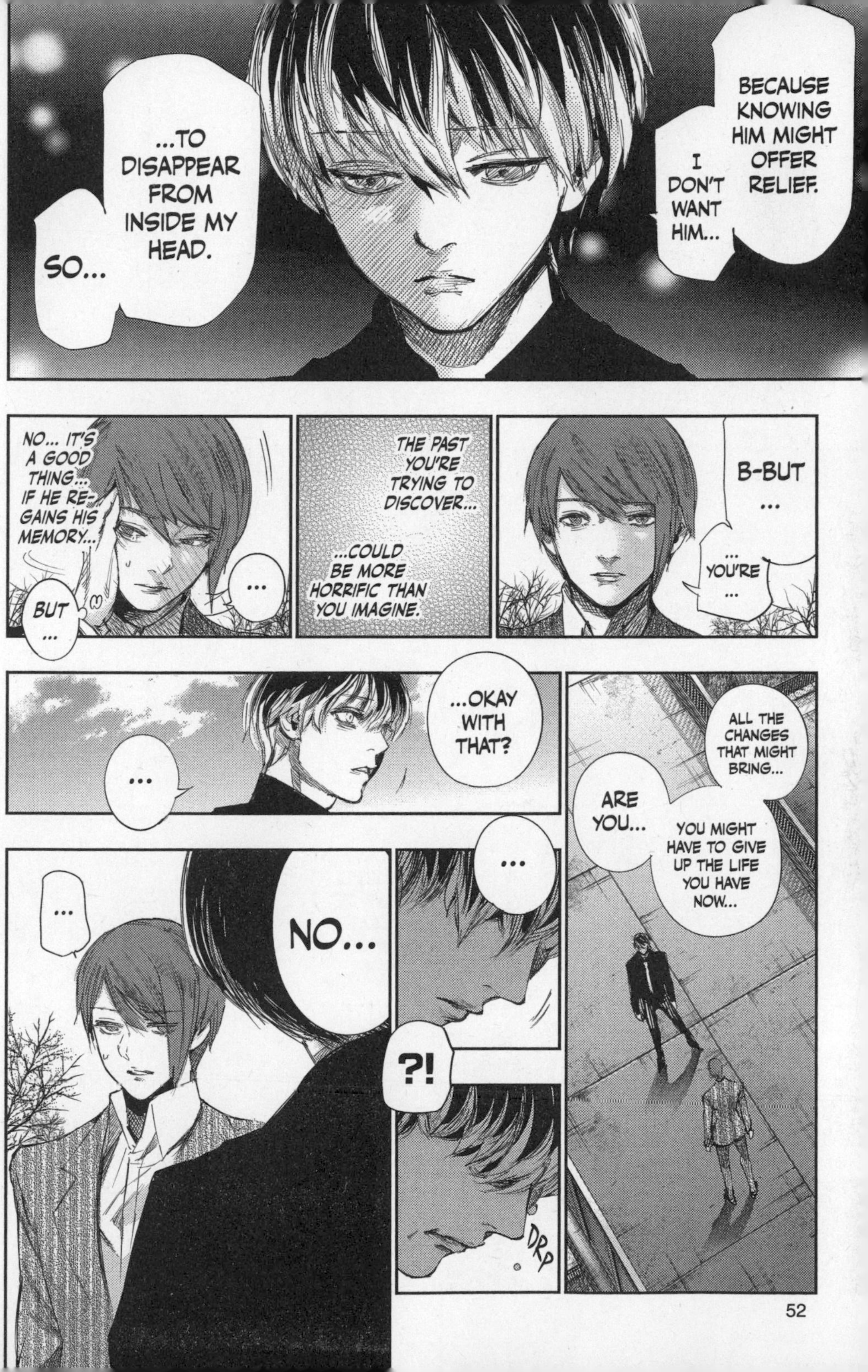
BECAUSE KNOWING HIM MIGHT OFFER RELIEF.
I DON'T WANT HIM...
SO...
...TO DISAPPEAR FROM INSIDE MY HEAD.
B-BUT ...
... YOU'RE ...
THE PAST YOU'RE TRYING TO DISCOVER...
...COULD BE MORE HORRIFIC THAN YOU IMAGINE.
...
NO... IT'S A GOOD THING... IF HE RE-GAINS HIS MEMORY...
BUT ...
ALL THE CHANGES THAT MIGHT BRING...
ARE YOU...
YOU MIGHT HAVE TO GIVE UP THE LIFE YOU HAVE NOW...
...OKAY WITH THAT?
...
...
?!
DRP
NO...
...

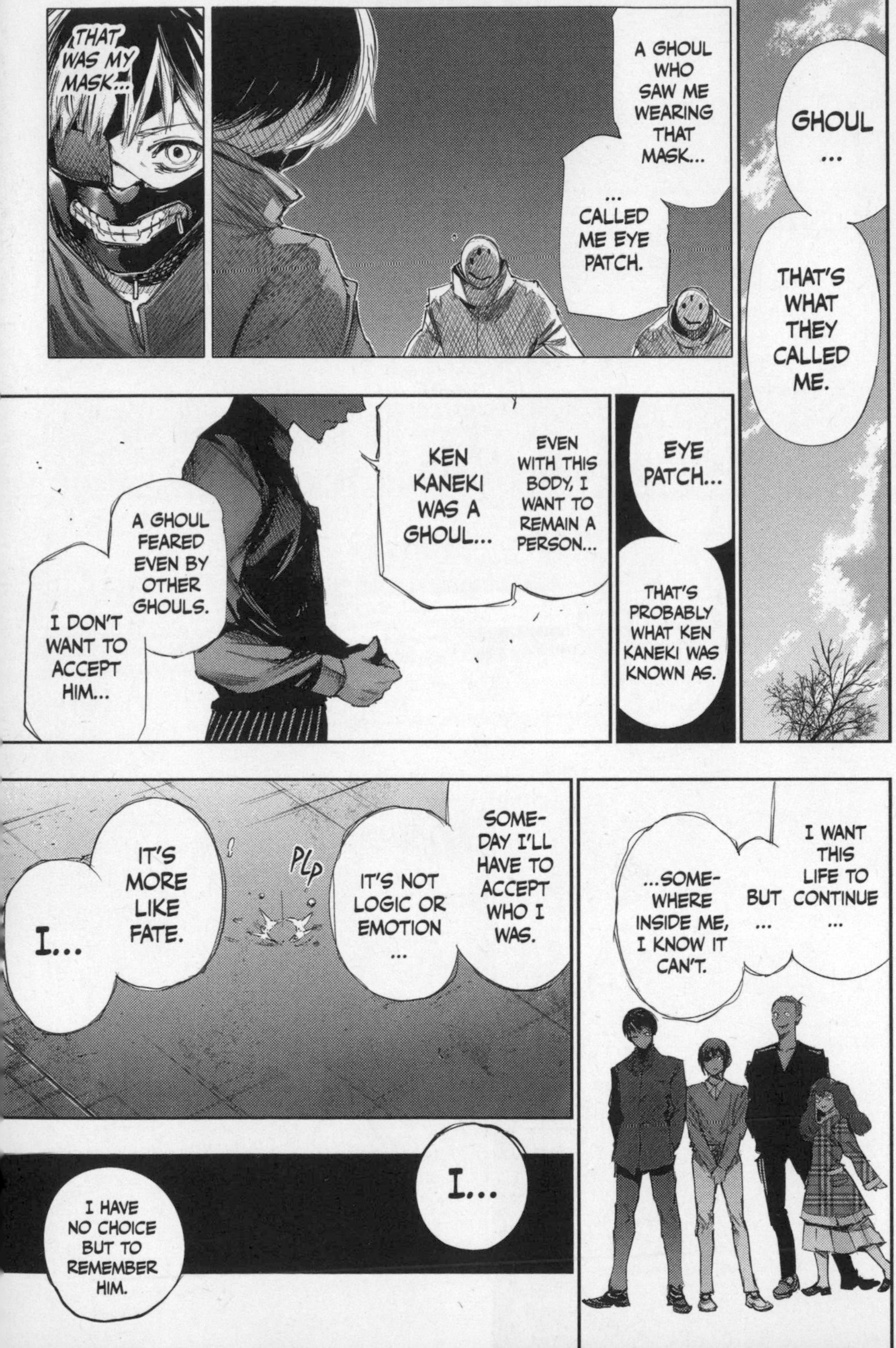
GHOUL ...
THAT'S WHAT THEY CALLED ME.
A GHOUL WHO SAW ME WEARING THAT MASK...
... CALLED ME EYE PATCH.
THAT WAS MY MASK...
EYE PATCH...
THAT'S PROBABLY WHAT KEN KANEKI WAS KNOWN AS.
EVEN WITH THIS BODY, I WANT TO REMAIN A PERSON...
KEN KANEKI WAS A GHOUL...
A GHOUL FEARED EVEN BY OTHER GHOULS.
I DON'T WANT TO ACCEPT HIM...
I WANT THIS LIFE TO CONTINUE ...
BUT ...
...SOME-WHERE INSIDE ME, I KNOW IT CAN'T.
SOME-DAY I'LL HAVE TO ACCEPT WHO I WAS.
IT'S NOT LOGIC OR EMOTION ...
PLP
IT'S MORE LIKE FATE.
I...
I...
I HAVE NO CHOICE BUT TO REMEMBER HIM.

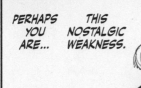

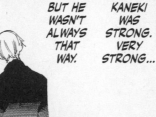

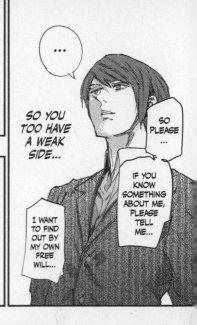

...
SO YOU TOO HAVE A WEAK SIDE...
SO PLEASE...
IF YOU KNOW SOMETHING ABOUT ME, PLEASE TELL ME...
I WANT TO FIND OUT BY MY OWN FREE WILL...
KANEKI WAS STRONG. VERY STRONG...
BUT HE WASN'T ALWAYS THAT WAY.
THIS NOSTALGIC WEAKNESS.
PERHAPS YOU ARE...
...AN EXTENSION OF KANEKI...
...WHO DID NOT MAKE A CHOICE.
WHO ONCE WAS NOT STRONG ENOUGH TO MAKE A CHOICE.
SUCH A WHOLESOME WEAKNESS...
...
"COULD YOU HAVE DIED FOR AN INGREDIENT?"
I'M NOT SURE.
HORI...
THERE ARE TOO MANY PRECIOUS THINGS IN THIS WORLD TO LIVE FOR.
ISN'T THAT RIGHT...?
"YOU CAN'T..."
IS THAT WHAT YOU WERE GOING TO SAY?
HORI, MY LITTLE FRIEND...
DID YOU KNOW...?
THAT I COULDN'T?
TIME TO BAIL.

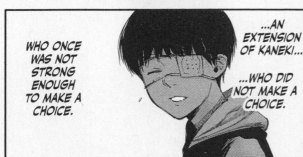

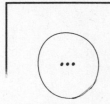

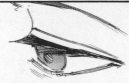

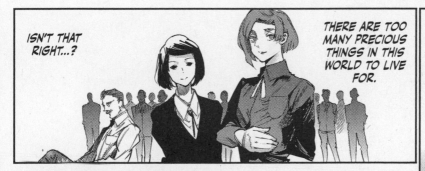

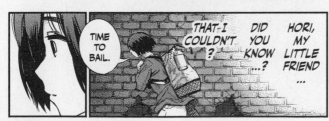

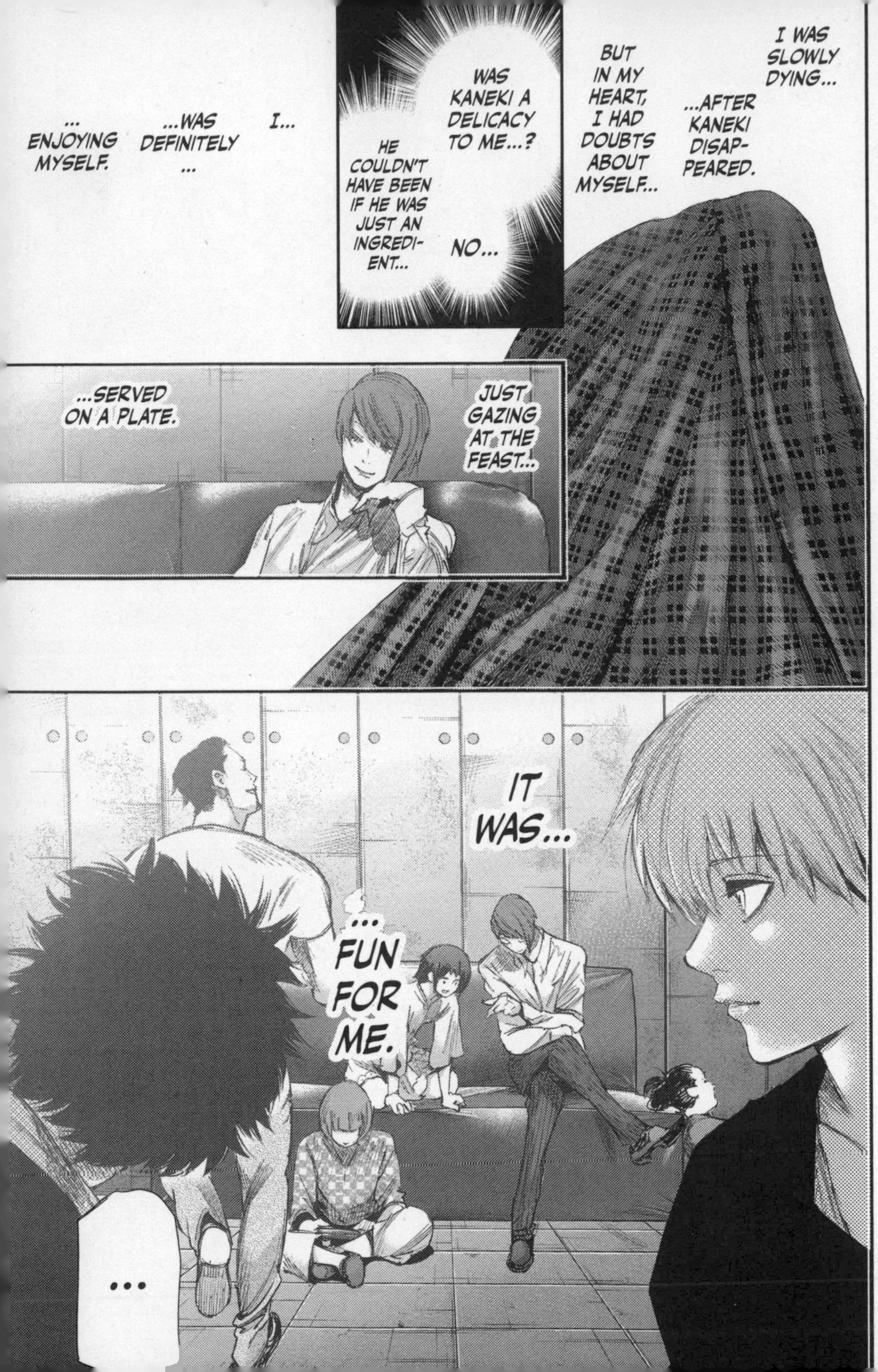
I WAS SLOWLY DYING...
...AFTER KANEKI DISAPPEARED.
BUT IN MY HEART, I HAD DOUBTS ABOUT MYSELF...
WAS KANEKI A DELICACY TO ME...?
NO...
HE COULDN'T HAVE BEEN IF HE WAS JUST AN INGREDIENT...
I...
...WAS DEFINITELY ...
... ENJOYING MYSELF.
JUST GAZING AT THE FEAST...
...SERVED ON A PLATE.
IT WAS...
... FUN FOR ME.
...

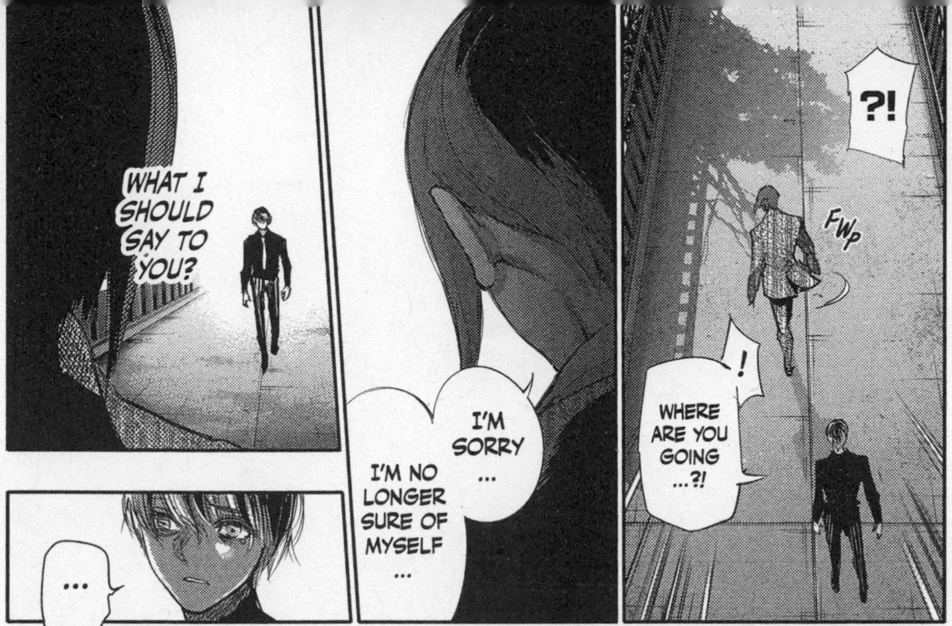
?!
FWP
!
WHERE ARE YOU GOING ...?!
I'M SORRY ...
I'M NO LONGER SURE OF MYSELF ...
WHAT I SHOULD SAY TO YOU?
...

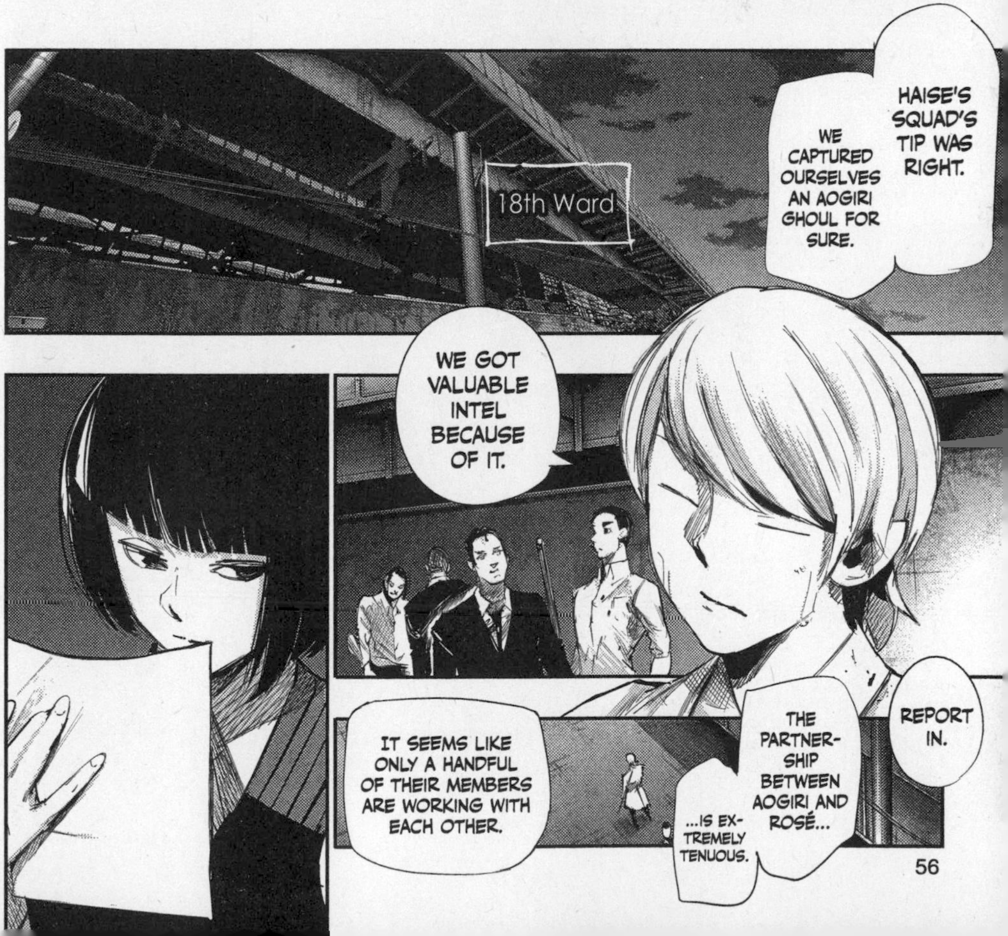
18th Ward
HAISE'S SQUAD'S TIP WAS RIGHT.
WE CAPTURED OURSELVES AN AOGIRI GHOUL FOR SURE.
WE GOT VALUABLE INTEL BECAUSE OF IT.
REPORT IN.
THE PARTNERSHIP BETWEEN AOGIRI AND ROSÉ...
...IS EXTREMELY TENUOUS.
IT SEEMS LIKE ONLY A HANDFUL OF THEIR MEMBERS ARE WORKING WITH EACH OTHER.

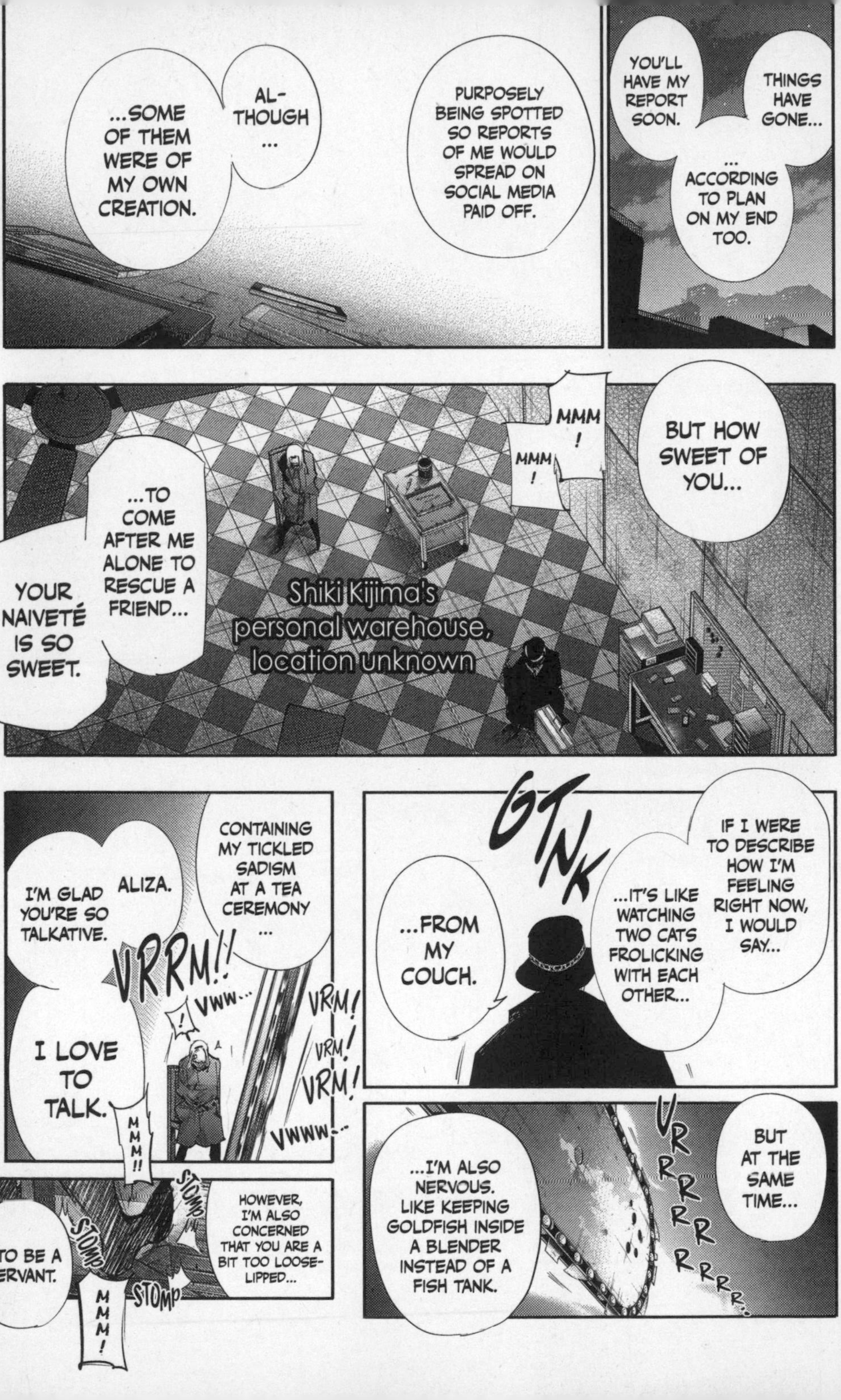
THINGS HAVE GONE...
...ACCORDING TO PLAN ON MY END TOO.
YOU'LL HAVE MY REPORT SOON.
PURPOSELY BEING SPOTTED SO REPORTS OF ME WOULD SPREAD ON SOCIAL MEDIA PAID OFF.
AL-THOUGH...
...SOME OF THEM WERE OF MY OWN CREATION.
BUT HOW SWEET OF YOU...
MMM!
MMM!
...TO COME AFTER ME ALONE TO RESCUE A FRIEND...
YOUR NAIVETÉ IS SO SWEET.
Shiki Kijima's personal warehouse, location unknown
GTNK
IF I WERE TO DESCRIBE HOW I'M FEELING RIGHT NOW, I WOULD SAY...
...IT'S LIKE WATCHING TWO CATS FROLICKING WITH EACH OTHER...
...FROM MY COUCH.
BUT AT THE SAME TIME...
VRRRRRRRRR...
...I'M ALSO NERVOUS. LIKE KEEPING GOLDFISH INSIDE A BLENDER INSTEAD OF A FISH TANK.
CONTAINING MY TICKLED SADISM AT A TEA CEREMONY...
ALIZA.
I'M GLAD YOU'RE SO TALKATIVE.
VRRM!!
VWW...
!
VRM!
VRM!
VRM!
I LOVE TO TALK.
MMM!!
VWWW...
HOWEVER, I'M ALSO CONCERNED THAT YOU ARE A BIT TOO LOOSE-LIPPED...
STOMP
STOMP
...TO BE A SERVANT.
STOMP
MMM!

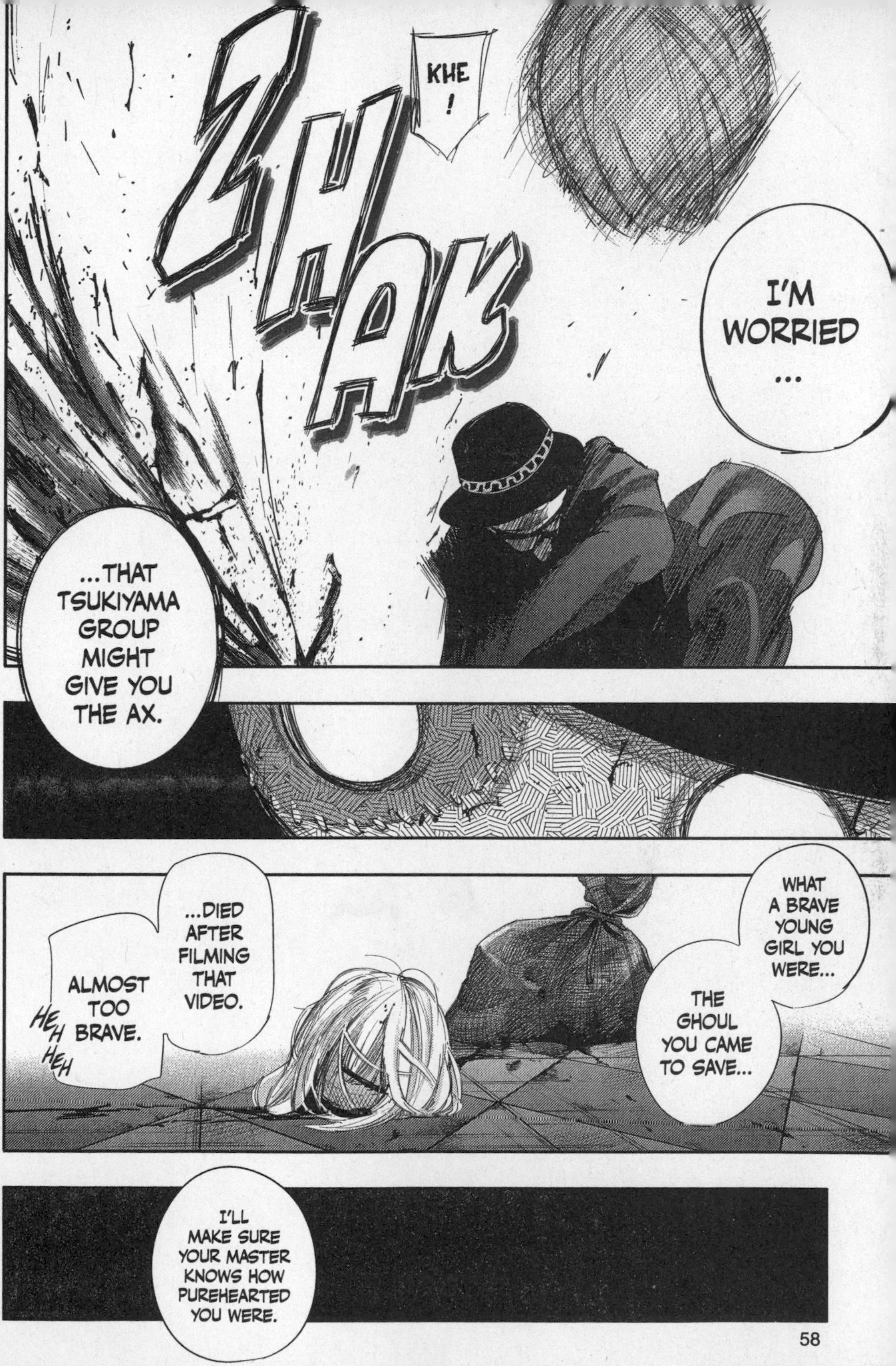
KHE !
I'M WORRIED ...
SHAK
...THAT TSUKIYAMA GROUP MIGHT GIVE YOU THE AX.
WHAT A BRAVE YOUNG GIRL YOU WERE...
THE GHOUL YOU CAME TO SAVE...
...DIED AFTER FILMING THAT VIDEO.
ALMOST TOO BRAVE.
HEH HEH HEH
I'LL MAKE SURE YOUR MASTER KNOWS HOW PUREHEARTED YOU WERE.

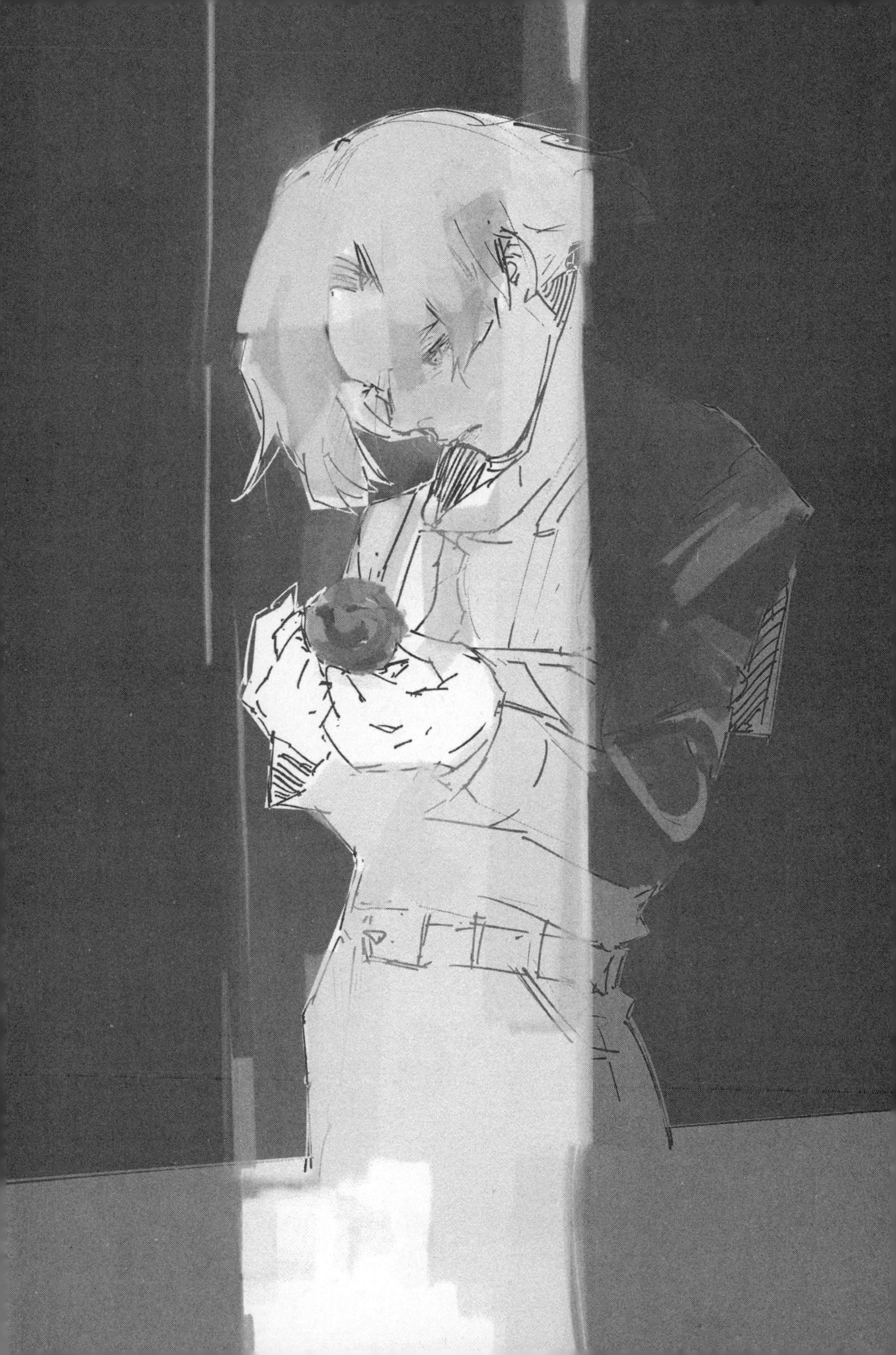

Plant :45

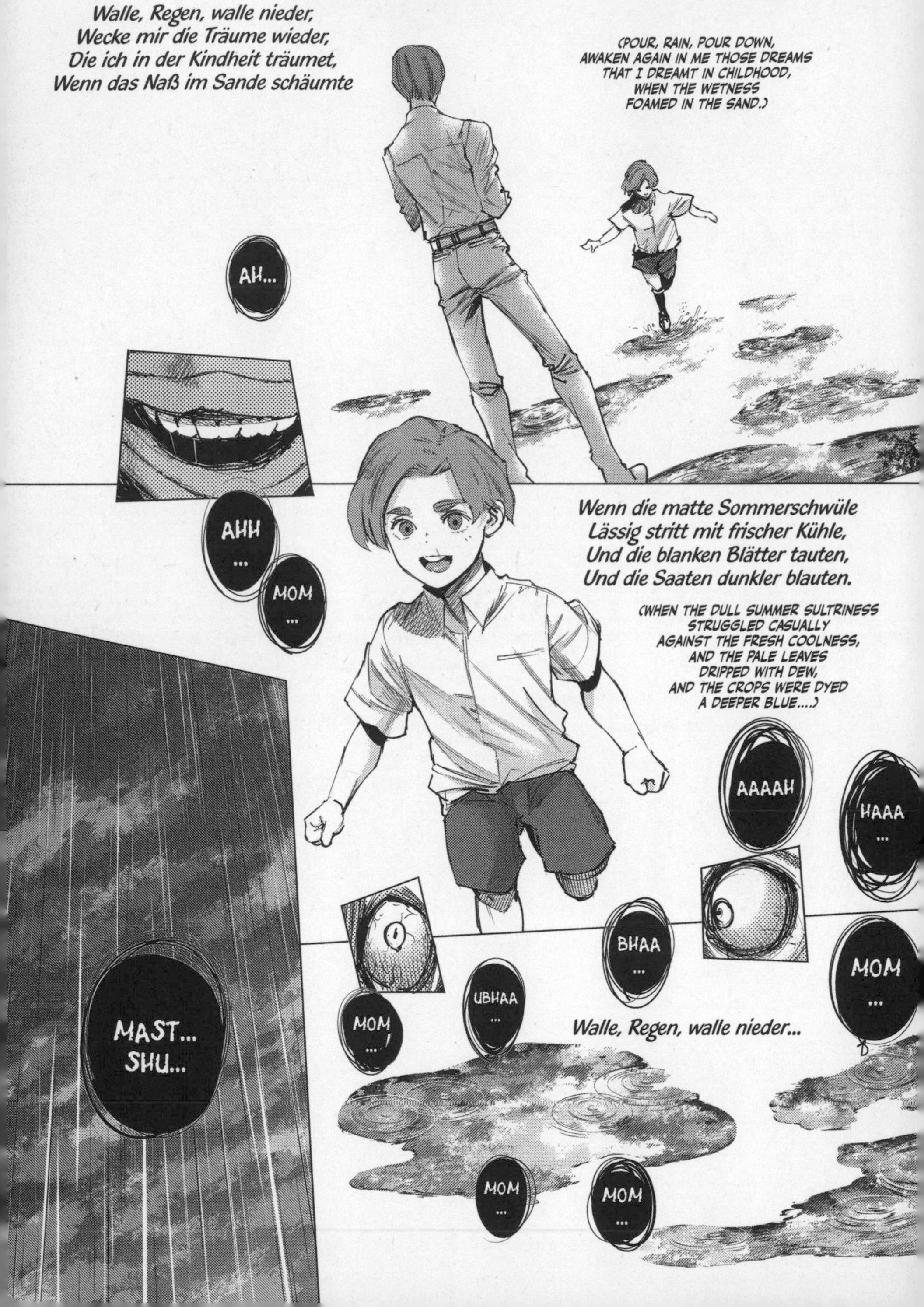

Walle, Regen, walle nieder,
Wecke mir die Träume wieder,
Die ich in der Kindheit träumet,
Wenn das Naß im Sande schäumte
(POUR, RAIN, POUR DOWN,
AWAKEN AGAIN IN ME THOSE DREAMS
THAT I DREAMT IN CHILDHOOD,
WHEN THE WETNESS
FOAMED IN THE SAND.)
AH...
AHH ...
MOM ...
Wenn die matte Sommerschwüle
Lässig stritt mit frischer Kühle,
Und die blanken Blätter tauten,
Und die Saaten dunkler blauten.
(WHEN THE DULL SUMMER SULTRINESS
STRUGGLED CASUALLY
AGAINST THE FRESH COOLNESS,
AND THE PALE LEAVES
DRIPPED WITH DEW,
AND THE CROPS WERE DYED
A DEEPER BLUE....)
HAAA ...
AAAAH
MOM ...
BHAA ...
UBHAA ...
MOM ...
Walle, Regen, walle nieder...
MOM ...
MOM ...
MAST... SHU...

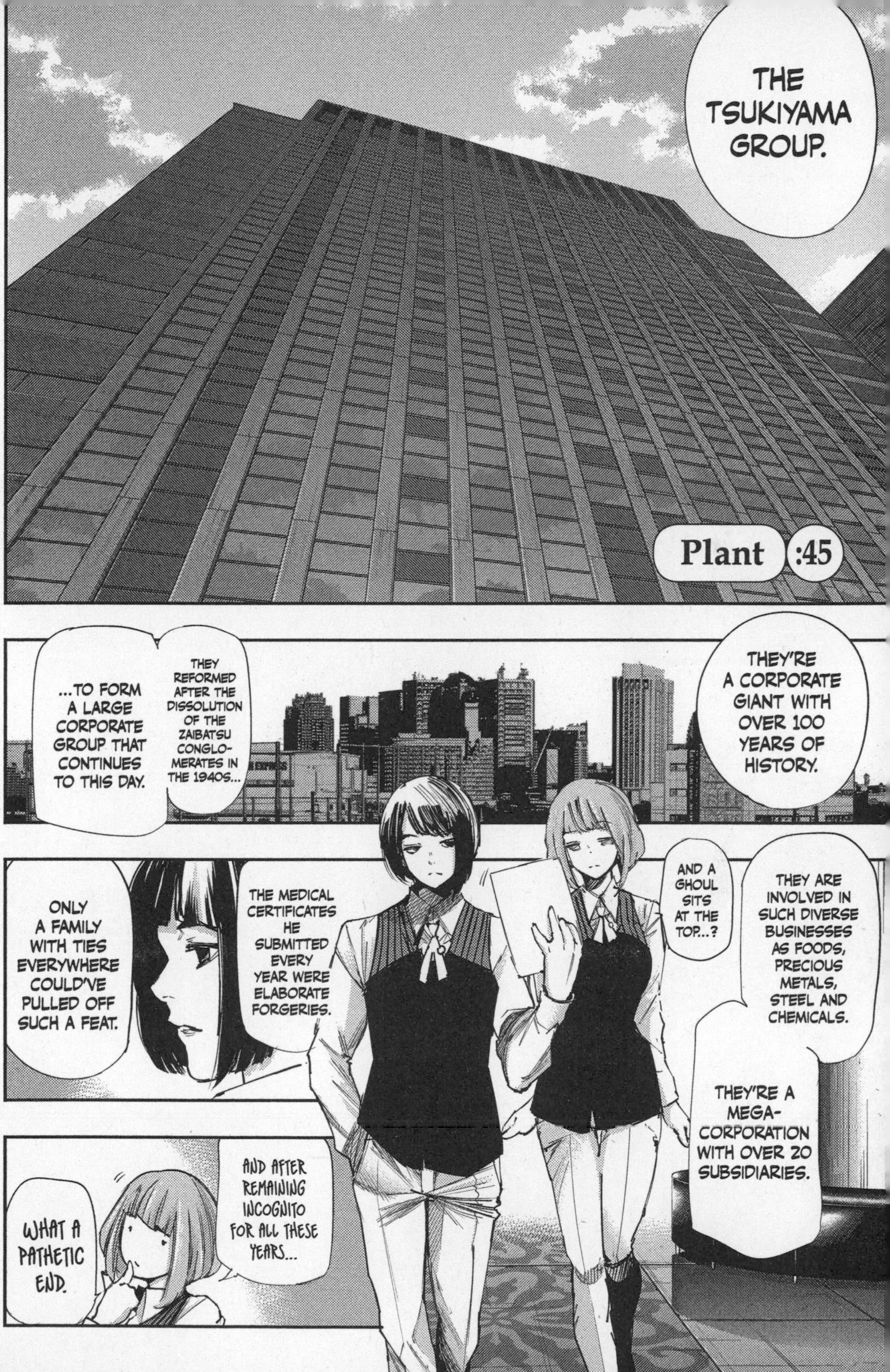
THE TSUKIYAMA GROUP.
Plant :45
THEY'RE A CORPORATE GIANT WITH OVER 100 YEARS OF HISTORY.
THEY REFORMED AFTER THE DISSOLUTION OF THE ZAIBATSU CONGLO-MERATES IN THE 1940S...
...TO FORM A LARGE CORPORATE GROUP THAT CONTINUES TO THIS DAY.
THEY ARE INVOLVED IN SUCH DIVERSE BUSINESSES AS FOODS, PRECIOUS METALS, STEEL AND CHEMICALS.
AND A GHOUL SITS AT THE TOP...?
THEY'RE A MEGA-CORPORATION WITH OVER 20 SUBSIDIARIES.
THE MEDICAL CERTIFICATES HE SUBMITTED EVERY YEAR WERE ELABORATE FORGERIES.
ONLY A FAMILY WITH TIES EVERYWHERE COULD'VE PULLED OFF SUCH A FEAT.
AND AFTER REMAINING INCOGNITO FOR ALL THESE YEARS...
WHAT A PATHETIC END.

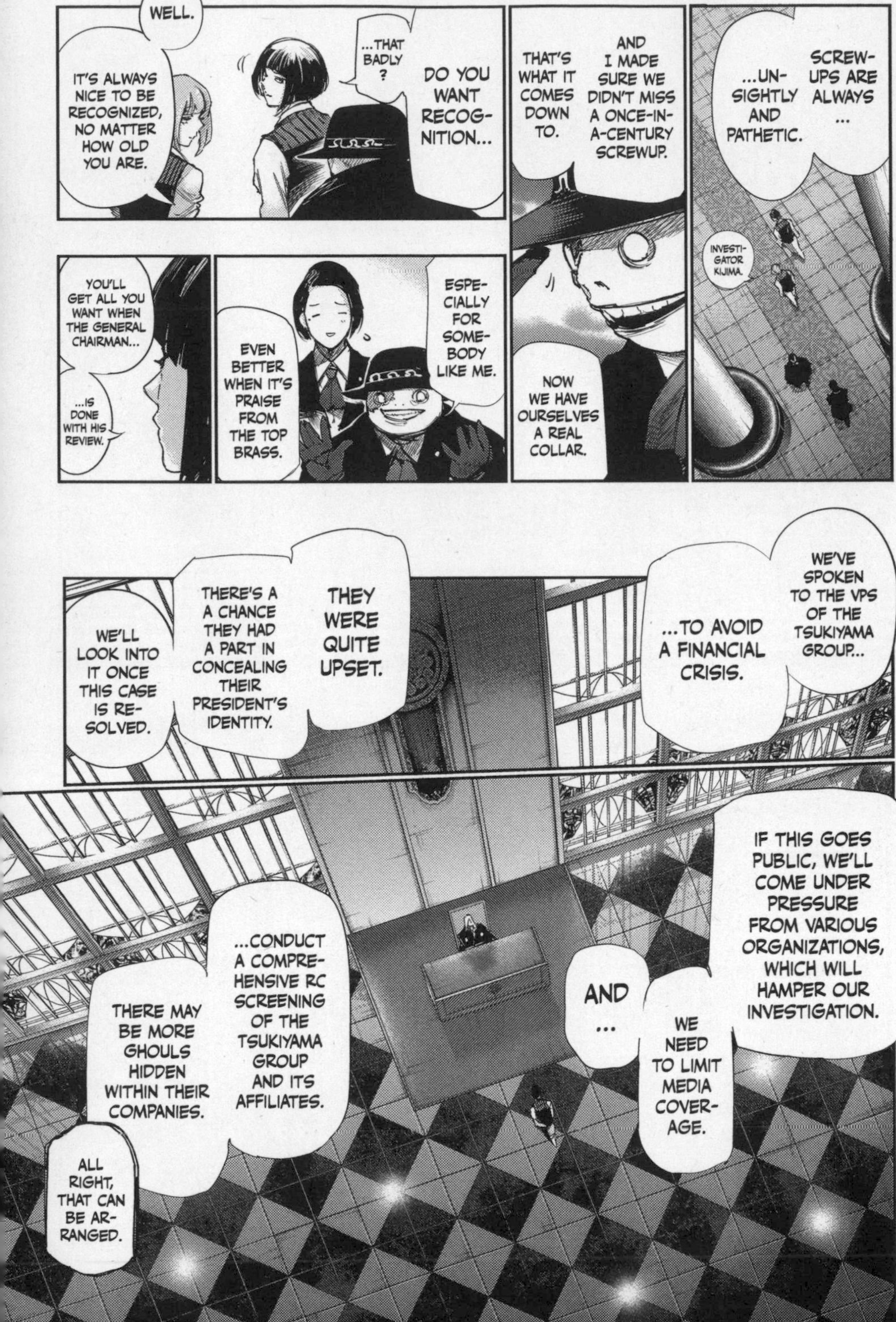
SCREW-UPS ARE ALWAYS ...
...UNSIGHTLY AND PATHETIC.
INVESTIGATOR KIJIMA.
AND I MADE SURE WE DIDN'T MISS A ONCE-IN-A-CENTURY SCREWUP.
THAT'S WHAT IT COMES DOWN TO.
NOW WE HAVE OURSELVES A REAL COLLAR.
DO YOU WANT RECOGNITION...
...THAT BADLY?
WELL.
IT'S ALWAYS NICE TO BE RECOGNIZED, NO MATTER HOW OLD YOU ARE.
ESPECIALLY FOR SOMEBODY LIKE ME.
EVEN BETTER WHEN IT'S PRAISE FROM THE TOP BRASS.
YOU'LL GET ALL YOU WANT WHEN THE GENERAL CHAIRMAN...
...IS DONE WITH HIS REVIEW.
WE'VE SPOKEN TO THE VPS OF THE TSUKIYAMA GROUP...
...TO AVOID A FINANCIAL CRISIS.
THEY WERE QUITE UPSET.
THERE'S A CHANCE THEY HAD A PART IN CONCEALING THEIR PRESIDENT'S IDENTITY.
WE'LL LOOK INTO IT ONCE THIS CASE IS RESOLVED.
IF THIS GOES PUBLIC, WE'LL COME UNDER PRESSURE FROM VARIOUS ORGANIZATIONS, WHICH WILL HAMPER OUR INVESTIGATION.
AND ...
WE NEED TO LIMIT MEDIA COVERAGE.
...CONDUCT A COMPREHENSIVE RC SCREENING OF THE TSUKIYAMA GROUP AND ITS AFFILIATES.
THERE MAY BE MORE GHOULS HIDDEN WITHIN THEIR COMPANIES.
ALL RIGHT, THAT CAN BE ARRANGED.

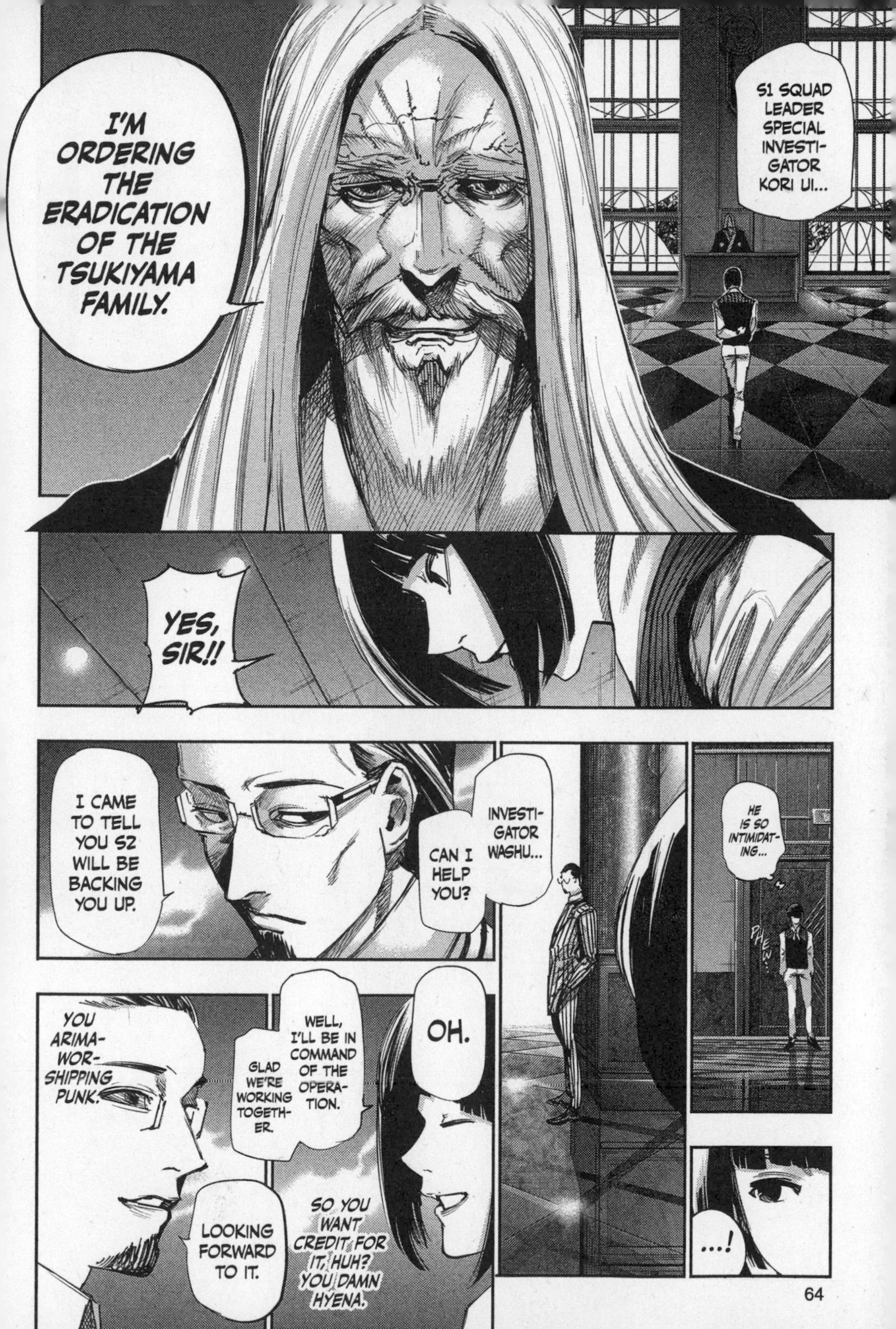
S1 SQUAD LEADER SPECIAL INVESTIGATOR KORI UI...
I'M ORDERING THE ERADICATION OF THE TSUKIYAMA FAMILY.
YES, SIR!!
HE IS SO INTIMIDATING...
PHEW...
...!
INVESTIGATOR WASHU...
CAN I HELP YOU?
I CAME TO TELL YOU S2 WILL BE BACKING YOU UP.
OH.
WELL, I'LL BE IN COMMAND OF THE OPERATION.
SO YOU WANT CREDIT FOR IT, HUH? YOU DAMN HYENA.
GLAD WE'RE WORKING TOGETHER.
YOU ARIMA-WORSHIPPING PUNK.
LOOKING FORWARD TO IT.

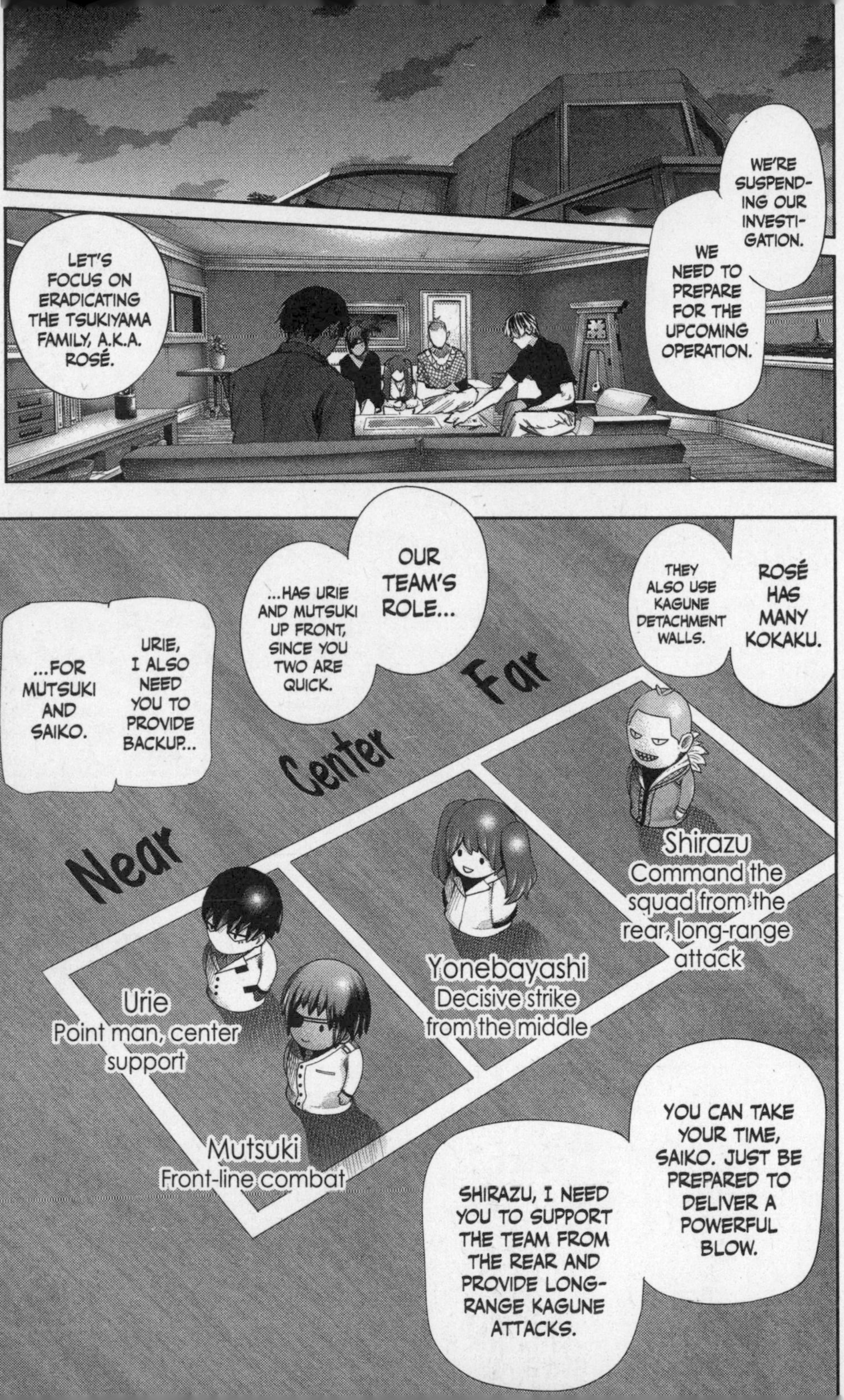
WE'RE SUSPENDING OUR INVESTIGATION.
WE NEED TO PREPARE FOR THE UPCOMING OPERATION.
LET'S FOCUS ON ERADICATING THE TSUKIYAMA FAMILY, A.K.A. ROSÉ.
ROSÉ HAS MANY KOKAKU.
THEY ALSO USE KAGUNE DETACHMENT WALLS.
OUR TEAM'S ROLE...
...HAS URIE AND MUTSUKI UP FRONT, SINCE YOU TWO ARE QUICK.
URIE, I ALSO NEED YOU TO PROVIDE BACKUP...
...FOR MUTSUKI AND SAIKO.
Far
Center
Near
Shirazu
Command the squad from the rear, long-range attack
Yonebayashi
Decisive strike from the middle
Urie
Point man, center support
Mutsuki
Front-line combat
YOU CAN TAKE YOUR TIME, SAIKO. JUST BE PREPARED TO DELIVER A POWERFUL BLOW.
SHIRAZU, I NEED YOU TO SUPPORT THE TEAM FROM THE REAR AND PROVIDE LONG-RANGE KAGUNE ATTACKS.

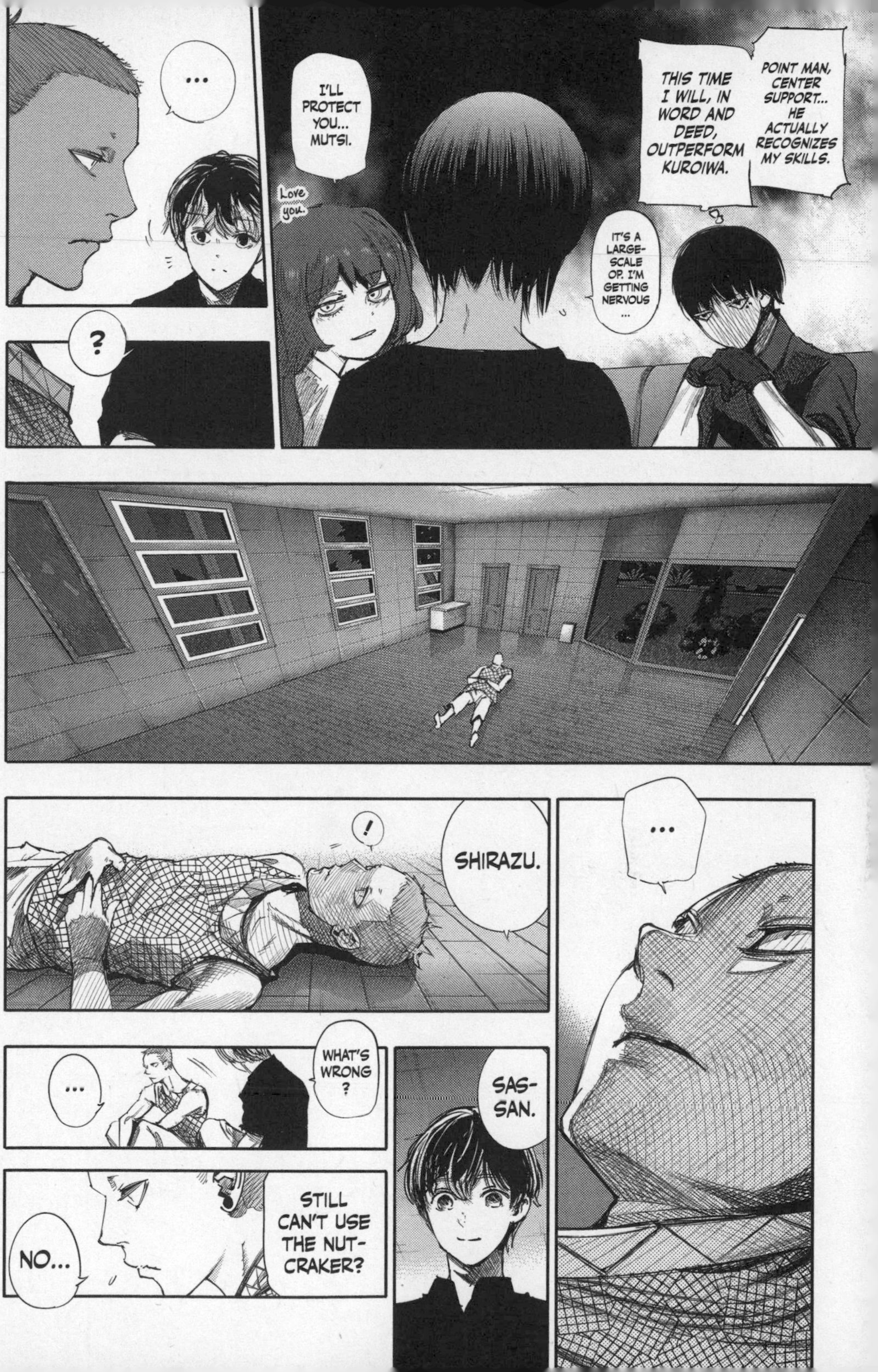
POINT MAN, CENTER SUPPORT... HE ACTUALLY RECOGNIZES MY SKILLS.
THIS TIME I WILL, IN WORD AND DEED, OUTPERFORM KUROIWA.
IT'S A LARGE-SCALE OP. I'M GETTING NERVOUS ...
I'LL PROTECT YOU... MUTSI.
Love you.
...
?
SHIRAZU.
...
SAS-SAN.
WHAT'S WRONG?
...
STILL CAN'T USE THE NUT-CRAKER?
NO...

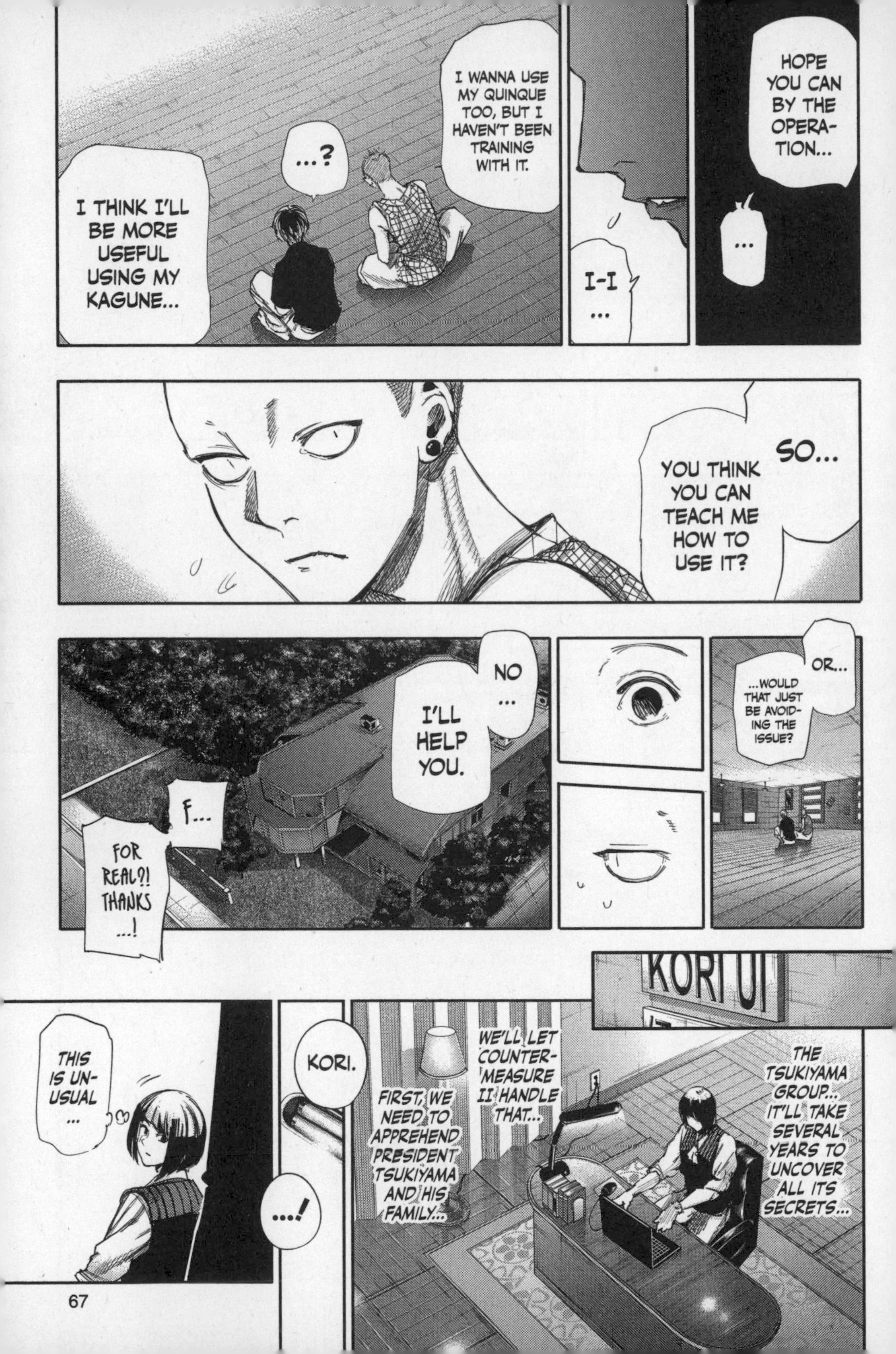
HOPE YOU CAN BY THE OPERATION...
...
I-I ...
I WANNA USE MY QUINQUE TOO, BUT I HAVEN'T BEEN TRAINING WITH IT.
...?
I THINK I'LL BE MORE USEFUL USING MY KAGUNE...
SO...
YOU THINK YOU CAN TEACH ME HOW TO USE IT?
OR...
...WOULD THAT JUST BE AVOIDING THE ISSUE?
NO ...
I'LL HELP YOU.
F...
FOR REAL?! THANKS ...!
KORI UI
THE TSUKIYAMA GROUP... IT'LL TAKE SEVERAL YEARS TO UNCOVER ALL ITS SECRETS...
WE'LL LET COUNTER-MEASURE II HANDLE THAT...
FIRST, WE NEED TO APPREHEND PRESIDENT TSUKIYAMA AND HIS FAMILY...
KORI.
...!
THIS IS UN-USUAL ...

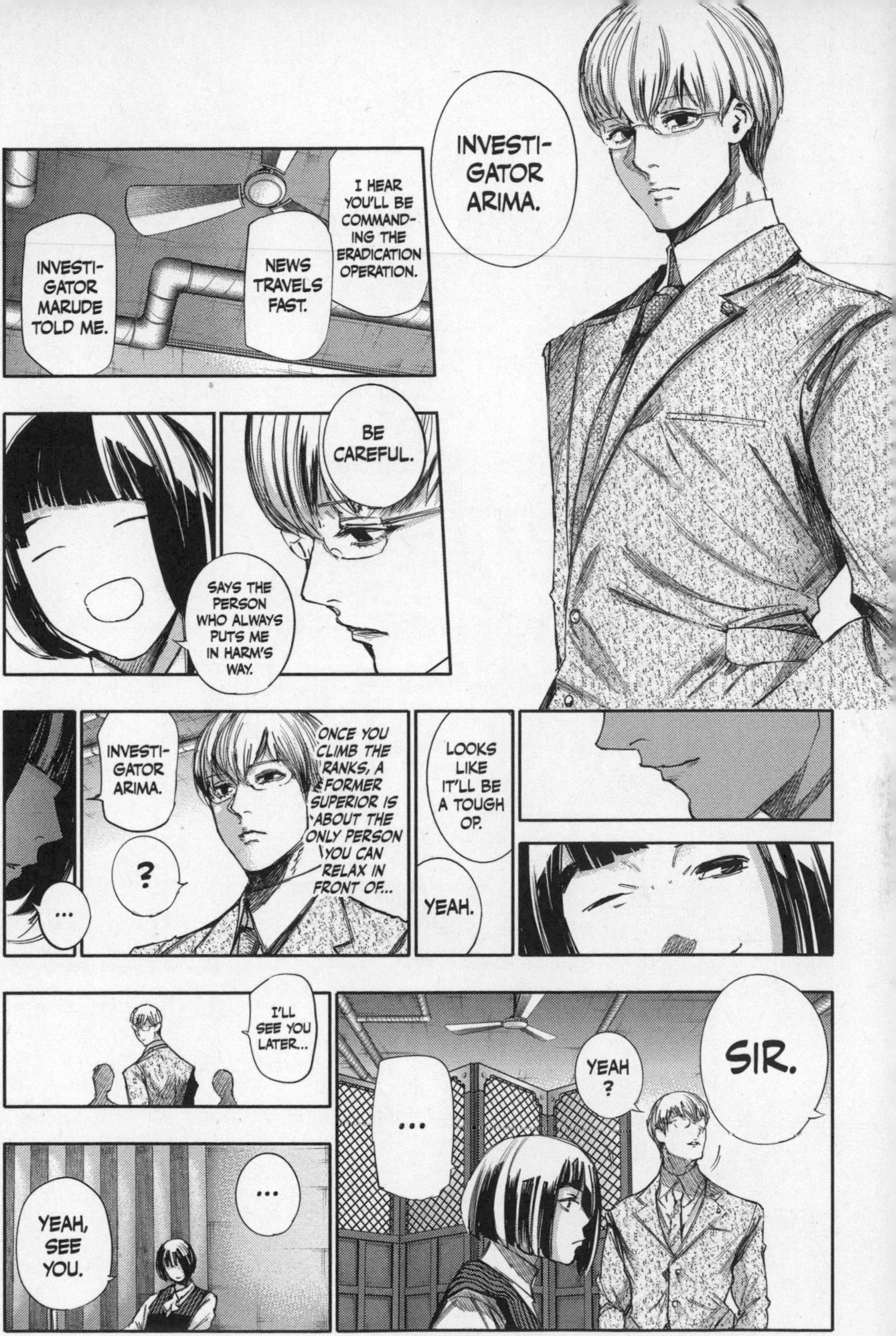
INVESTI-GATOR ARIMA.
I HEAR YOU'LL BE COMMAND-ING THE ERADICATION OPERATION.
NEWS TRAVELS FAST.
INVESTI-GATOR MARUDE TOLD ME.
BE CAREFUL.
SAYS THE PERSON WHO ALWAYS PUTS ME IN HARM'S WAY.
LOOKS LIKE IT'LL BE A TOUGH OP.
YEAH.
ONCE YOU CLIMB THE RANKS, A FORMER SUPERIOR IS ABOUT THE ONLY PERSON YOU CAN RELAX IN FRONT OF...
INVESTI-GATOR ARIMA.
?
...
SIR.
YEAH?
...
I'LL SEE YOU LATER...
...
YEAH, SEE YOU.

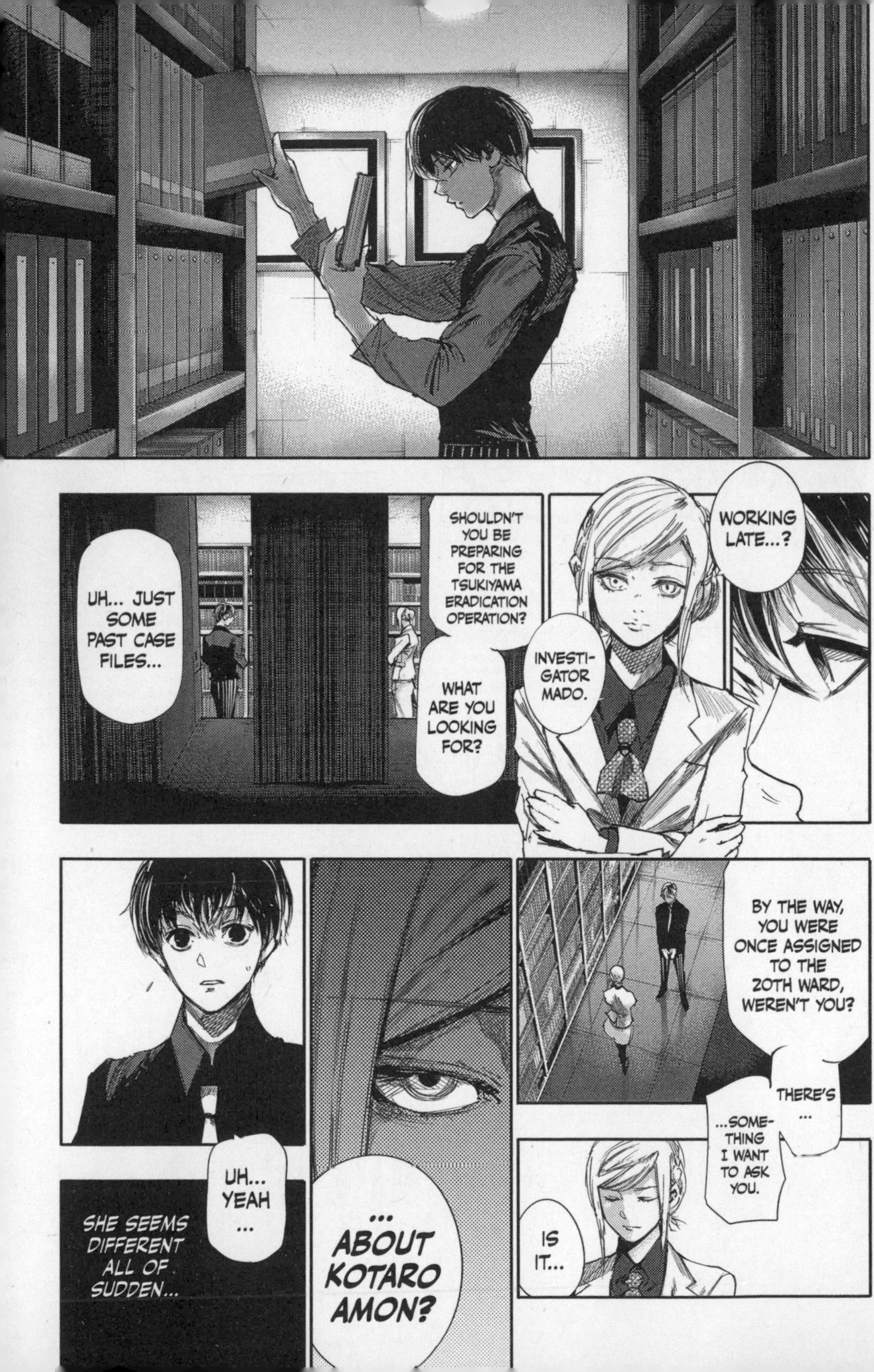
WORKING LATE...?
INVESTIGATOR MADO.
SHOULDN'T YOU BE PREPARING FOR THE TSUKIYAMA ERADICATION OPERATION?
WHAT ARE YOU LOOKING FOR?
UH... JUST SOME PAST CASE FILES...
BY THE WAY, YOU WERE ONCE ASSIGNED TO THE 20TH WARD, WEREN'T YOU?
UH... YEAH...
THERE'S...
...SOMETHING I WANT TO ASK YOU.
IS IT...
...ABOUT KOTARO AMON?
SHE SEEMS DIFFERENT ALL OF SUDDEN...

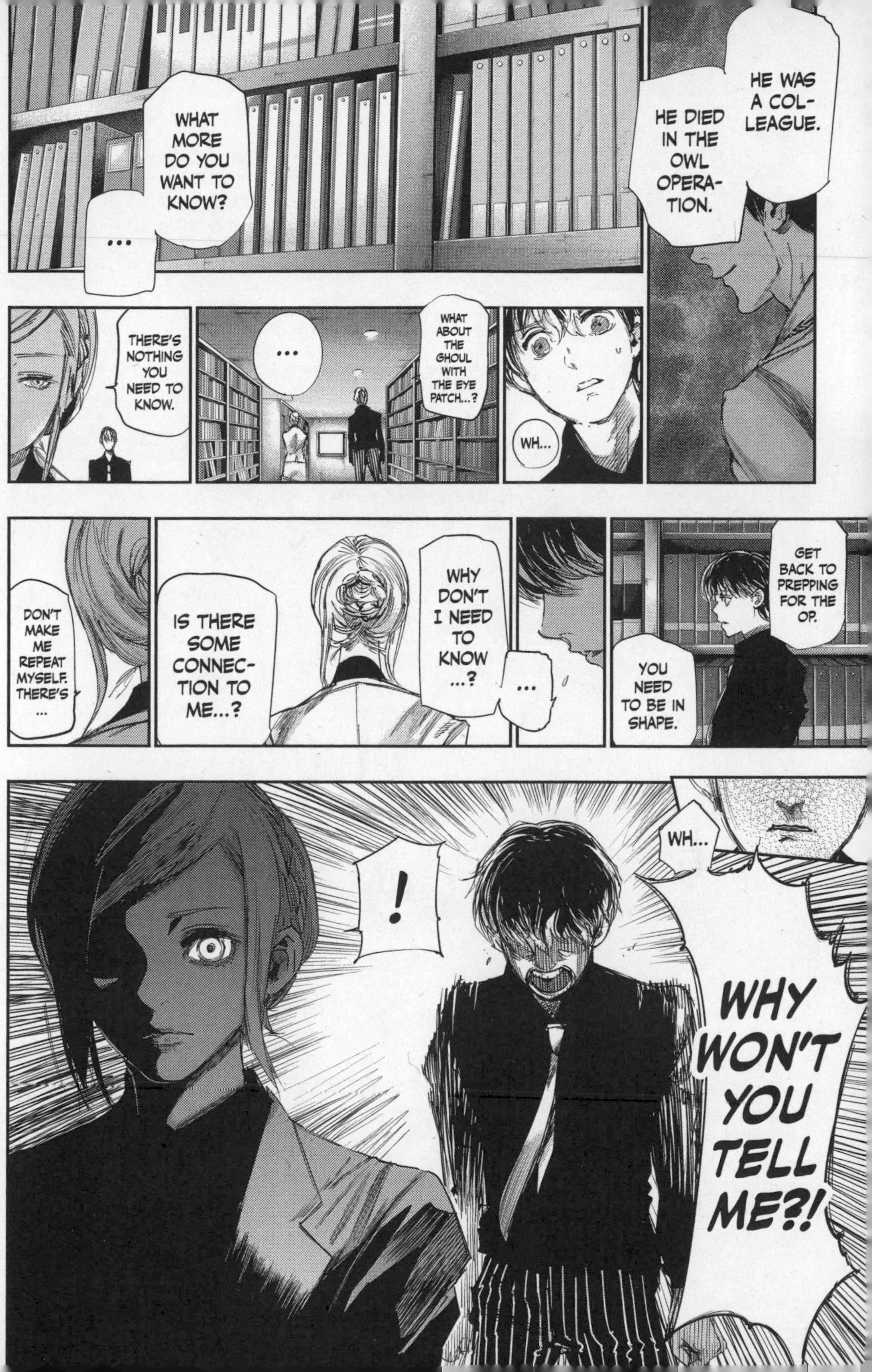
HE WAS A COL-LEAGUE.
HE DIED IN THE OWL OPERA-TION.
WHAT MORE DO YOU WANT TO KNOW?
...
WH...
WHAT ABOUT THE GHOUL WITH THE EYE PATCH...?
...
THERE'S NOTHING YOU NEED TO KNOW.
GET BACK TO PREPPING FOR THE OP.
YOU NEED TO BE IN SHAPE.
...
WHY DON'T I NEED TO KNOW...?
IS THERE SOME CONNECTION TO ME...?
DON'T MAKE ME REPEAT MYSELF. THERE'S ...
WH...
WHY WON'T YOU TELL ME?!
!

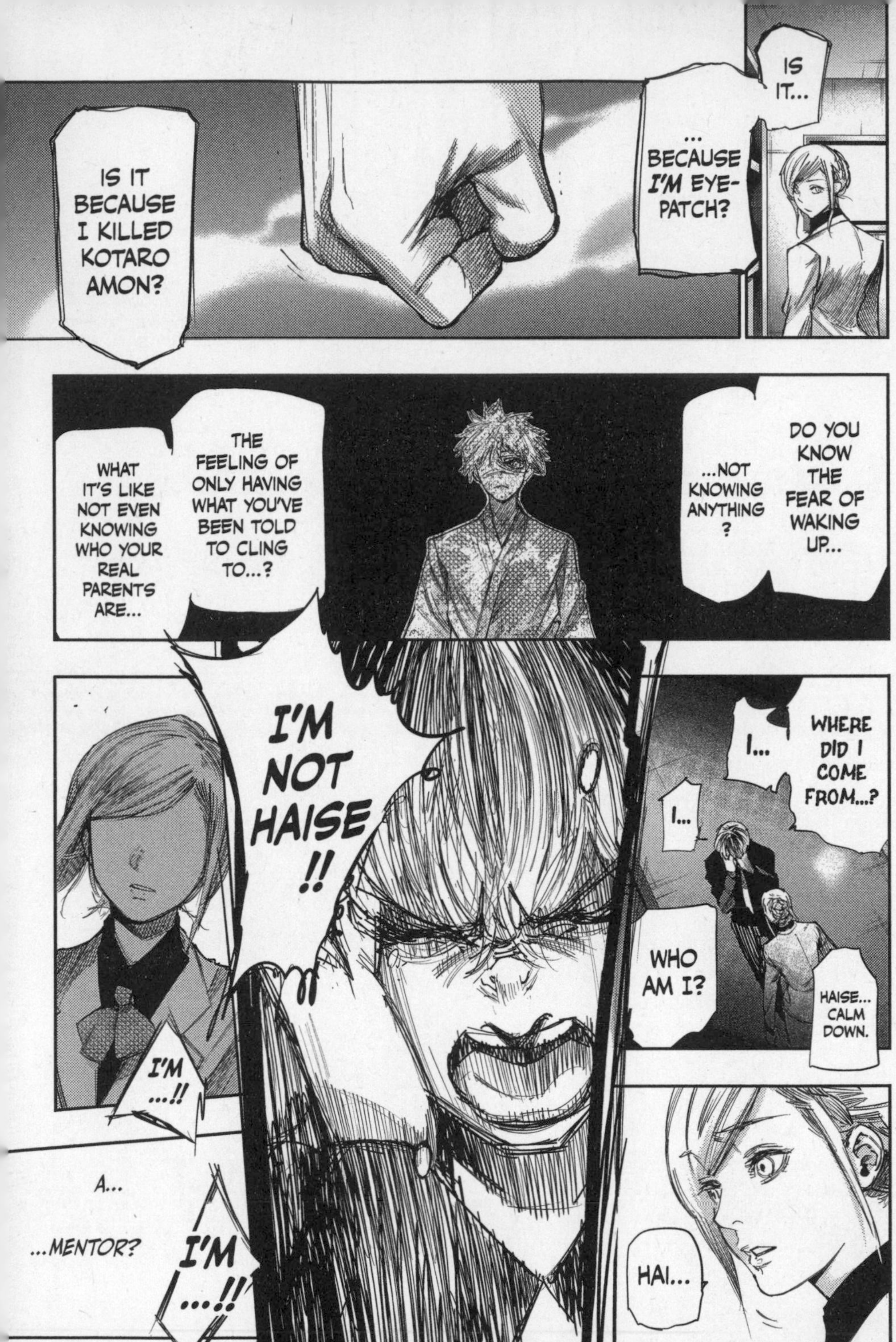
IS IT...
...BECAUSE I'M EYE-PATCH?
IS IT BECAUSE I KILLED KOTARO AMON?
DO YOU KNOW THE FEAR OF WAKING UP...
...NOT KNOWING ANYTHING?
THE FEELING OF ONLY HAVING WHAT YOU'VE BEEN TOLD TO CLING TO...?
WHAT IT'S LIKE NOT EVEN KNOWING WHO YOUR REAL PARENTS ARE...
WHERE DID I COME FROM...?
I...
I...
WHO AM I?
HAISE... CALM DOWN.
I'M NOT HAISE!!
I'M ...!!
HAI...
I'M ...!!
A...
...MENTOR?

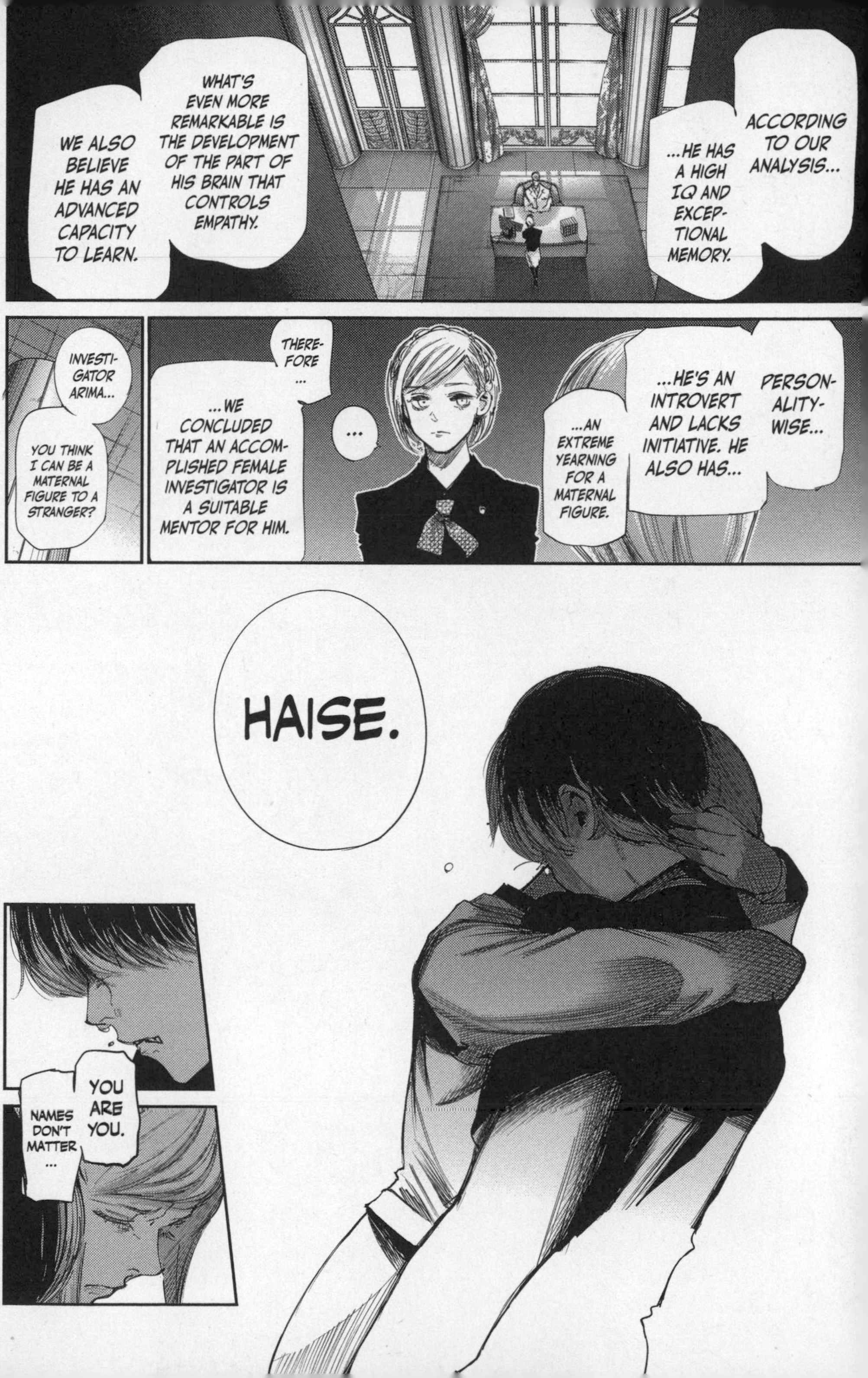
ACCORDING TO OUR ANALYSIS...
...HE HAS A HIGH IQ AND EXCEPTIONAL MEMORY.
WHAT'S EVEN MORE REMARKABLE IS THE DEVELOPMENT OF THE PART OF HIS BRAIN THAT CONTROLS EMPATHY.
WE ALSO BELIEVE HE HAS AN ADVANCED CAPACITY TO LEARN.
PERSONALITY-WISE...
...HE'S AN INTROVERT AND LACKS INITIATIVE. HE ALSO HAS...
...AN EXTREME YEARNING FOR A MATERNAL FIGURE.
THEREFORE...
...
...WE CONCLUDED THAT AN ACCOMPLISHED FEMALE INVESTIGATOR IS A SUITABLE MENTOR FOR HIM.
INVESTIGATOR ARIMA...
YOU THINK I CAN BE A MATERNAL FIGURE TO A STRANGER?
HAISE.
YOU ARE YOU.
NAMES DON'T MATTER...

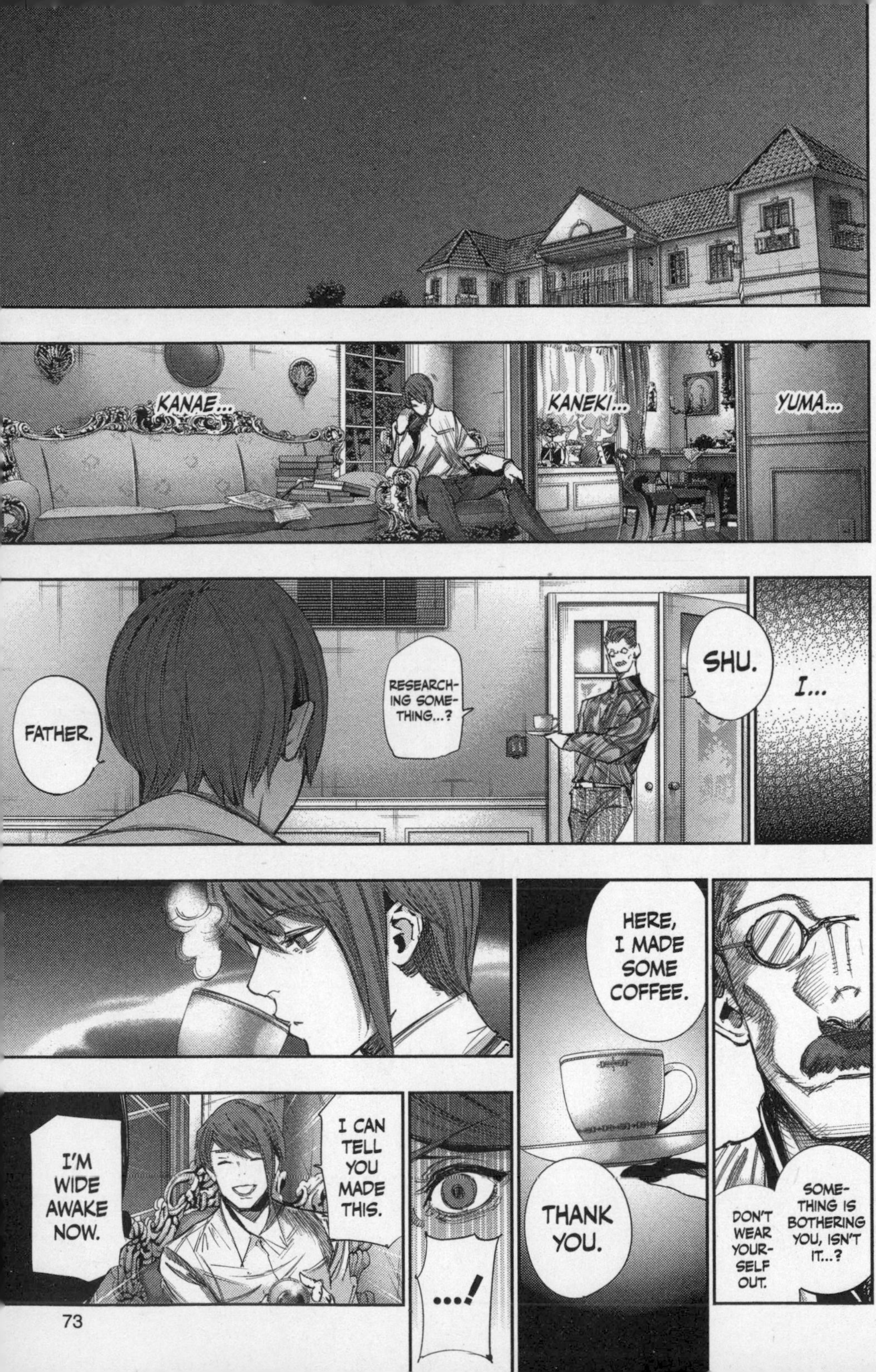
YUMA...
KANEKI...
KANAE...
I...
SHU.
RESEARCHING SOMETHING...?
FATHER.
SOMETHING IS BOTHERING YOU, ISN'T IT...?
DON'T WEAR YOURSELF OUT.
HERE, I MADE SOME COFFEE.
THANK YOU.
...!
I CAN TELL YOU MADE THIS.
I'M WIDE AWAKE NOW.

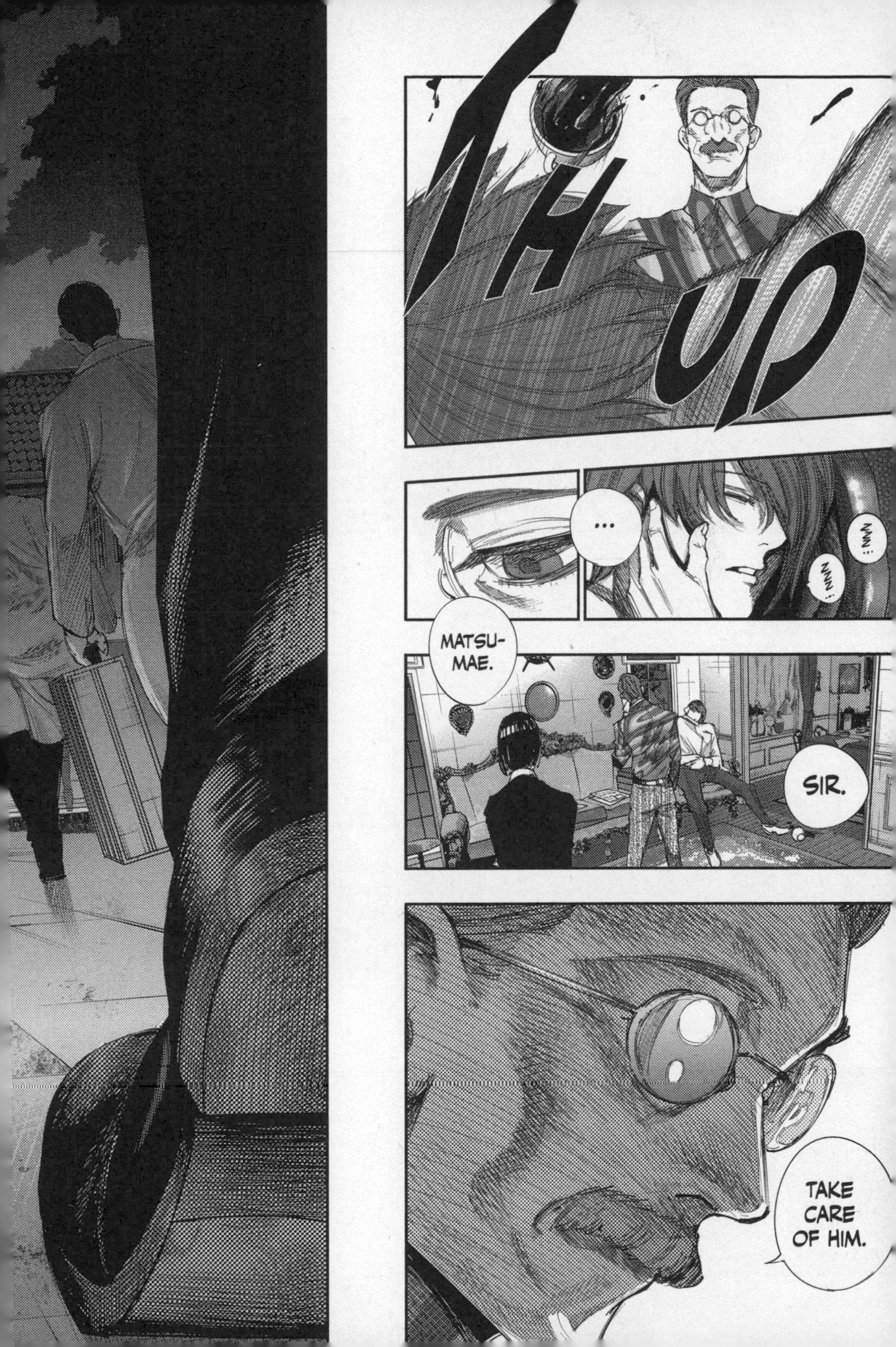

WHUP
...
Zzz...
Zzz...
MATSU-MAE.
SIR.
TAKE CARE OF HIM.

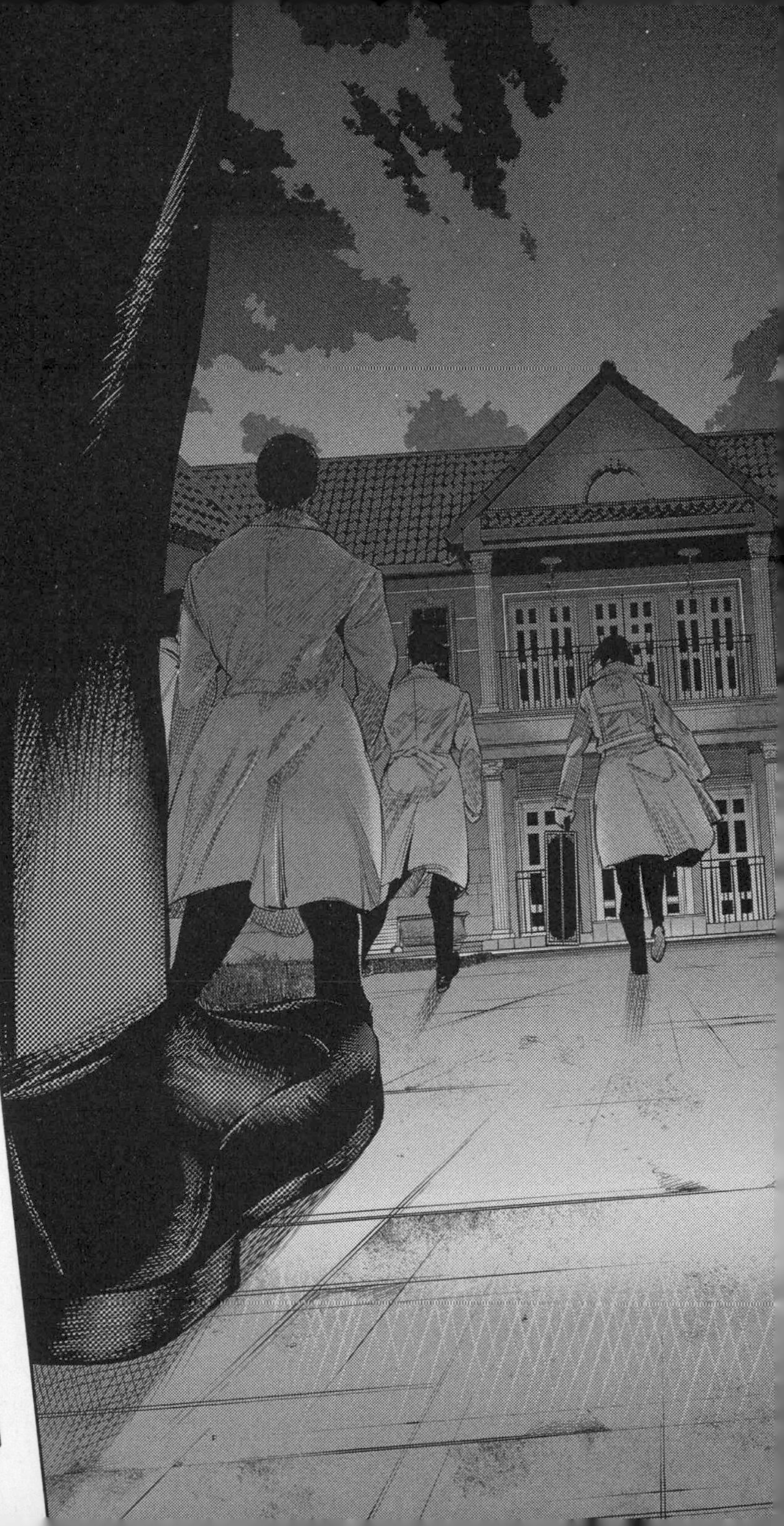

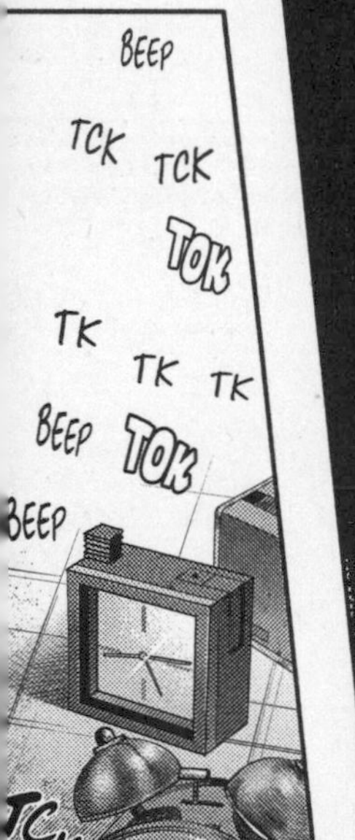
BEEP
TCK TCK
TOK
TK
TK TK
BEEP TOK
BEEP
TCK
TCK

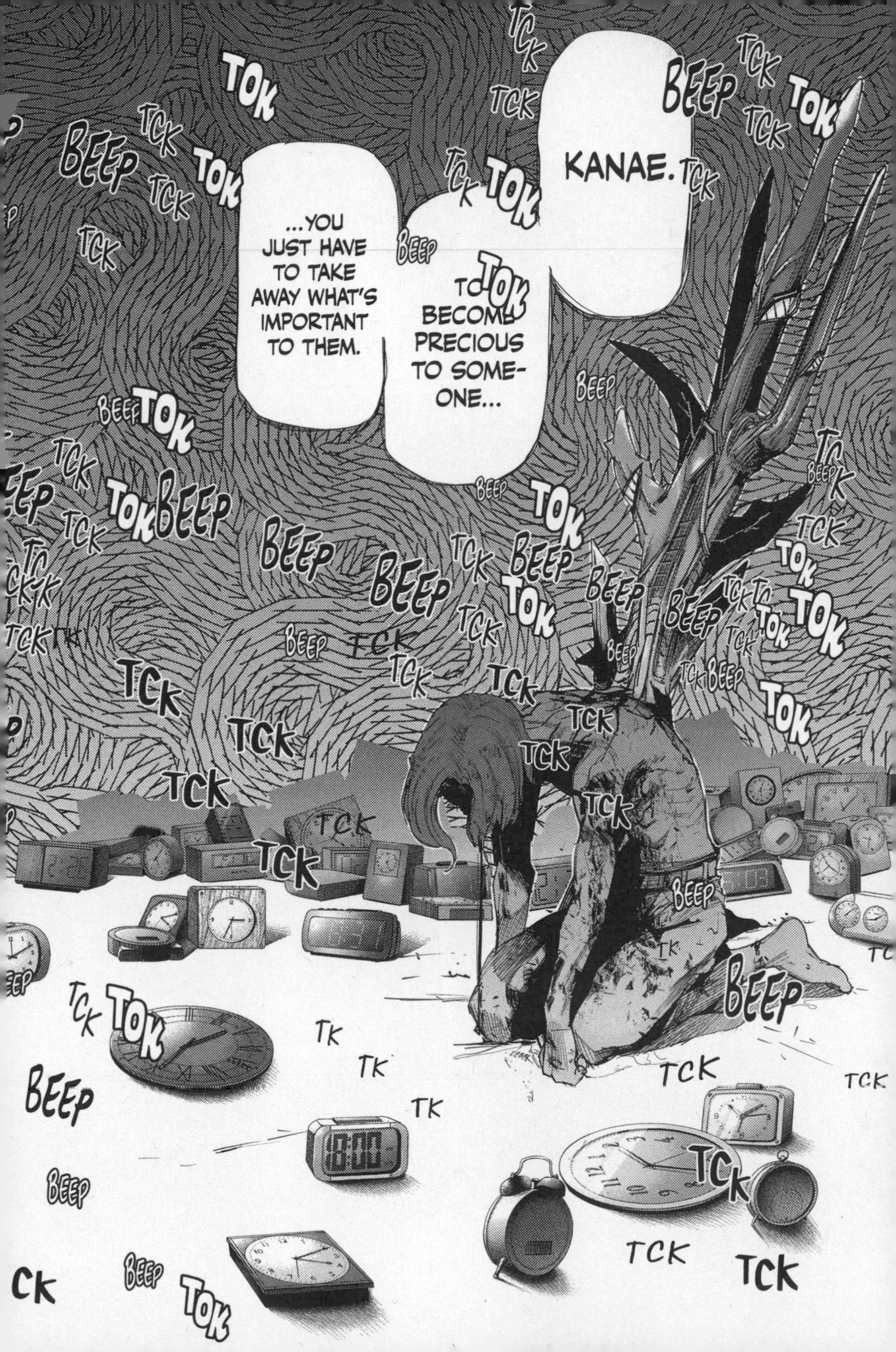
KANAE.
TO BECOME PRECIOUS TO SOME-ONE...
...YOU JUST HAVE TO TAKE AWAY WHAT'S IMPORTANT TO THEM.
TCK
BEEP
TOK
TCK
TOK
BEEP
TCK
TOK
TCK
BEEP
TOK
TCK
BEEP
TOK
TCK
BEEP
TCK
TK
TCK
BEEP
TOK
CK

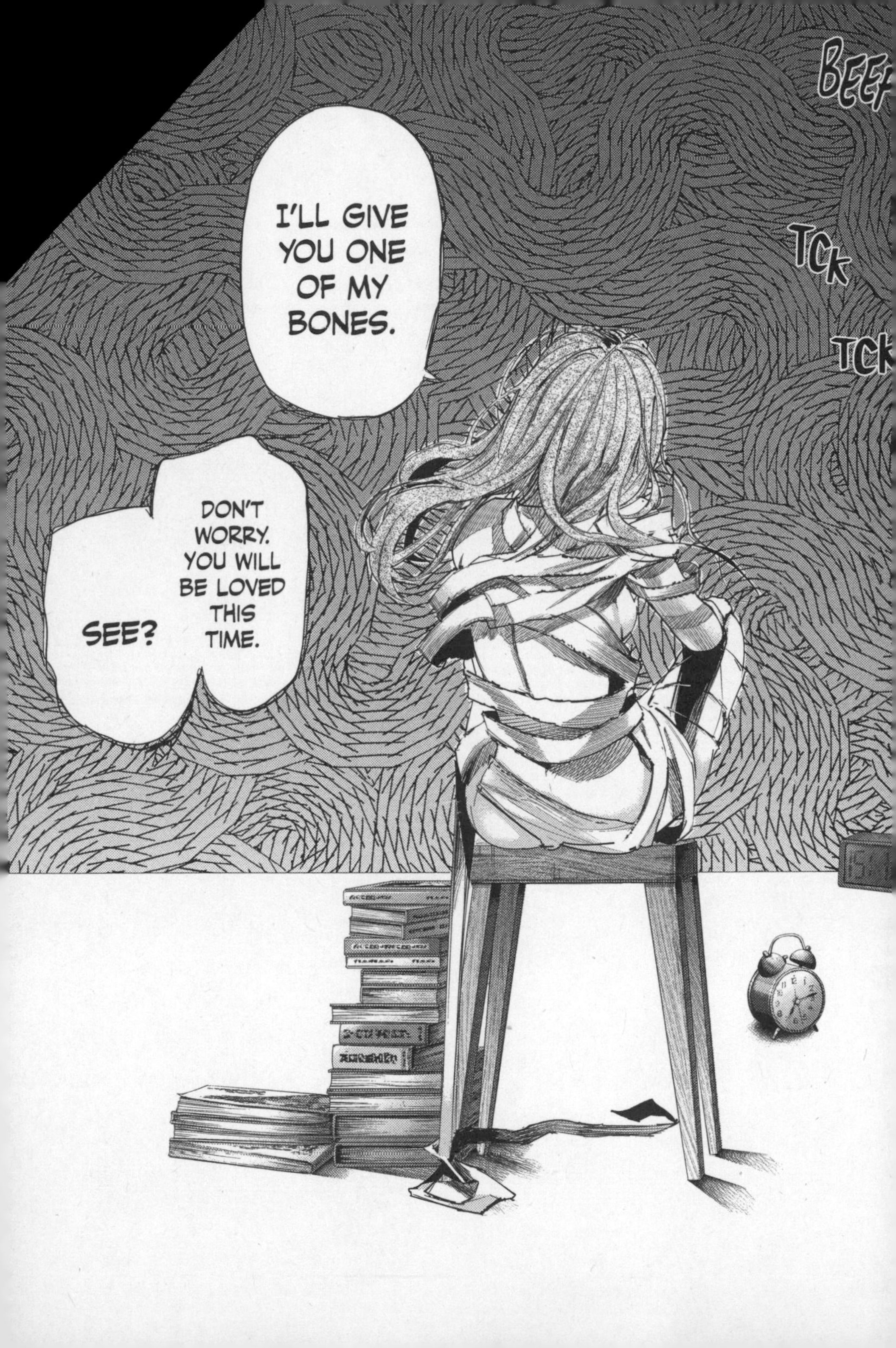
I'LL GIVE YOU ONE OF MY BONES.
TCK
TCK
DON'T WORRY. YOU WILL BE LOVED THIS TIME.
SEE?

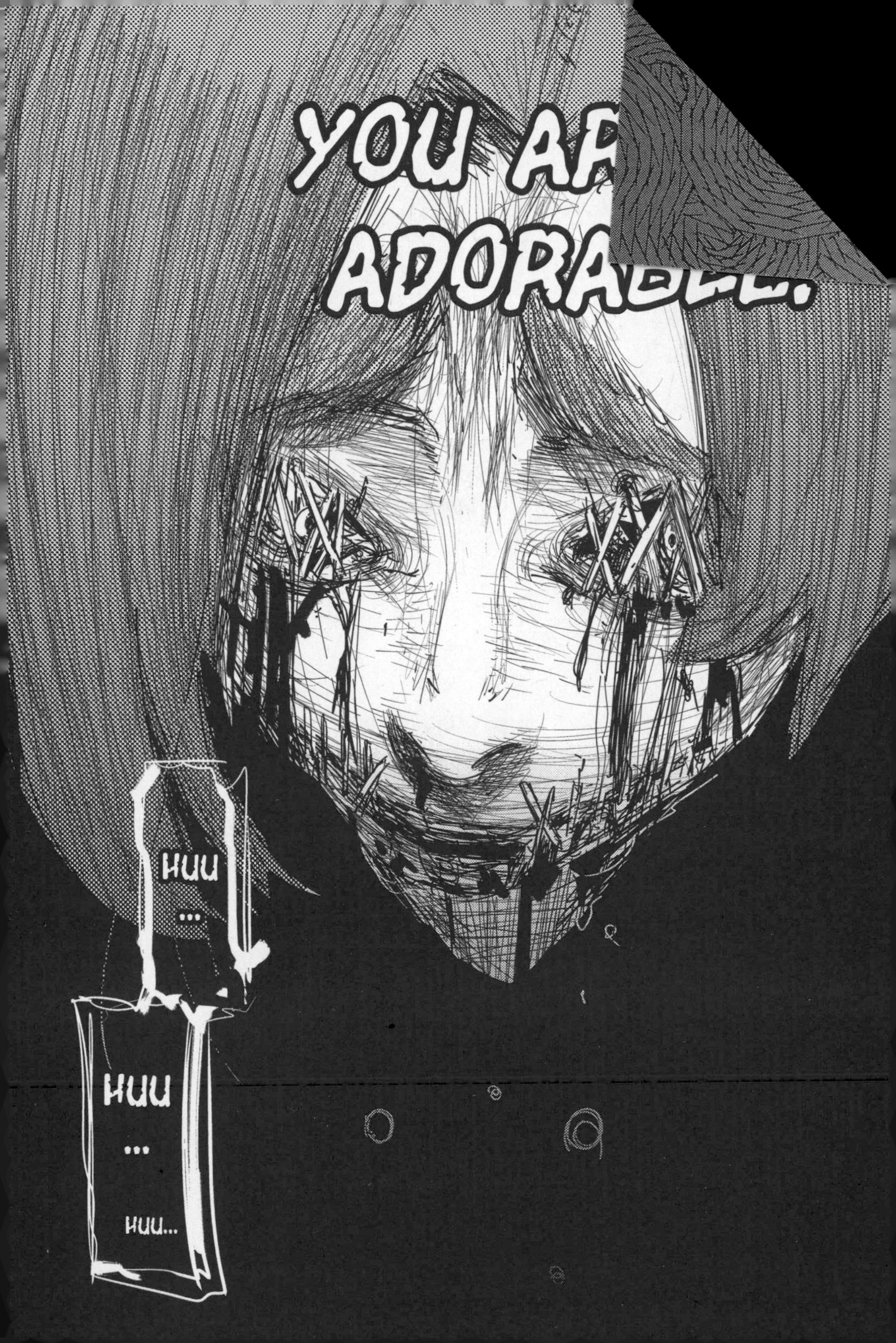
YOU AR
ADORABLE.
HUU ...
HUU ...
HUU...

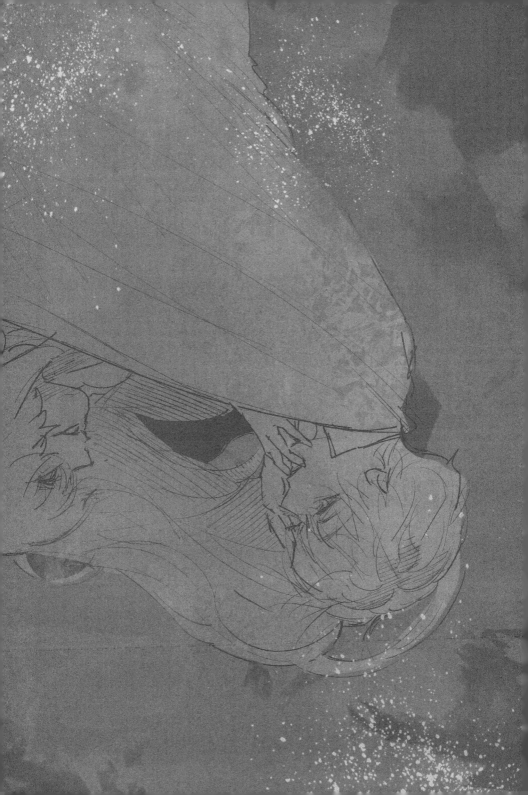

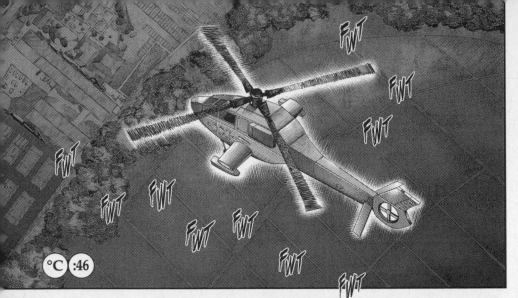

°C :46

FWT FWT FWT FWT FWT FWT FWT FWT FWT FWT

FWT FWT FWT FWT FWT

ZSH

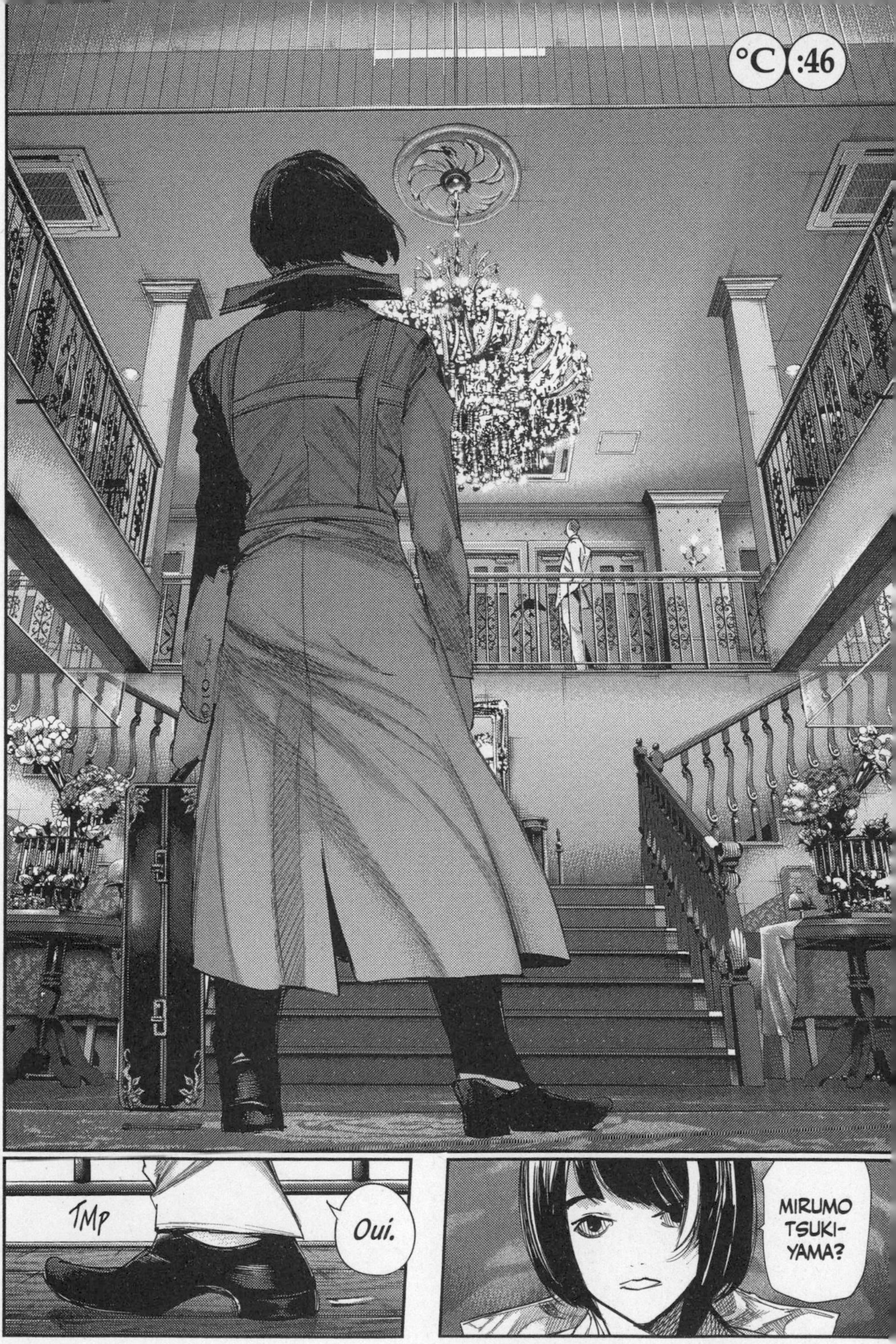
°C :46
MIRUMO TSUKIYAMA?
TMP
Oui.

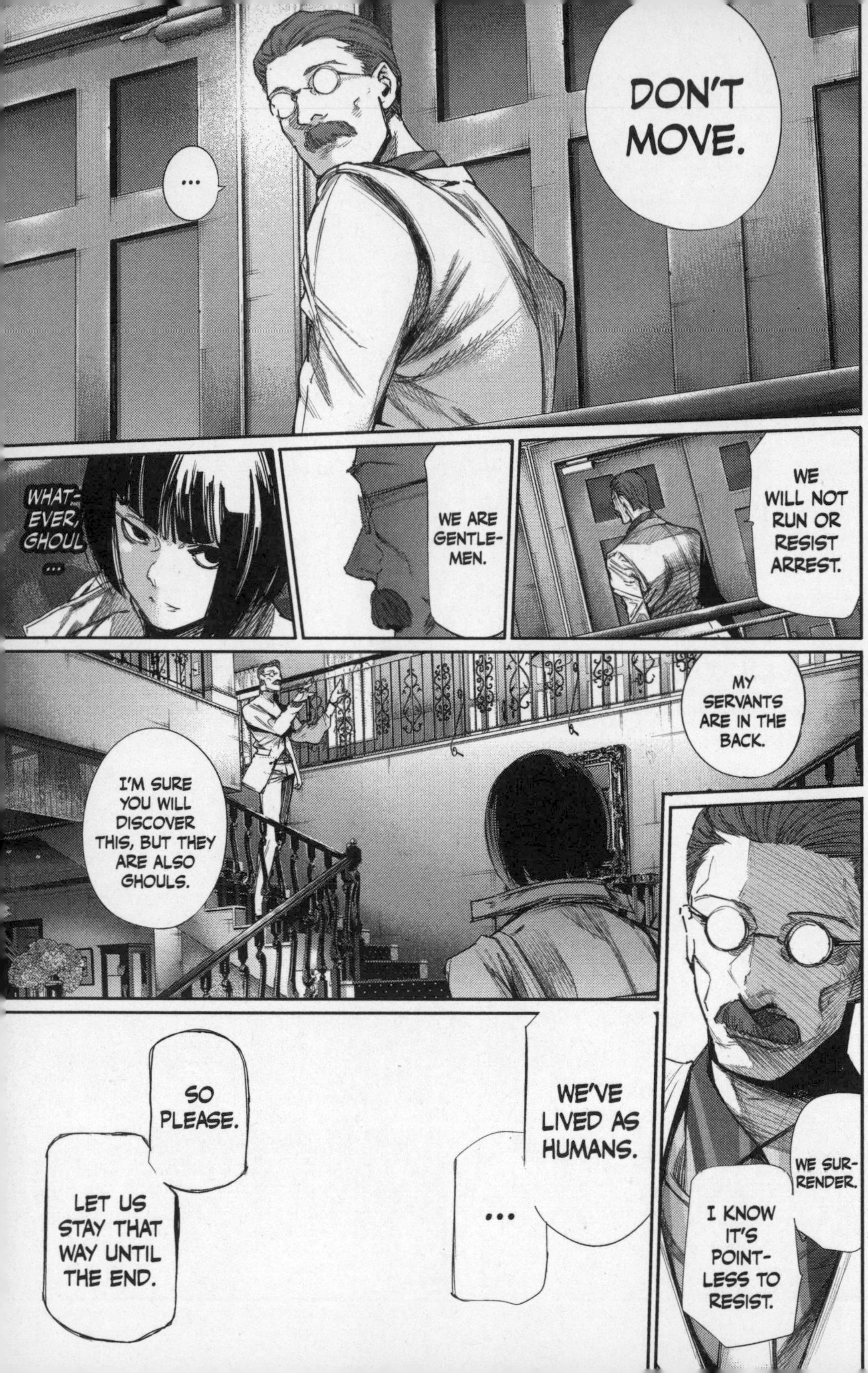
DON'T MOVE.
...
WE WILL NOT RUN OR RESIST ARREST.
WE ARE GENTLEMEN.
WHATEVER, GHOUL ...
MY SERVANTS ARE IN THE BACK.
I'M SURE YOU WILL DISCOVER THIS, BUT THEY ARE ALSO GHOULS.
WE SURRENDER.
I KNOW IT'S POINTLESS TO RESIST.
WE'VE LIVED AS HUMANS.
...
SO PLEASE.
LET US STAY THAT WAY UNTIL THE END.

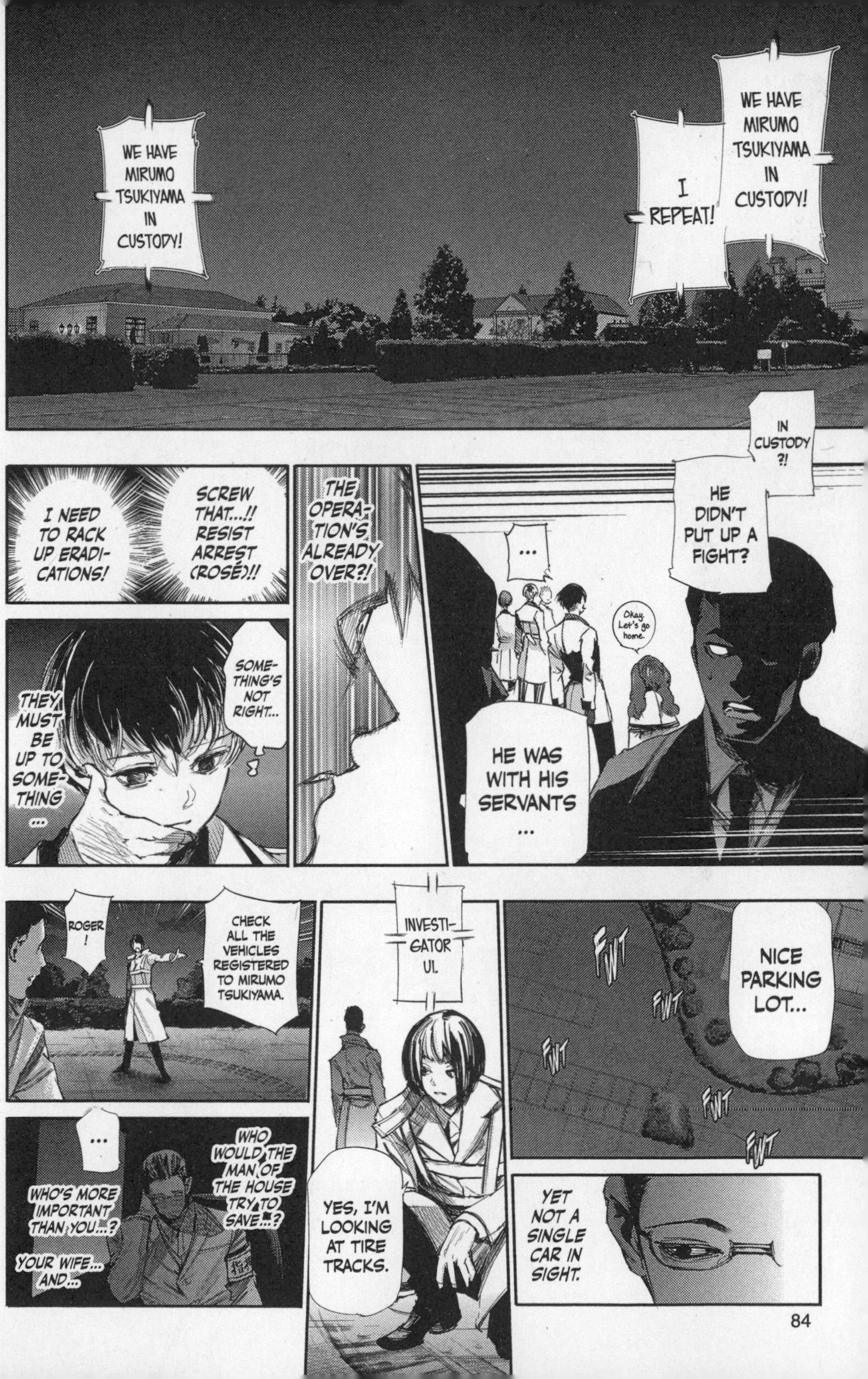

WE HAVE MIRUMO TSUKIYAMA IN CUSTODY!
I REPEAT!
WE HAVE MIRUMO TSUKIYAMA IN CUSTODY!
IN CUSTODY ?!
HE DIDN'T PUT UP A FIGHT?
...
Okay. Let's go home.
HE WAS WITH HIS SERVANTS ...
THE OPERATION'S ALREADY OVER?!
SCREW THAT...!! RESIST ARREST (ROSÉ)!!
I NEED TO RACK UP ERADICATIONS!
SOMETHING'S NOT RIGHT...
THEY MUST BE UP TO SOMETHING ...
NICE PARKING LOT...
FWT
FWT
FWT
FWT
FWT
YET NOT A SINGLE CAR IN SIGHT.
INVESTIGATOR UI.
YES, I'M LOOKING AT TIRE TRACKS.
CHECK ALL THE VEHICLES REGISTERED TO MIRUMO TSUKIYAMA.
ROGER!
WHO WOULD THE MAN OF THE HOUSE TRY TO SAVE...?
...
WHO'S MORE IMPORTANT THAN YOU...?
YOUR WIFE... AND...

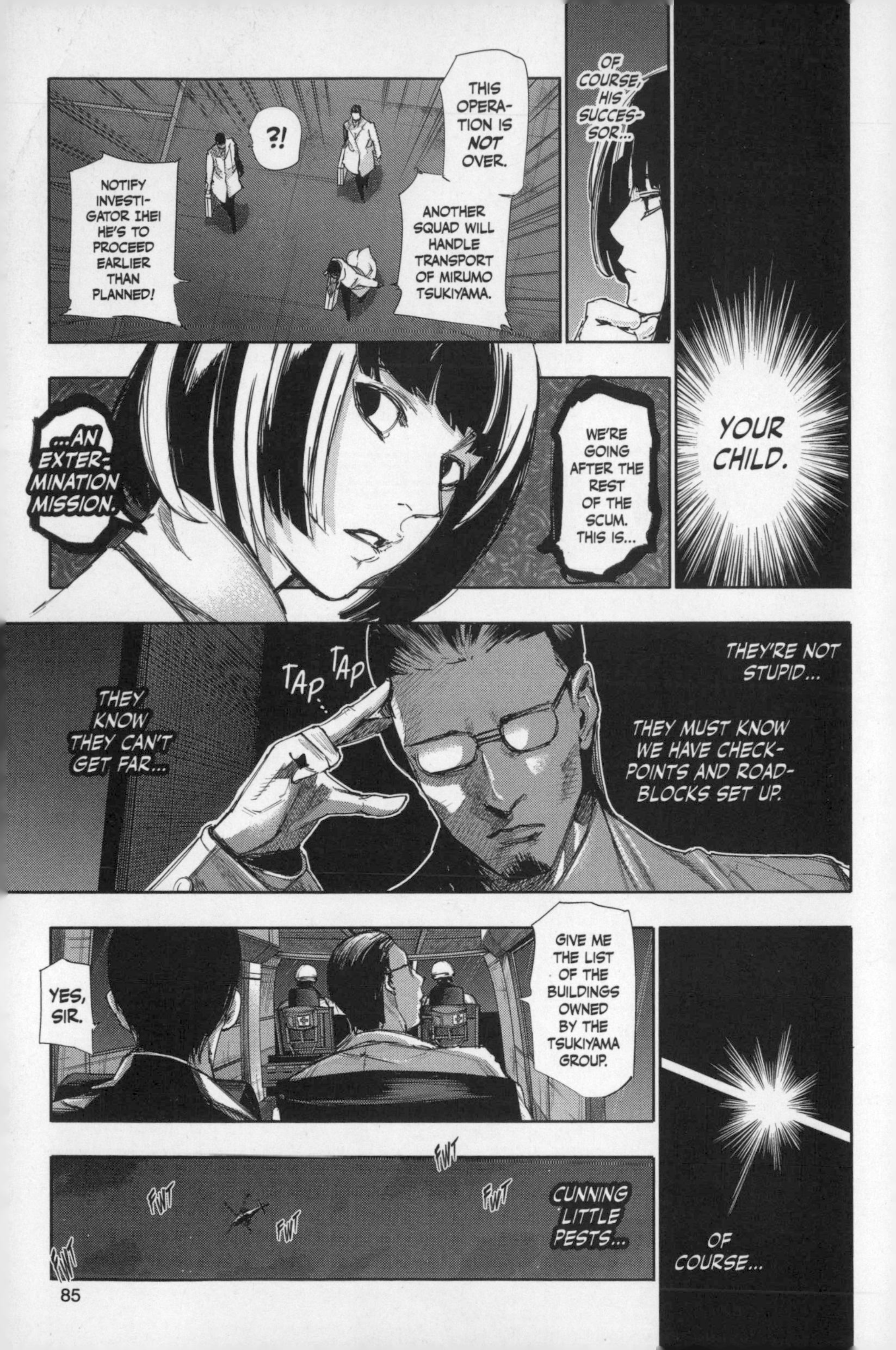
YOUR CHILD.
OF COURSE, HIS SUCCESSOR...
THIS OPERATION IS *NOT* OVER.
?!
ANOTHER SQUAD WILL HANDLE TRANSPORT OF MIRUMO TSUKIYAMA.
NOTIFY INVESTIGATOR IHEI HE'S TO PROCEED EARLIER THAN PLANNED!
WE'RE GOING AFTER THE REST OF THE SCUM. THIS IS...
...AN EXTERMINATION MISSION.
THEY'RE NOT STUPID...
THEY MUST KNOW WE HAVE CHECKPOINTS AND ROADBLOCKS SET UP.
TAP TAP
THEY KNOW THEY CAN'T GET FAR...
OF COURSE...
GIVE ME THE LIST OF THE BUILDINGS OWNED BY THE TSUKIYAMA GROUP.
YES, SIR.
FWT
FWT
CUNNING LITTLE PESTS...
FWT
FWT
FWT

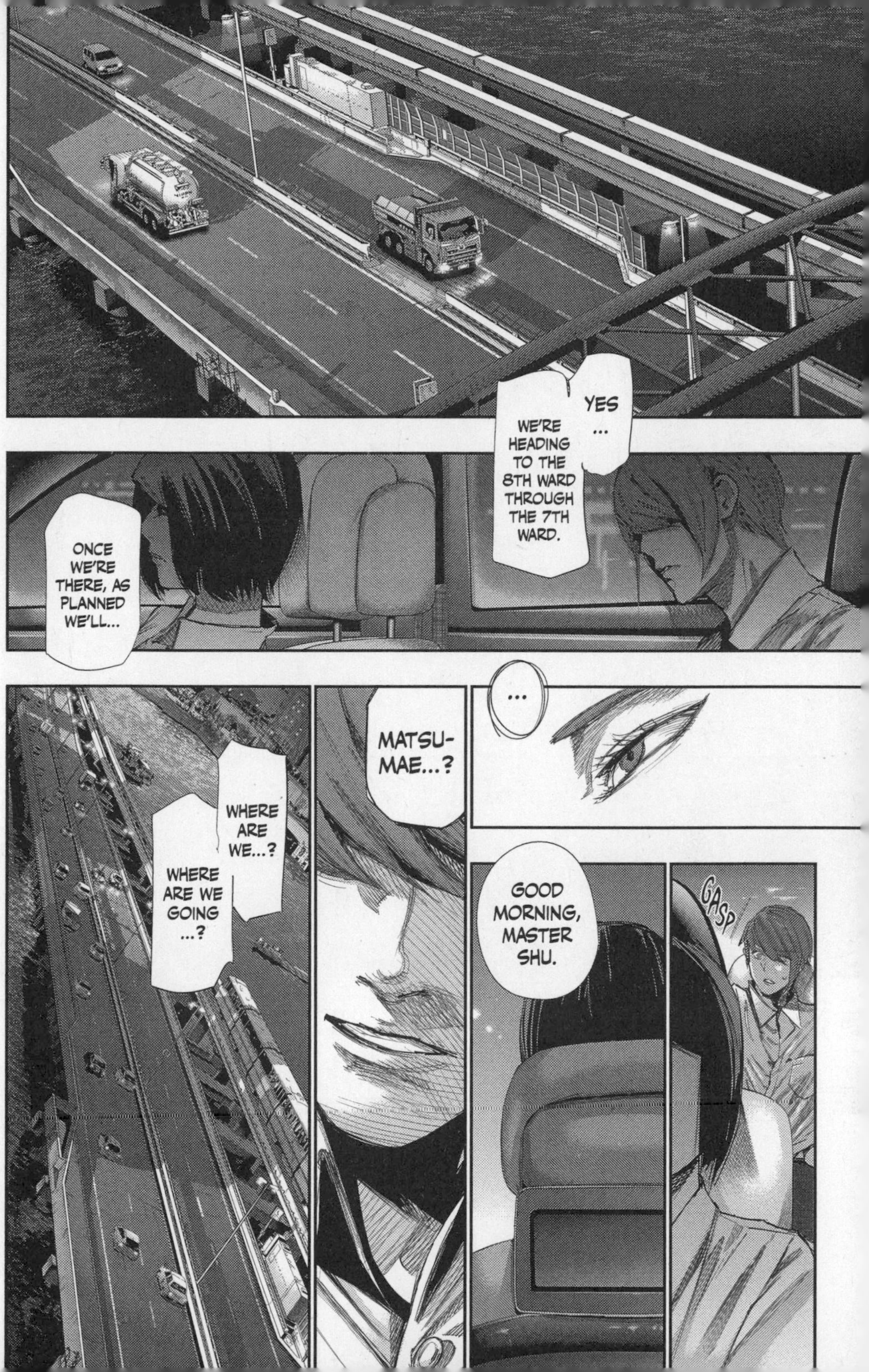
YES...
WE'RE HEADING TO THE 8TH WARD THROUGH THE 7TH WARD.
ONCE WE'RE THERE, AS PLANNED WE'LL...
...
GASP
GOOD MORNING, MASTER SHU.
MATSU-MAE...?
WHERE ARE WE...?
WHERE ARE WE GOING...?

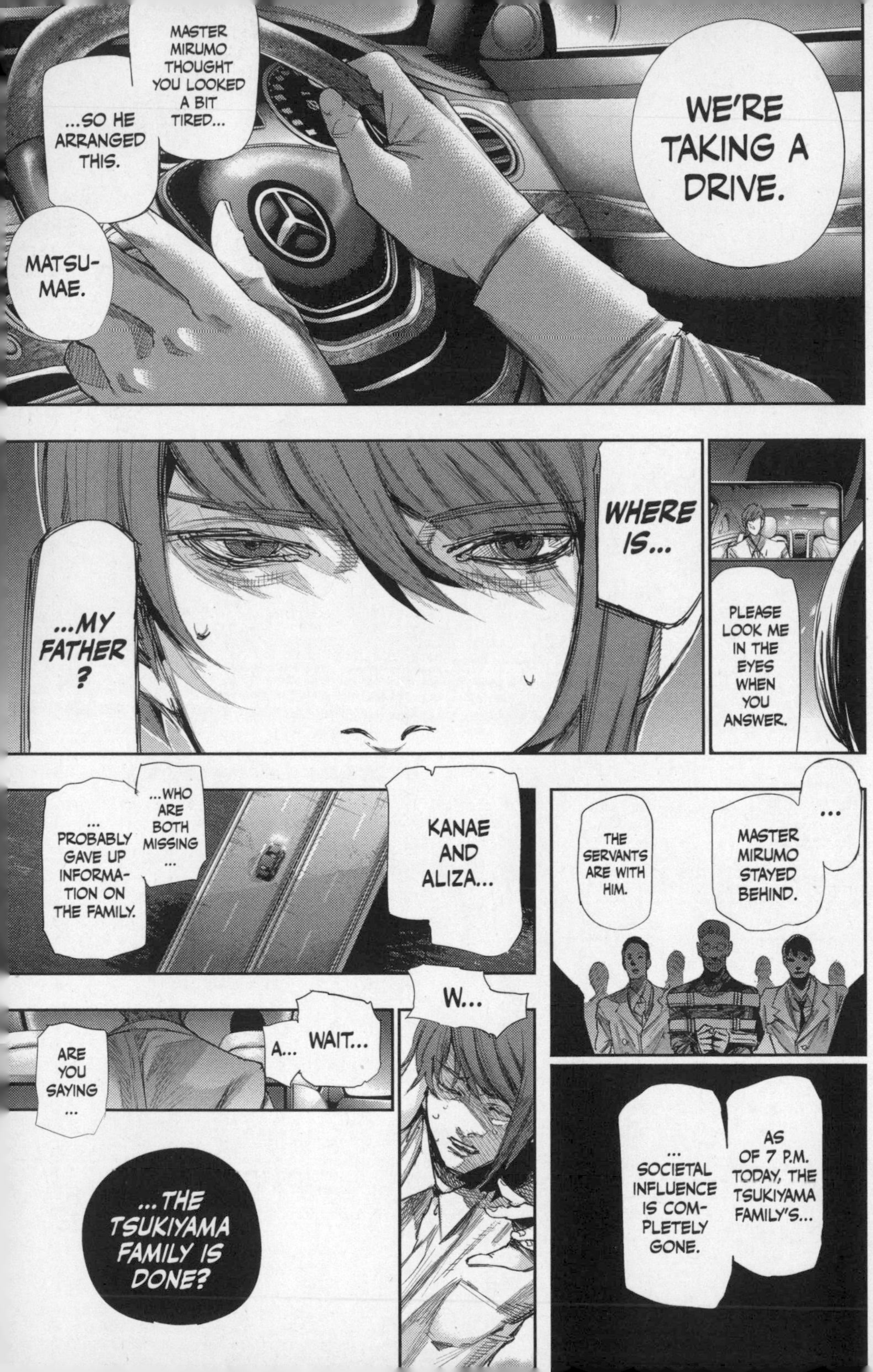
WE'RE TAKING A DRIVE.
MASTER MIRUMO THOUGHT YOU LOOKED A BIT TIRED...
...SO HE ARRANGED THIS.
MATSU-MAE.
PLEASE LOOK ME IN THE EYES WHEN YOU ANSWER.
WHERE IS...
...MY FATHER?
...
MASTER MIRUMO STAYED BEHIND.
THE SERVANTS ARE WITH HIM.
KANAE AND ALIZA...
...WHO ARE BOTH MISSING...
...PROBABLY GAVE UP INFORMATION ON THE FAMILY.
AS OF 7 P.M. TODAY, THE TSUKIYAMA FAMILY'S...
...SOCIETAL INFLUENCE IS COMPLETELY GONE.
W...
WAIT...
A...
ARE YOU SAYING...
...THE TSUKIYAMA FAMILY IS DONE?

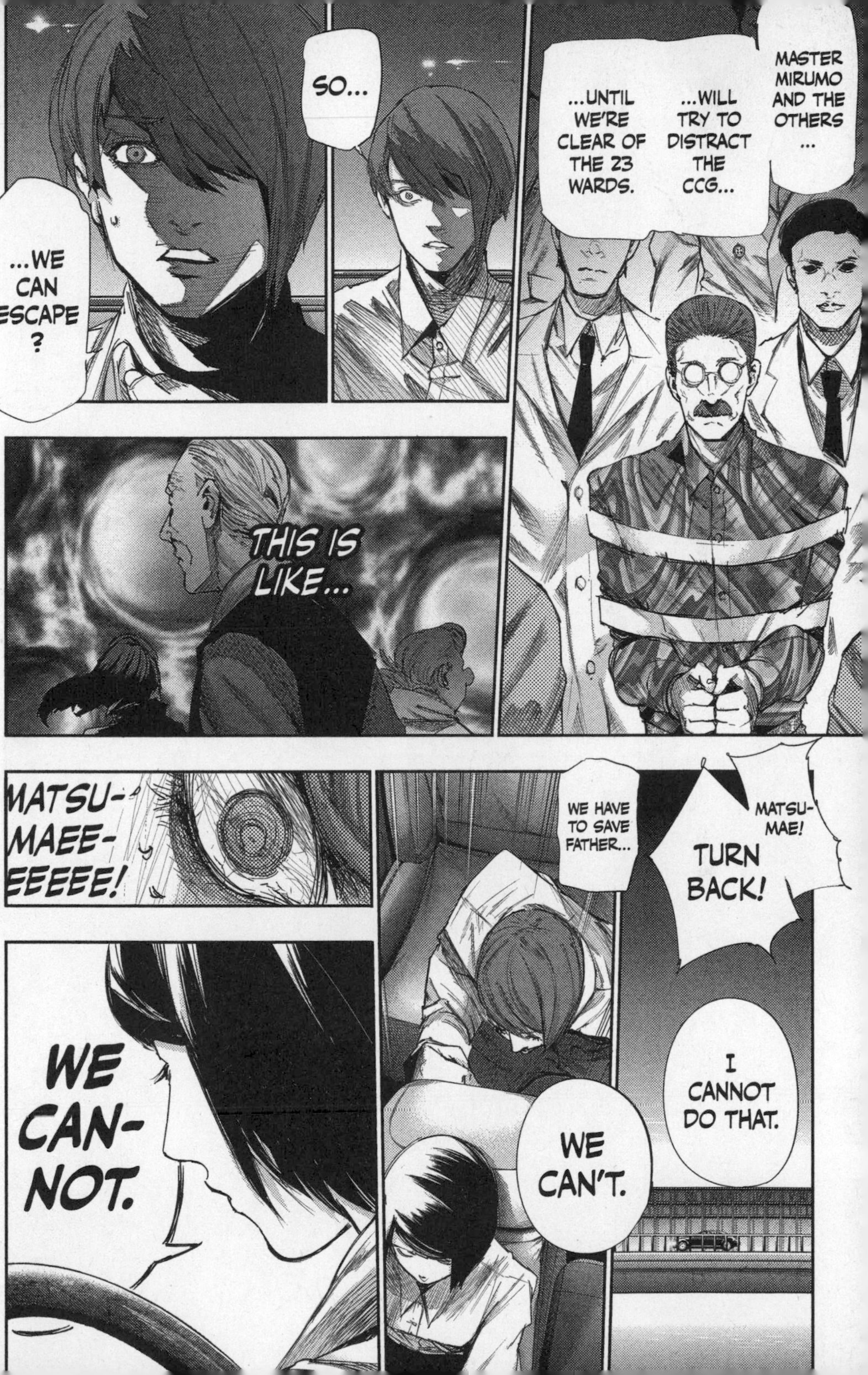
MASTER MIRUMO AND THE OTHERS ...
...WILL TRY TO DISTRACT THE CCG...
...UNTIL WE'RE CLEAR OF THE 23 WARDS.
SO...
...WE CAN ESCAPE?
THIS IS LIKE...
MATSU-MAE!
TURN BACK!
WE HAVE TO SAVE FATHER...
I CANNOT DO THAT.
WE CAN'T.
MATSU-MAEE-EEEEE!
WE CAN-NOT.

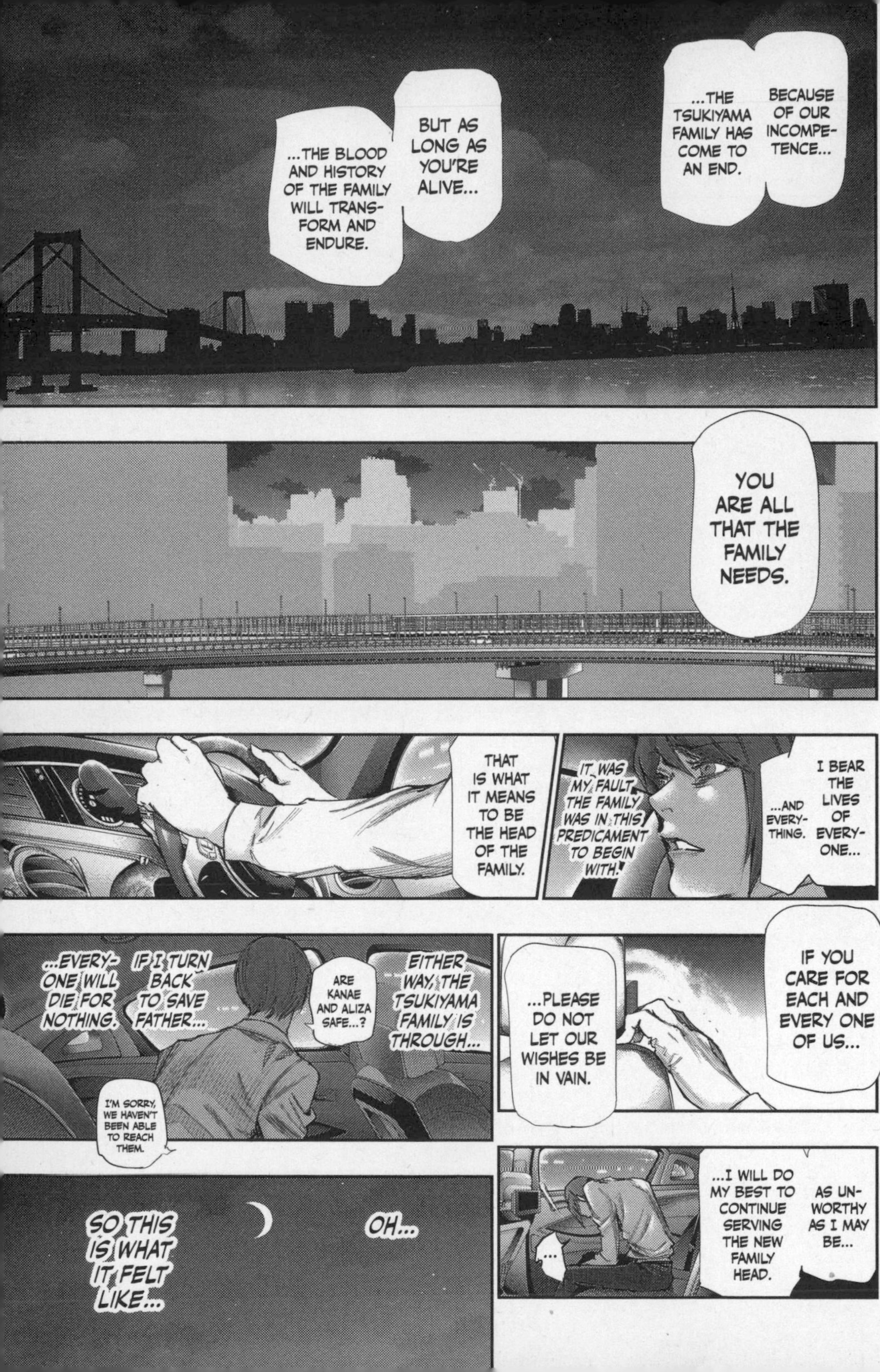
BECAUSE OF OUR INCOMPETENCE...
...THE TSUKIYAMA FAMILY HAS COME TO AN END.
BUT AS LONG AS YOU'RE ALIVE...
...THE BLOOD AND HISTORY OF THE FAMILY WILL TRANSFORM AND ENDURE.
YOU ARE ALL THAT THE FAMILY NEEDS.
I BEAR THE LIVES OF EVERYONE...
...AND EVERYTHING.
IT WAS MY FAULT THE FAMILY WAS IN THIS PREDICAMENT TO BEGIN WITH.
THAT IS WHAT IT MEANS TO BE THE HEAD OF THE FAMILY.
IF YOU CARE FOR EACH AND EVERY ONE OF US...
...PLEASE DO NOT LET OUR WISHES BE IN VAIN.
EITHER WAY, THE TSUKIYAMA FAMILY IS THROUGH...
ARE KANAE AND ALIZA SAFE...?
IF I TURN BACK TO SAVE FATHER...
...EVERYONE WILL DIE FOR NOTHING.
I'M SORRY, WE HAVEN'T BEEN ABLE TO REACH THEM.
AS UNWORTHY AS I MAY BE...
...I WILL DO MY BEST TO CONTINUE SERVING THE NEW FAMILY HEAD.
...
OH...
SO THIS IS WHAT IT FELT LIKE...

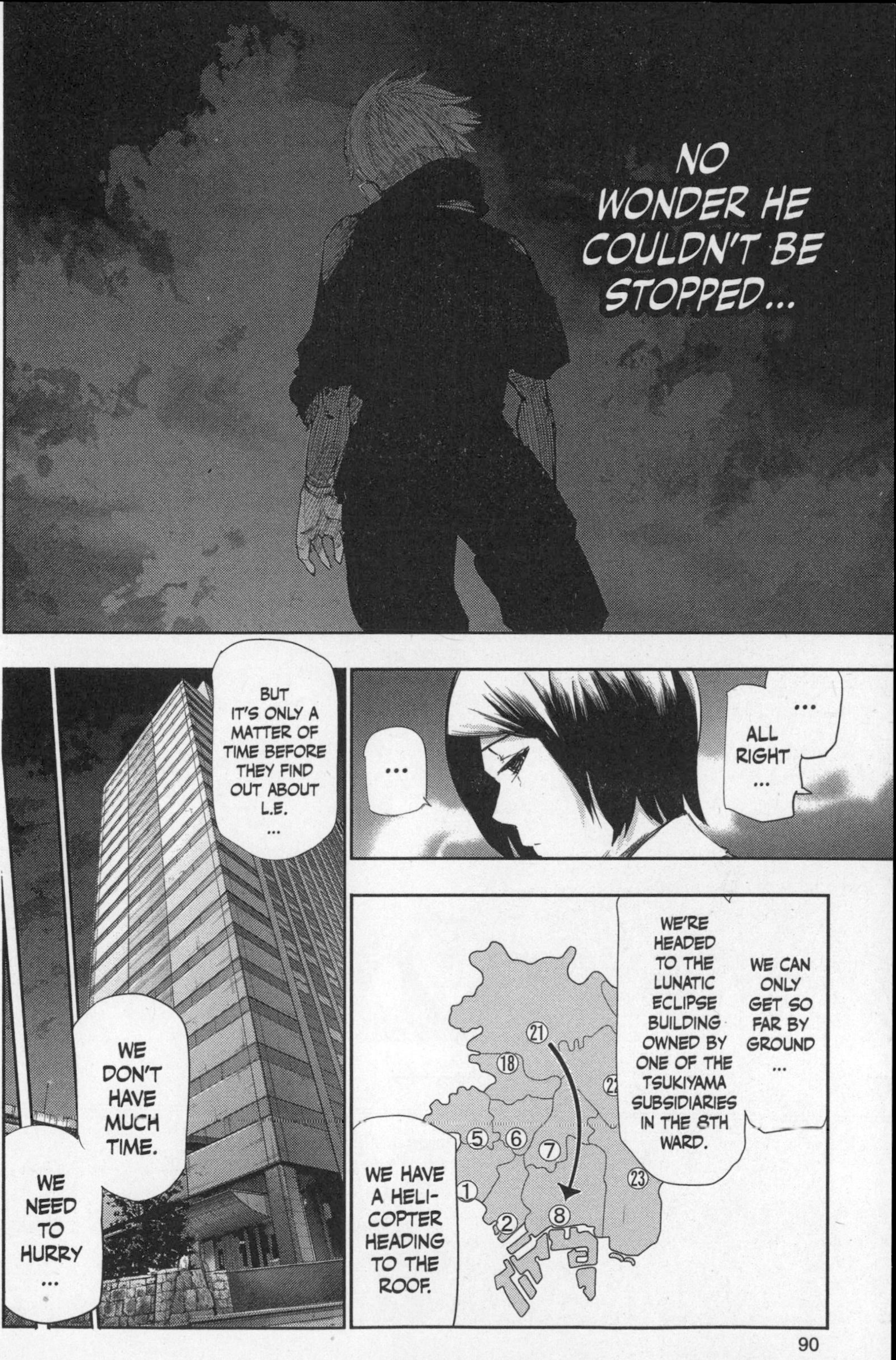

NO WONDER HE COULDN'T BE STOPPED...
... ALL RIGHT ...
...
WE CAN ONLY GET SO FAR BY GROUND ...
WE'RE HEADED TO THE LUNATIC ECLIPSE BUILDING OWNED BY ONE OF THE TSUKIYAMA SUBSIDIARIES IN THE 8TH WARD.
21
18
22
5
6
7
23
1
2
8
WE HAVE A HELI-COPTER HEADING TO THE ROOF.
BUT IT'S ONLY A MATTER OF TIME BEFORE THEY FIND OUT ABOUT L.E. ...
WE DON'T HAVE MUCH TIME.
WE NEED TO HURRY ...

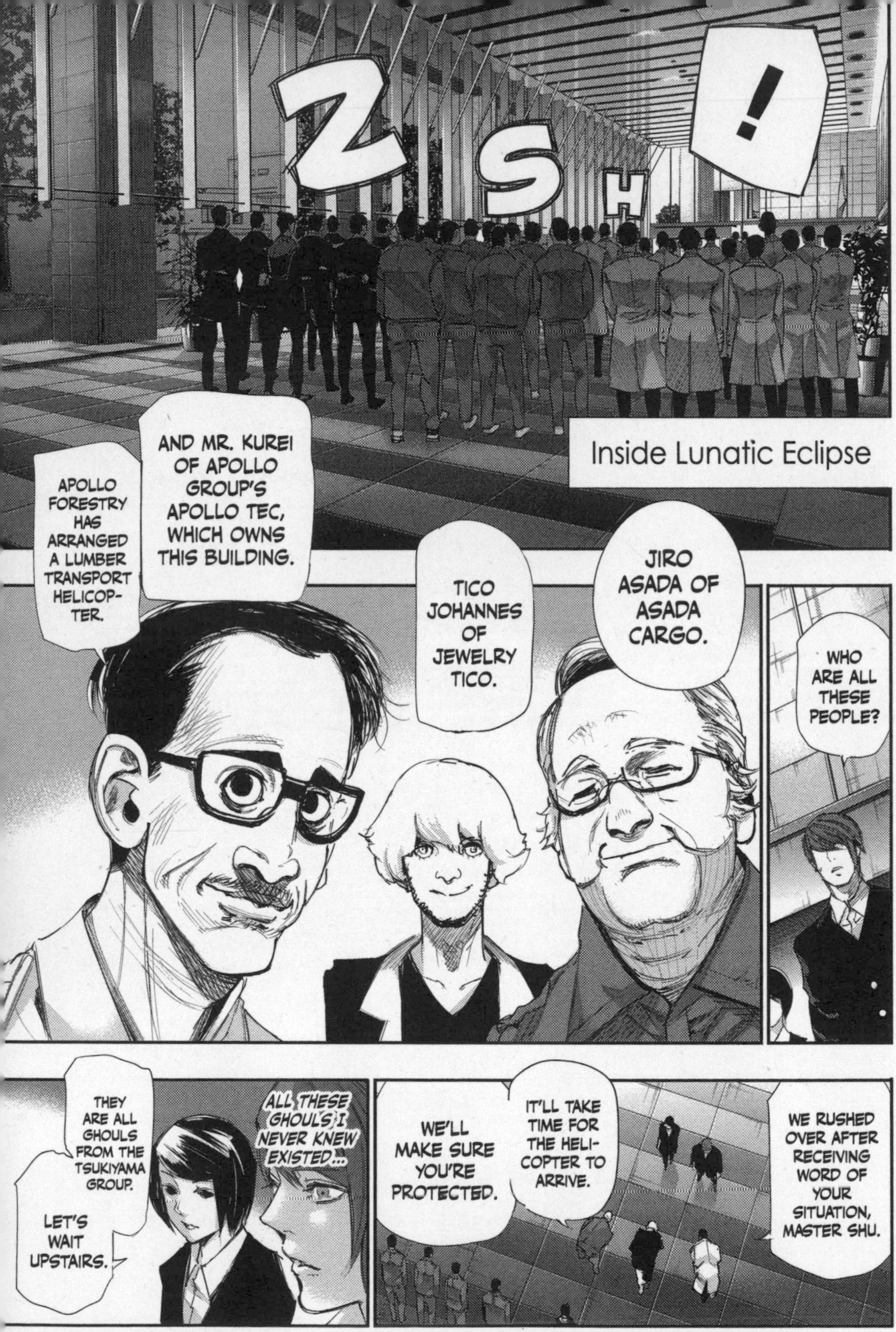
ZSH!
Inside Lunatic Eclipse
WHO ARE ALL THESE PEOPLE?
JIRO ASADA OF ASADA CARGO.
TICO JOHANNES OF JEWELRY TICO.
AND MR. KUREI OF APOLLO GROUP'S APOLLO TEC, WHICH OWNS THIS BUILDING.
APOLLO FORESTRY HAS ARRANGED A LUMBER TRANSPORT HELICOPTER.
WE RUSHED OVER AFTER RECEIVING WORD OF YOUR SITUATION, MASTER SHU.
IT'LL TAKE TIME FOR THE HELICOPTER TO ARRIVE.
WE'LL MAKE SURE YOU'RE PROTECTED.
ALL THESE GHOULS I NEVER KNEW EXISTED...
THEY ARE ALL GHOULS FROM THE TSUKIYAMA GROUP.
LET'S WAIT UPSTAIRS.

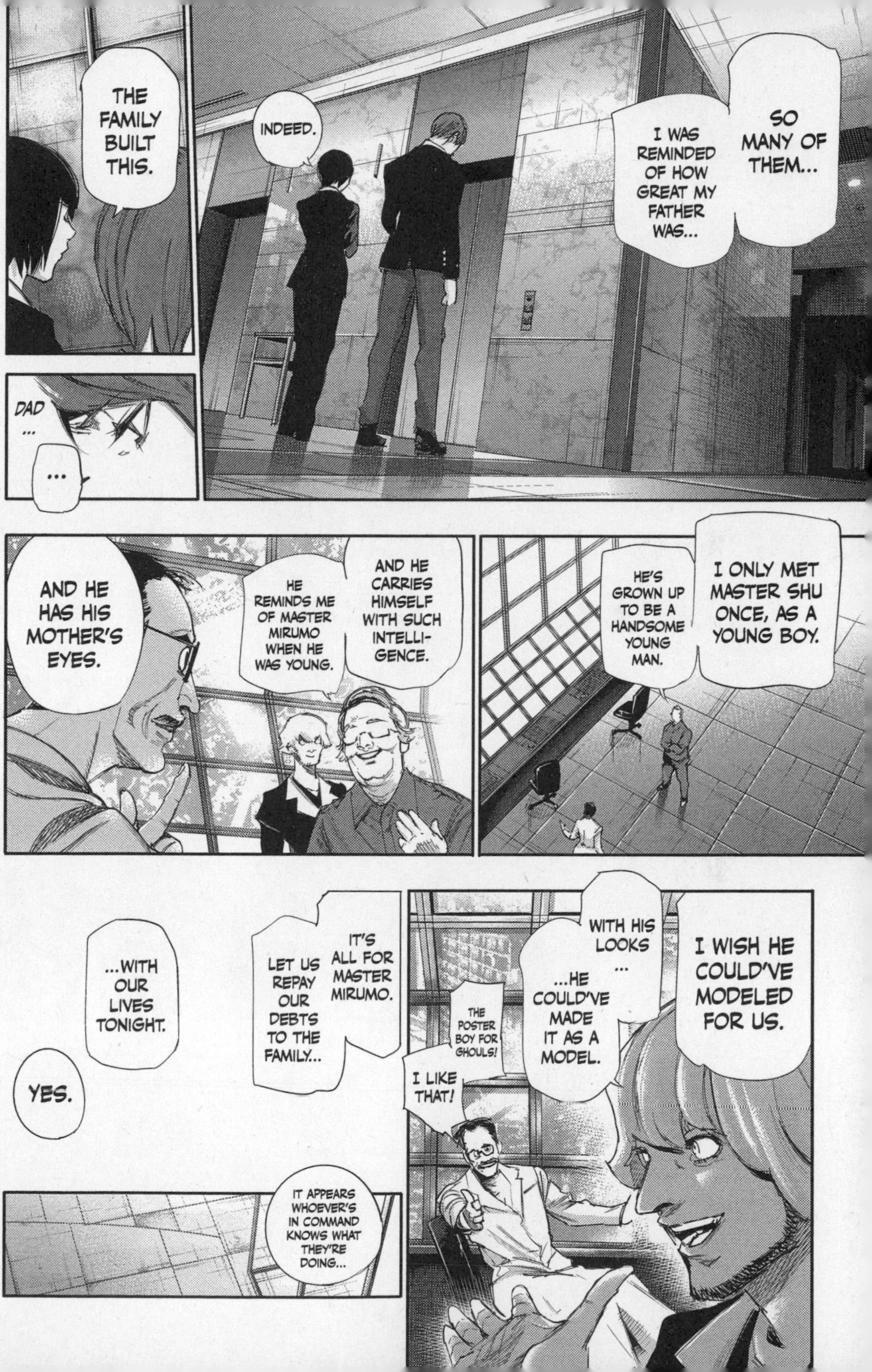
SO MANY OF THEM...
I WAS REMINDED OF HOW GREAT MY FATHER WAS...
INDEED.
THE FAMILY BUILT THIS.
DAD ...
...
I ONLY MET MASTER SHU ONCE, AS A YOUNG BOY.
HE'S GROWN UP TO BE A HANDSOME YOUNG MAN.
AND HE CARRIES HIMSELF WITH SUCH INTELLIGENCE.
HE REMINDS ME OF MASTER MIRUMO WHEN HE WAS YOUNG.
AND HE HAS HIS MOTHER'S EYES.
I WISH HE COULD'VE MODELED FOR US.
WITH HIS LOOKS ...
...HE COULD'VE MADE IT AS A MODEL.
THE POSTER BOY FOR GHOULS!
I LIKE THAT!
IT'S ALL FOR MASTER MIRUMO.
LET US REPAY OUR DEBTS TO THE FAMILY...
...WITH OUR LIVES TONIGHT.
YES.
IT APPEARS WHOEVER'S IN COMMAND KNOWS WHAT THEY'RE DOING...

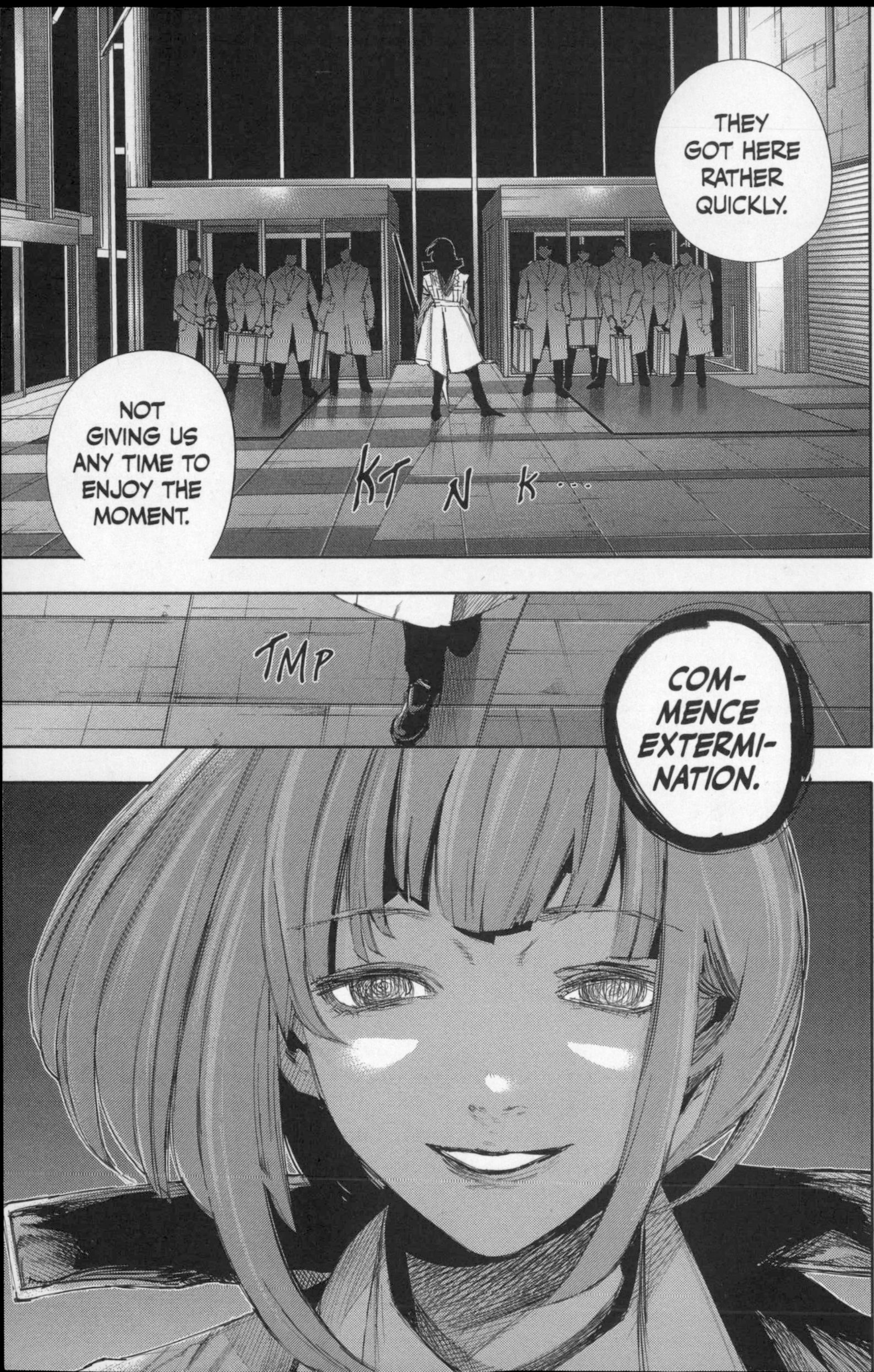
THEY GOT HERE RATHER QUICKLY.
NOT GIVING US ANY TIME TO ENJOY THE MOMENT.
KTNK...
TMP
COM-MENCE EXTERMI-NATION.

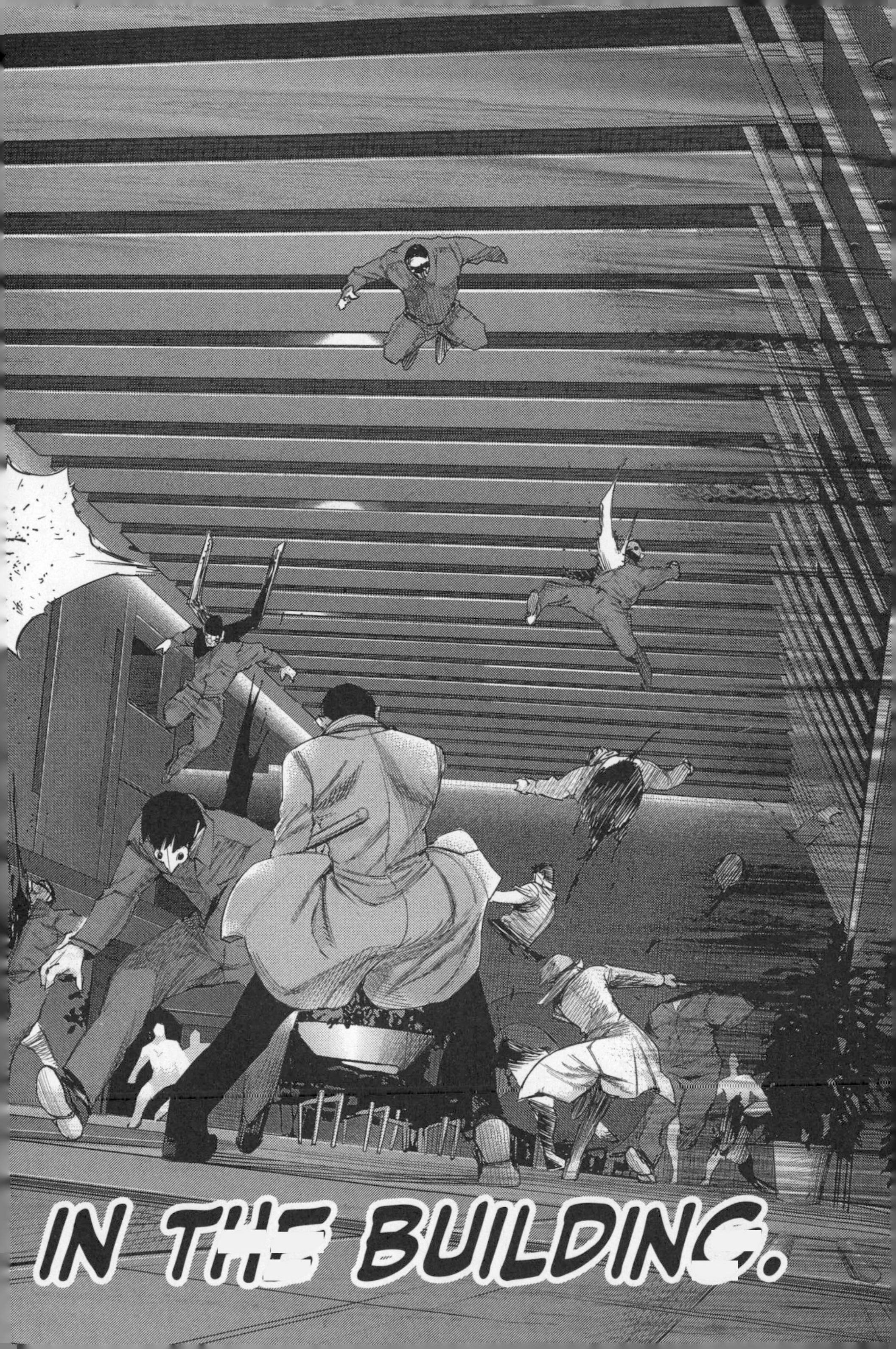
IN THE BUILDING.

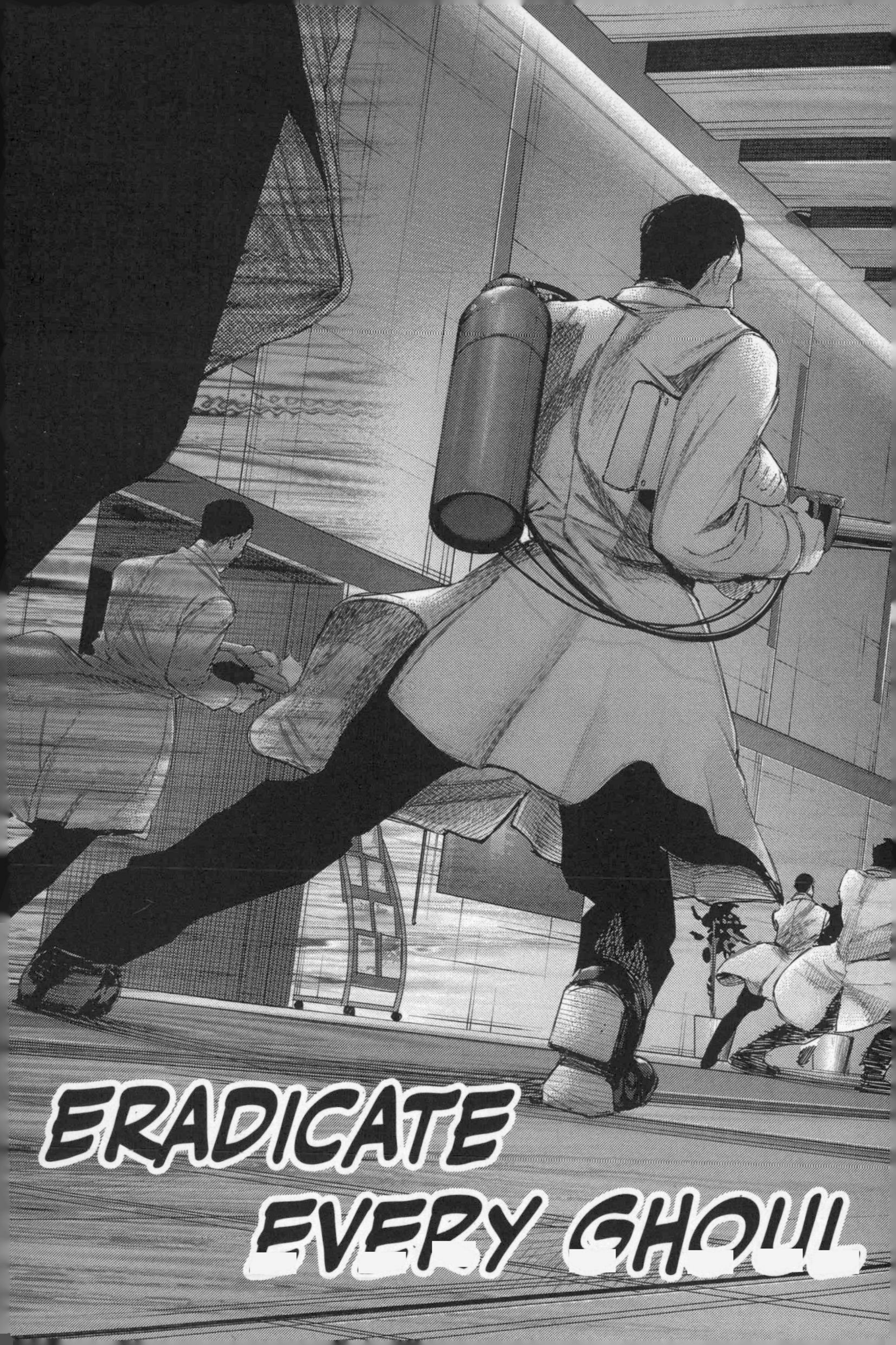
ERADICATE EVERY GHOUL

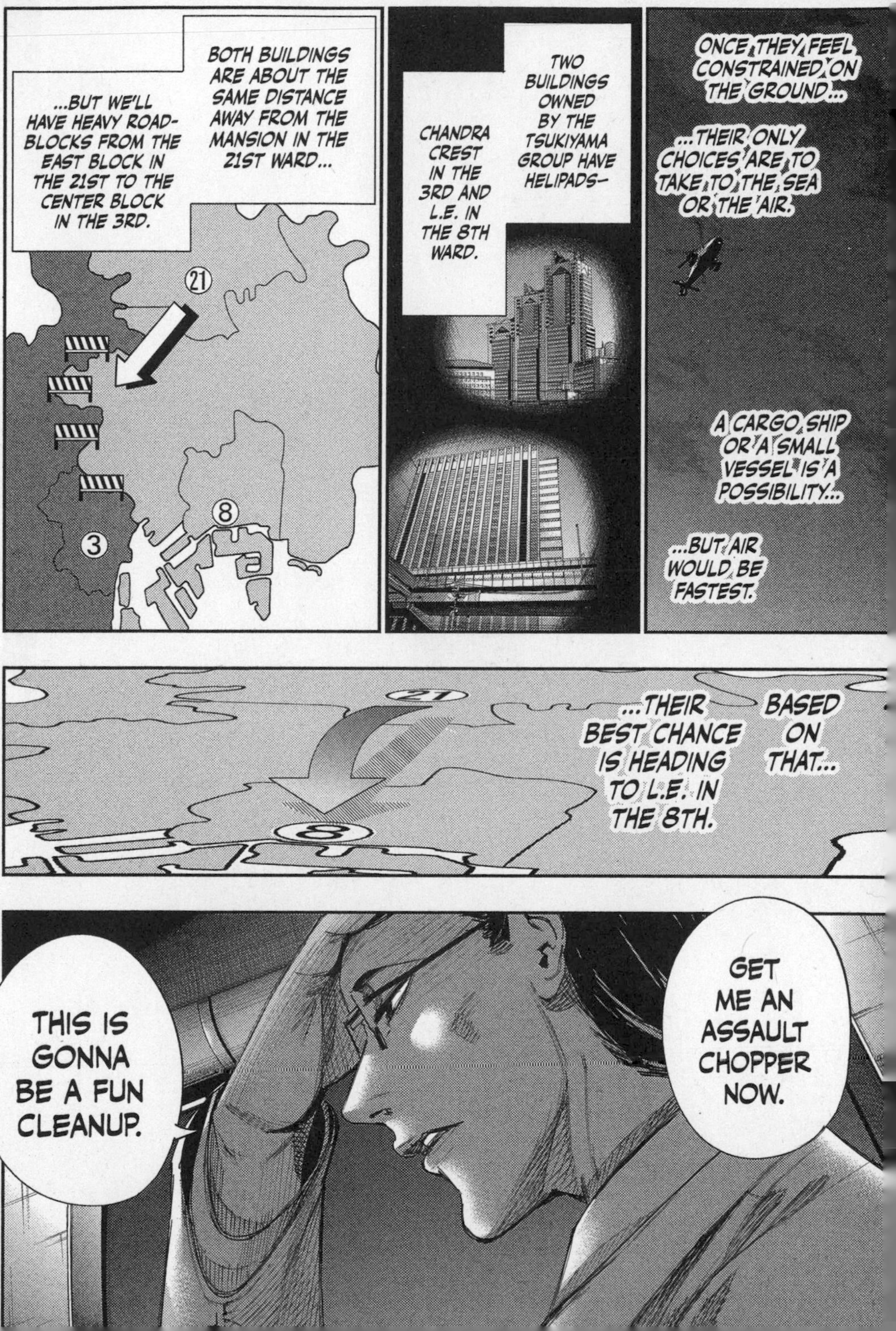
ONCE THEY FEEL CONSTRAINED ON THE GROUND...
...THEIR ONLY CHOICES ARE TO TAKE TO THE SEA OR THE AIR.
A CARGO SHIP OR A SMALL VESSEL IS A POSSIBILITY...
...BUT AIR WOULD BE FASTEST.
TWO BUILDINGS OWNED BY THE TSUKIYAMA GROUP HAVE HELIPADS—
CHANDRA CREST IN THE 3RD AND L.E. IN THE 8TH WARD.
BOTH BUILDINGS ARE ABOUT THE SAME DISTANCE AWAY FROM THE MANSION IN THE 21ST WARD...
...BUT WE'LL HAVE HEAVY ROAD-BLOCKS FROM THE EAST BLOCK IN THE 21ST TO THE CENTER BLOCK IN THE 3RD.
21
8
3
BASED ON THAT...
...THEIR BEST CHANCE IS HEADING TO L.E. IN THE 8TH.
21
8
GET ME AN ASSAULT CHOPPER NOW.
THIS IS GONNA BE A FUN CLEANUP.

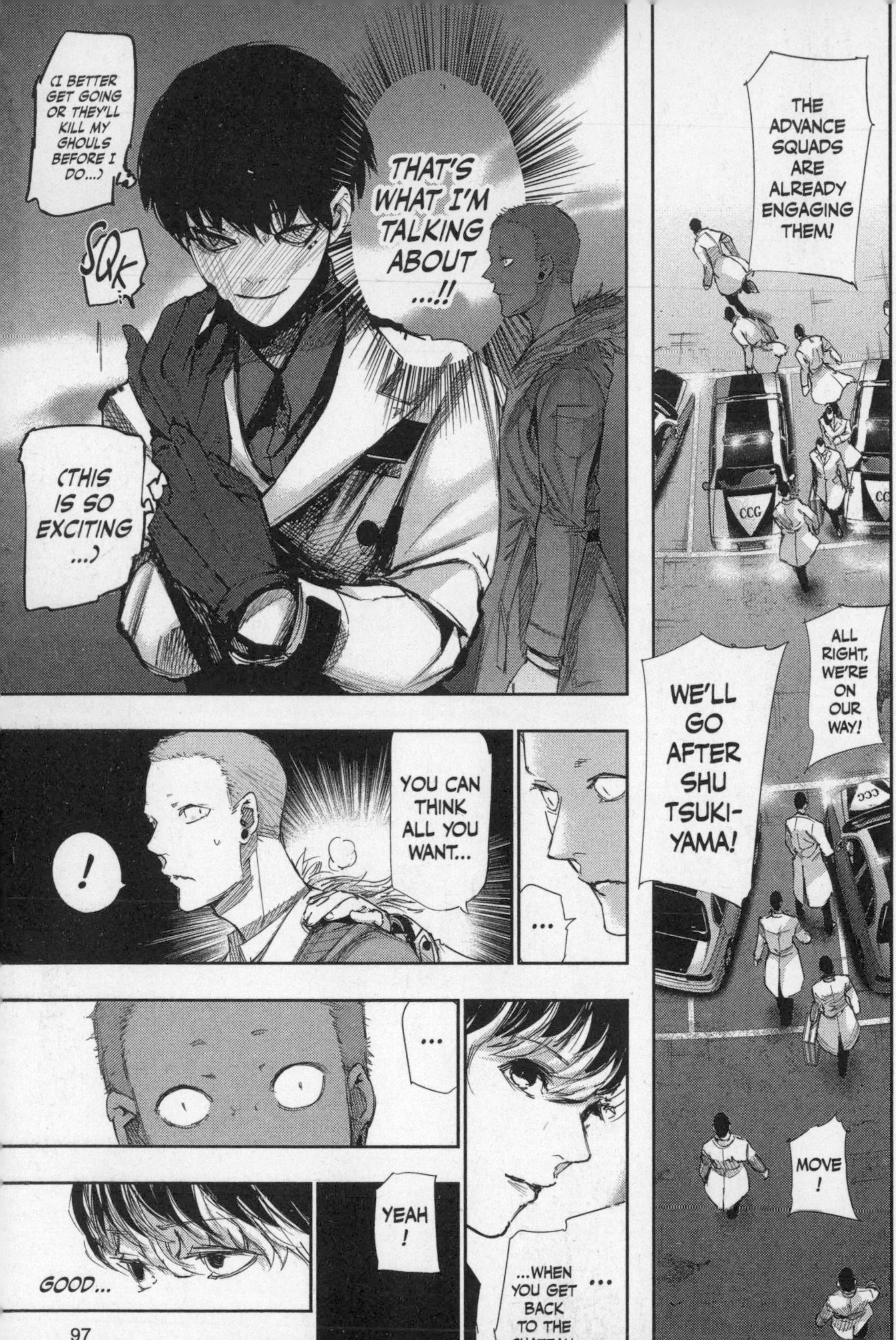

THE ADVANCE SQUADS ARE ALREADY ENGAGING THEM!
ALL RIGHT, WE'RE ON OUR WAY!
WE'LL GO AFTER SHU TSUKI-YAMA!
MOVE!
THAT'S WHAT I'M TALKING ABOUT ...!!
(I BETTER GET GOING OR THEY'LL KILL MY GHOULS BEFORE I DO...)
SQK
(THIS IS SO EXCITING ...)
...
YOU CAN THINK ALL YOU WANT...
!
...
...WHEN YOU GET BACK TO THE CHATEAU.
...
YEAH!
GOOD...

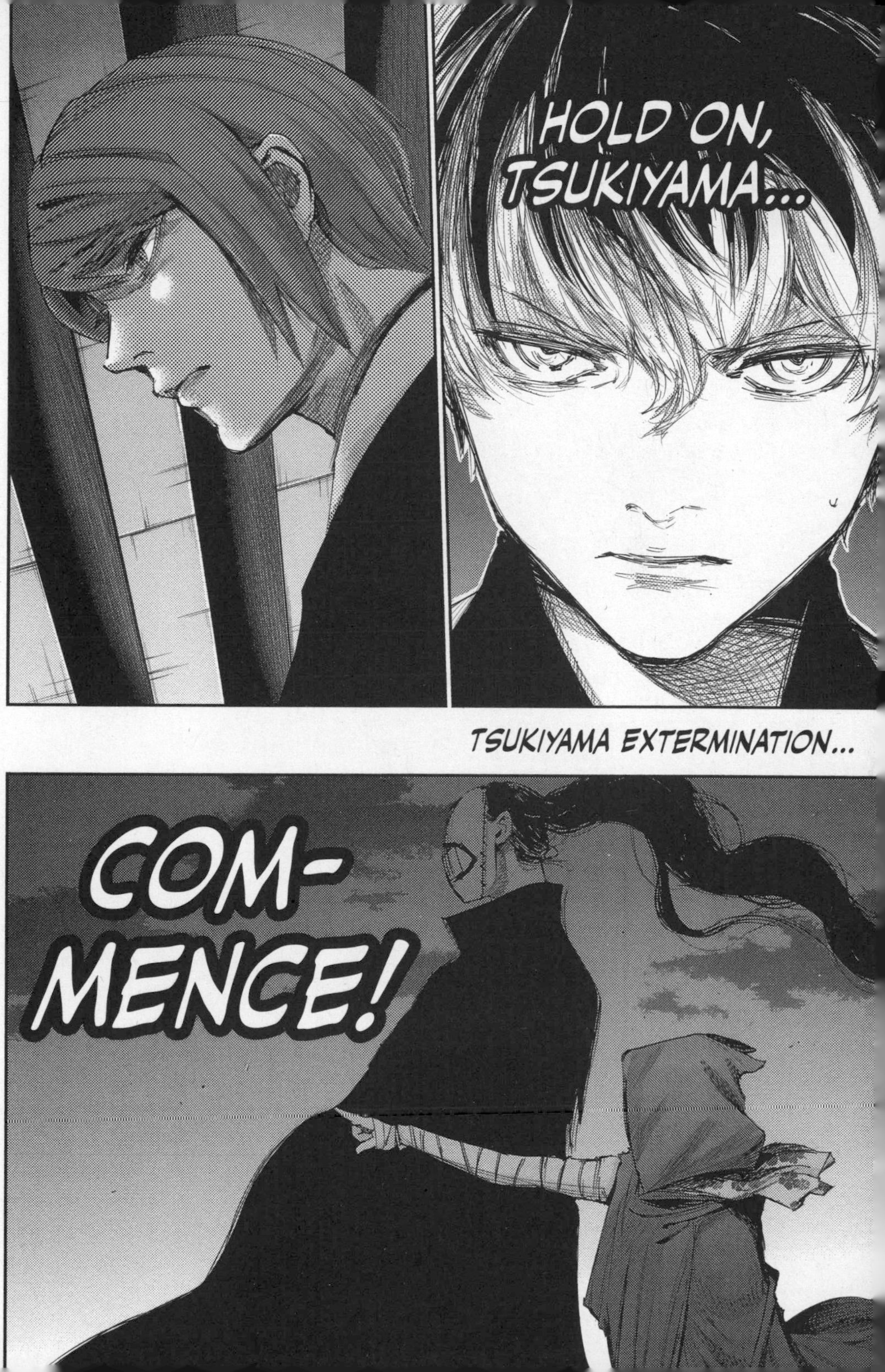
HOLD ON, TSUKIYAMA...
TSUKIYAMA EXTERMINATION...
COM-MENCE!

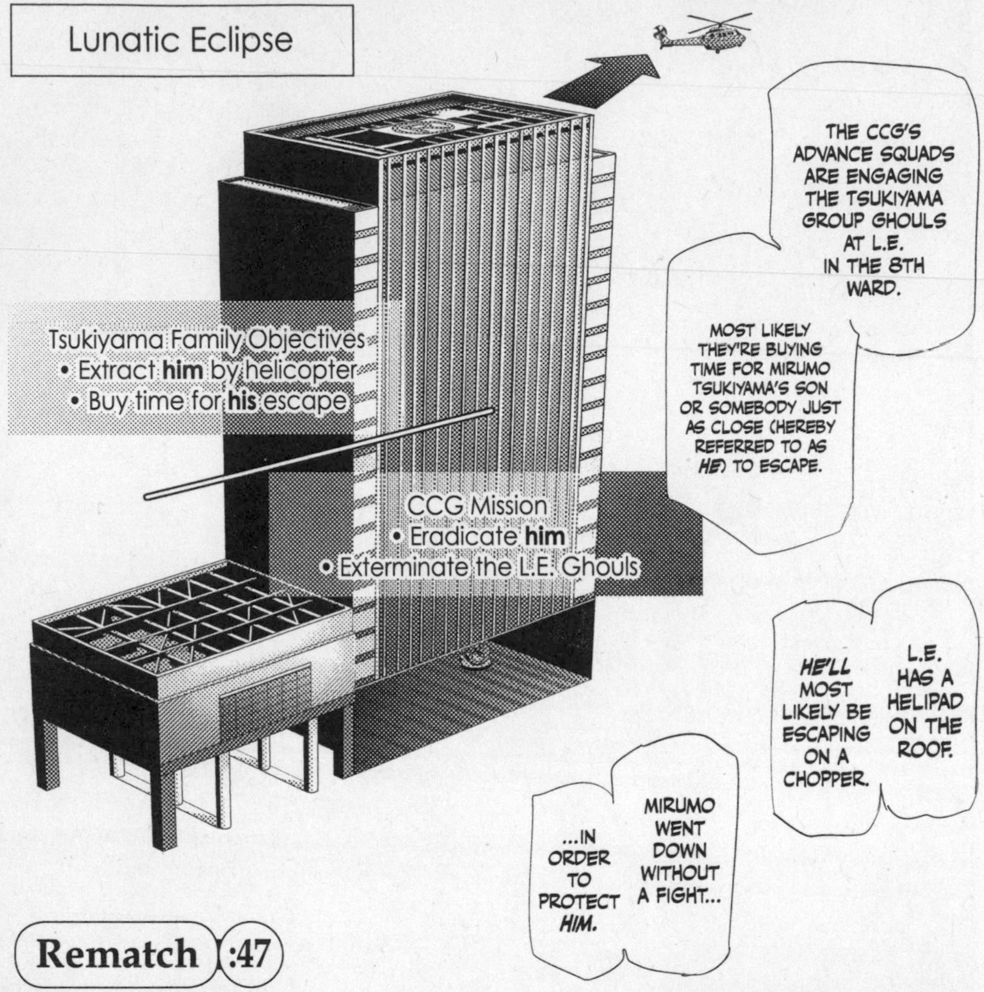
Lunatic Eclipse
THE CCG'S ADVANCE SQUADS ARE ENGAGING THE TSUKIYAMA GROUP GHOULS AT L.E. IN THE 8TH WARD.
MOST LIKELY THEY'RE BUYING TIME FOR MIRUMO TSUKIYAMA'S SON OR SOMEBODY JUST AS CLOSE (HEREBY REFERRED TO AS *HE*) TO ESCAPE.
Tsukiyama Family Objectives
• Extract **him** by helicopter
• Buy time for **his** escape
CCG Mission
• Eradicate **him**
• Exterminate the L.E. Ghouls
L.E. HAS A HELIPAD ON THE ROOF.
HE'LL MOST LIKELY BE ESCAPING ON A CHOPPER.
MIRUMO WENT DOWN WITHOUT A FIGHT...
...IN ORDER TO PROTECT *HIM*.

Rematch :47

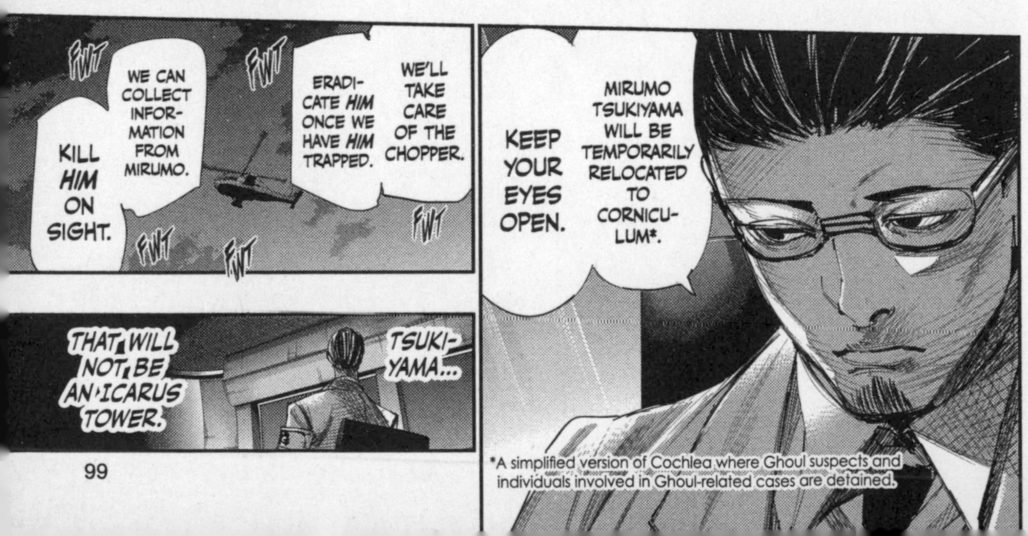
MIRUMO TSUKIYAMA WILL BE TEMPORARILY RELOCATED TO CORNICULUM*.
KEEP YOUR EYES OPEN.
WE'LL TAKE CARE OF THE CHOPPER.
ERADICATE *HIM* ONCE WE HAVE *HIM* TRAPPED.
WE CAN COLLECT INFORMATION FROM MIRUMO.
KILL *HIM* ON SIGHT.
FWT
FWT
FWT
FWT
FWT
TSUKIYAMA...
THAT WILL NOT BE AN "ICARUS TOWER."

*A simplified version of Cochlea where Ghoul suspects and individuals involved in Ghoul-related cases are detained.

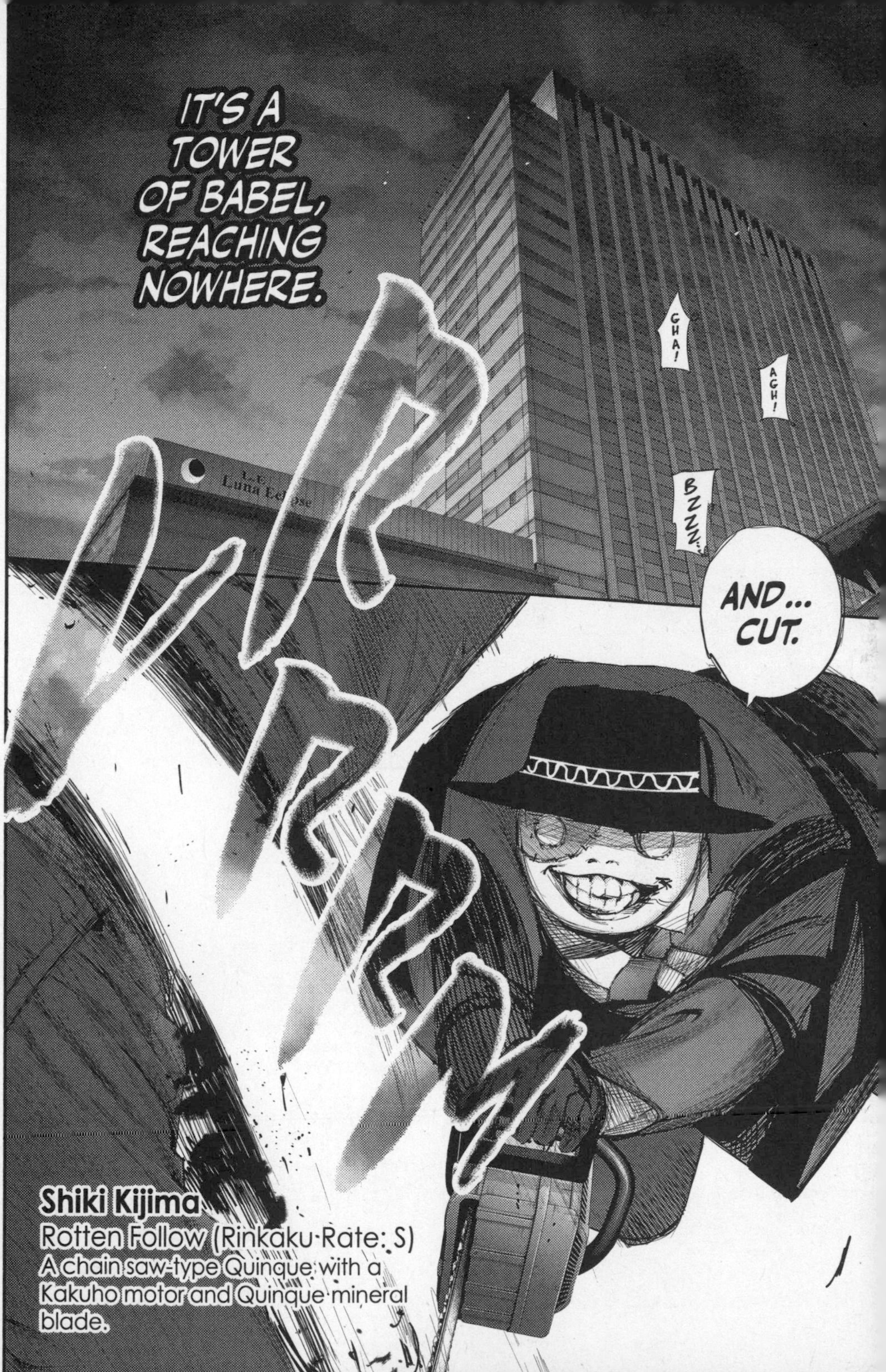
IT'S A TOWER OF BABEL, REACHING NOWHERE.
GHA!
AGH!
BZZZ...
AND... CUT.
Shiki Kijima
Rotten Follow (Rinkaku Rate: S)
A chain saw-type Quinque with a Kakuho motor and Quinque mineral blade.

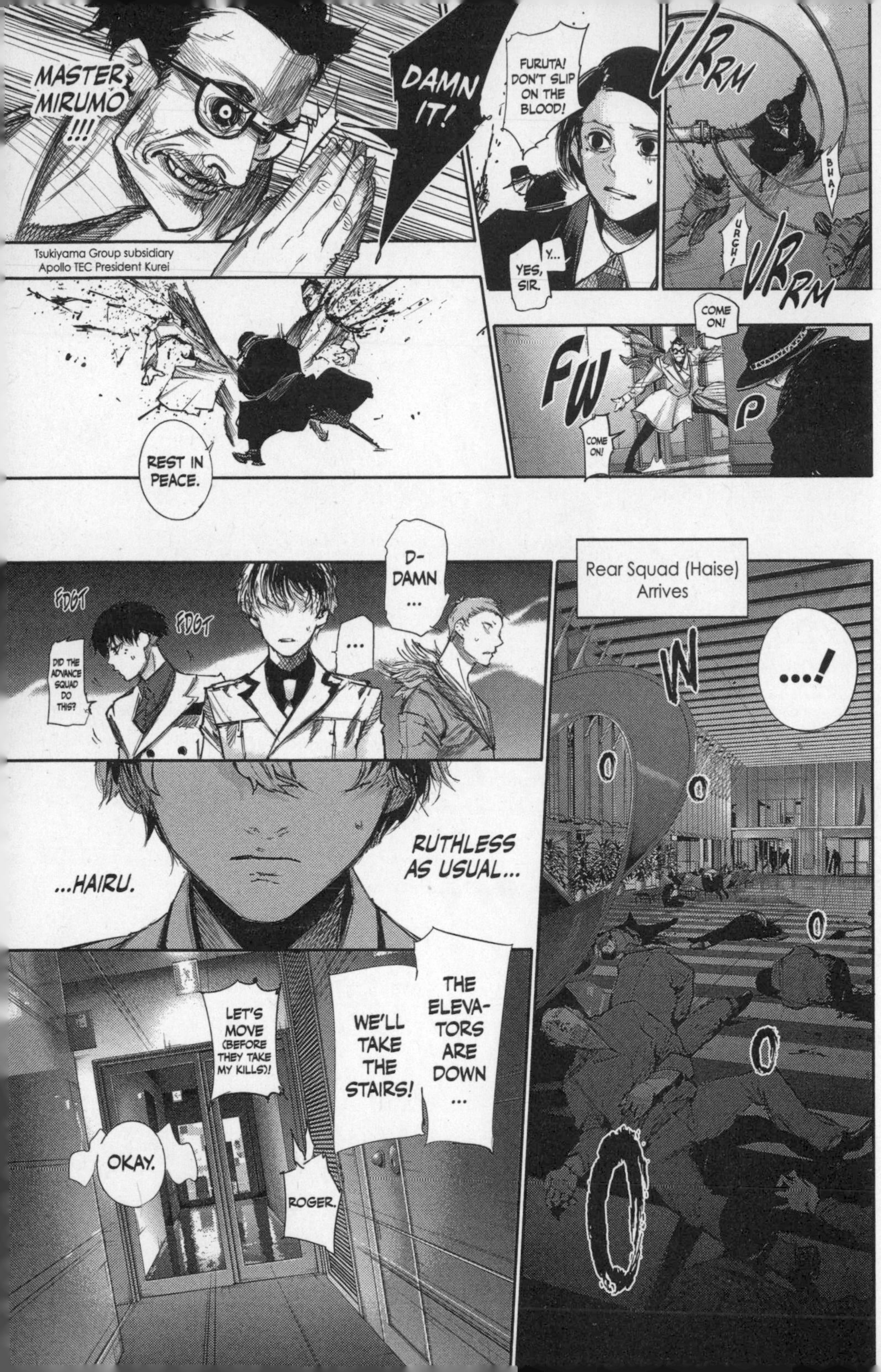
VRRM
BHA!
URGH!
VRRM
FURUTA! DON'T SLIP ON THE BLOOD!
Y... YES, SIR.
DAMN IT!
MASTER MIRUMO!!!
Tsukiyama Group subsidiary Apollo TEC President Kurei
COME ON!
P
FW
COME ON!
REST IN PEACE.
Rear Squad (Haise) Arrives
...!
W
D-DAMN...
...
FDGT
FDGT
DID THE ADVANCE SQUAD DO THIS?
RUTHLESS AS USUAL...
...HAIRU.
THE ELEVATORS ARE DOWN...
WE'LL TAKE THE STAIRS!
LET'S MOVE (BEFORE THEY TAKE MY KILLS)!
ROGER.
OKAY.

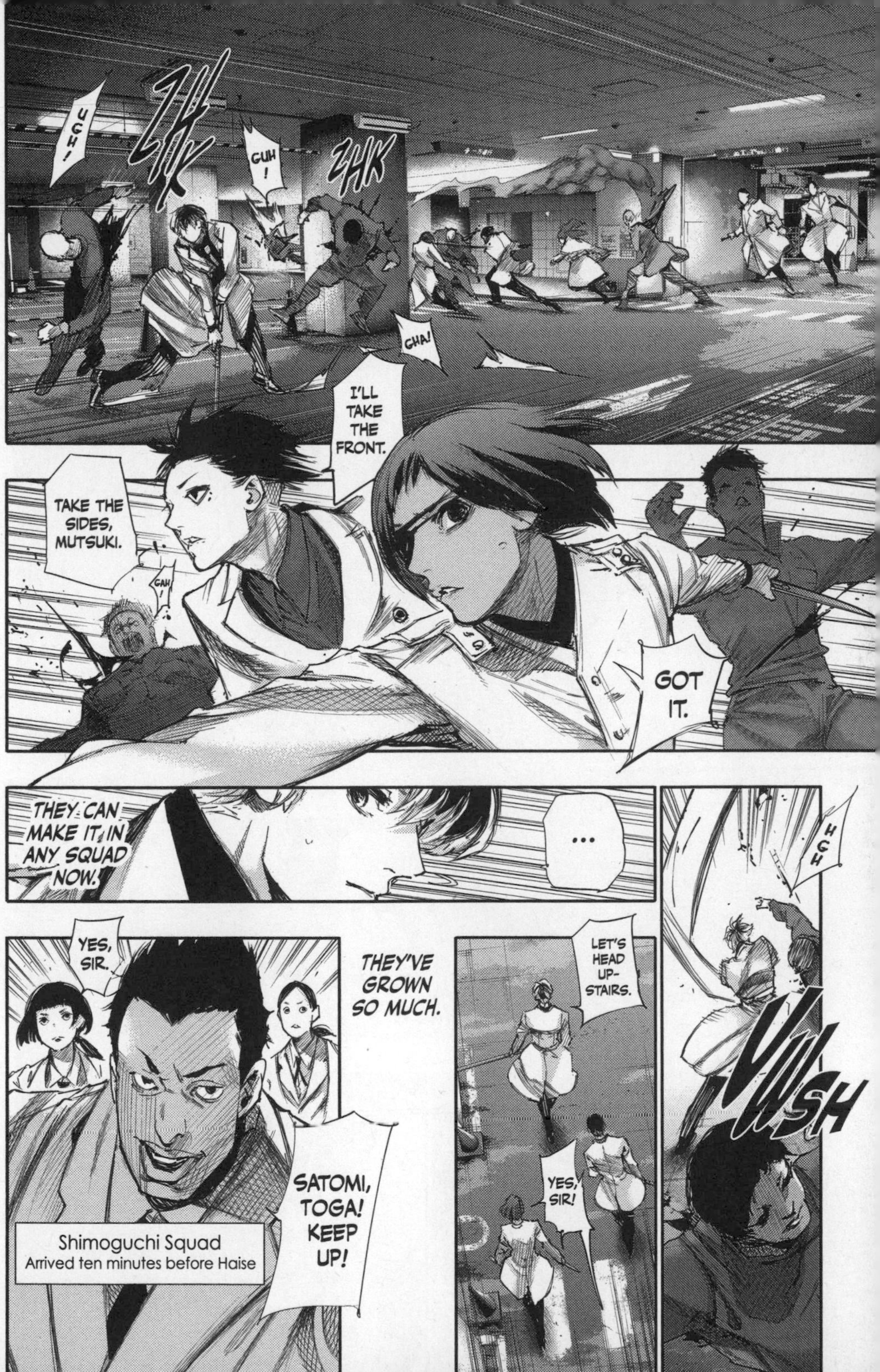
ZHK
GUH!
ZHK
UGH!
GHA!
I'LL TAKE THE FRONT.
TAKE THE SIDES, MUTSUKI.
GAH!
GOT IT.
HGH
VUSH
...
THEY CAN MAKE IT IN ANY SQUAD NOW.
LET'S HEAD UP-STAIRS.
YES, SIR!
THEY'VE GROWN SO MUCH.
YES, SIR.
SATOMI, TOGA! KEEP UP!
Shimoguchi Squad
Arrived ten minutes before Haise

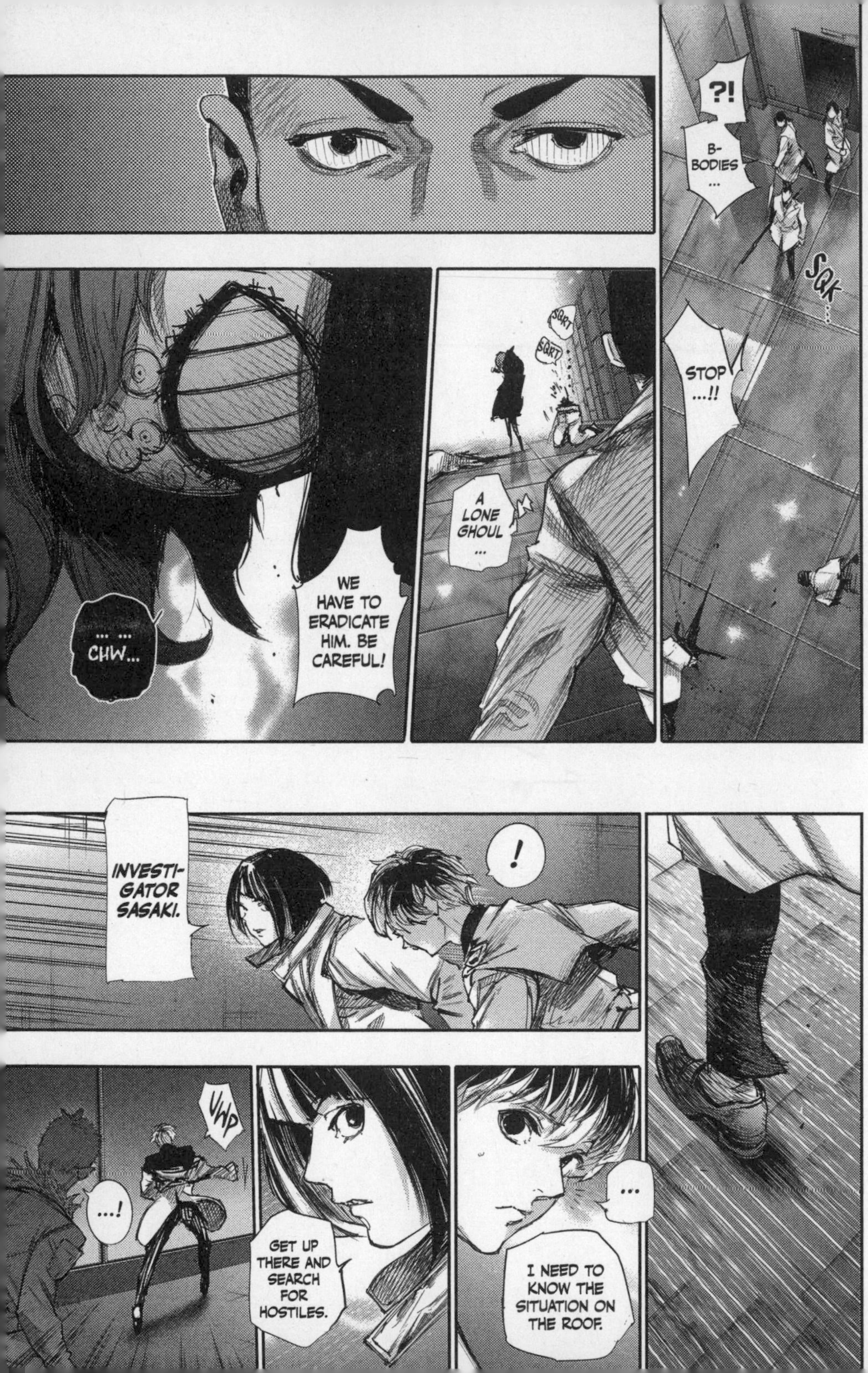
?!
B-BODIES...
SQK...
STOP...!!
SQRT
SQRT
A LONE GHOUL...
WE HAVE TO ERADICATE HIM. BE CAREFUL!
... ... CHW...
INVESTI-GATOR SASAKI.
!
...
I NEED TO KNOW THE SITUATION ON THE ROOF.
GET UP THERE AND SEARCH FOR HOSTILES.
UWP
...!

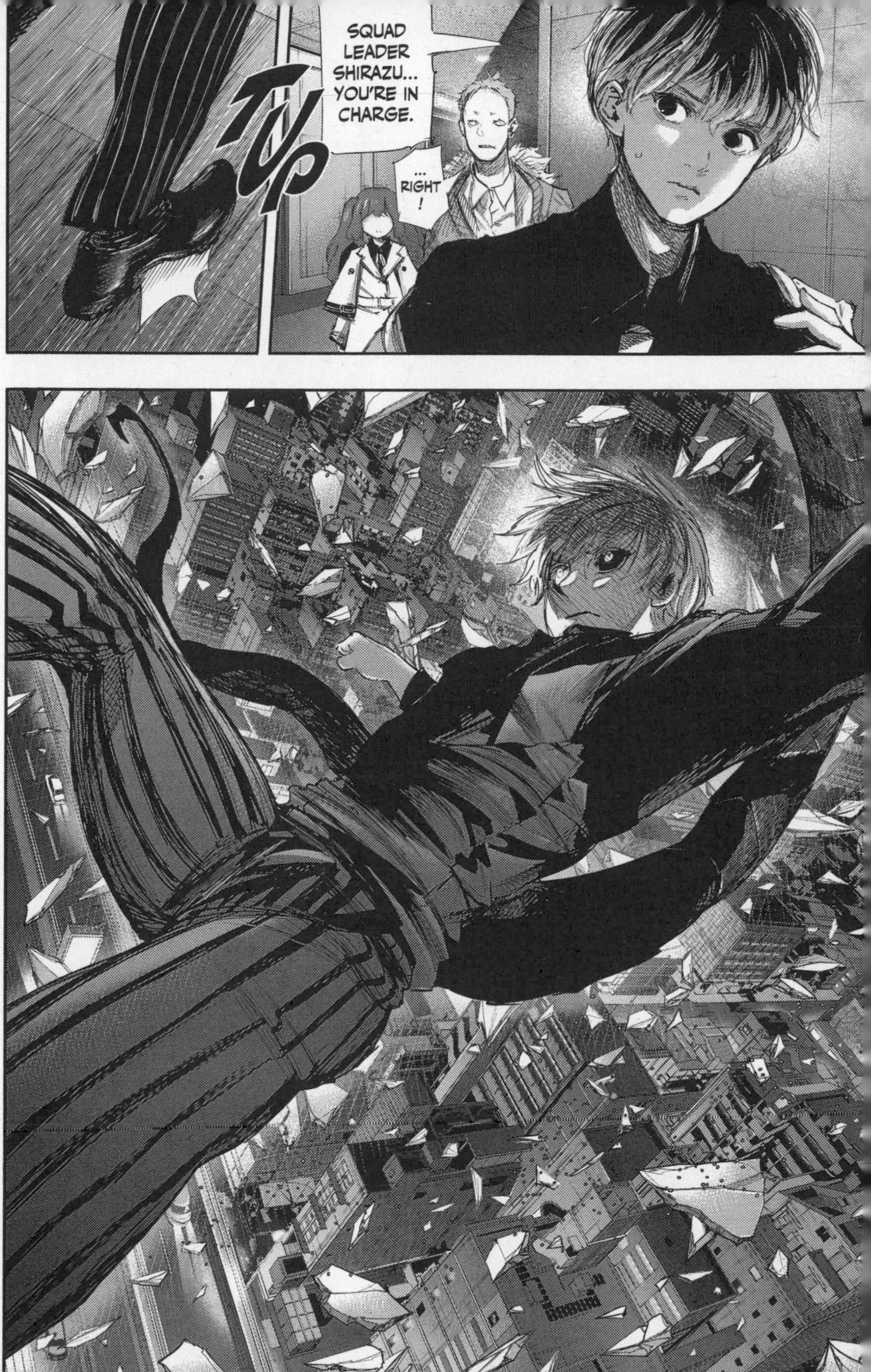
SQUAD LEADER SHIRAZU... YOU'RE IN CHARGE.
...RIGHT!
TUP

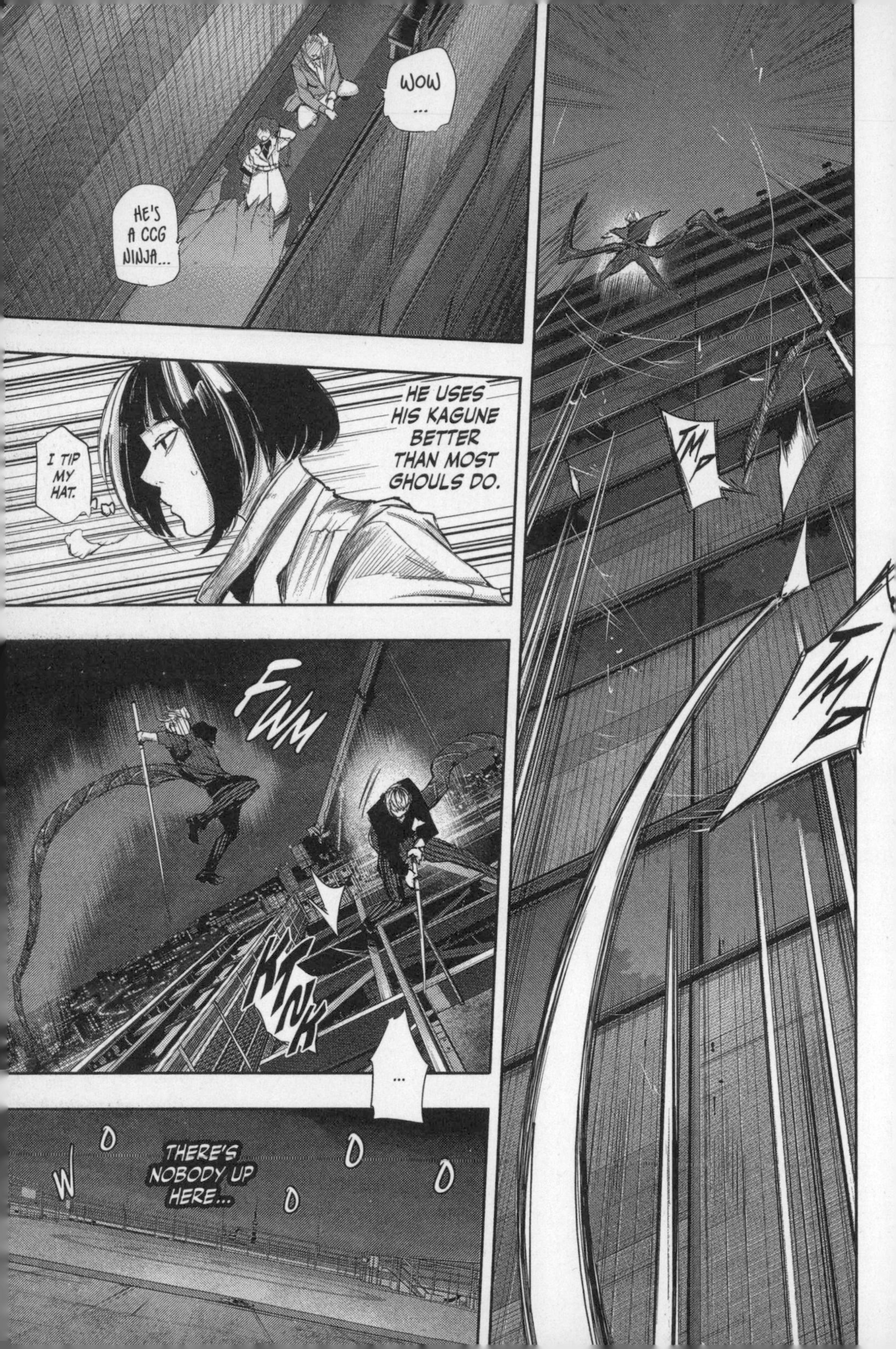
TMP
TMP
WOW...
HE'S A CCG NINJA...
HE USES HIS KAGUNE BETTER THAN MOST GHOULS DO.
I TIP MY HAT.
FWM
KTCK
...
WOOOO
THERE'S NOBODY UP HERE...

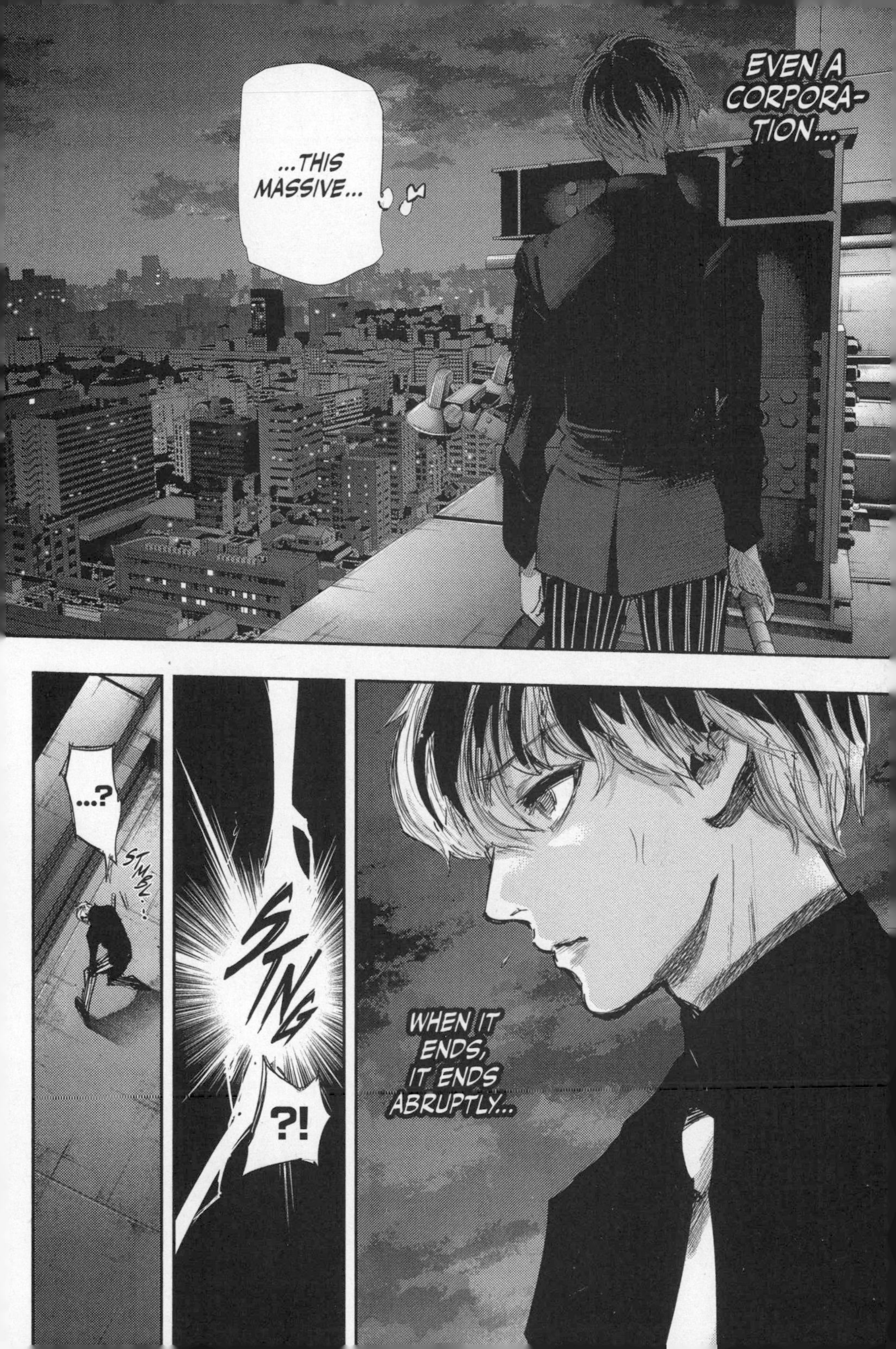
EVEN A CORPORATION...
...THIS MASSIVE...
WHEN IT ENDS, IT ENDS ABRUPTLY...
STING
?!
...?
STMBL...

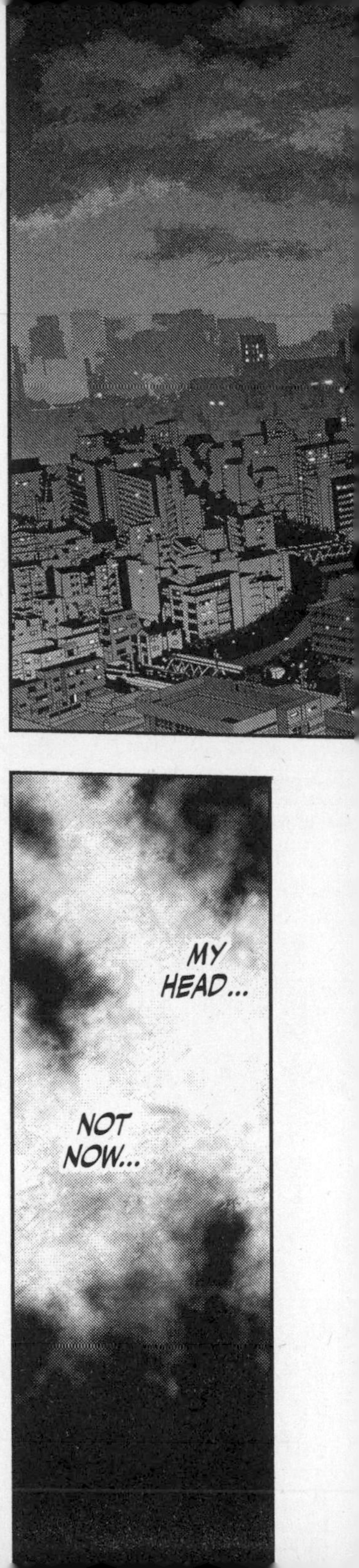
MY HEAD...
NOT NOW...

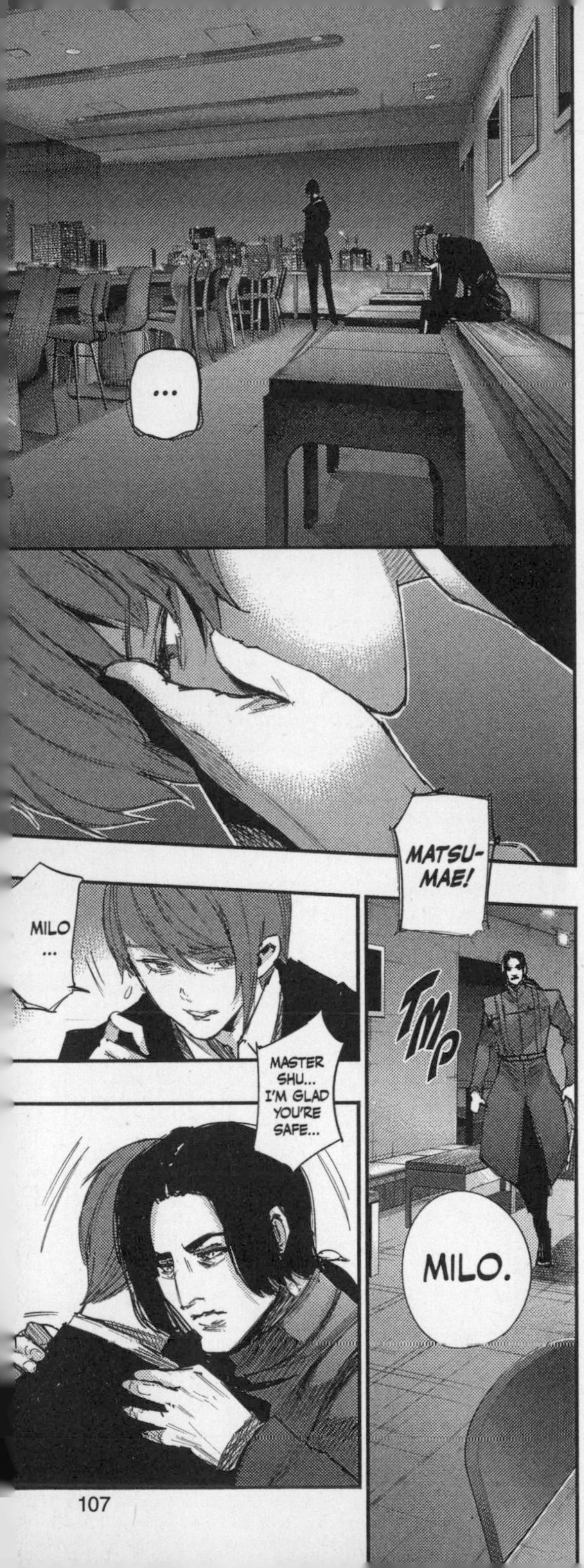
...
MATSU-MAE!
TMP
MILO.
MILO ...
MASTER SHU... I'M GLAD YOU'RE SAFE...

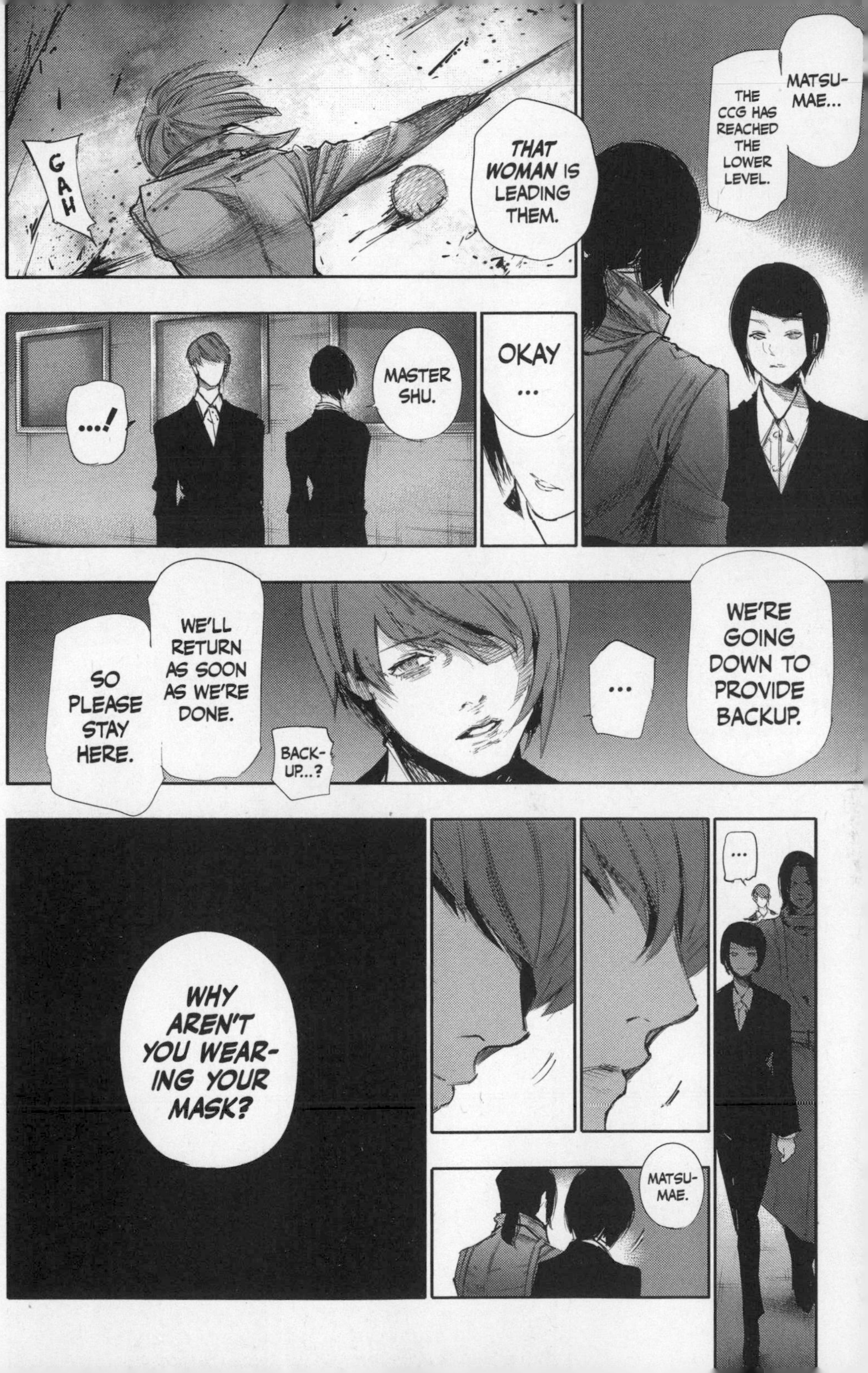
MATSU-MAE...
THE CCG HAS REACHED THE LOWER LEVEL.
GAH
THAT WOMAN IS LEADING THEM.
OKAY...
MASTER SHU.
...!
WE'RE GOING DOWN TO PROVIDE BACKUP.
...
BACK-UP...?
WE'LL RETURN AS SOON AS WE'RE DONE.
SO PLEASE STAY HERE.
...
MATSU-MAE.
WHY AREN'T YOU WEAR-ING YOUR MASK?

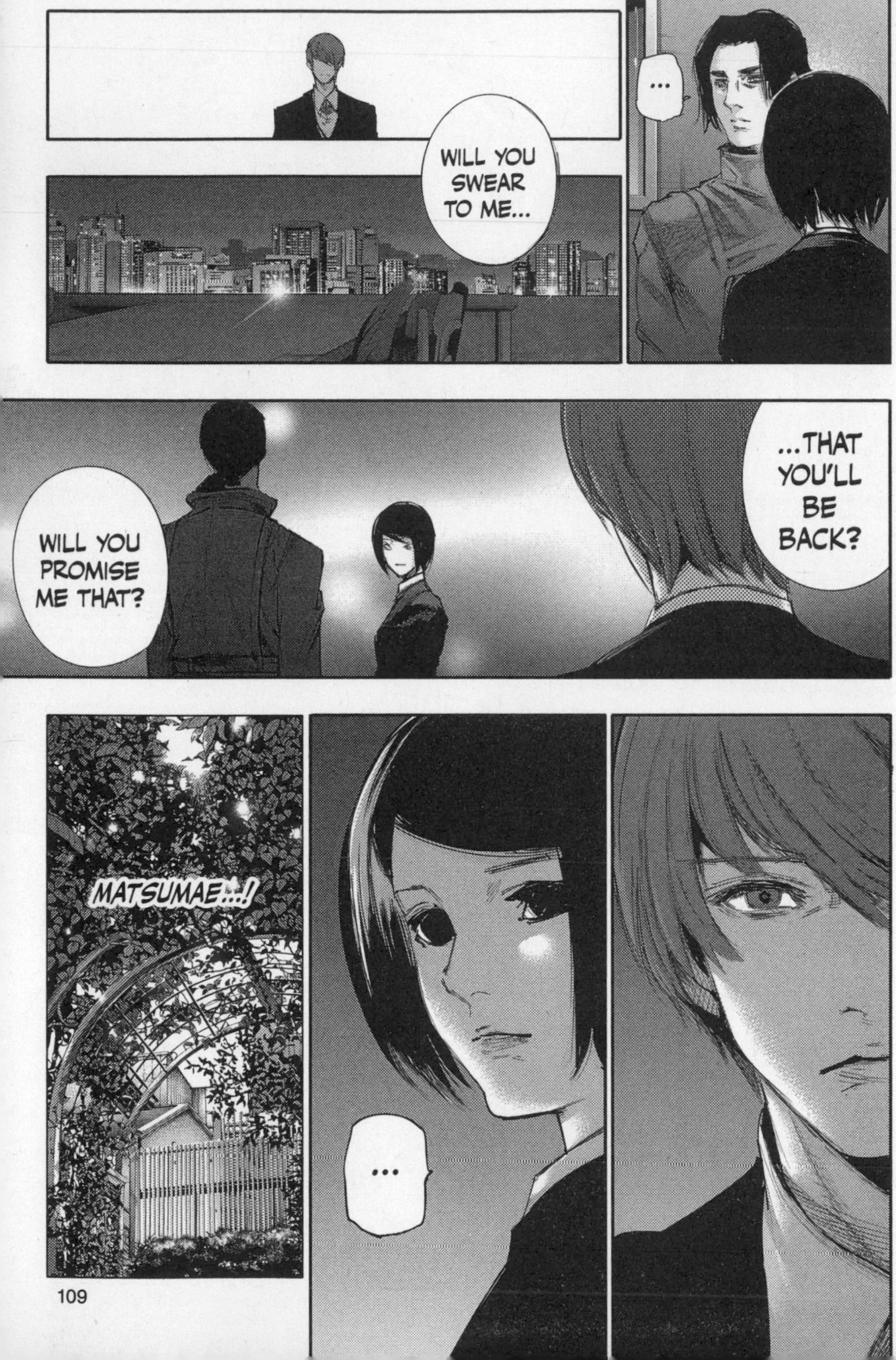
...
WILL YOU SWEAR TO ME...
...THAT YOU'LL BE BACK?
WILL YOU PROMISE ME THAT?
...
MATSUMAE...!

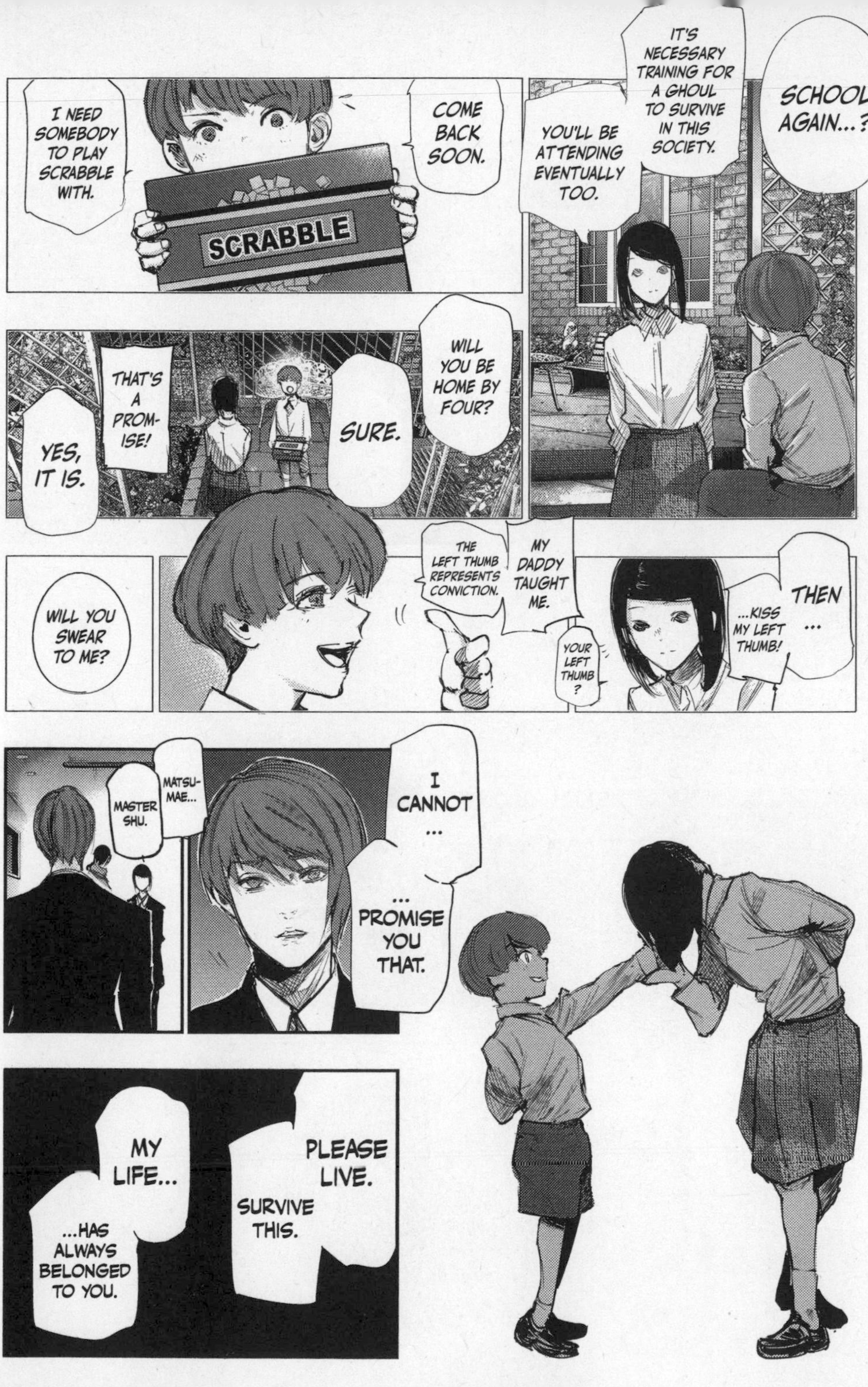
SCHOOL AGAIN...?
IT'S NECESSARY TRAINING FOR A GHOUL TO SURVIVE IN THIS SOCIETY.
YOU'LL BE ATTENDING EVENTUALLY TOO.
COME BACK SOON.
I NEED SOMEBODY TO PLAY SCRABBLE WITH.
SCRABBLE
WILL YOU BE HOME BY FOUR?
SURE.
THAT'S A PROMISE!
YES, IT IS.
THEN ...
...KISS MY LEFT THUMB!
YOUR LEFT THUMB ?
MY DADDY TAUGHT ME.
THE LEFT THUMB REPRESENTS CONVICTION.
WILL YOU SWEAR TO ME?
I CANNOT ...
... PROMISE YOU THAT.
MATSU-MAE...
MASTER SHU.
PLEASE LIVE.
SURVIVE THIS.
MY LIFE...
...HAS ALWAYS BELONGED TO YOU.

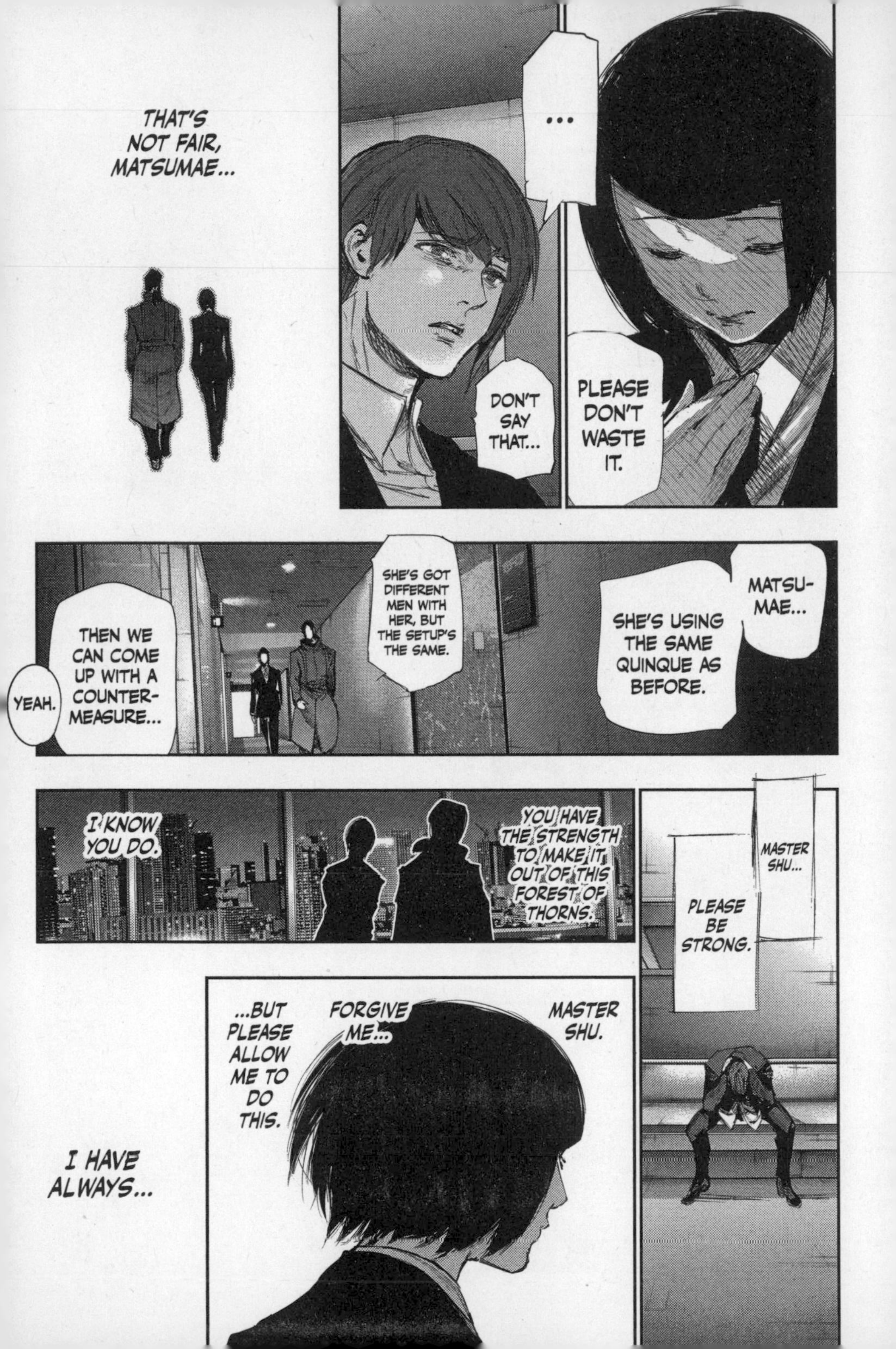
PLEASE DON'T WASTE IT.
...
DON'T SAY THAT...
THAT'S NOT FAIR, MATSUMAE...
MATSUMAE...
SHE'S USING THE SAME QUINQUE AS BEFORE.
SHE'S GOT DIFFERENT MEN WITH HER, BUT THE SETUP'S THE SAME.
THEN WE CAN COME UP WITH A COUNTER-MEASURE...
YEAH.
MASTER SHU...
PLEASE BE STRONG.
YOU HAVE THE STRENGTH TO MAKE IT OUT OF THIS FOREST OF THORNS.
I KNOW YOU DO.
MASTER SHU.
FORGIVE ME...
...BUT PLEASE ALLOW ME TO DO THIS.
I HAVE ALWAYS...

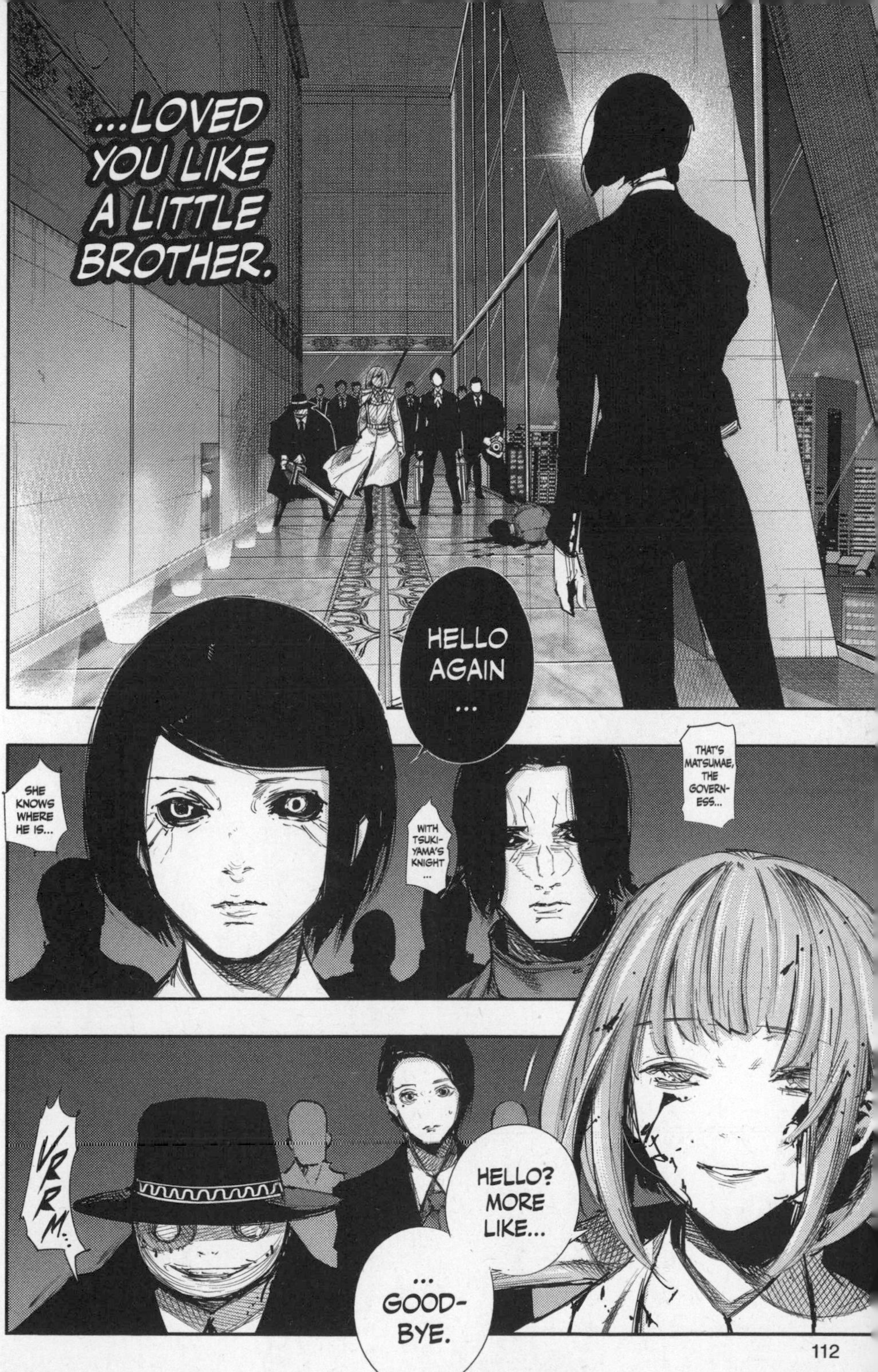
...LOVED YOU LIKE A LITTLE BROTHER.
HELLO AGAIN ...
THAT'S MATSUMAE, THE GOVERN-ESS...
WITH TSUKI-YAMA'S KNIGHT ...
SHE KNOWS WHERE HE IS...
HELLO? MORE LIKE...
... GOOD-BYE.
VRRM...

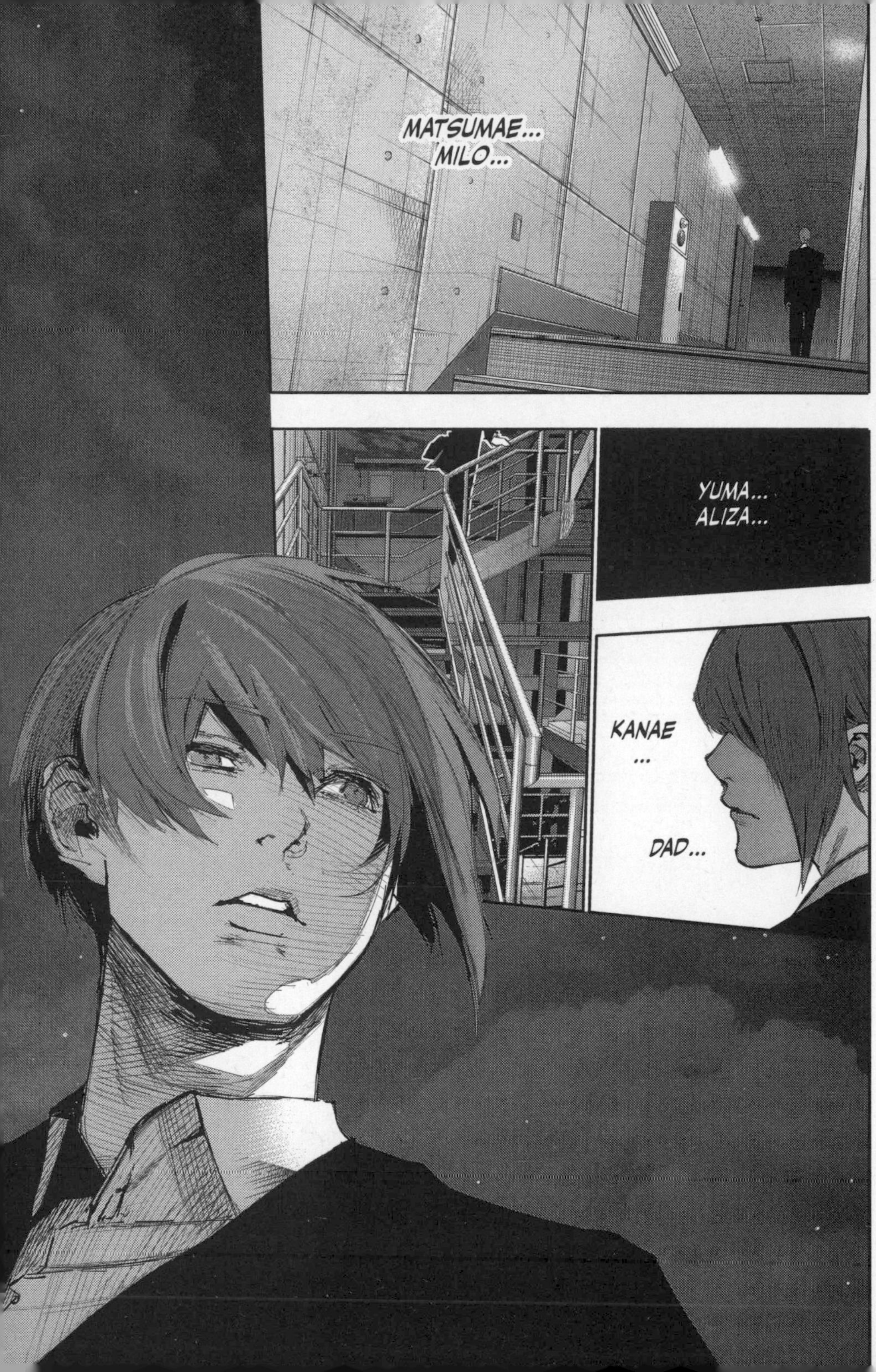
MATSUMAE...
MILO...
YUMA...
ALIZA...
KANAE
...
DAD...

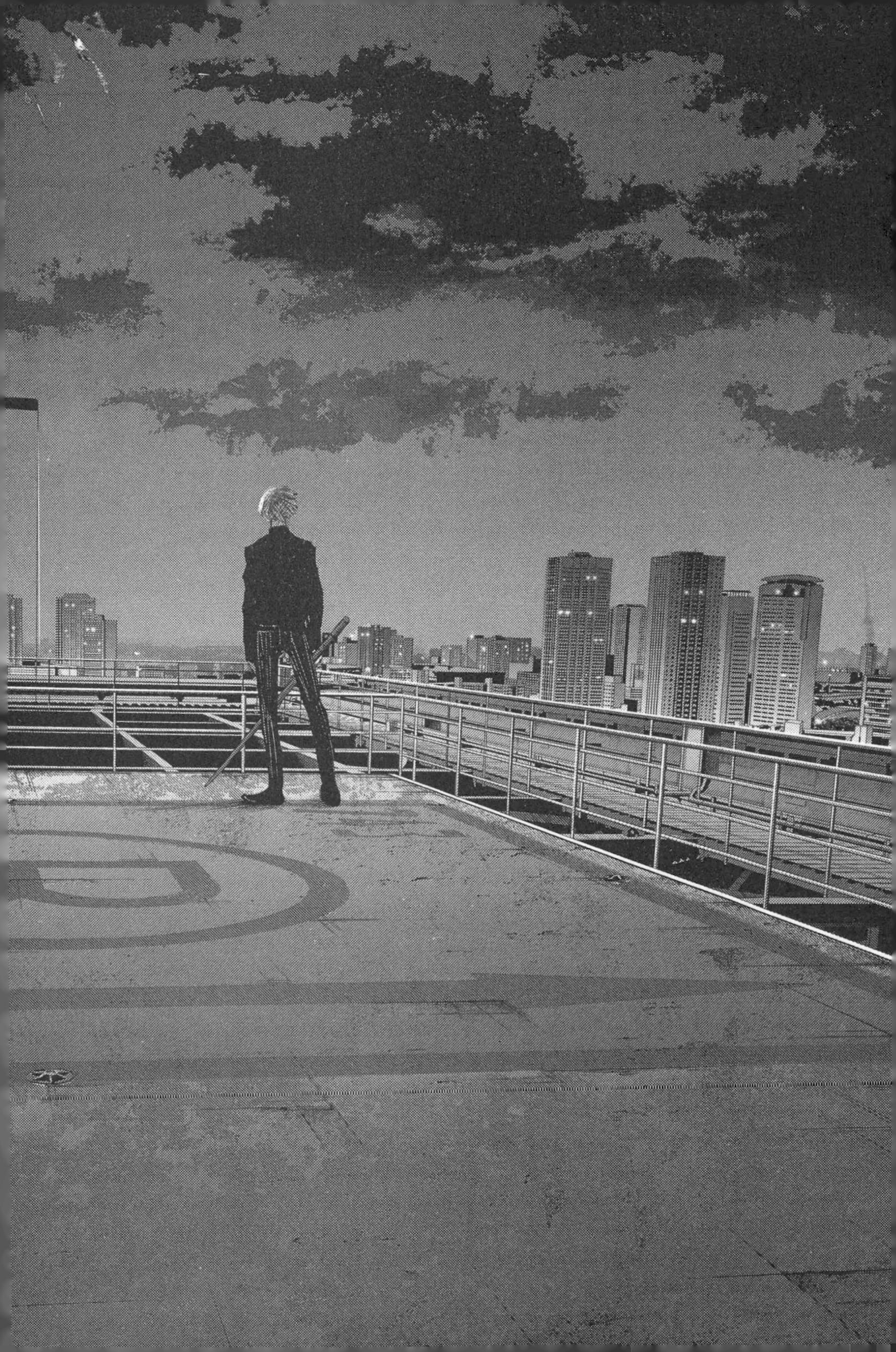

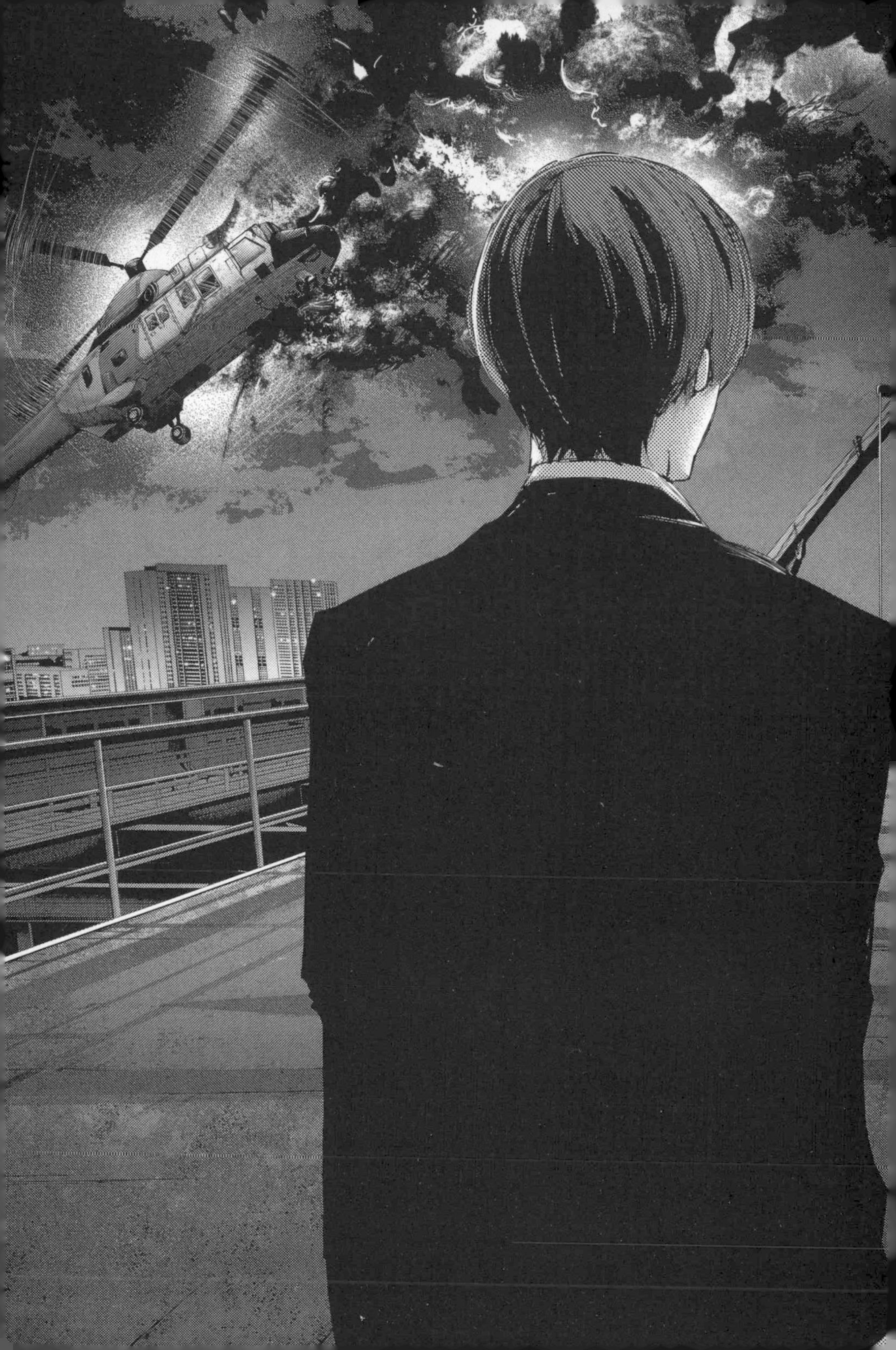

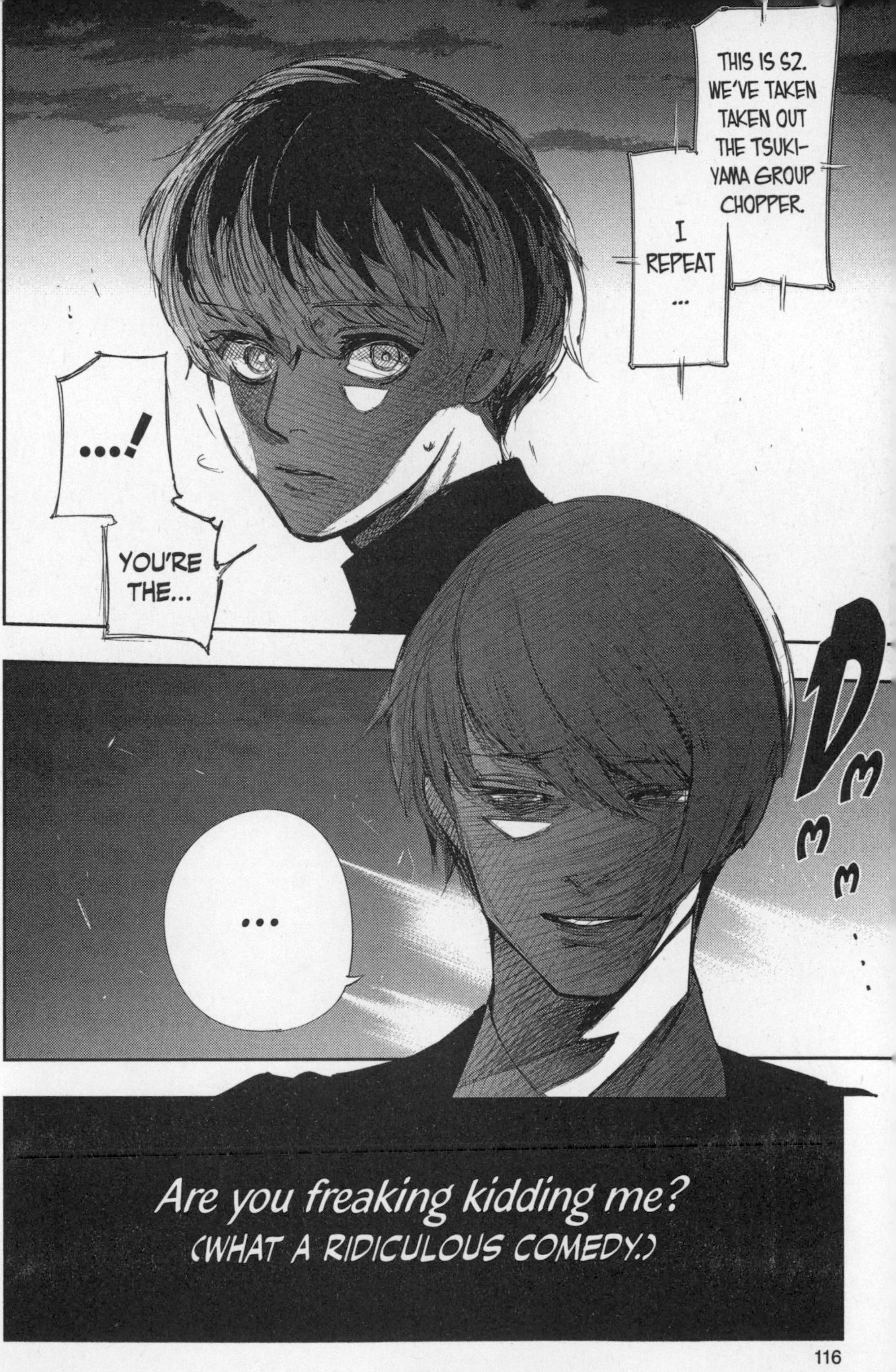
THIS IS S2. WE'VE TAKEN TAKEN OUT THE TSUKI-YAMA GROUP CHOPPER.
I REPEAT ...
...!
YOU'RE THE...
DMMMM...
...
Are you freaking kidding me?
(WHAT A RIDICULOUS COMEDY.)

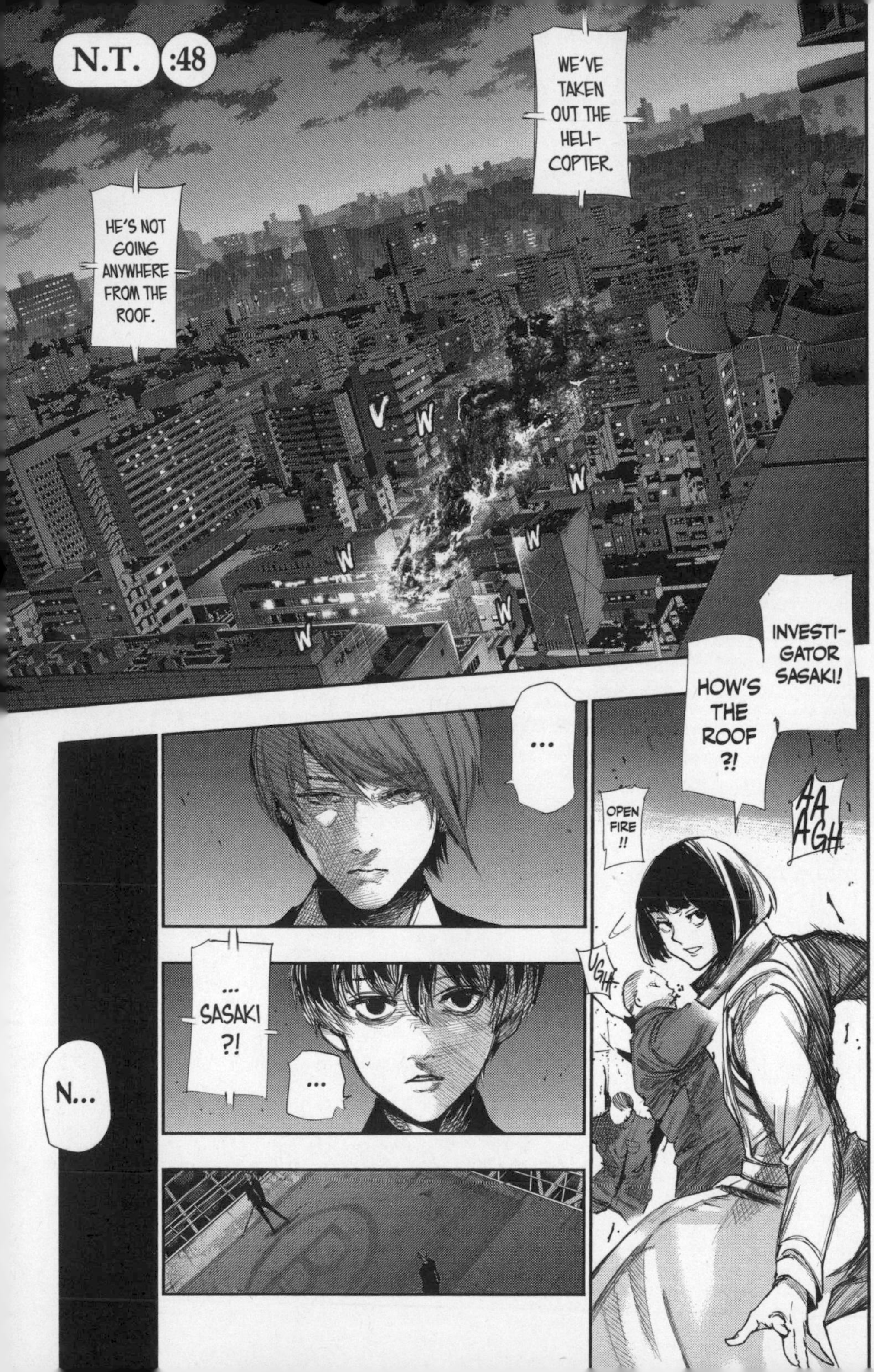
N.T. :48
WE'VE TAKEN OUT THE HELI-COPTER.
HE'S NOT GOING ANYWHERE FROM THE ROOF.
INVESTI-GATOR SASAKI!
HOW'S THE ROOF ?!
AAAGH
OPEN FIRE !!
UGH
...
... SASAKI ?!
...
N...

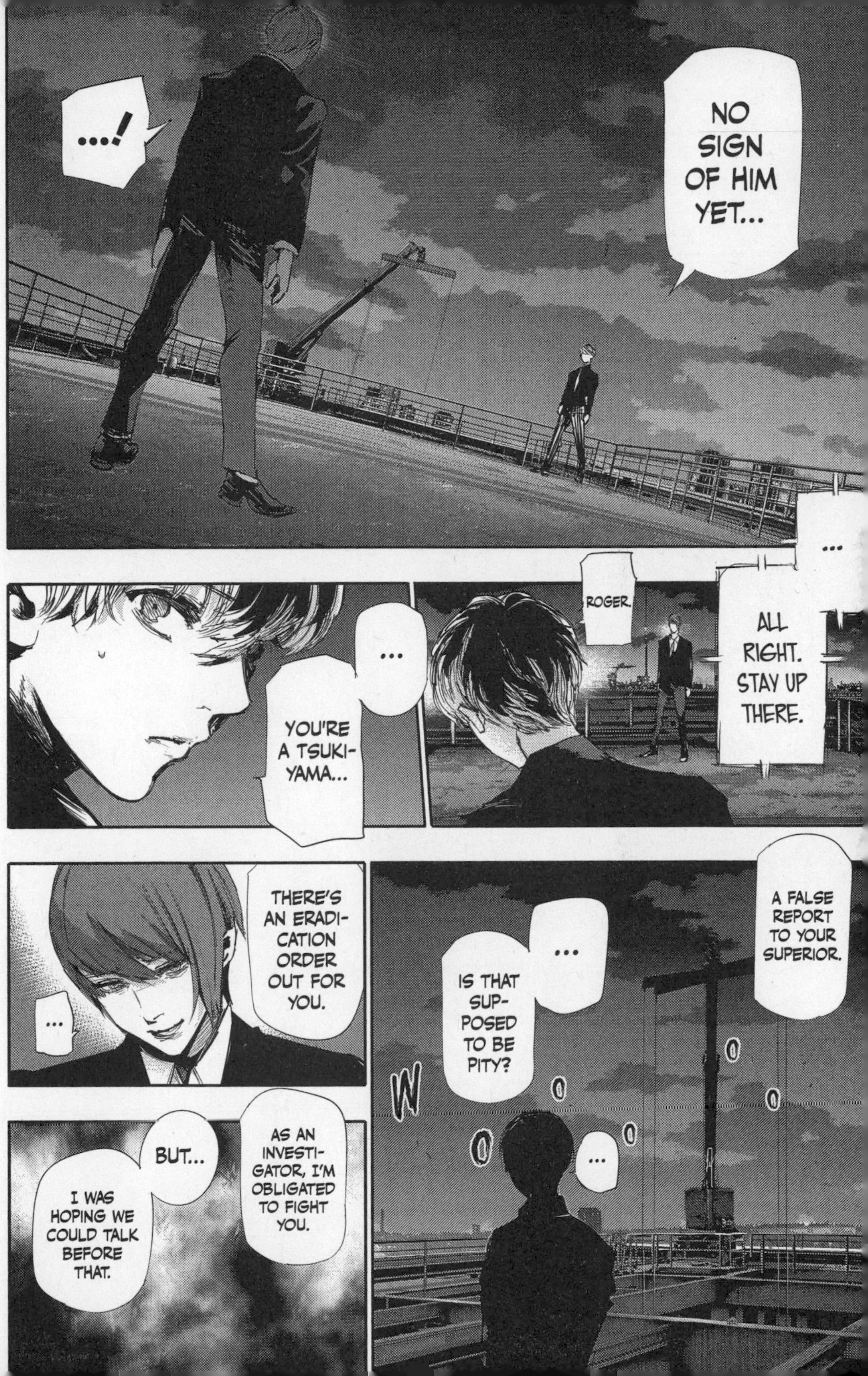
NO SIGN OF HIM YET...
...!
...
ALL RIGHT. STAY UP THERE.
ROGER.
...
YOU'RE A TSUKI-YAMA...
A FALSE REPORT TO YOUR SUPERIOR.
...
IS THAT SUP-POSED TO BE PITY?
WOOOOO
...
THERE'S AN ERADI-CATION ORDER OUT FOR YOU.
...
AS AN INVESTI-GATOR, I'M OBLIGATED TO FIGHT YOU.
BUT...
I WAS HOPING WE COULD TALK BEFORE THAT.

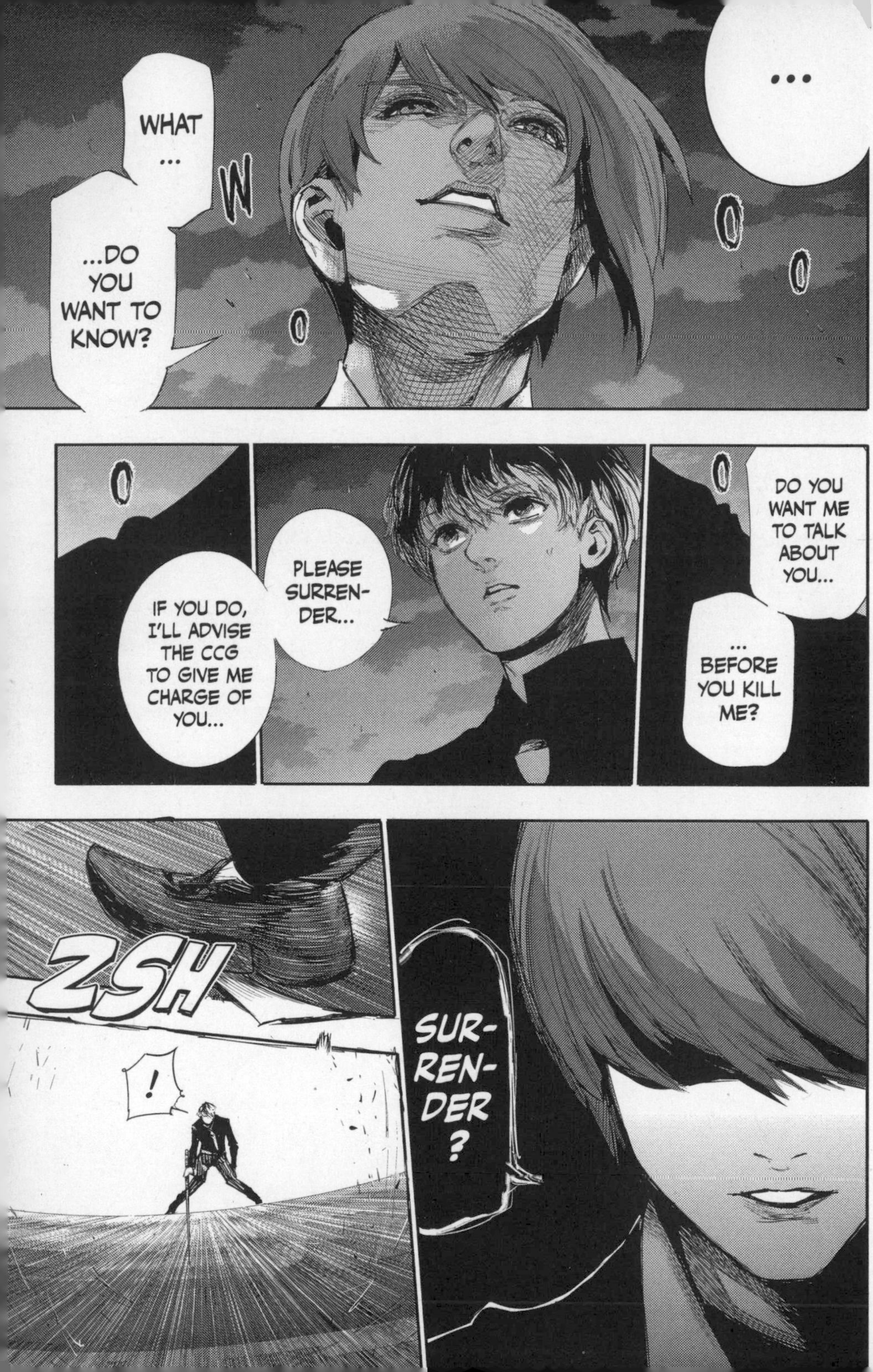
...
WHAT ...
...DO YOU WANT TO KNOW?
WOOO
O
DO YOU WANT ME TO TALK ABOUT YOU...
... BEFORE YOU KILL ME?
PLEASE SURREN-DER...
IF YOU DO, I'LL ADVISE THE CCG TO GIVE ME CHARGE OF YOU...
O
SUR-REN-DER?
ZSH
!

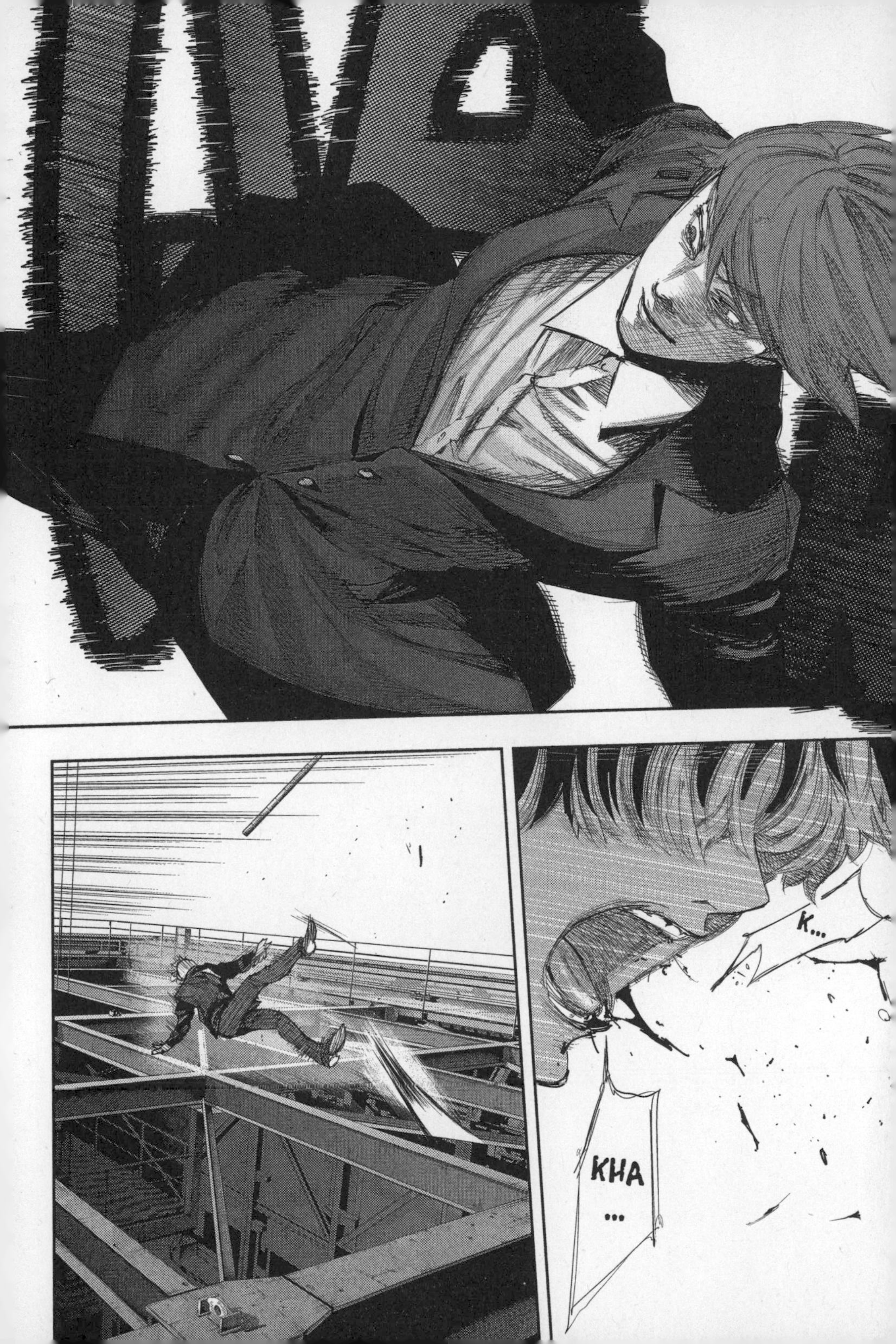
K...
KHA
...

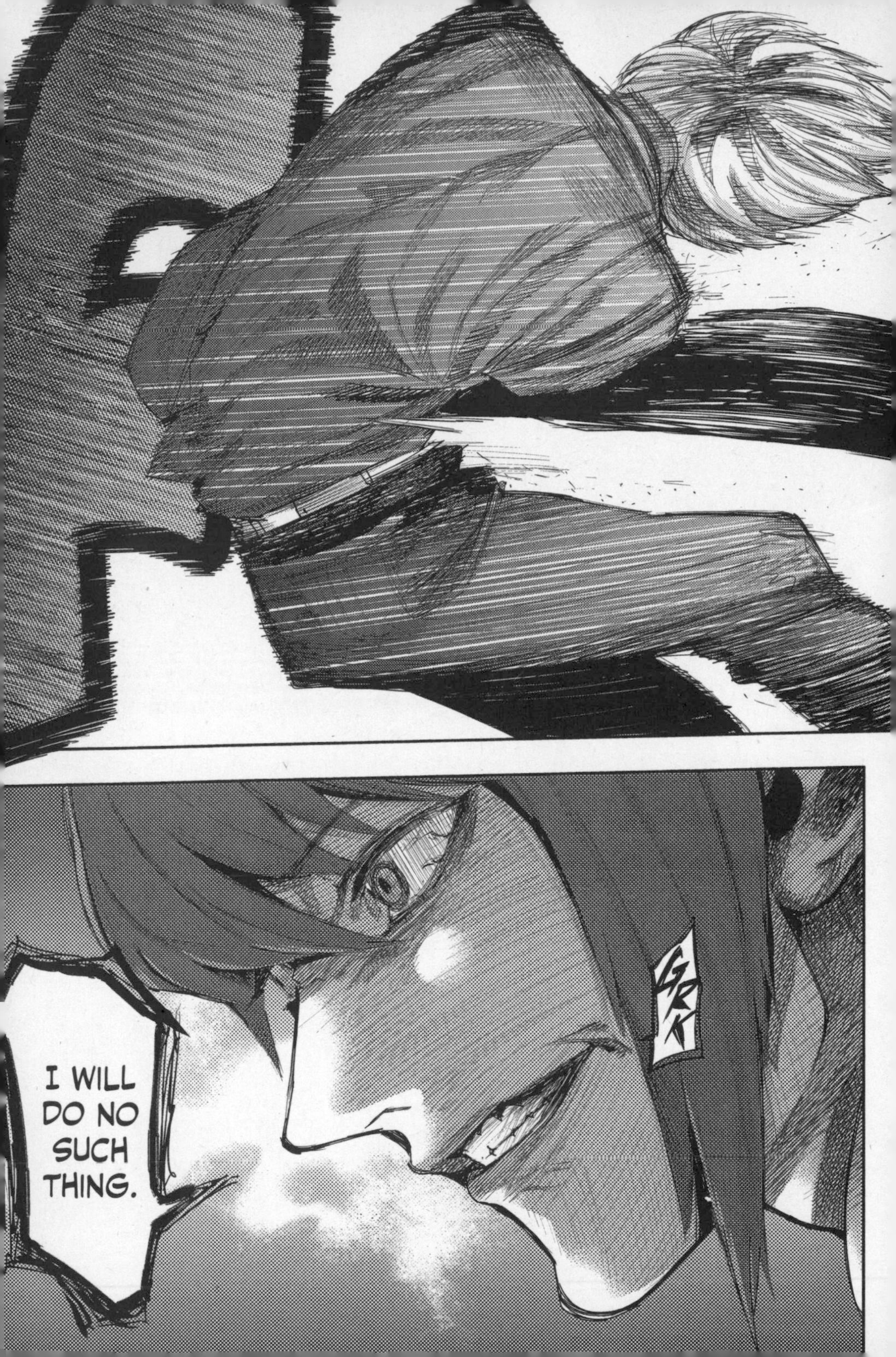
GRK
I WILL DO NO SUCH THING.

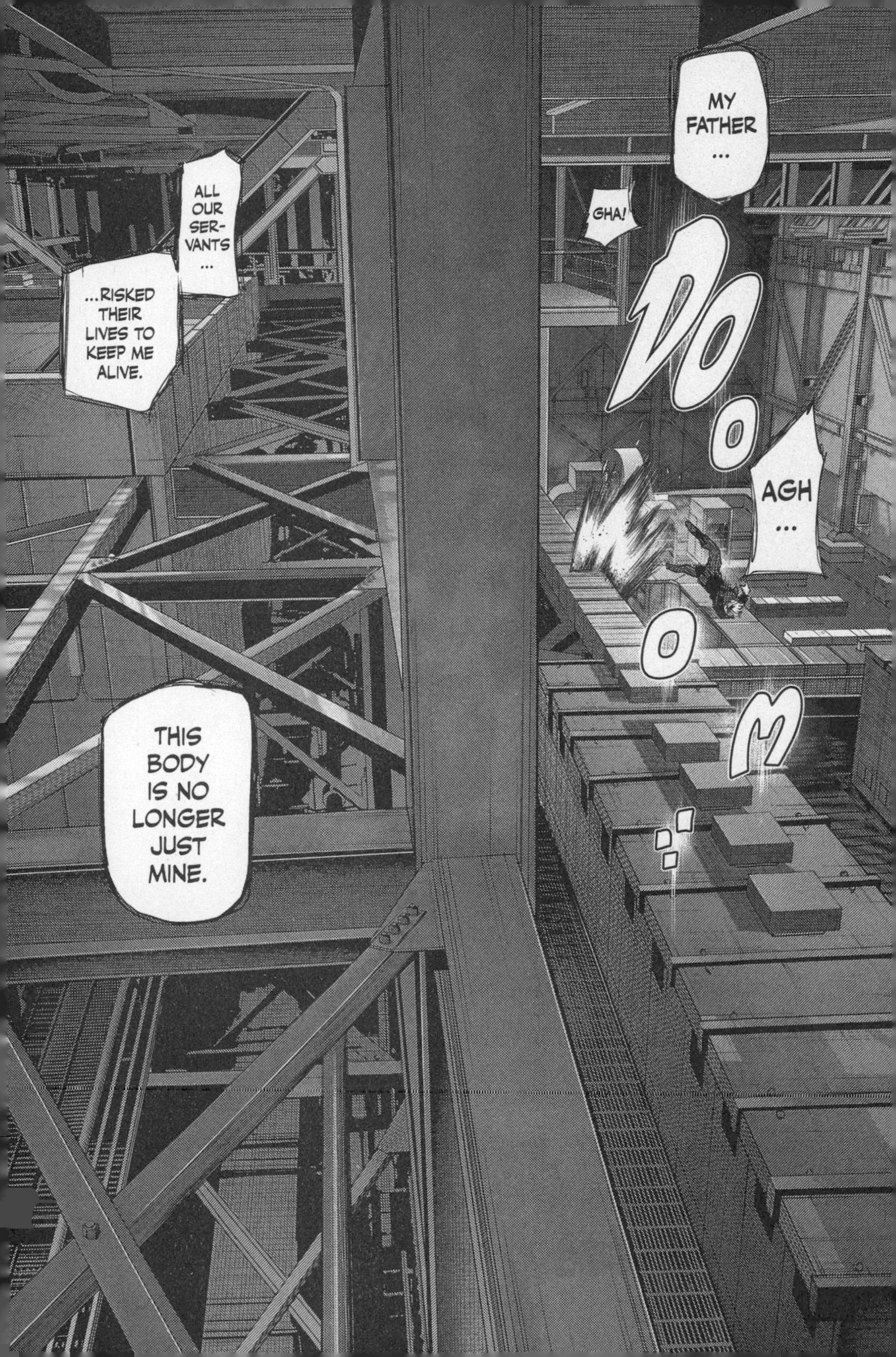
MY FATHER ...
GHA!
DOOOM
AGH ...
ALL OUR SER- VANTS ...
...RISKED THEIR LIVES TO KEEP ME ALIVE.
THIS BODY IS NO LONGER JUST MINE.

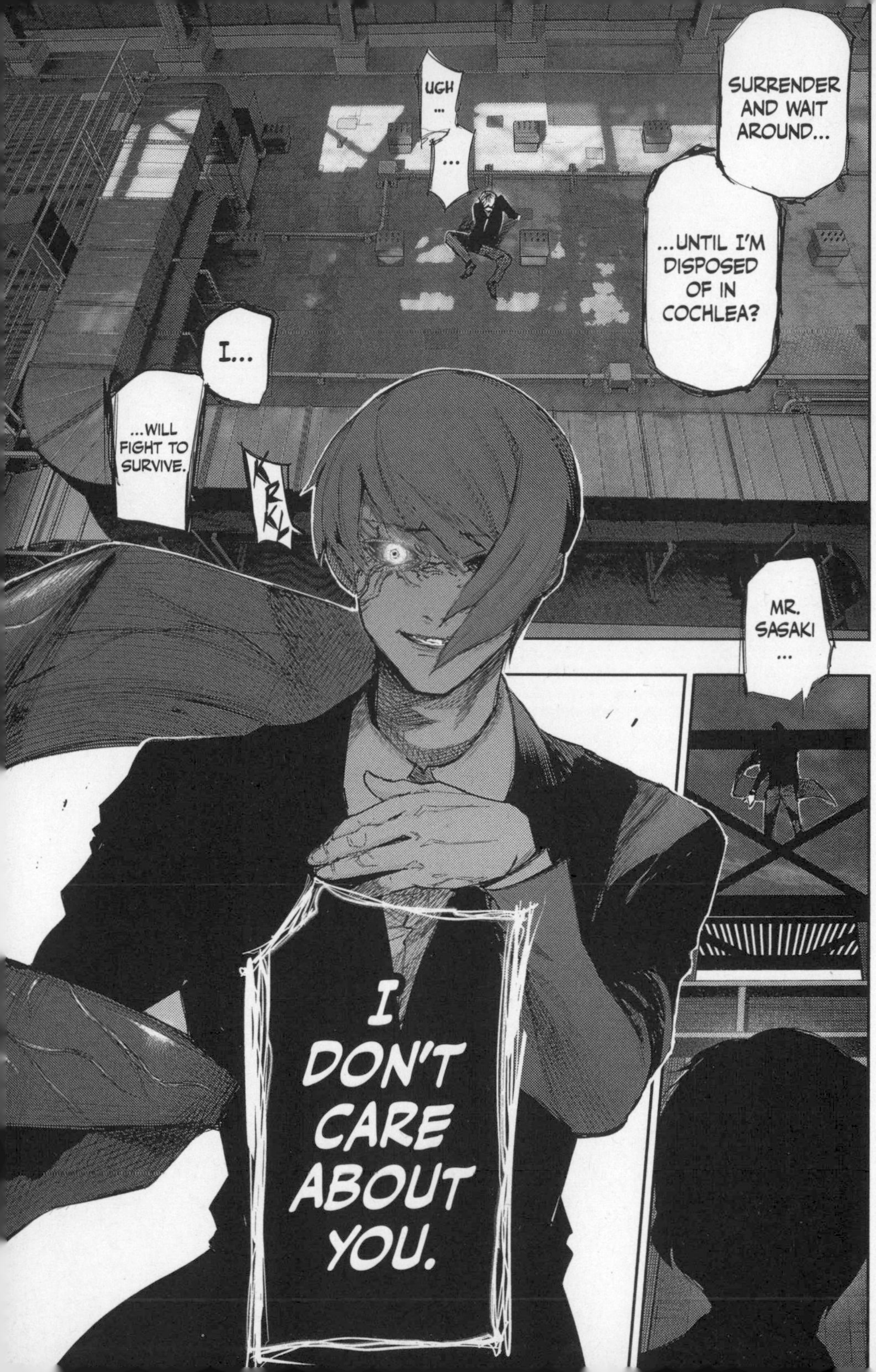
SURRENDER AND WAIT AROUND...
...UNTIL I'M DISPOSED OF IN COCHLEA?
UGH ...
...
I...
...WILL FIGHT TO SURVIVE.
MR. SASAKI ...
I DON'T CARE ABOUT YOU.

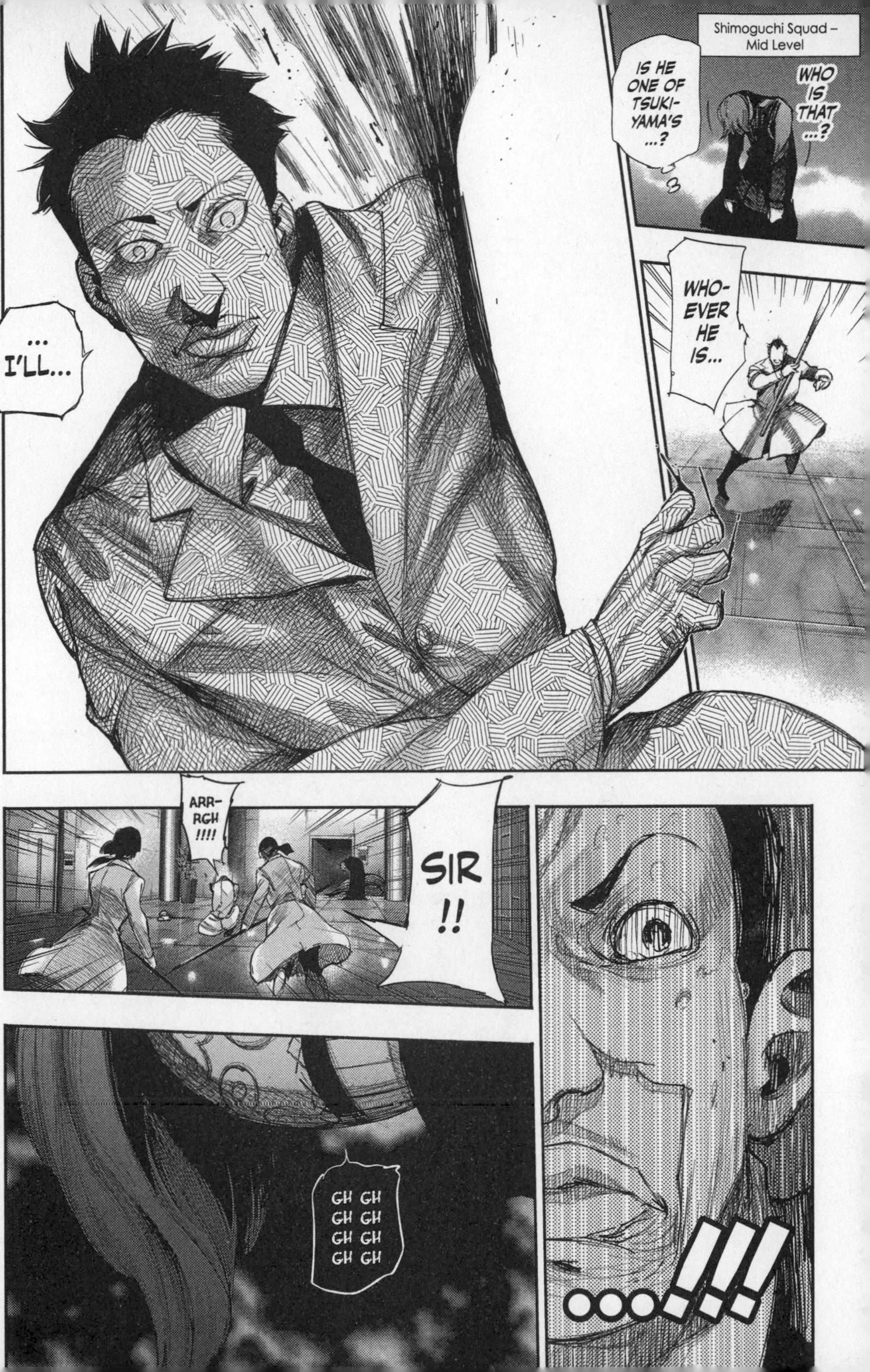

Shimoguchi Squad – Mid Level
WHO IS THAT ...?
IS HE ONE OF TSUKIYAMA'S ...?
WHO-EVER HE IS...
... I'LL...
...!!!
SIR !!
ARR-RGH !!!!
GH GH GH GH GH GH GH GH

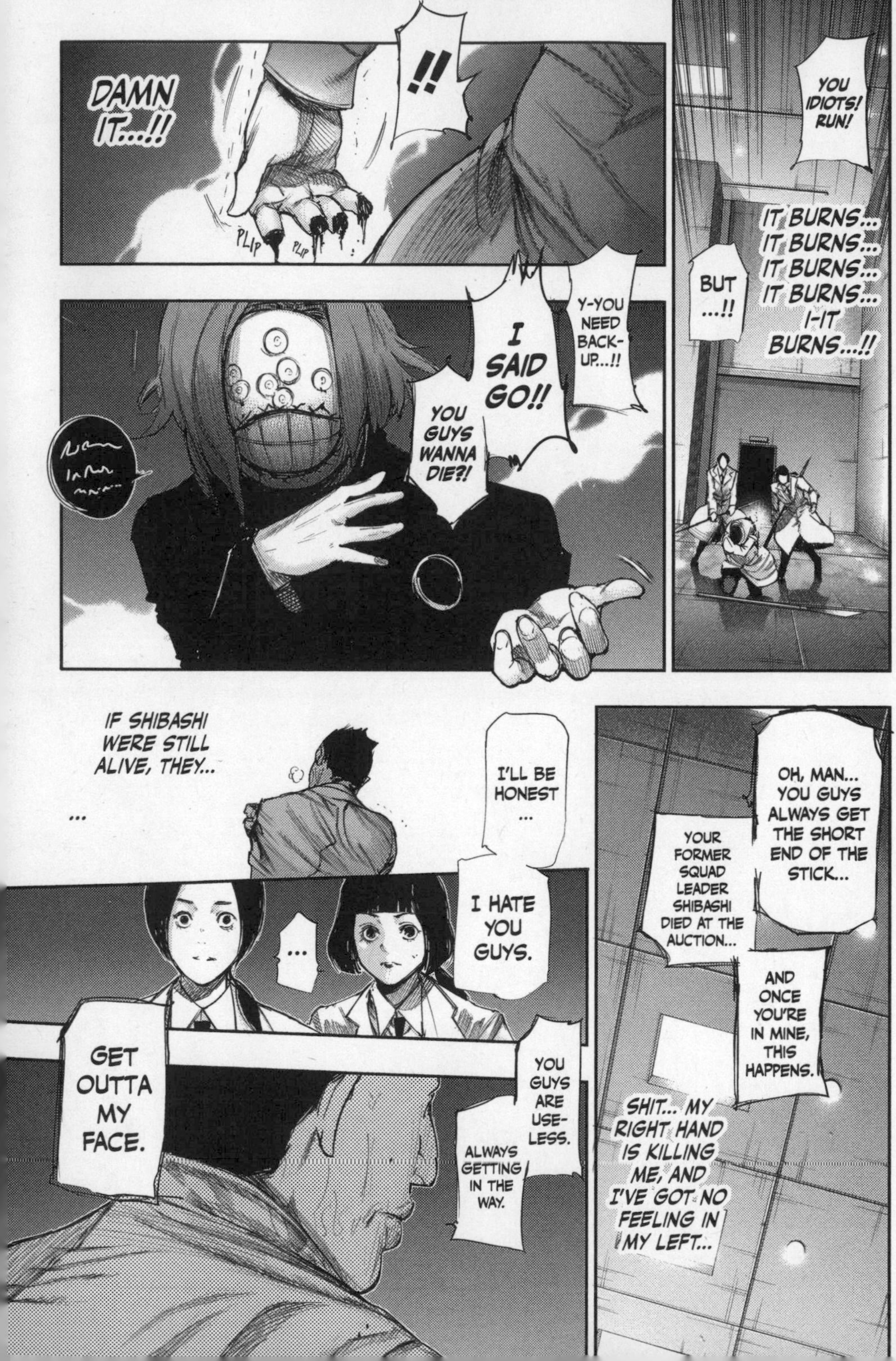
YOU IDIOTS! RUN!
BUT ...!!
IT BURNS... IT BURNS... IT BURNS... IT BURNS... I-IT BURNS...!!
!!
DAMN IT...!!
PLIP
PLIP
Y-YOU NEED BACK-UP...!!
I SAID GO!!
YOU GUYS WANNA DIE?!
OH, MAN... YOU GUYS ALWAYS GET THE SHORT END OF THE STICK...
YOUR FORMER SQUAD LEADER SHIBASHI DIED AT THE AUCTION...
AND ONCE YOU'RE IN MINE, THIS HAPPENS.
SHIT... MY RIGHT HAND IS KILLING ME, AND I'VE GOT NO FEELING IN MY LEFT...
IF SHIBASHI WERE STILL ALIVE, THEY...
...
I'LL BE HONEST ...
...
I HATE YOU GUYS.
YOU GUYS ARE USE-LESS.
ALWAYS GETTING IN THE WAY.
GET OUTTA MY FACE.

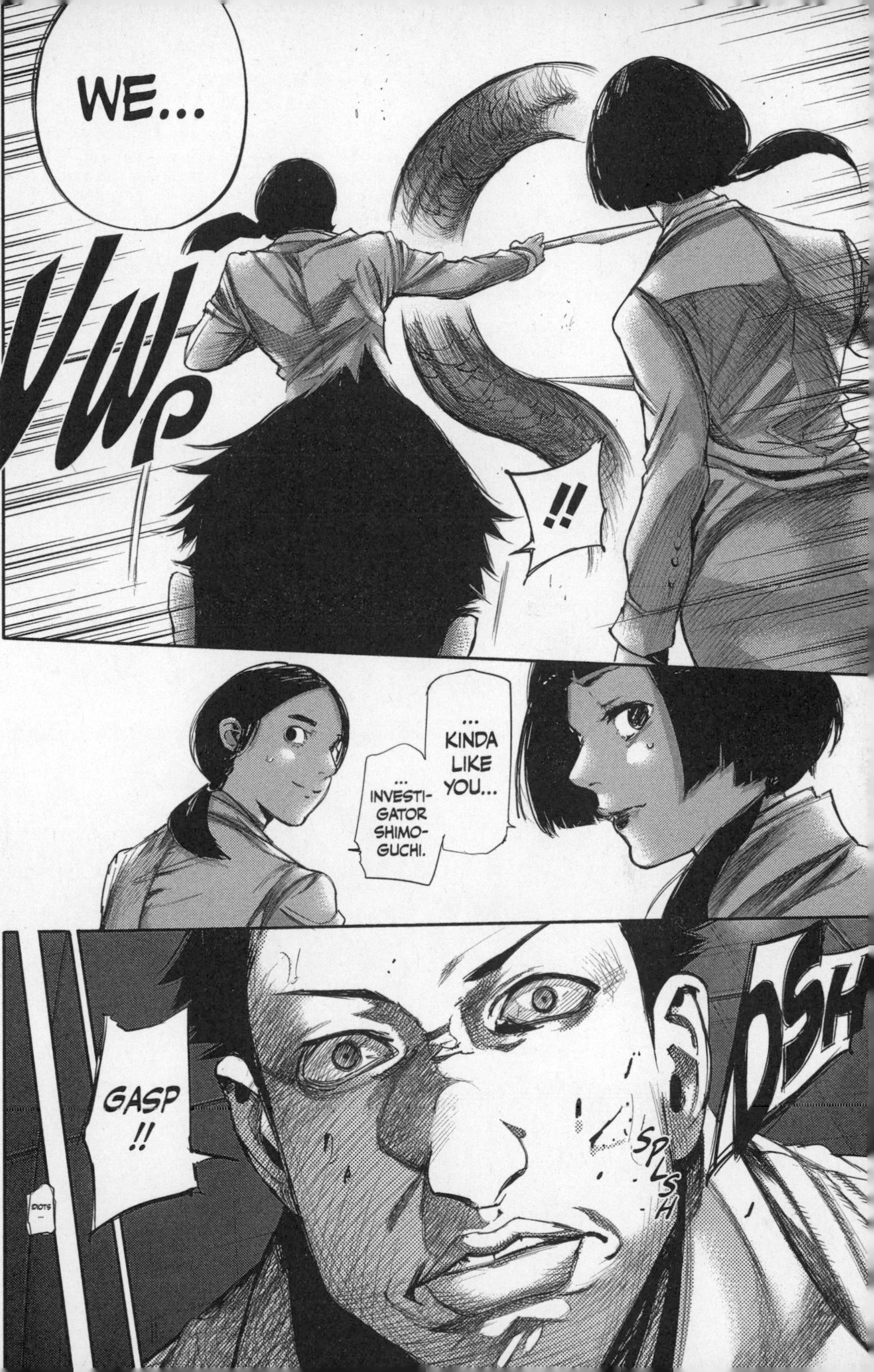
WE...
!!
VWP
...KINDA LIKE YOU...
...INVESTIGATOR SHIMOGUCHI.
DSH
SPLSH
GASP!!
IDIOTS...

WHEN DID I START LAUGHING WITH THE CORNERS OF MY LIPS LIFTED?

I KNEW THAT WHEN I LAUGHED LIKE THAT, MY UGLY FACE GOT EVEN UGLIER.

"HAVEN'T YOU MET ANYBODY NICE?"

MY MOM SAID THAT WITH HER BACK ROLLED UP LIKE A ROLY-POLY.

I CAN'T. BECAUSE I'M MEAN AND UGLY.

BECAUSE I'M A LONELY GUY WHO BARELY HAS ANY FRIENDS THAT I CAN REMEMBER.

(WHAT'LL HAPPEN TO MY MOM IF I'M GONE?)

I'M CHASING A BALL. I'M LAUGHING.

"NOBU! OVER HERE, OVER HERE!"

I HEARD A VOICE...

A GUY I WAS KIND OF FRIENDS WITH IN ELEMENTARY SCHOOL. I THINK IT WAS YAMAKAWA. YEAH, THAT'S WHO IT WAS. I'D FORGOTTEN ABOUT HIM.

WHY DID WE STOP PLAYING TOGETHER...?

I'M RUNNING IN THE SCHOOL YARD CHASING A BALL. YAMAKAWA'S CALLING ME. PASS.

I'M LAUGHING.

I'VE ALWAYS BEEN A QUIET, MEAN, UGLY GUY.

WHY DID WE STOP PLAYING TOGETHER...?

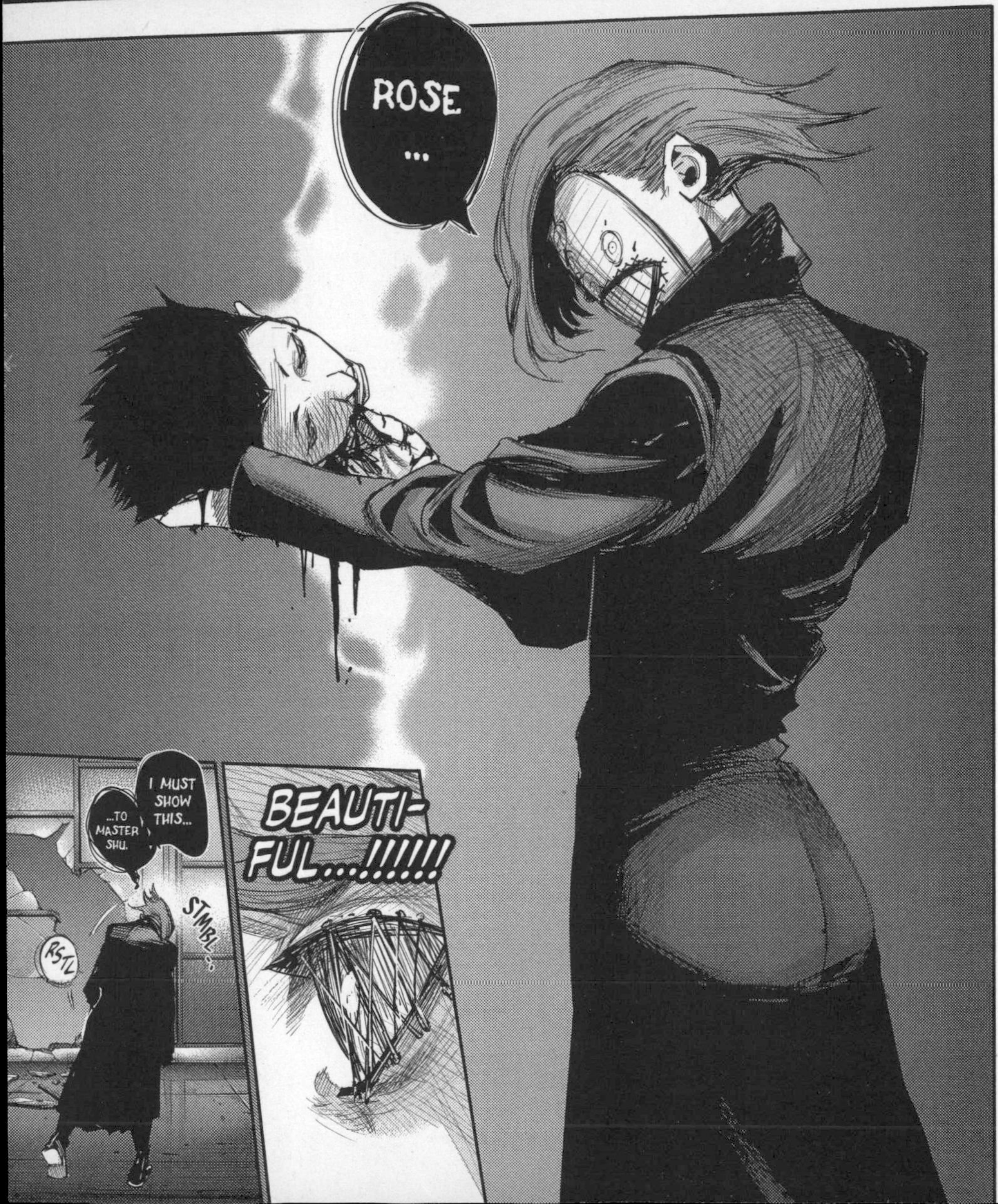
ROSE ...
BEAUTI-FUL...!!!!!!
I MUST SHOW THIS...
...TO MASTER SHU.
STMBL...
RSTL

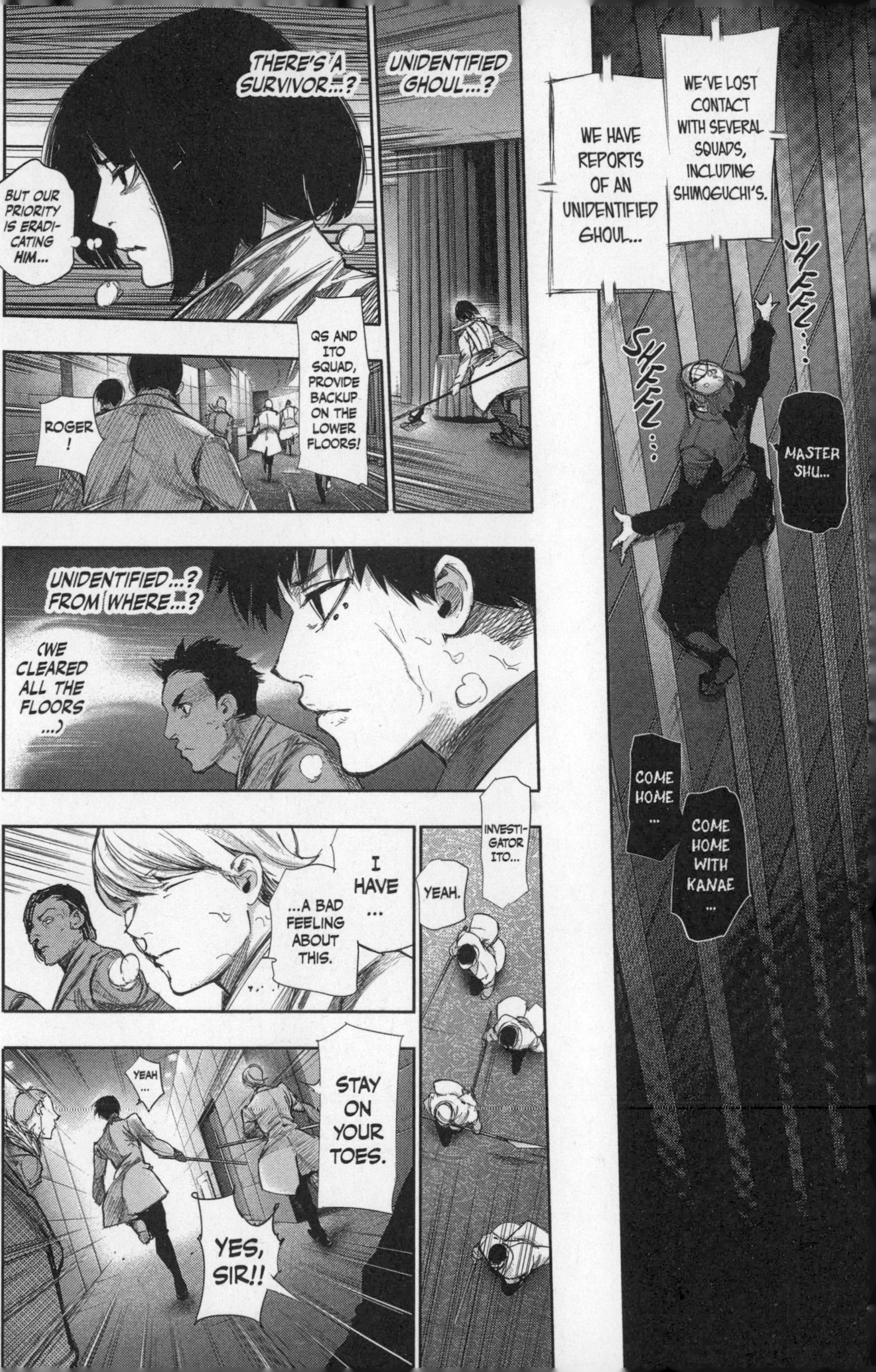
WE'VE LOST CONTACT WITH SEVERAL SQUADS, INCLUDING SHIMOGUCHI'S.
WE HAVE REPORTS OF AN UNIDENTIFIED GHOUL...
SHFFL...
SHFFL...
MASTER SHU...
COME HOME ...
COME HOME WITH KANAE ...
UNIDENTIFIED GHOUL...?
QS AND ITO SQUAD, PROVIDE BACKUP ON THE LOWER FLOORS!
THERE'S A SURVIVOR...?
BUT OUR PRIORITY IS ERADICATING HIM...
ROGER!
UNIDENTIFIED...? FROM WHERE...?
(WE CLEARED ALL THE FLOORS ...)
INVESTIGATOR ITO...
YEAH.
I HAVE ...
...A BAD FEELING ABOUT THIS.
STAY ON YOUR TOES.
YEAH ...
YES, SIR!!

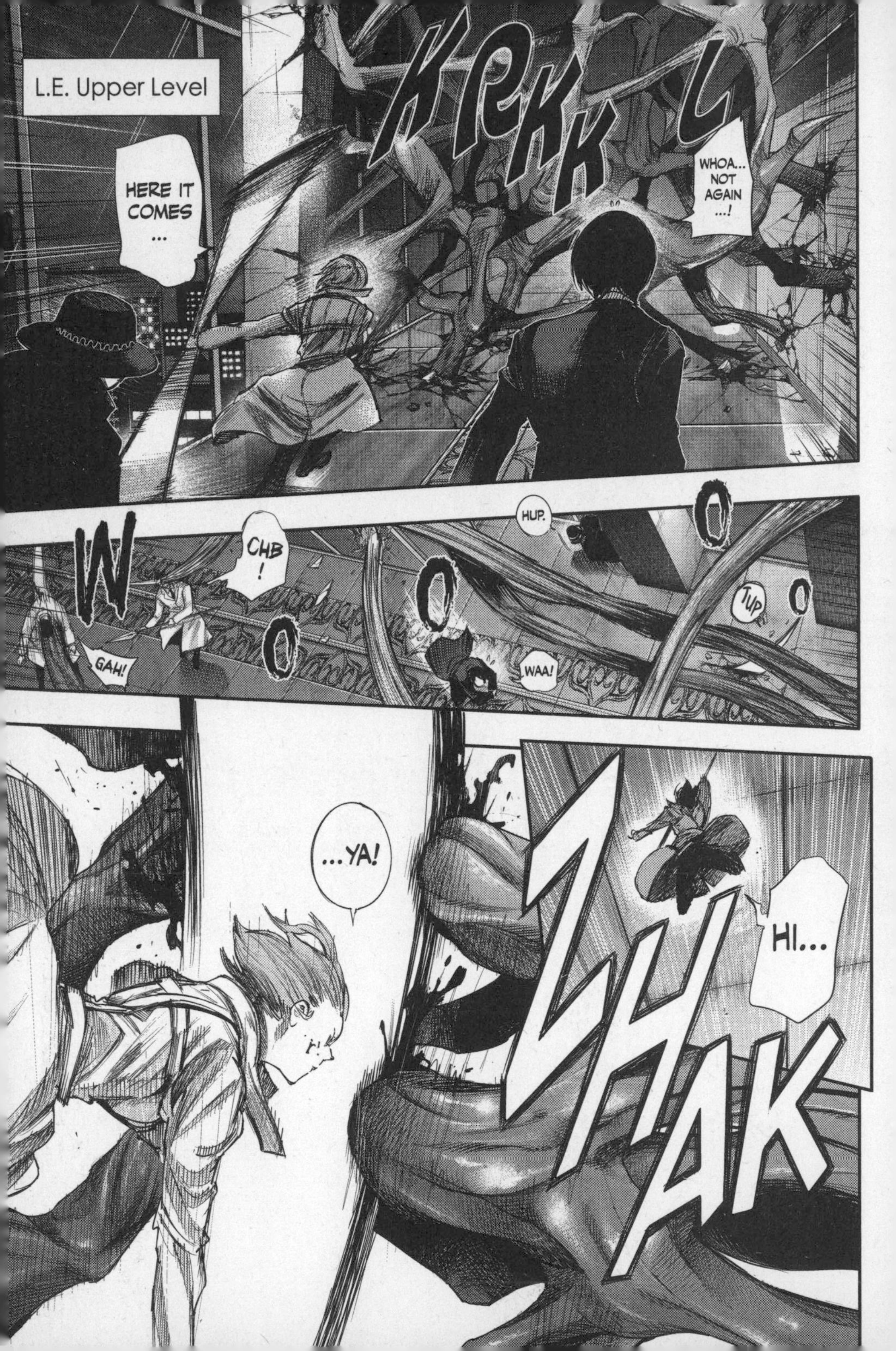
KRKKL
WHOA... NOT AGAIN ...!
L.E. Upper Level
HERE IT COMES ...
HUP.
TUP
WOOOO
WAA!
CHB!
GAH!
HI...
ZHAK
...YA!

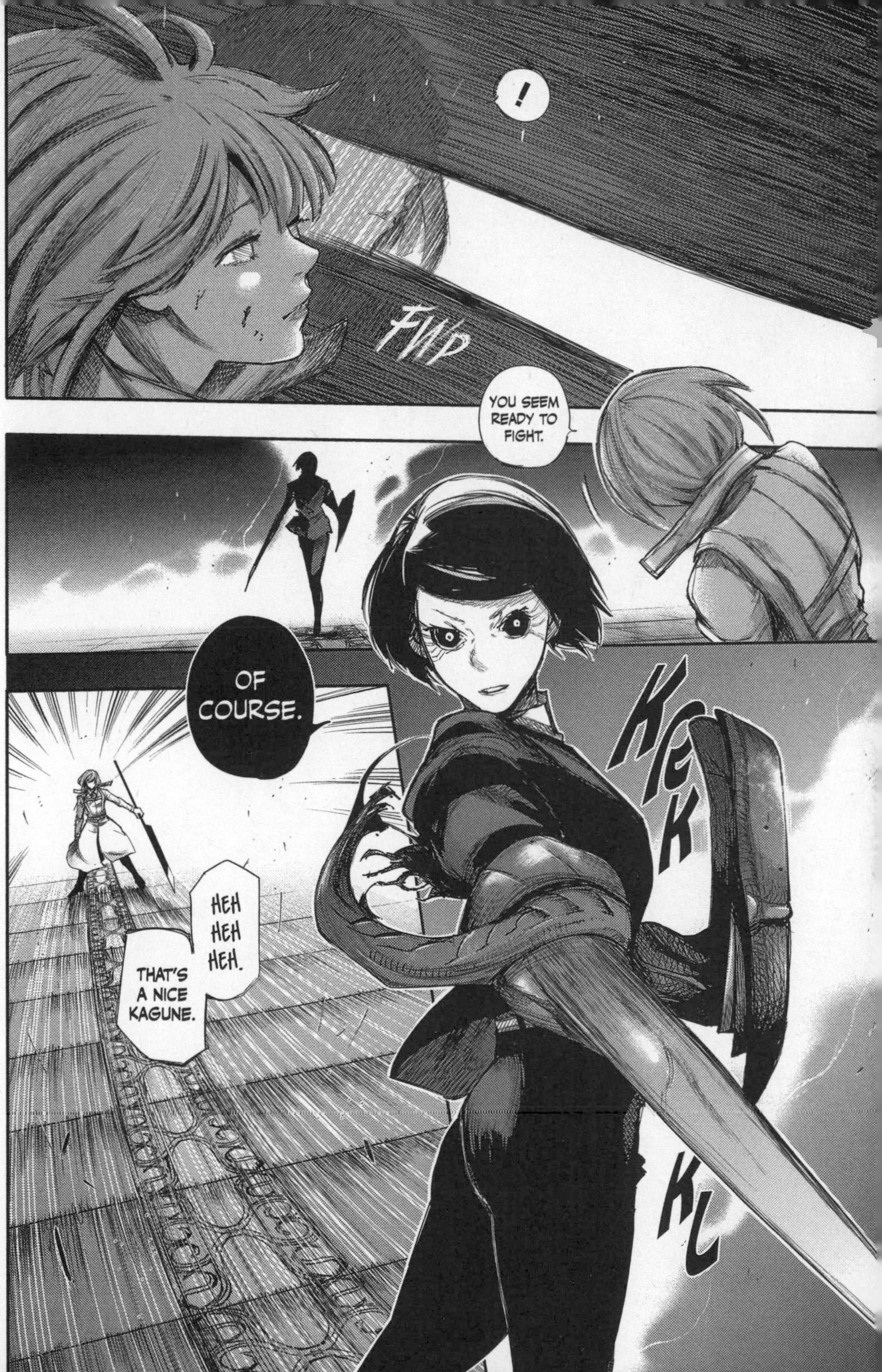
!
FWP
YOU SEEM READY TO FIGHT.
OF COURSE.
KREK
HEH HEH HEH.
THAT'S A NICE KAGUNE.
KL

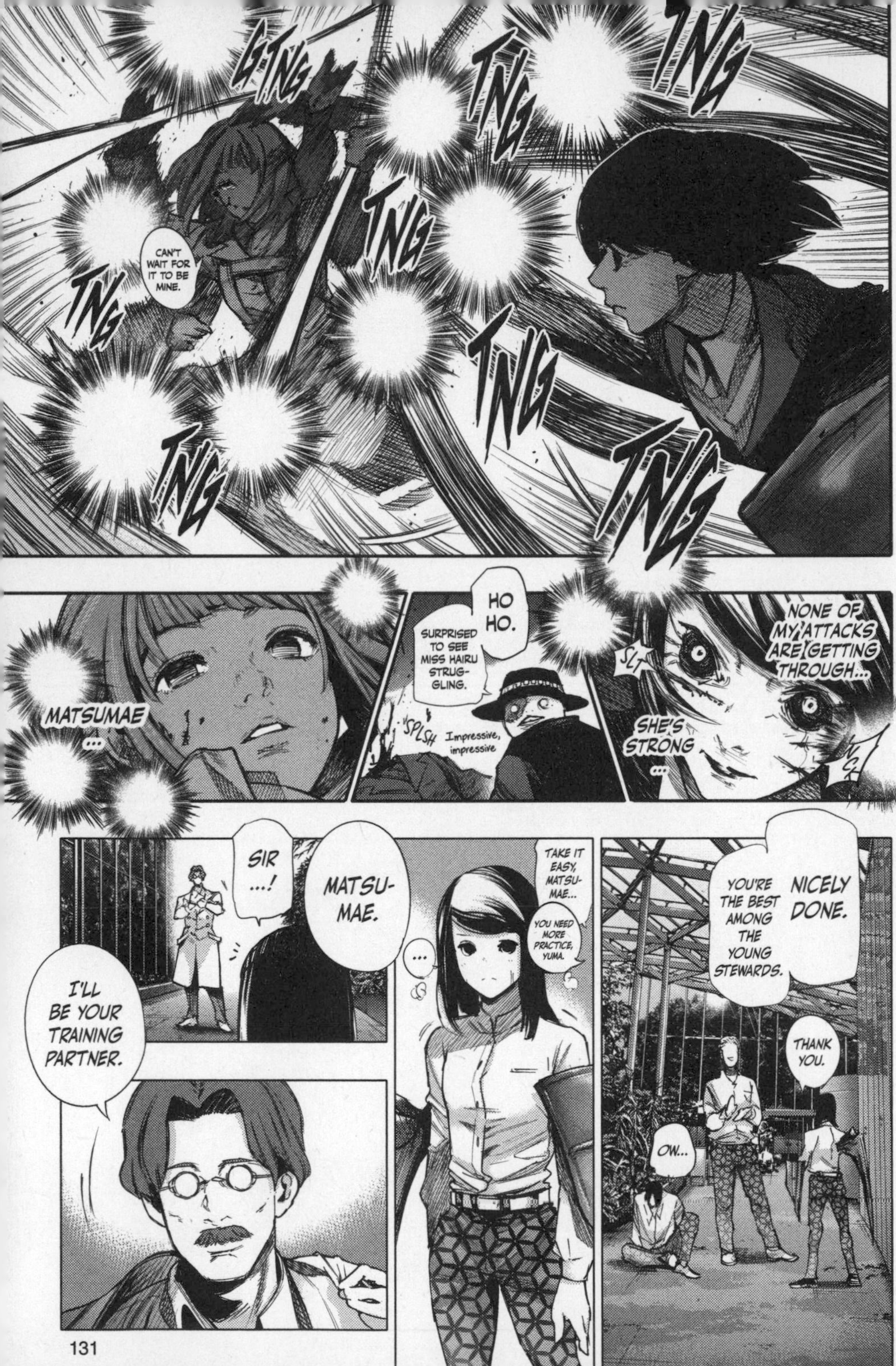
TNG
TNG
TNG
TNG
TNG
TNG
TNG
CAN'T WAIT FOR IT TO BE MINE.
NONE OF MY ATTACKS ARE GETTING THROUGH...
SLT
SHE'S STRONG...
HO HO.
SURPRISED TO SEE MISS HAIRU STRUG-GLING.
SPLSH
Impressive, impressive
MATSUMAE...
NICELY DONE.
YOU'RE THE BEST AMONG THE YOUNG STEWARDS.
THANK YOU.
OW...
TAKE IT EASY, MATSU-MAE...
YOU NEED MORE PRACTICE, YUMA.
...
MATSU-MAE.
SIR ...!
I'LL BE YOUR TRAINING PARTNER.

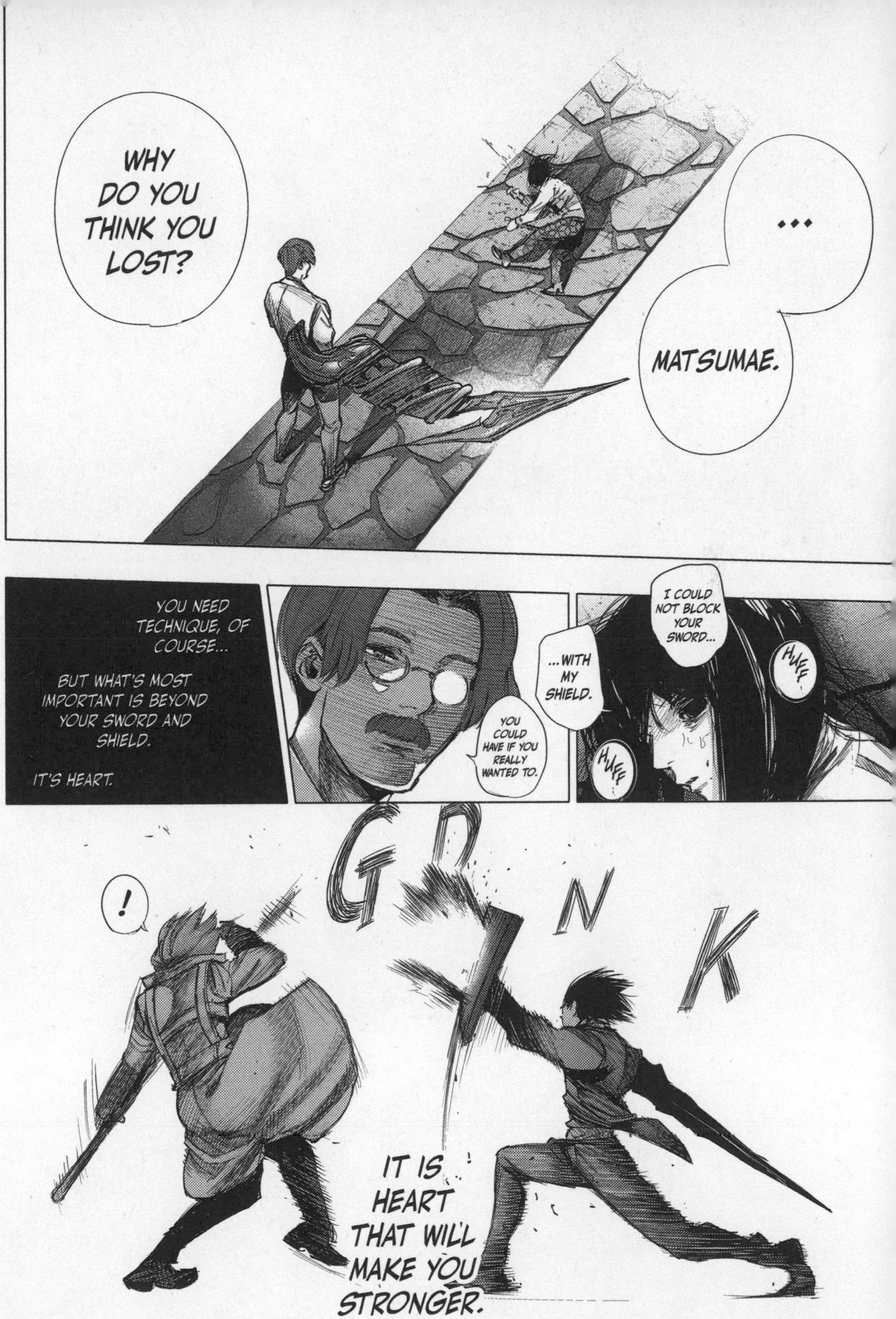
...
MATSUMAE.
WHY DO YOU THINK YOU LOST?
I COULD NOT BLOCK YOUR SWORD...
HUFF
...WITH MY SHIELD.
HUFF
YOU COULD HAVE IF YOU REALLY WANTED TO.
YOU NEED TECHNIQUE, OF COURSE...
BUT WHAT'S MOST IMPORTANT IS BEYOND YOUR SWORD AND SHIELD.
IT'S HEART.
GDNK
!
IT IS HEART THAT WILL MAKE YOU STRONGER.

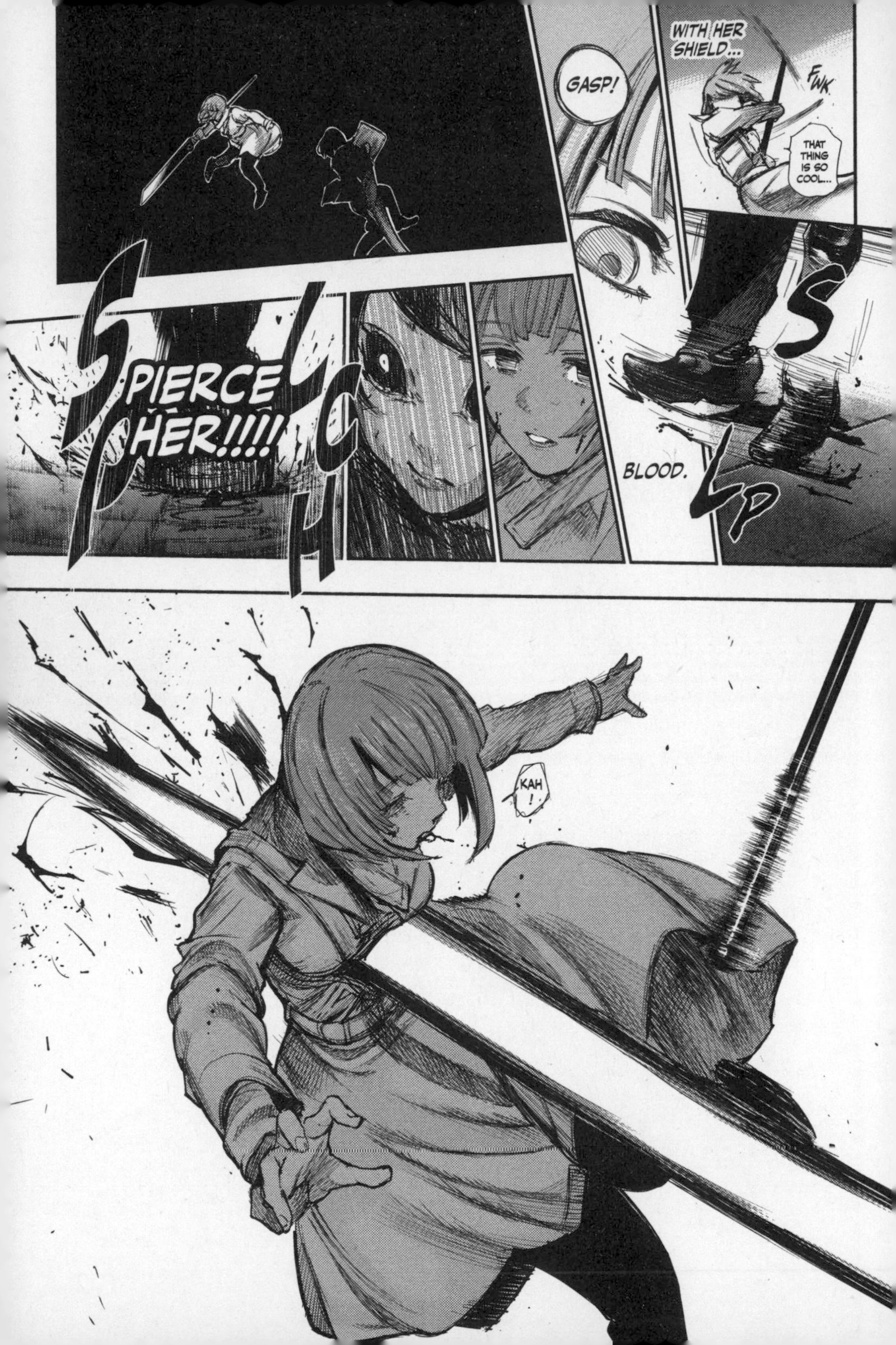
WITH HER SHIELD...
FWK
THAT THING IS SO COOL...
GASP!
BLOOD.
PIERCE HER!!!!!
KAH!

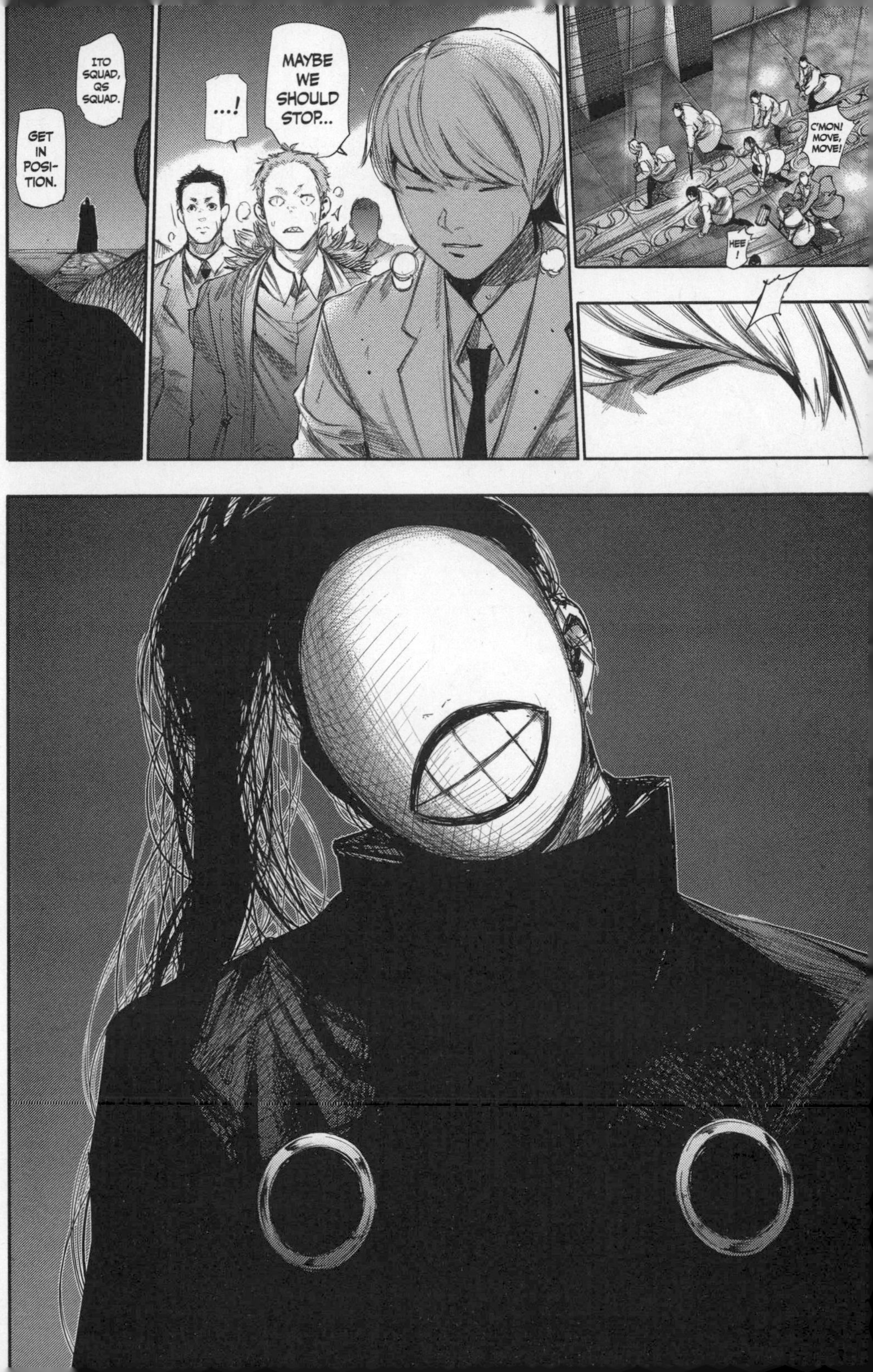
C'MON! MOVE, MOVE!
HEE!
MAYBE WE SHOULD STOP...
...!
ITO SQUAD, QS SQUAD.
GET IN POSITION.

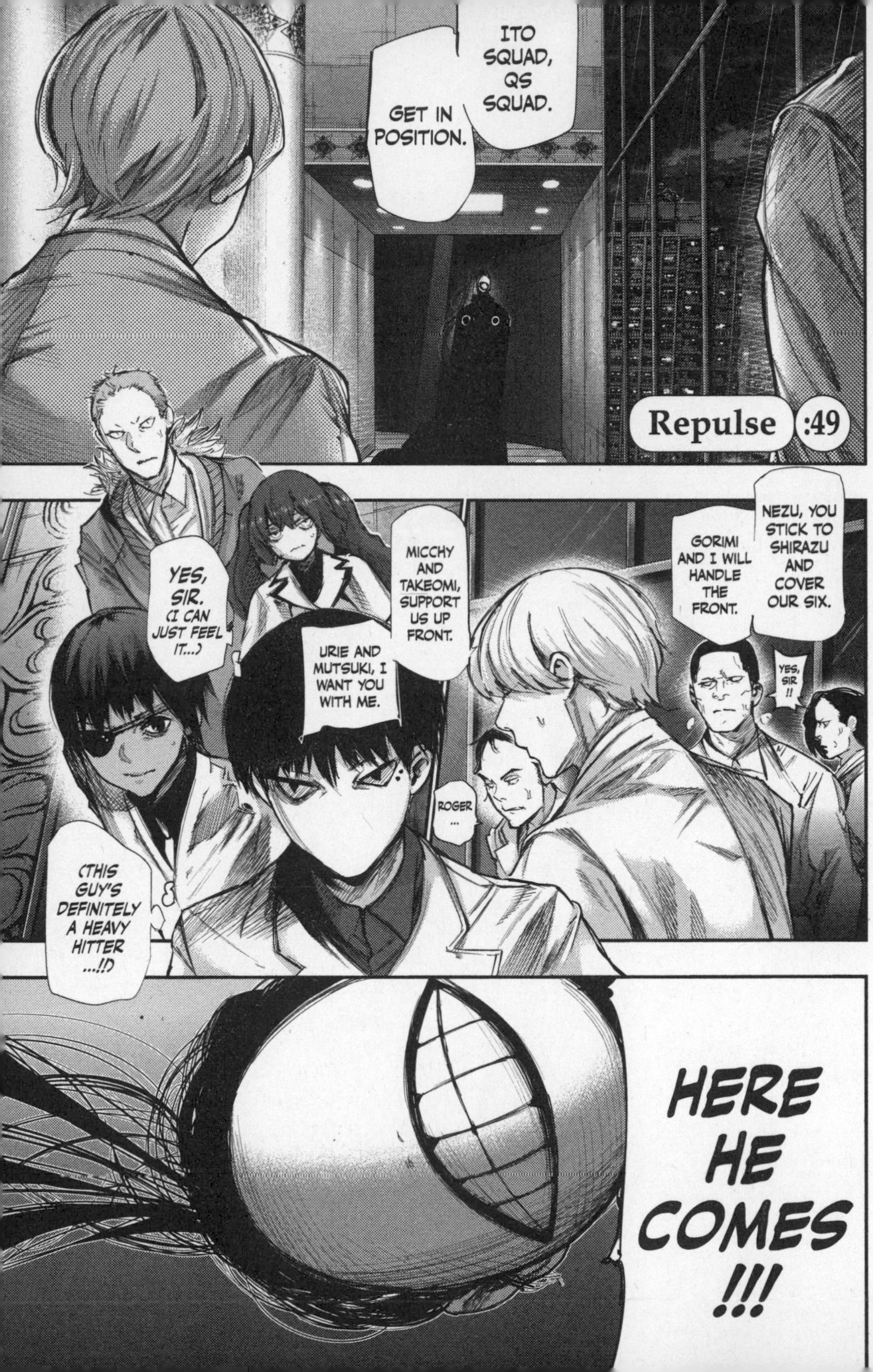
ITO SQUAD, QS SQUAD.
GET IN POSITION.
Repulse :49
NEZU, YOU STICK TO SHIRAZU AND COVER OUR SIX.
GORIMI AND I WILL HANDLE THE FRONT.
YES, SIR!!
MICCHY AND TAKEOMI, SUPPORT US UP FRONT.
URIE AND MUTSUKI, I WANT YOU WITH ME.
ROGER...
YES, SIR. (I CAN JUST FEEL IT...)
(THIS GUY'S DEFINITELY A HEAVY HITTER...!?)
HERE HE COMES!!!

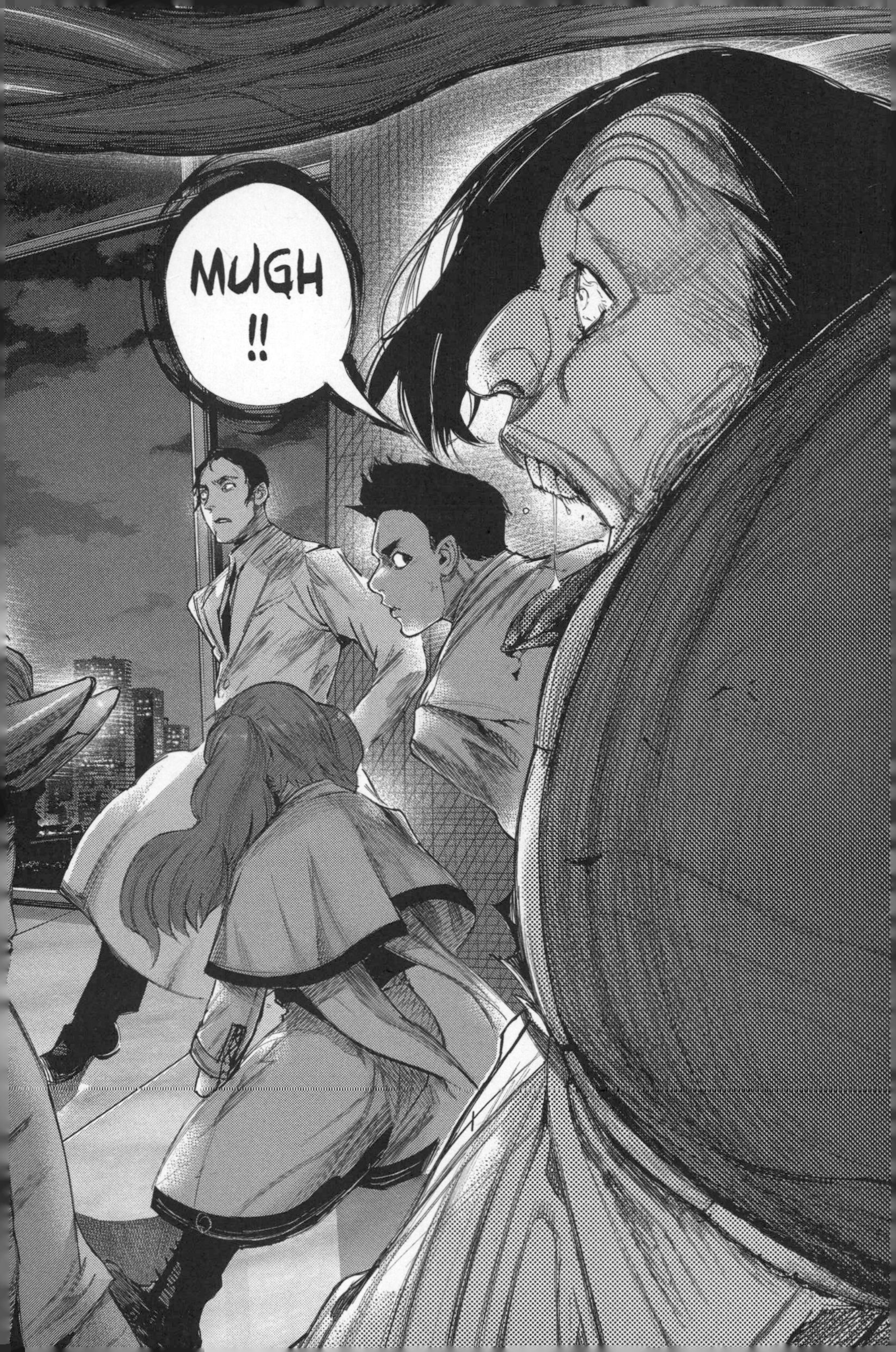
MUGH !!

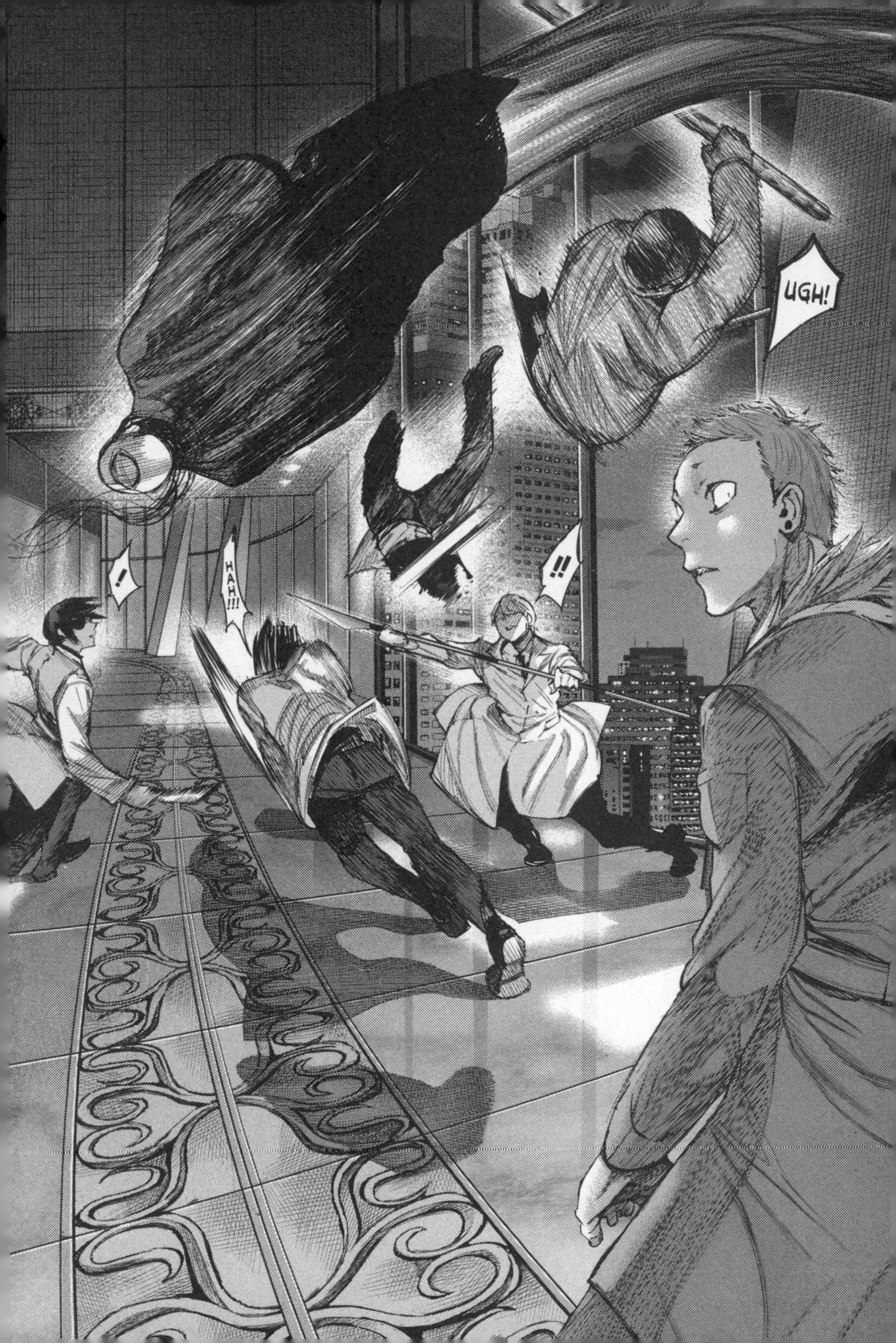
UGH!
!!
HAH!!!
!

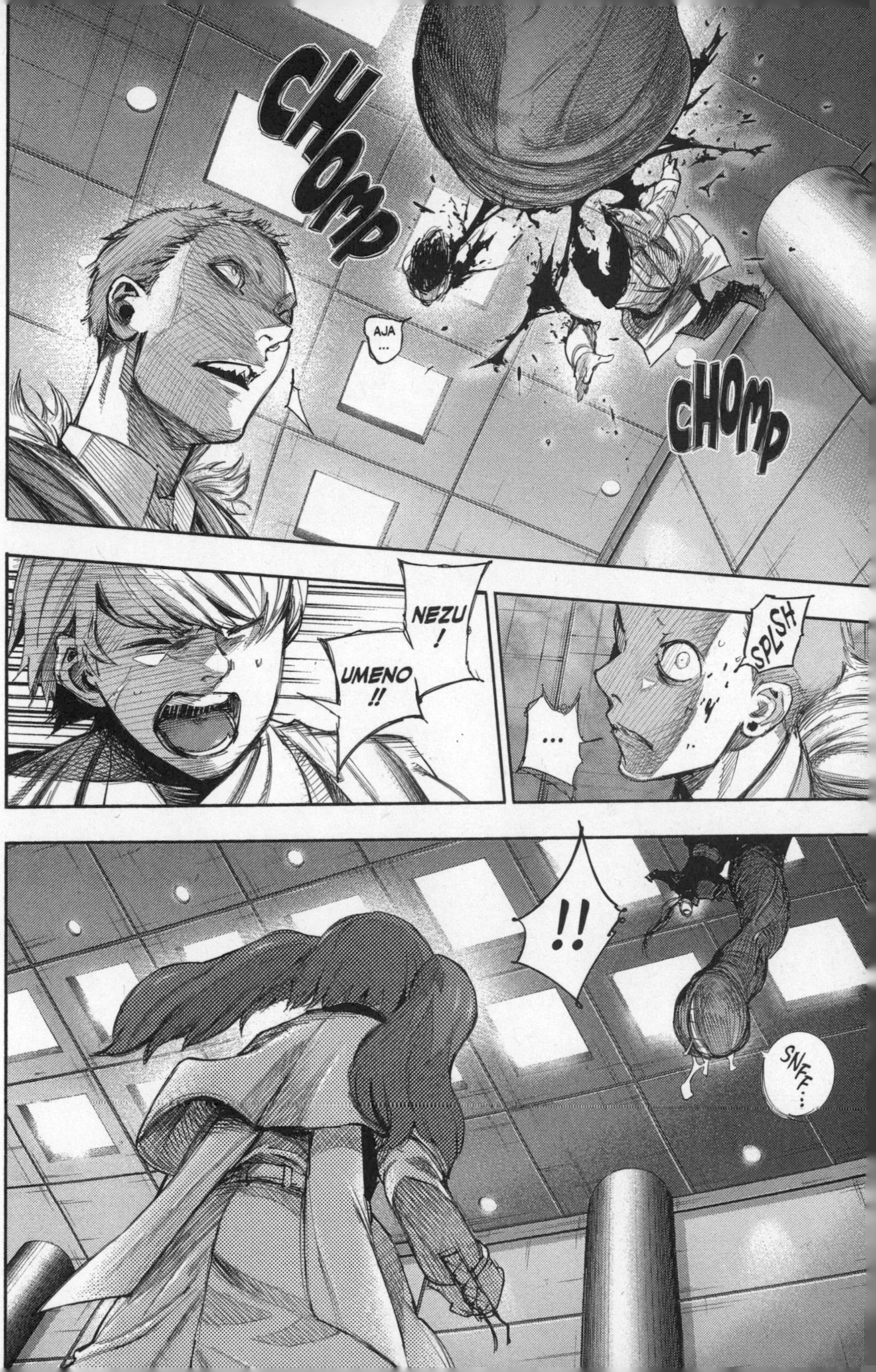
CHOMP
AJA ...
CHOMP
NEZU!
UMENO!!
SPLSH
...
!!
SNFF...

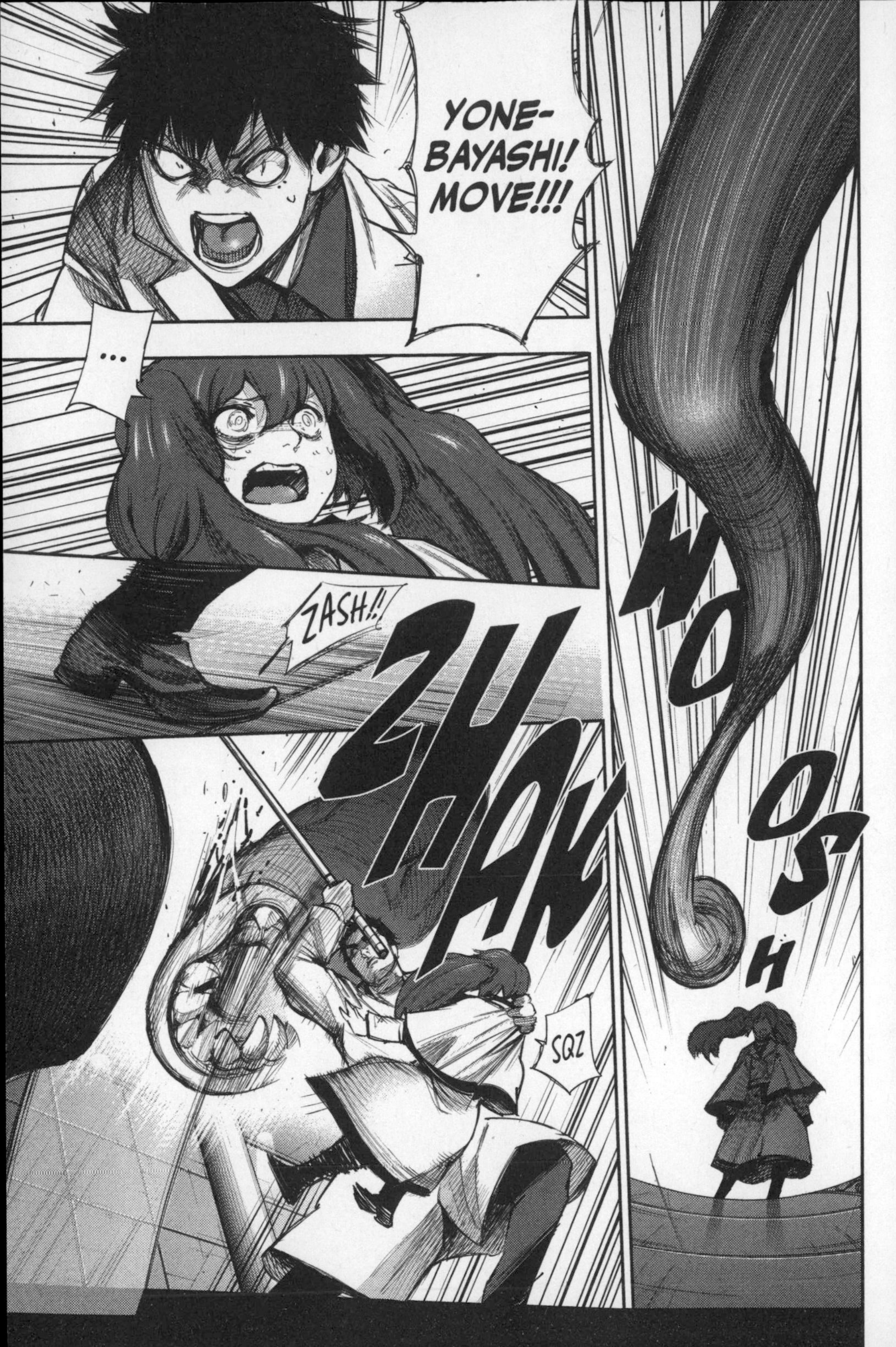
WHOOSH
YONE-BAYASHI! MOVE!!!
...
ZASH!!
ZHAK
SQZ

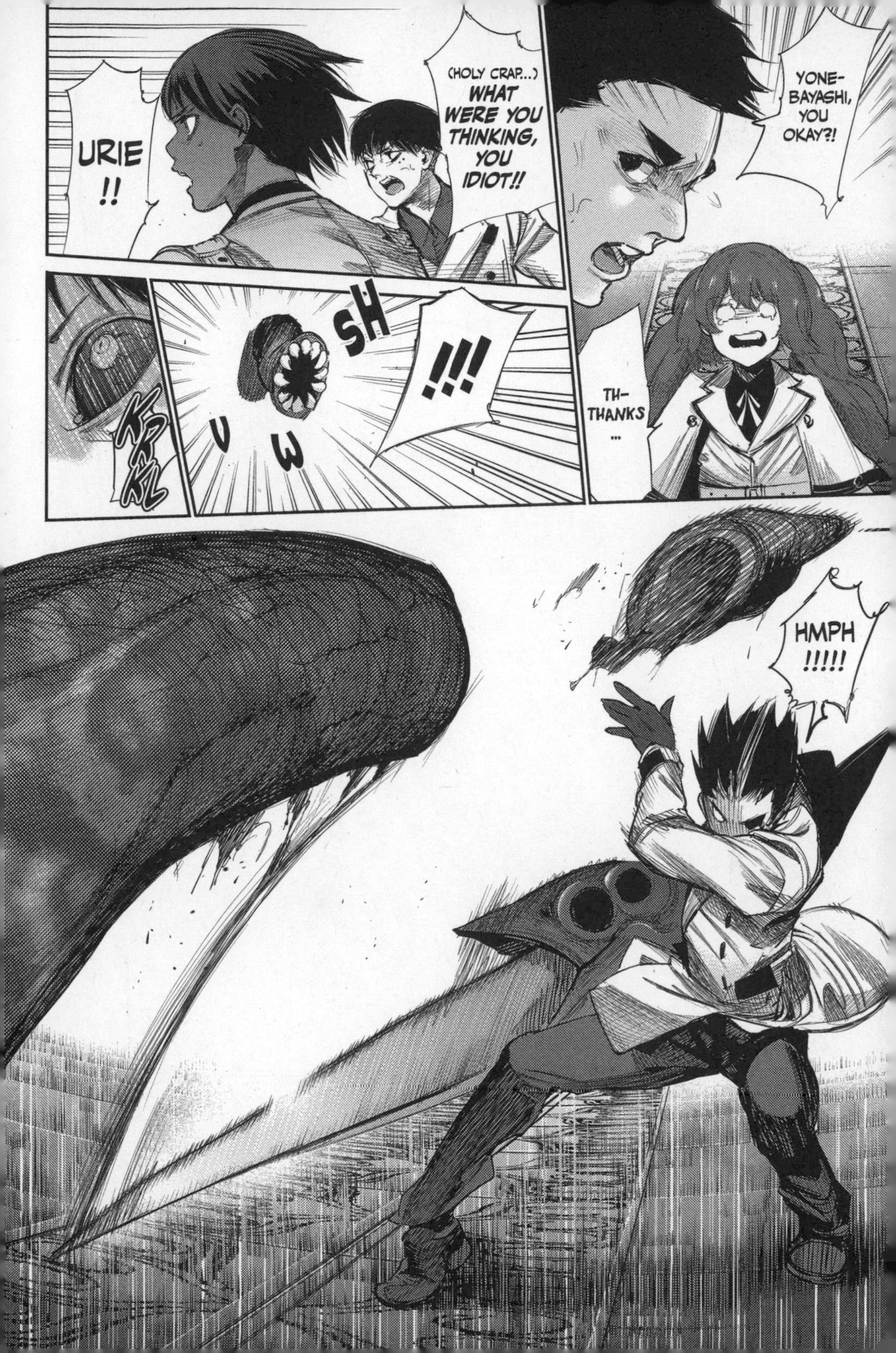
YONE-BAYASHI, YOU OKAY?!
TH-THANKS ...
(HOLY CRAP...) WHAT WERE YOU THINKING, YOU IDIOT!!
URIE !!
!!!
VWSH
KRKL
HMPH !!!!!

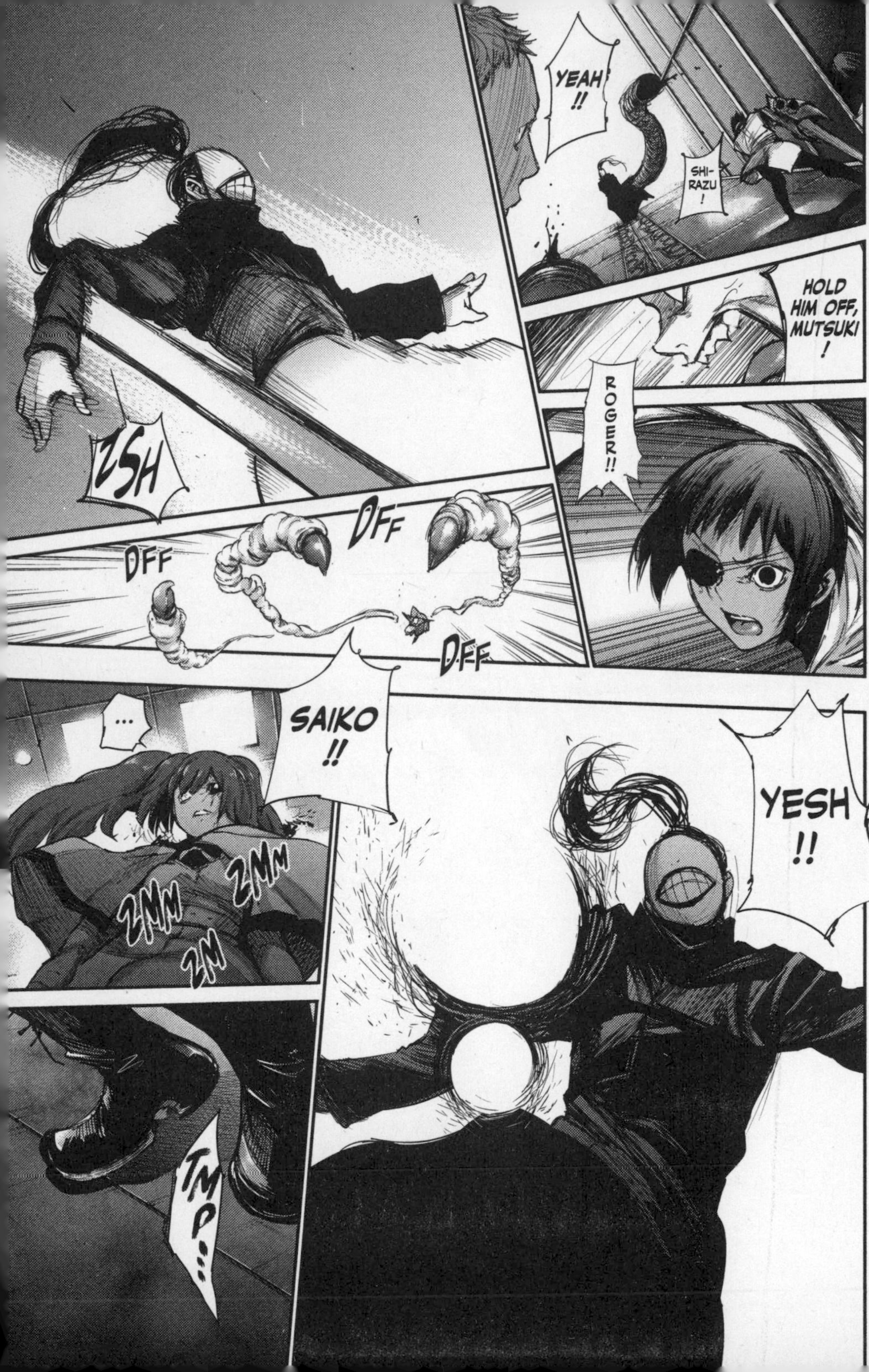

YEAH!!
SHI-RAZU!
HOLD HIM OFF, MUTSUKI!
ROGER!!
ZSH
DFF
DFF
DFF
SAIKO!!
YESH!!
...
ZMM
ZMM
ZM
TMP...

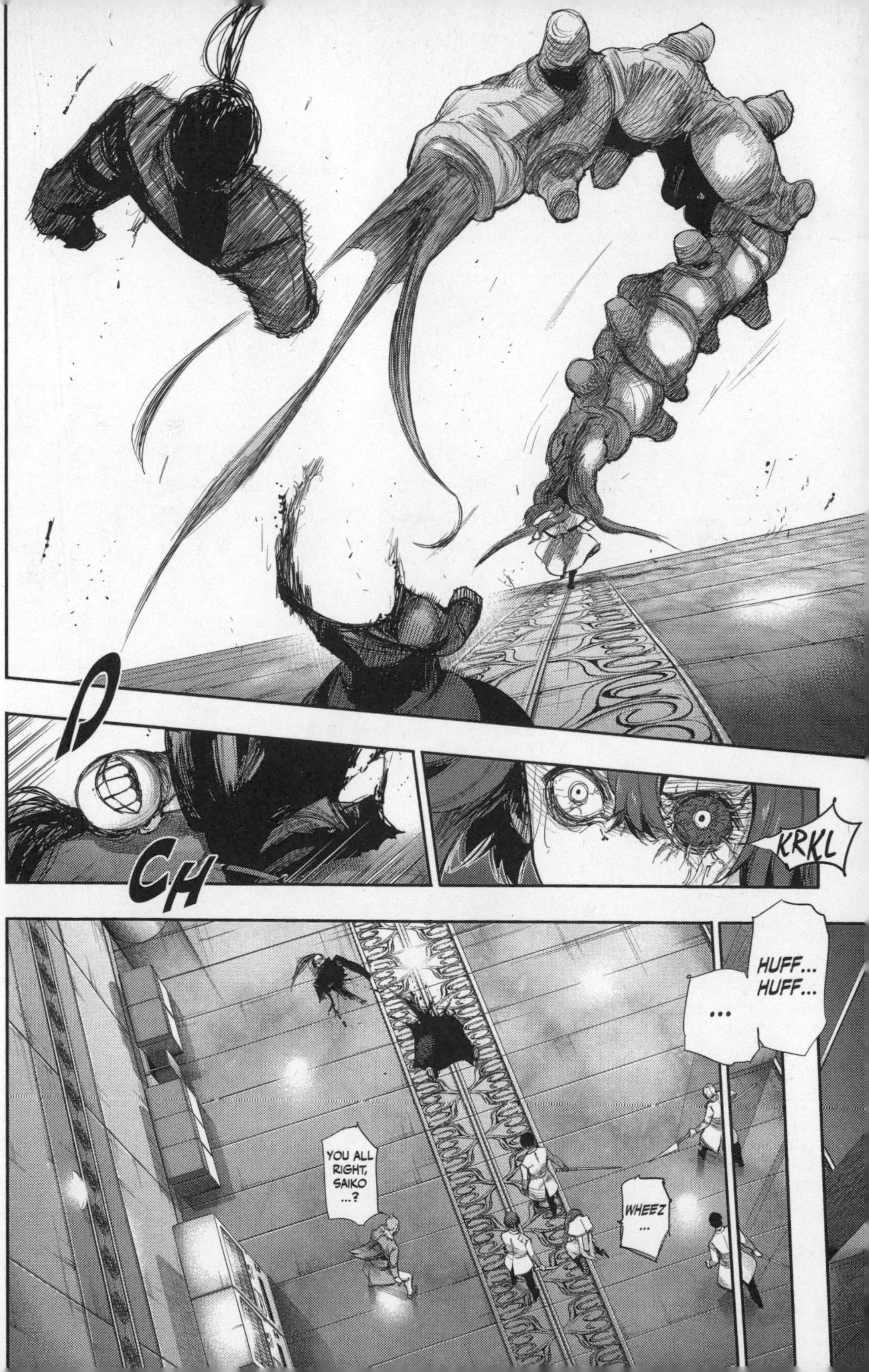

P
KRKL
CH
HUFF... HUFF...
...
WHEEZ ...
YOU ALL RIGHT, SAIKO ...?

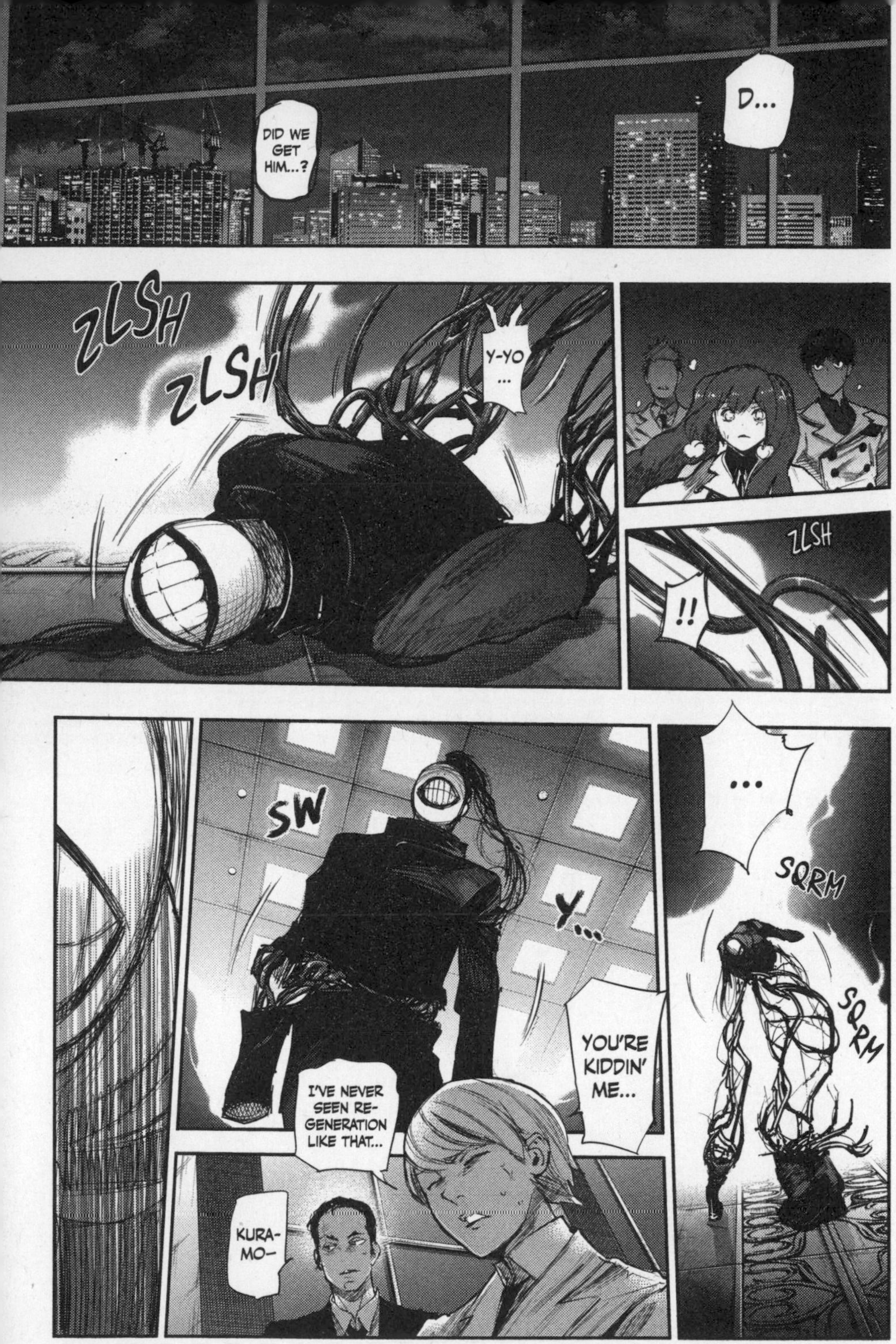
D...
DID WE GET HIM...?
ZLSH
!!
Y-YO ...
ZLSH
ZLSH
...
SQRM
SQRM
SW
Y...
YOU'RE KIDDIN' ME...
I'VE NEVER SEEN RE-GENERATION LIKE THAT...
KURA-MO-

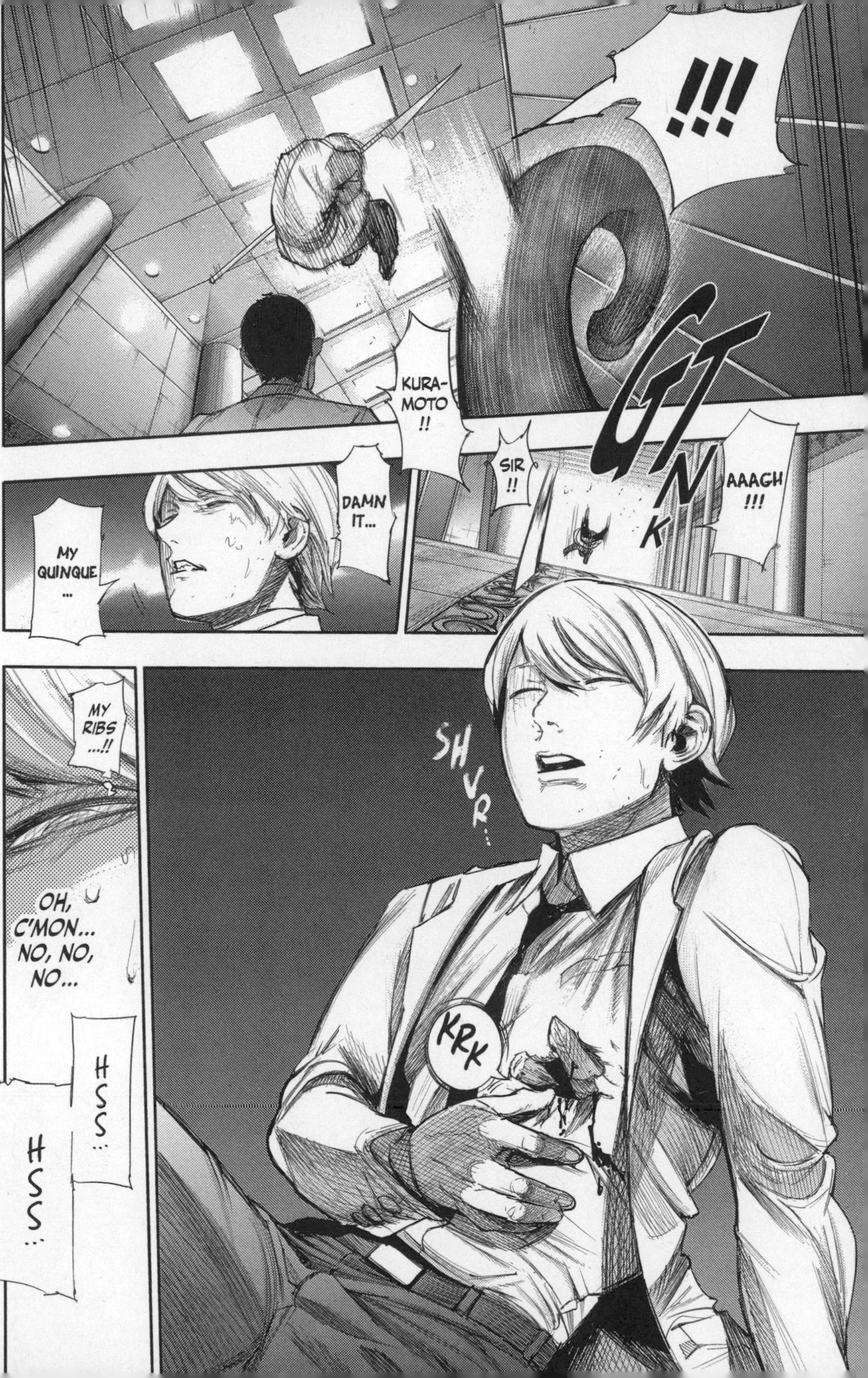
!!!
KURA-MOTO !!
GINK
AAAGH !!!
SIR !!
DAMN IT...
MY QUINQUE ...
SHVR...
KRK
MY RIBS ...!!
OH, C'MON... NO, NO, NO...
HSS..
HSS..

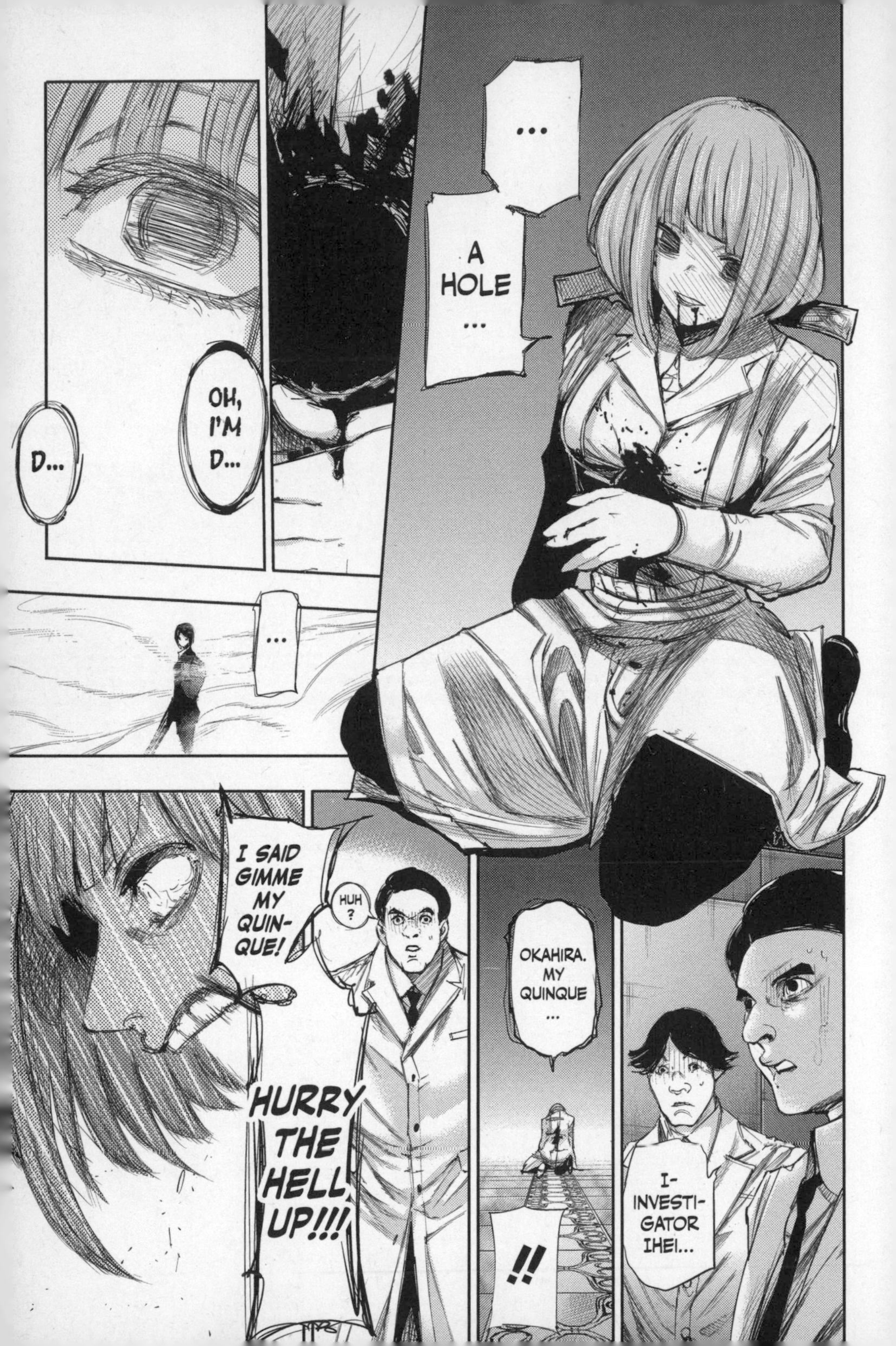
...
A HOLE ...
OH, I'M D...
D...
...
I- INVESTIGATOR IHEI...
OKAHIRA. MY QUINQUE ...
!!
HUH?
I SAID GIMME MY QUINQUE!
HURRY THE HELL UP!!!

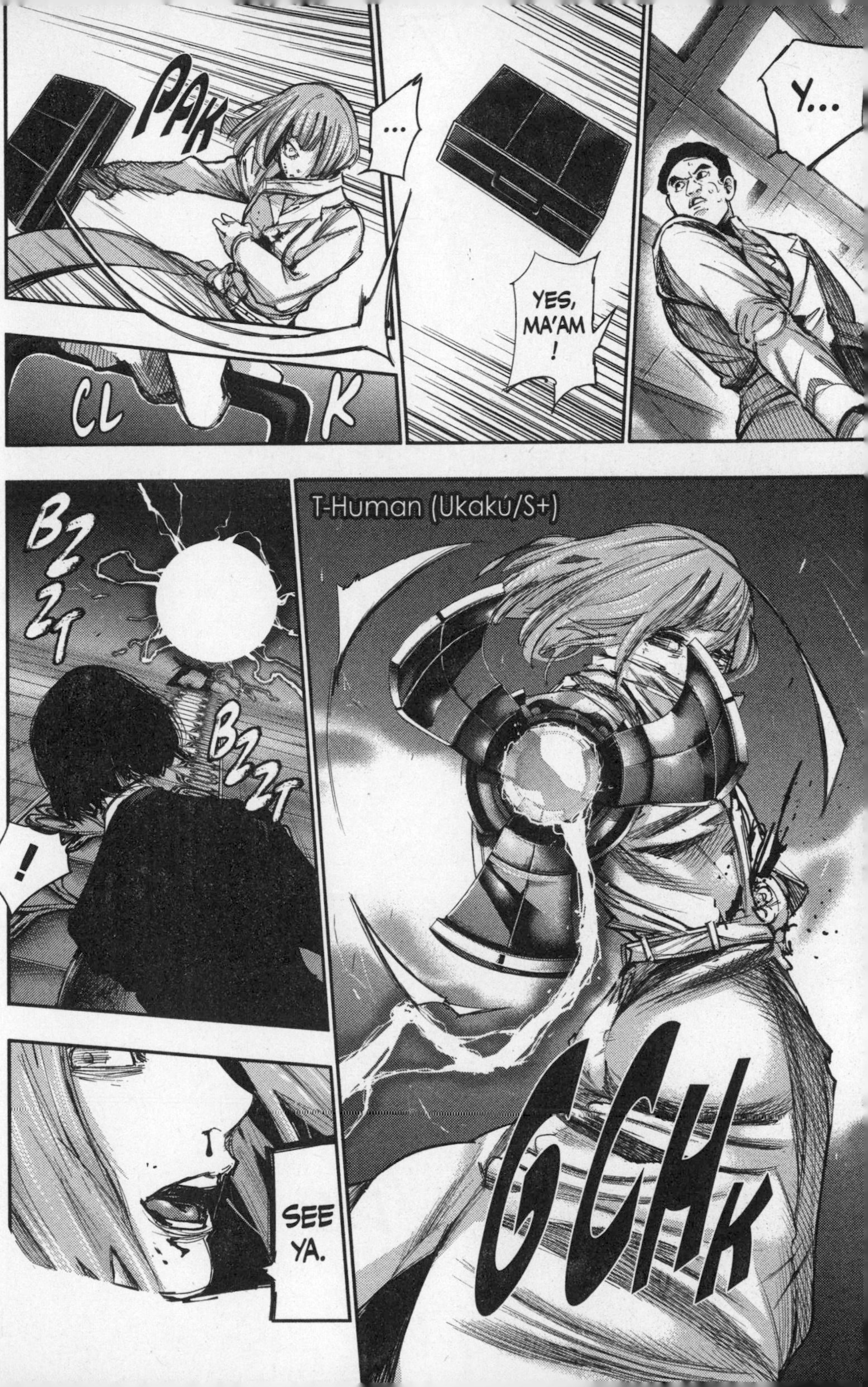
Y...
...
YES, MA'AM !
PAK
CL K
T-Human (Ukakú/S+)
...
GCHK
BZZT
BZZT
!
SEE YA.

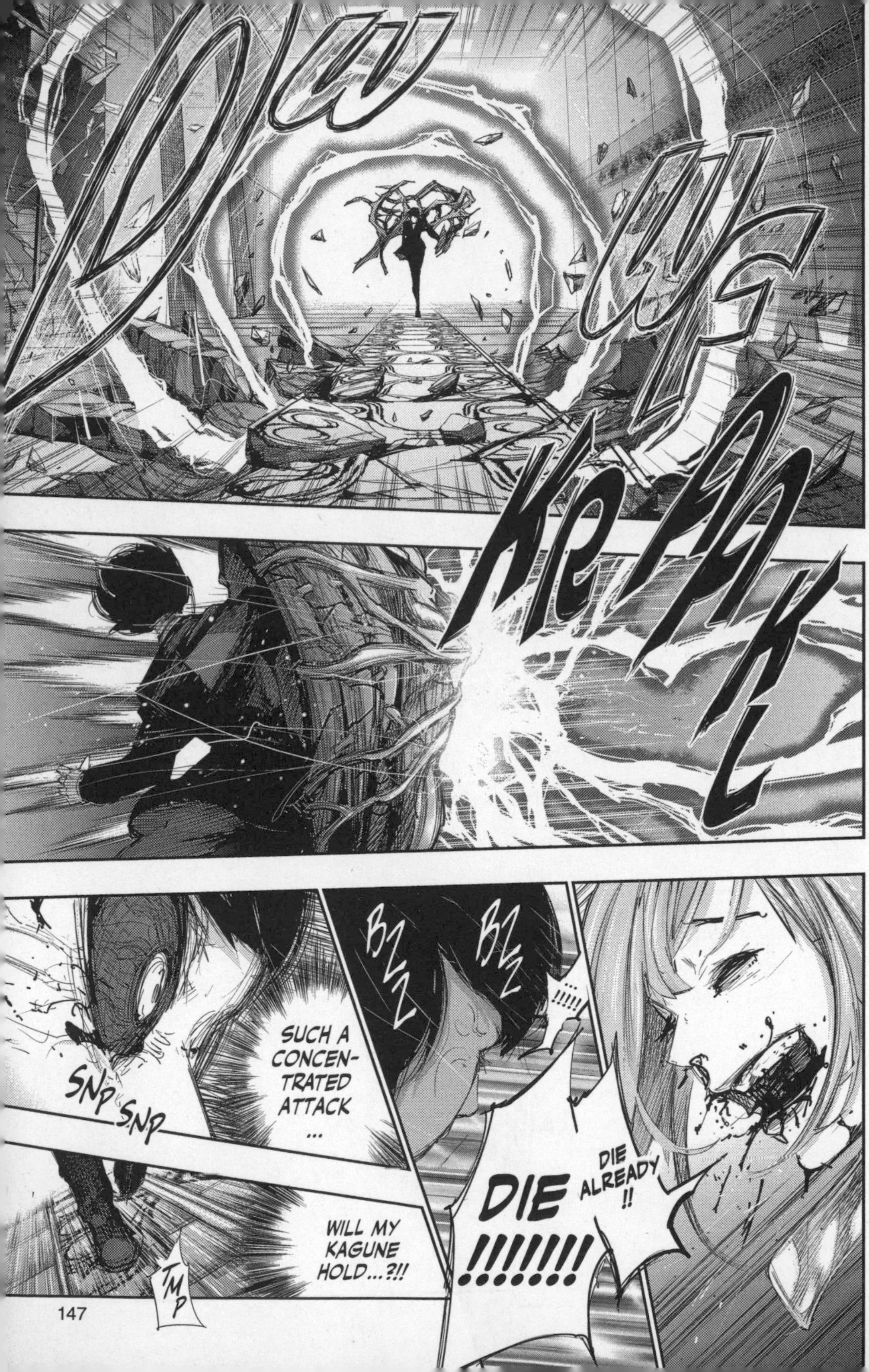
...!!!!!
DIE ALREADY !!
DIE !!!!!!!!
BZZ
BZZ
SUCH A CONCENTRATED ATTACK ...
WILL MY KAGUNE HOLD...?!!
SNP SNP
TMP

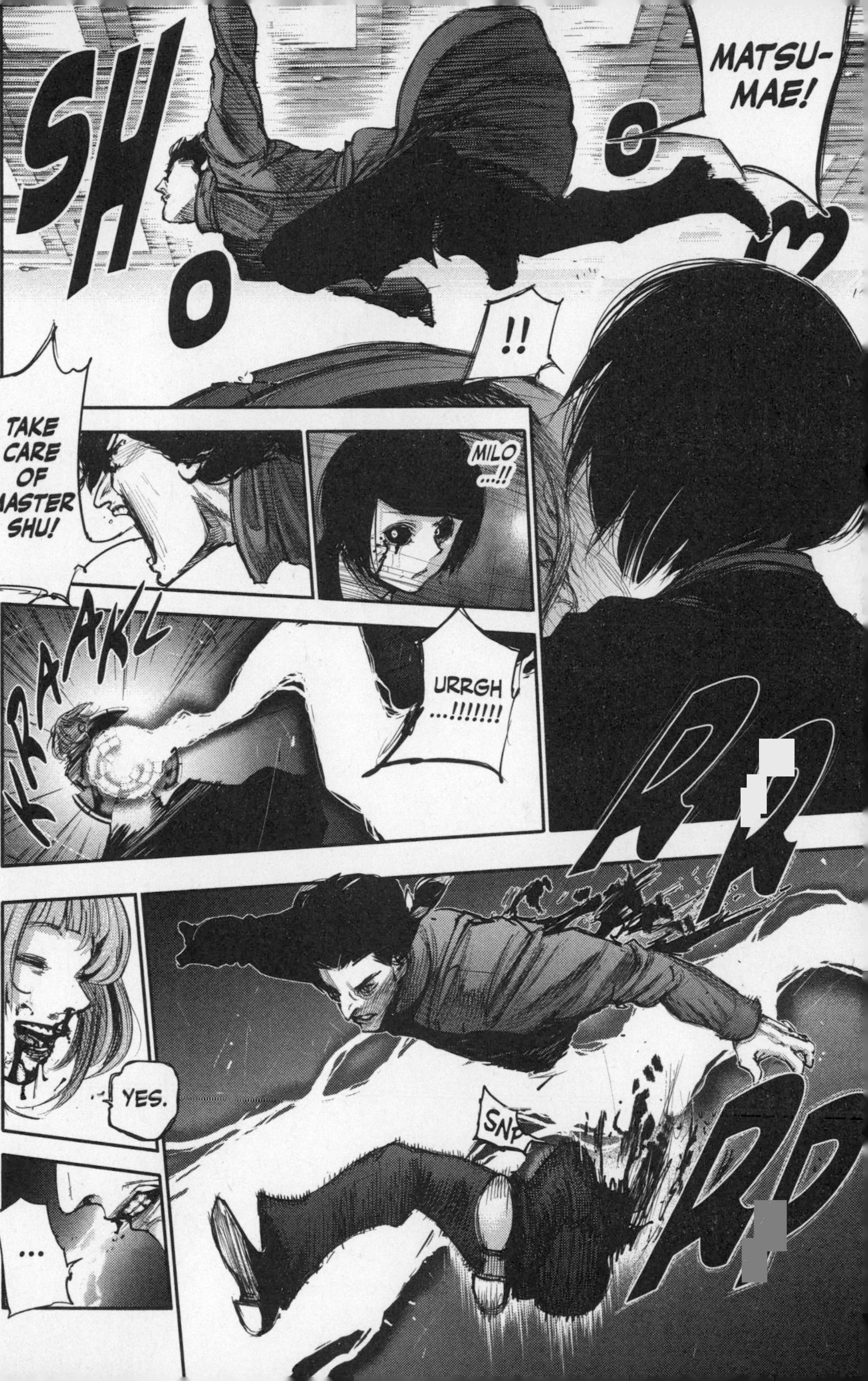
MATSU-MAE!
SHOOM
!!
MILO ...!!
TAKE CARE OF MASTER SHU!
URRGH ...!!!!!!!
KRRAKL
YES.
SNP
...

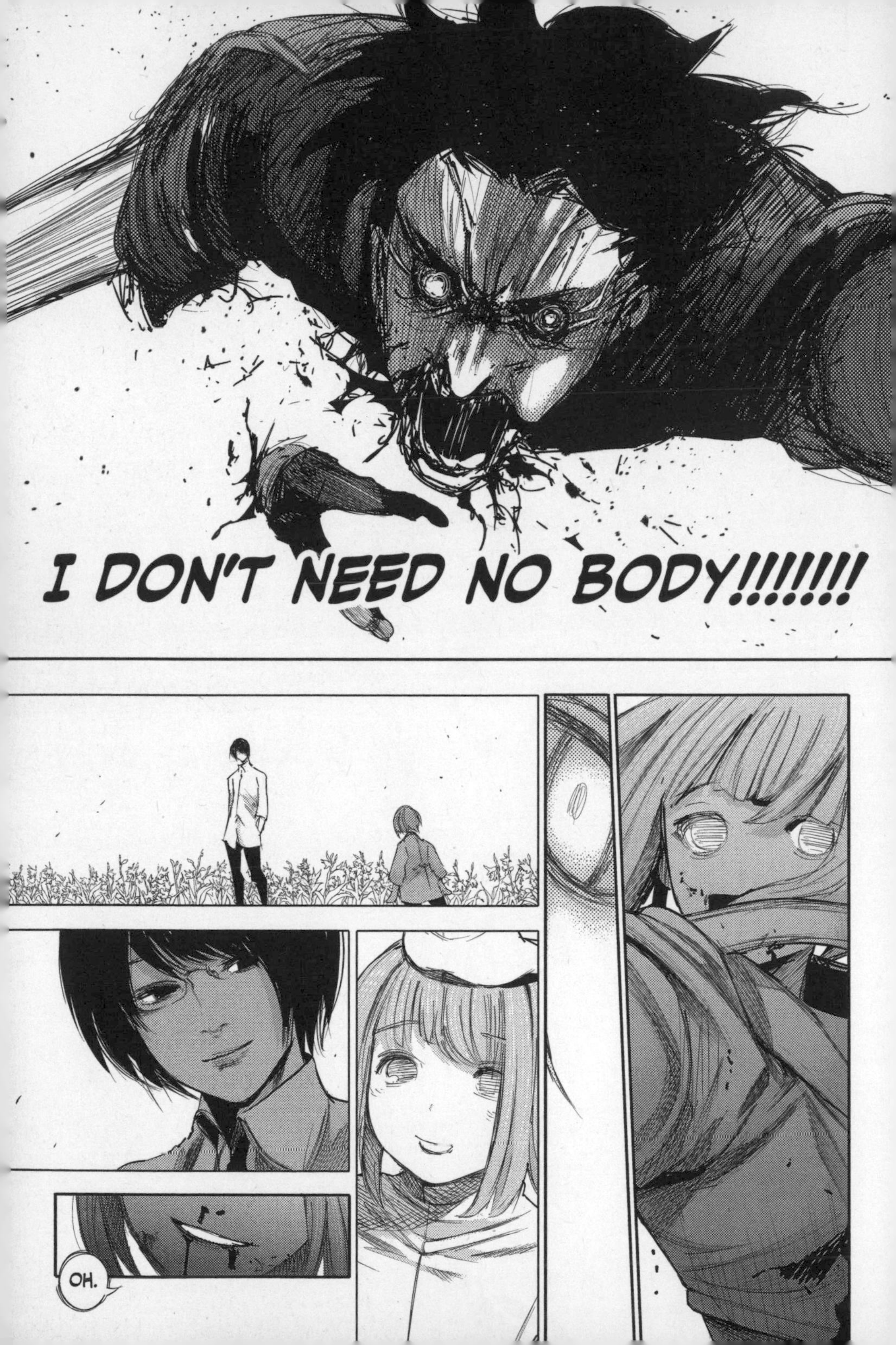
I DON'T NEED NO BODY!!!!!!!
OH.

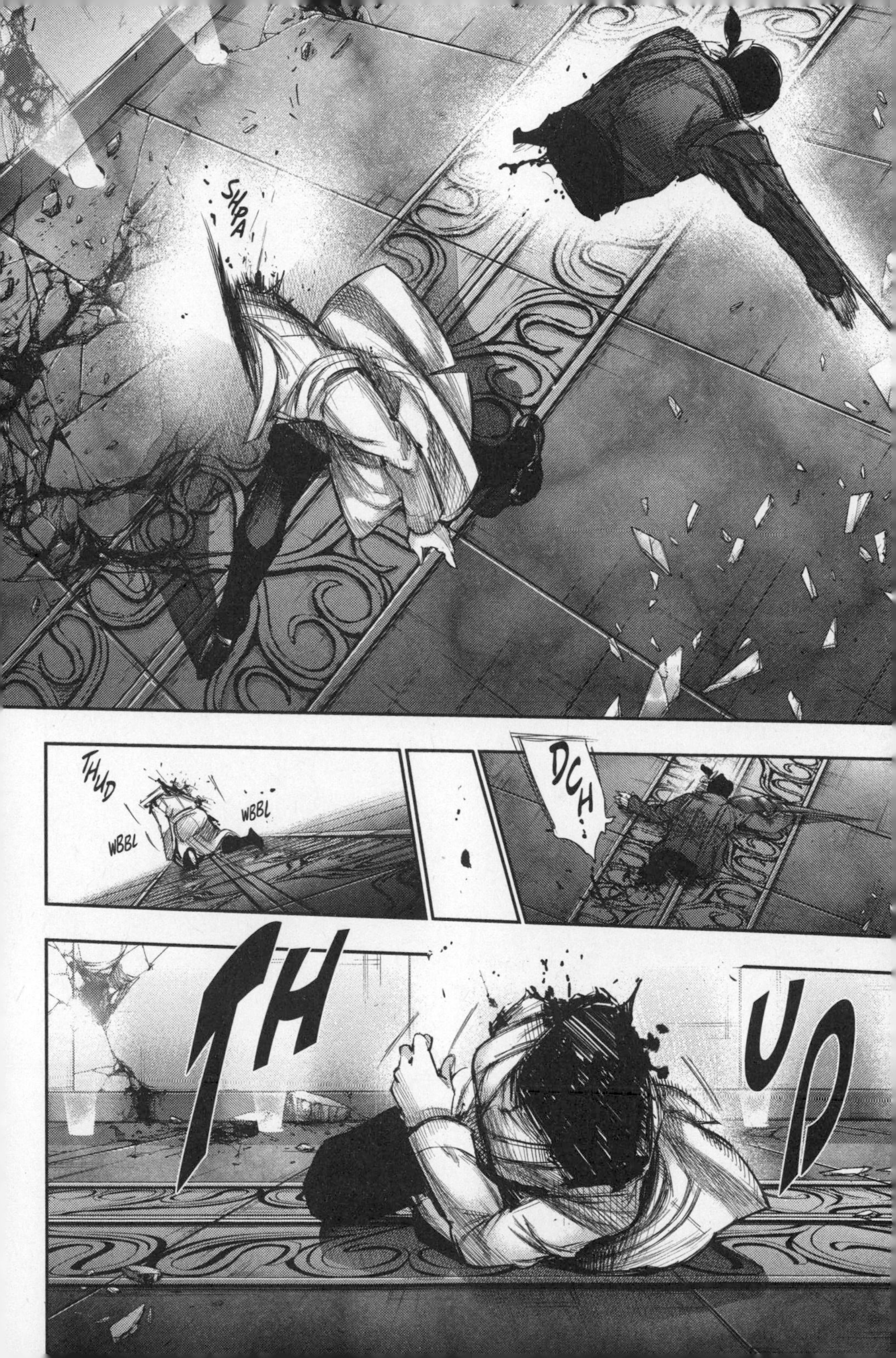
SHPA
DCH!
THUD
WBBL
WBBL
TH UD

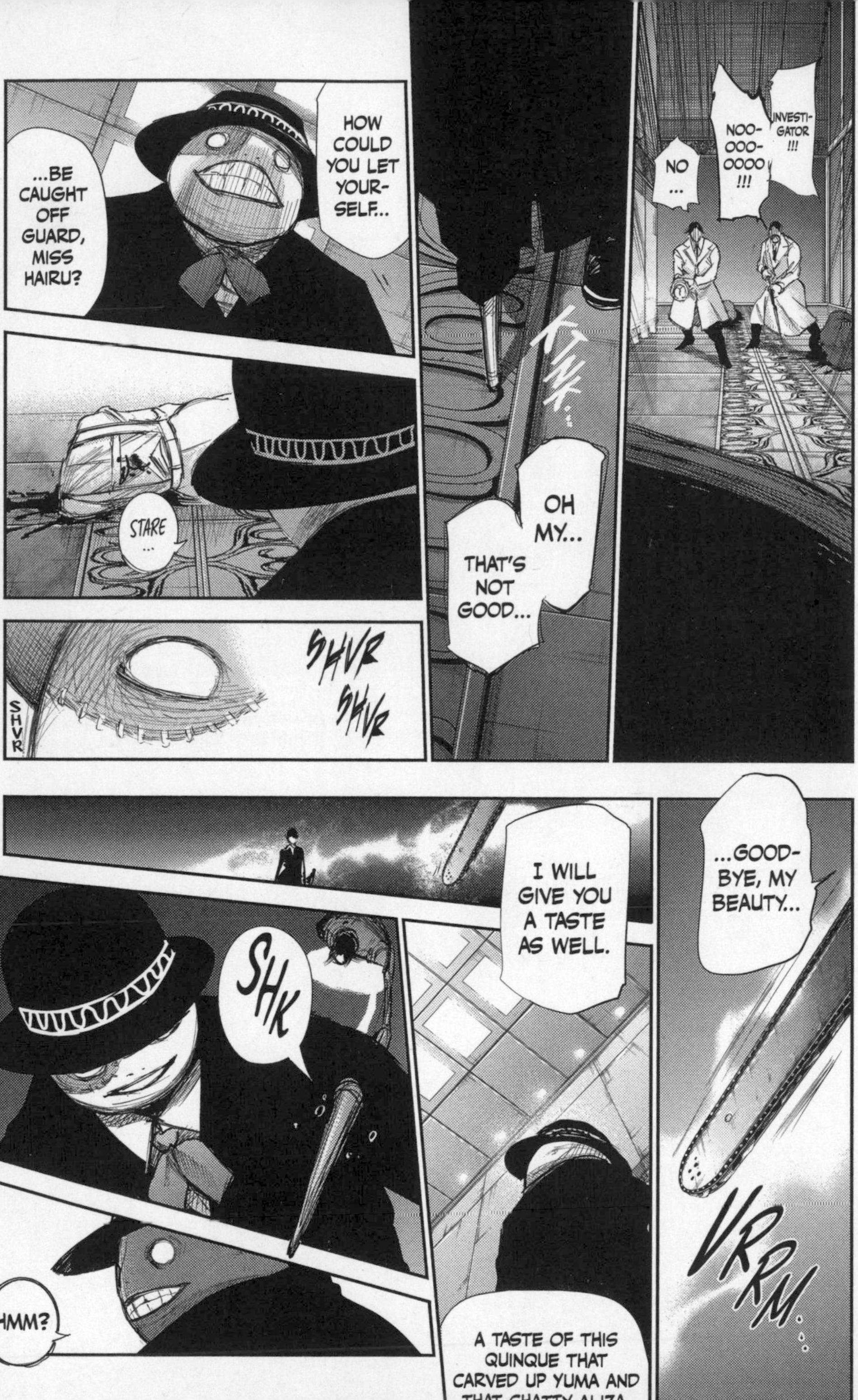
INVESTI-GATOR!!!
NOO-OOO-OOOO!!!
NO...
KNK...
OH MY...
THAT'S NOT GOOD...
HOW COULD YOU LET YOUR-SELF...
...BE CAUGHT OFF GUARD, MISS HAIRU?
STARE...
SHVR SHVR
SHVR
...GOOD-BYE, MY BEAUTY...
VRRM...
I WILL GIVE YOU A TASTE AS WELL.
A TASTE OF THIS QUINQUE THAT CARVED UP YUMA AND THAT CHATTY ALIZA.
SHK
HMM?

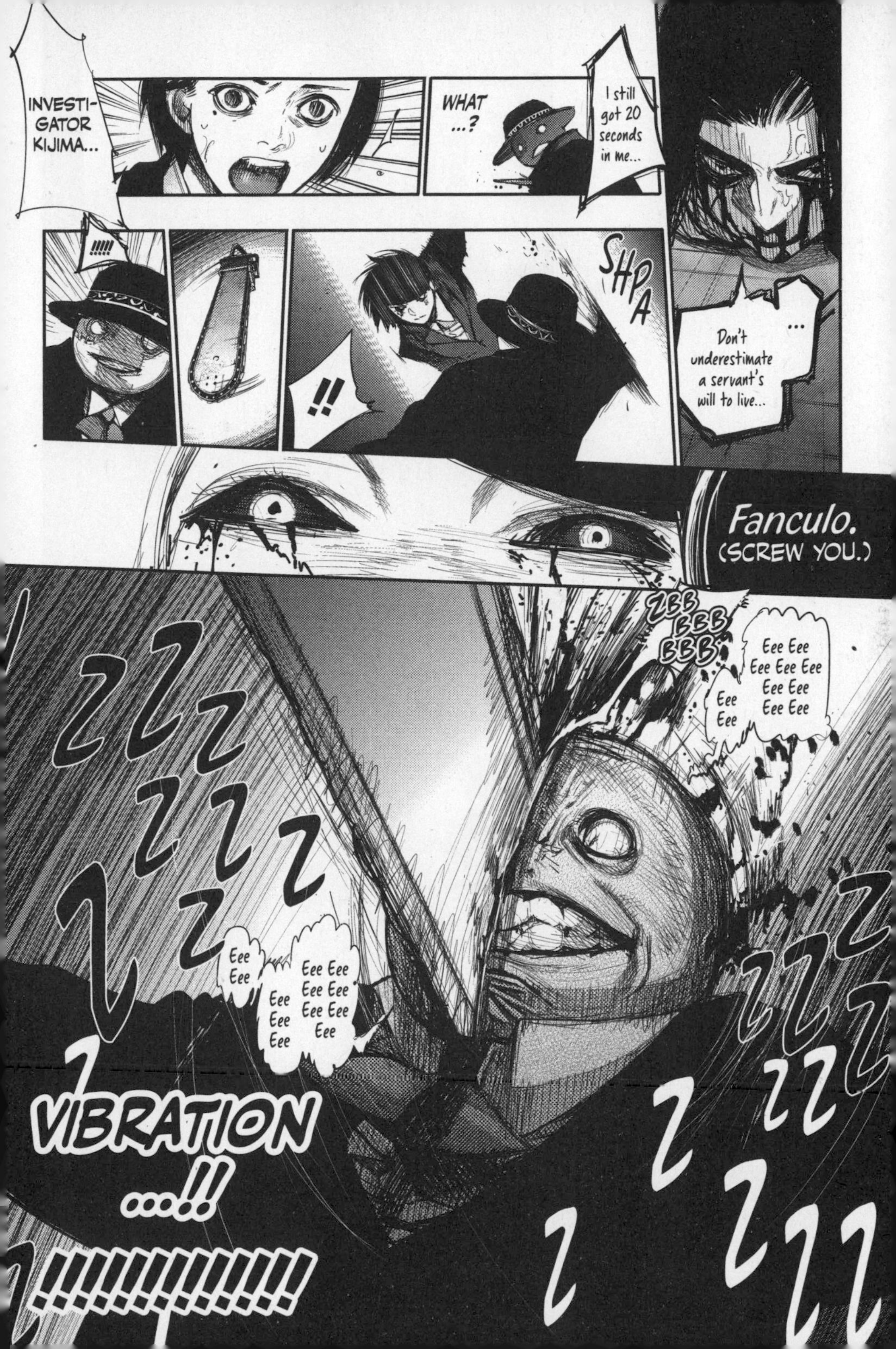
I still got 20 seconds in me...
...
Don't underestimate a servant's will to live...
WHAT ...?
INVESTI-GATOR KIJIMA...
SHPA
!!
!!!!!
Fanculo.
(SCREW YOU.)
ZBB BBB BBB
Eee Eee Eee Eee Eee Eee Eee Eee Eee
Eee Eee
Eee Eee Eee Eee Eee Eee Eee
Eee Eee Eee
Eee Eee
VIBRATION ...!!
!!!!!!!!!!!!!

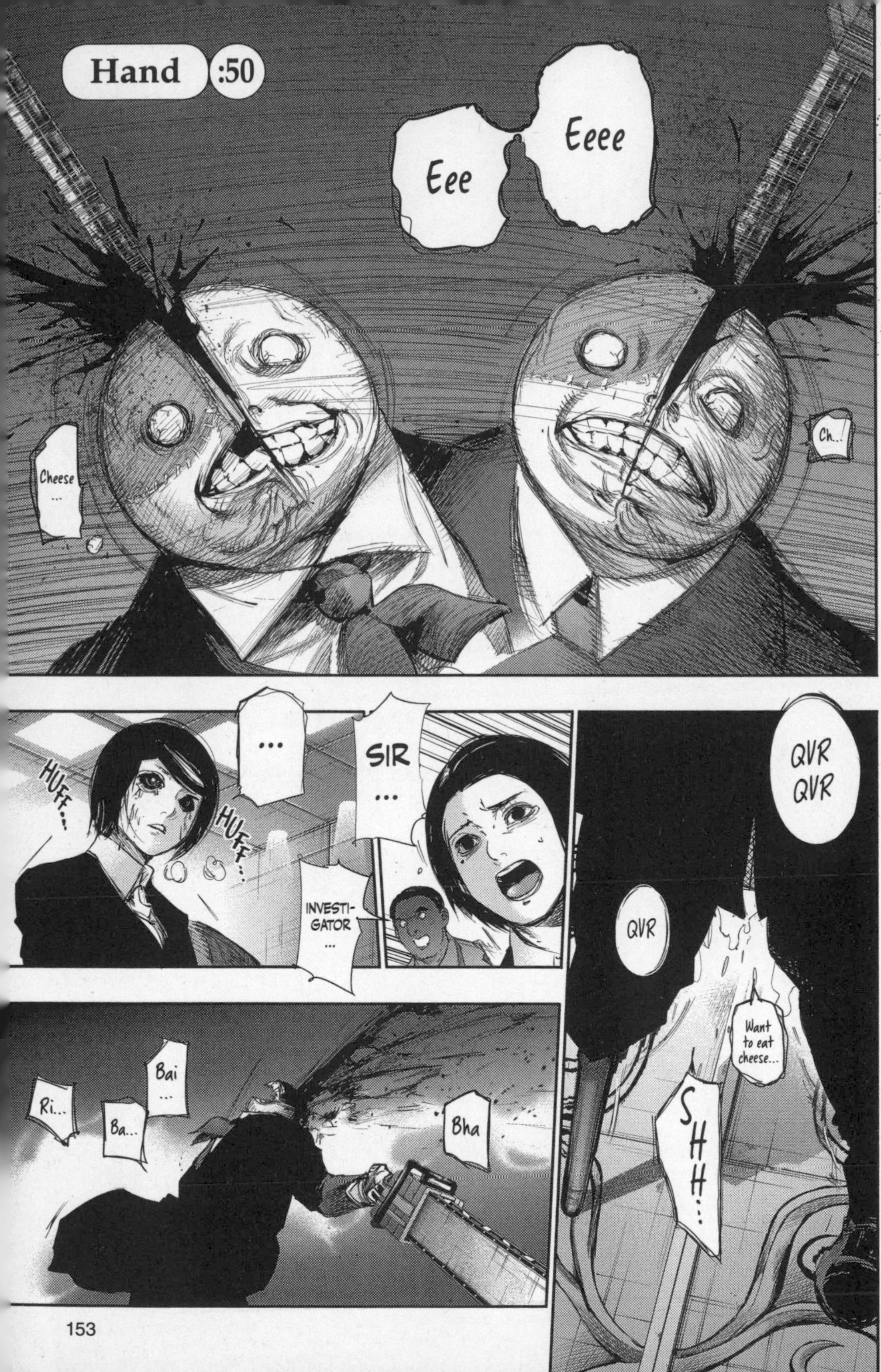

Hand :50
Eeee
Eee
Ch...
Cheese ...
QVR QVR
QVR
Want to eat cheese...
SHH...
SIR ...
INVESTIGATOR ...
...
HUFF...
HUFF...
Bha
Bai ...
Ba...
Ri...

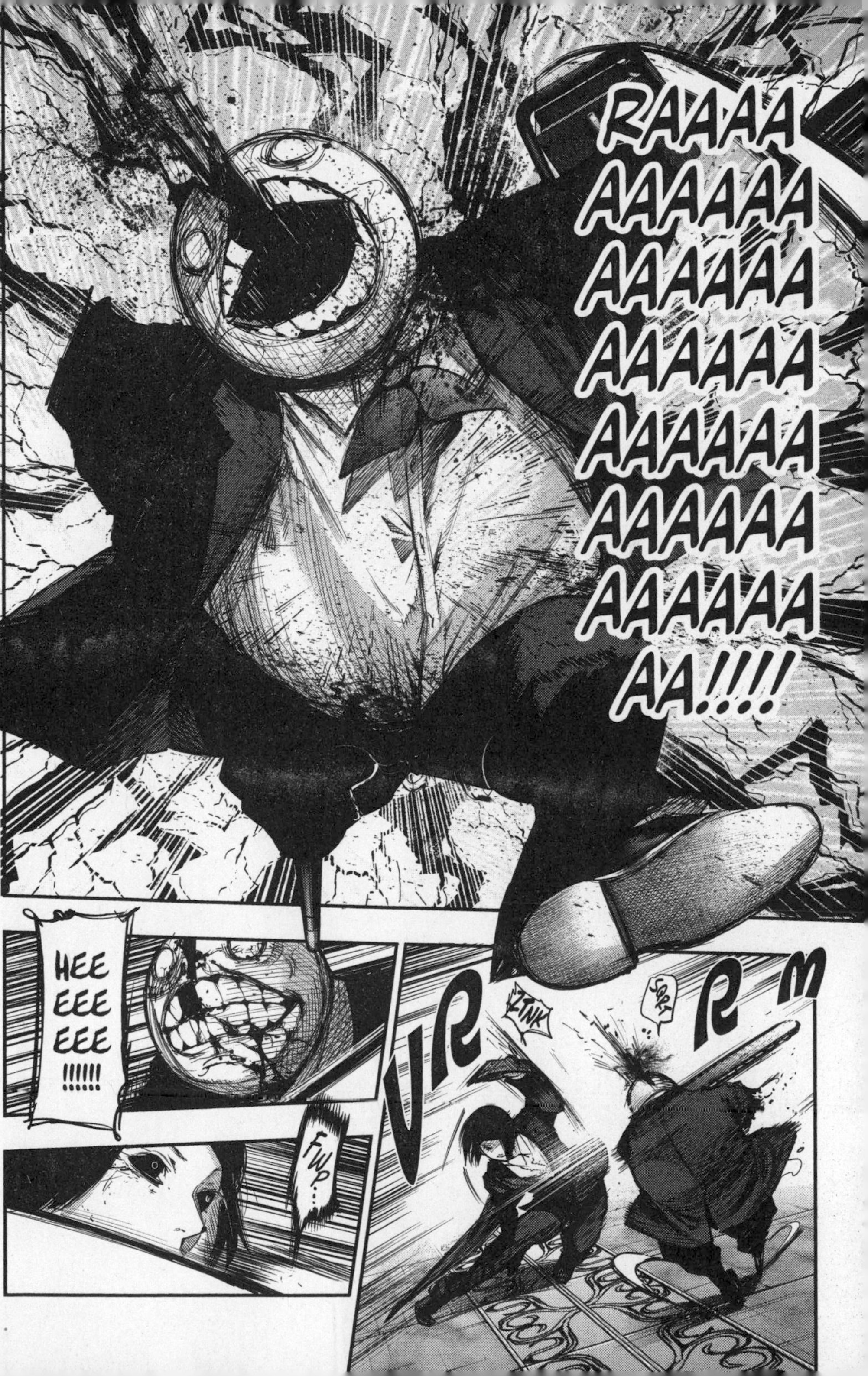
RAAAA AAAAAA AAAAAA AAAAAA AAAAAA AAAAAA AAAAAA AA!!!!
VRRM
SQRT
ZINK
HEE EEE EEE !!!!!!
FWP...

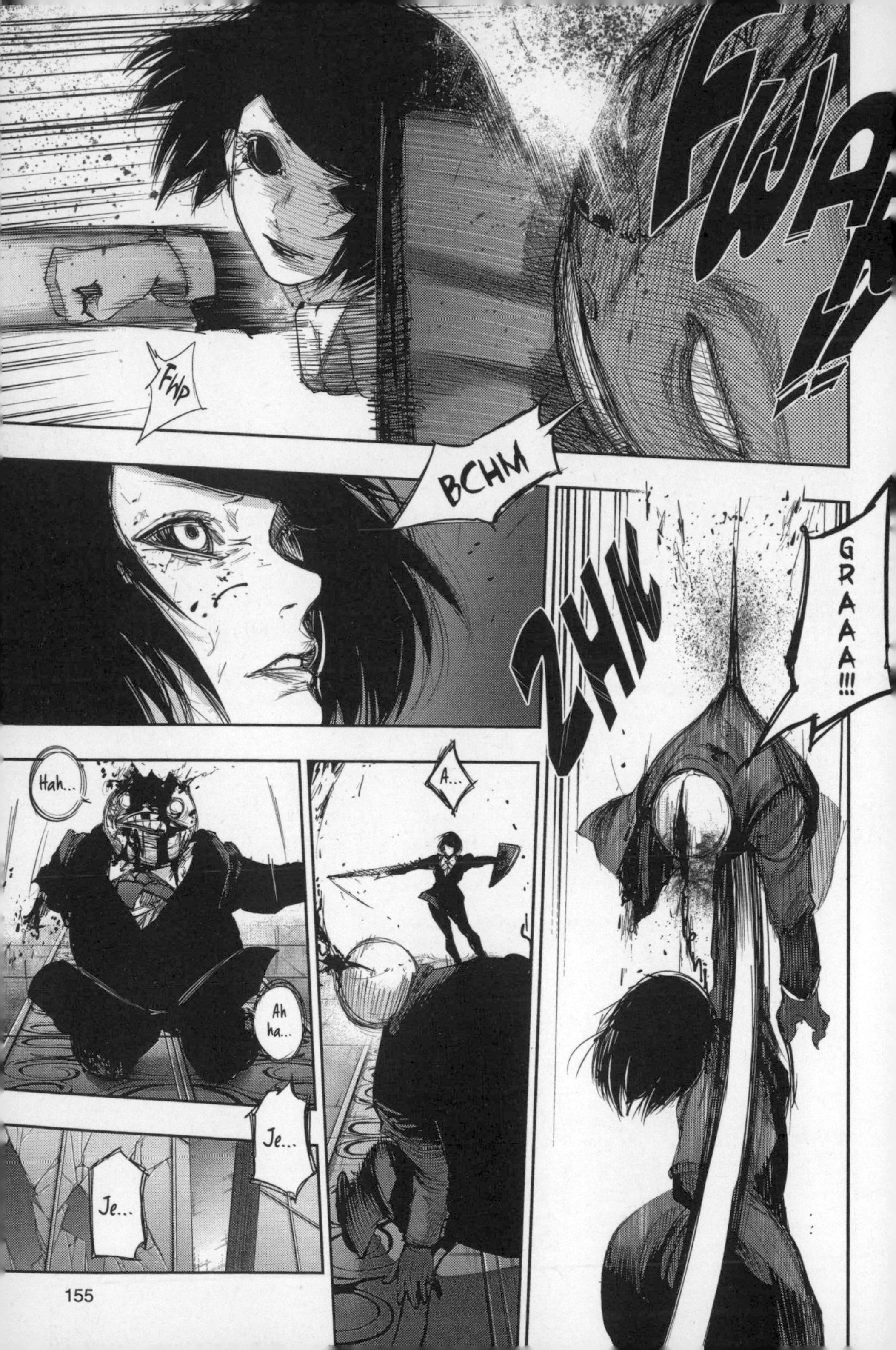
GWAH!!
Fwp
GRAAAA!!!
ZHK
BCHM
A...
Hah...
Ah ha...
Je...
Je...

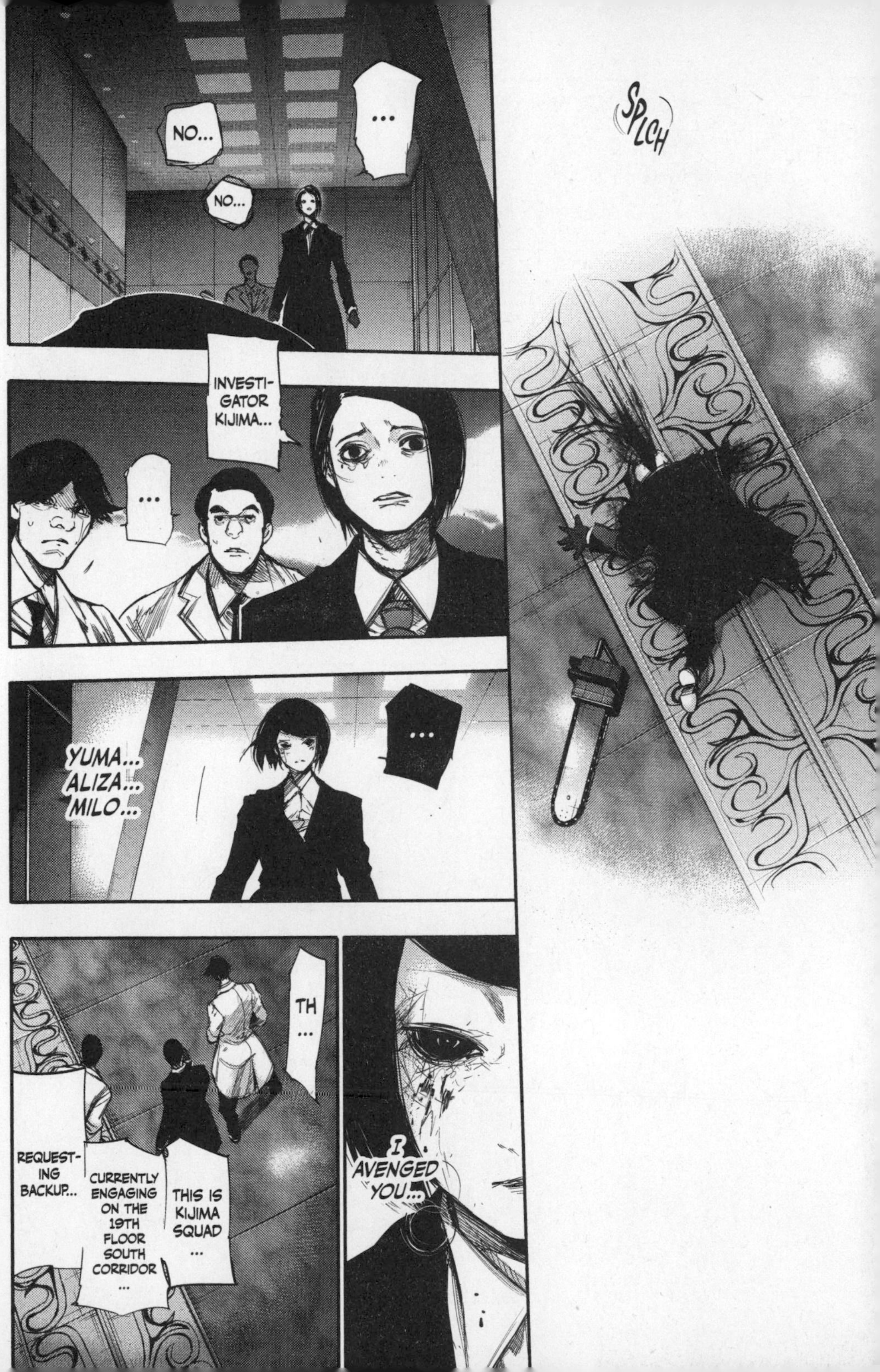
SPLCH
...
NO...
NO...
INVESTIGATOR KIJIMA...
...
...
YUMA... ALIZA... MILO...
TH...
I AVENGED YOU...
THIS IS KIJIMA SQUAD...
CURRENTLY ENGAGING ON THE 19TH FLOOR SOUTH CORRIDOR...
REQUESTING BACKUP...

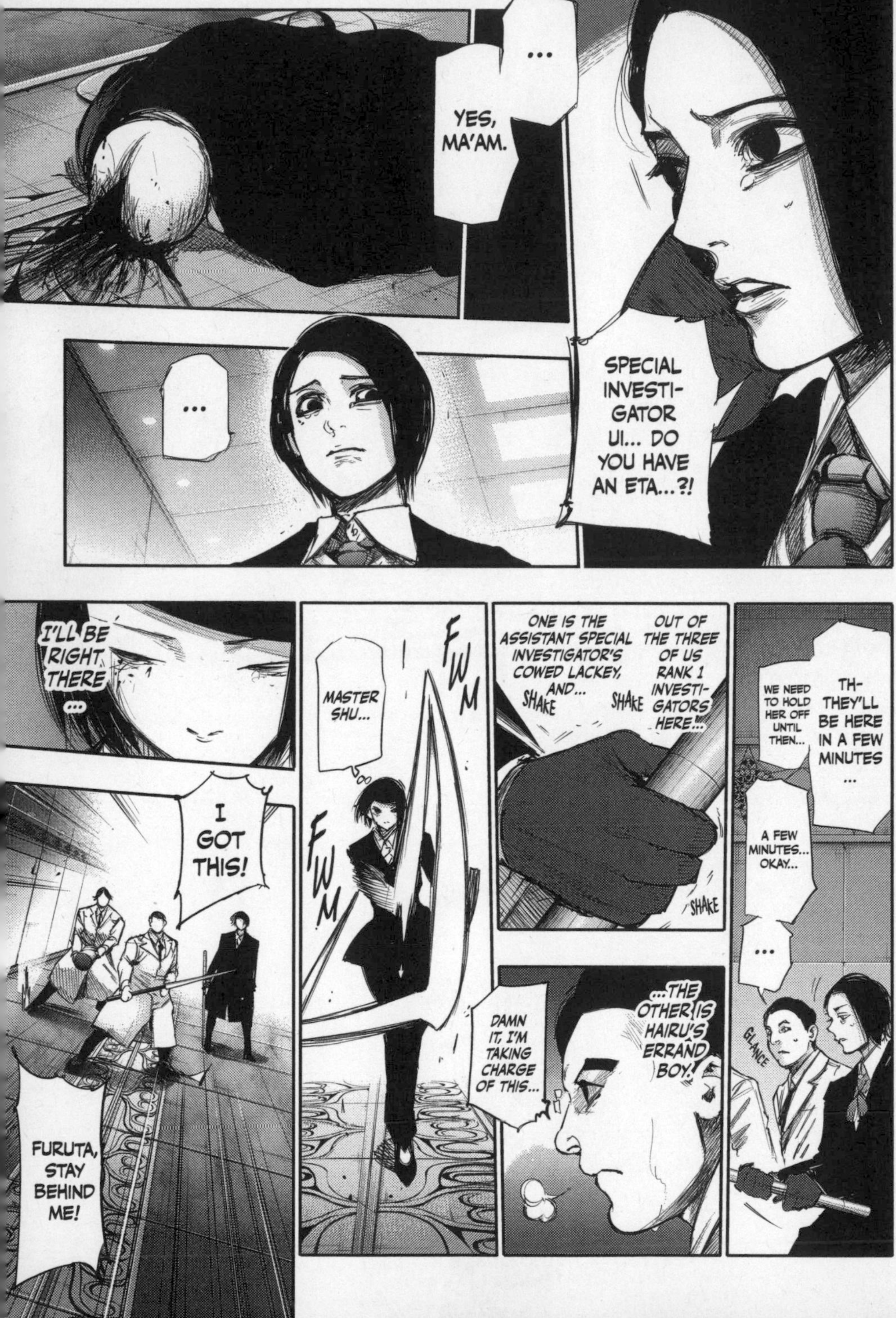
SPECIAL INVESTIGATOR UI... DO YOU HAVE AN ETA...?!
...
YES, MA'AM.
...
TH- THEY'LL BE HERE IN A FEW MINUTES...
WE NEED TO HOLD HER OFF UNTIL THEN...
A FEW MINUTES... OKAY...
...
GLANCE
OUT OF THE THREE OF US RANK 1 INVESTIGATORS HERE...
ONE IS THE ASSISTANT SPECIAL INVESTIGATOR'S COWED LACKEY, AND...
SHAKE
SHAKE
SHAKE
...THE OTHER IS HAIRU'S ERRAND BOY!
DAMN IT, I'M TAKING CHARGE OF THIS...
FWM
MASTER SHU...
FWM
I'LL BE RIGHT THERE...
I GOT THIS!
FURUTA, STAY BEHIND ME!

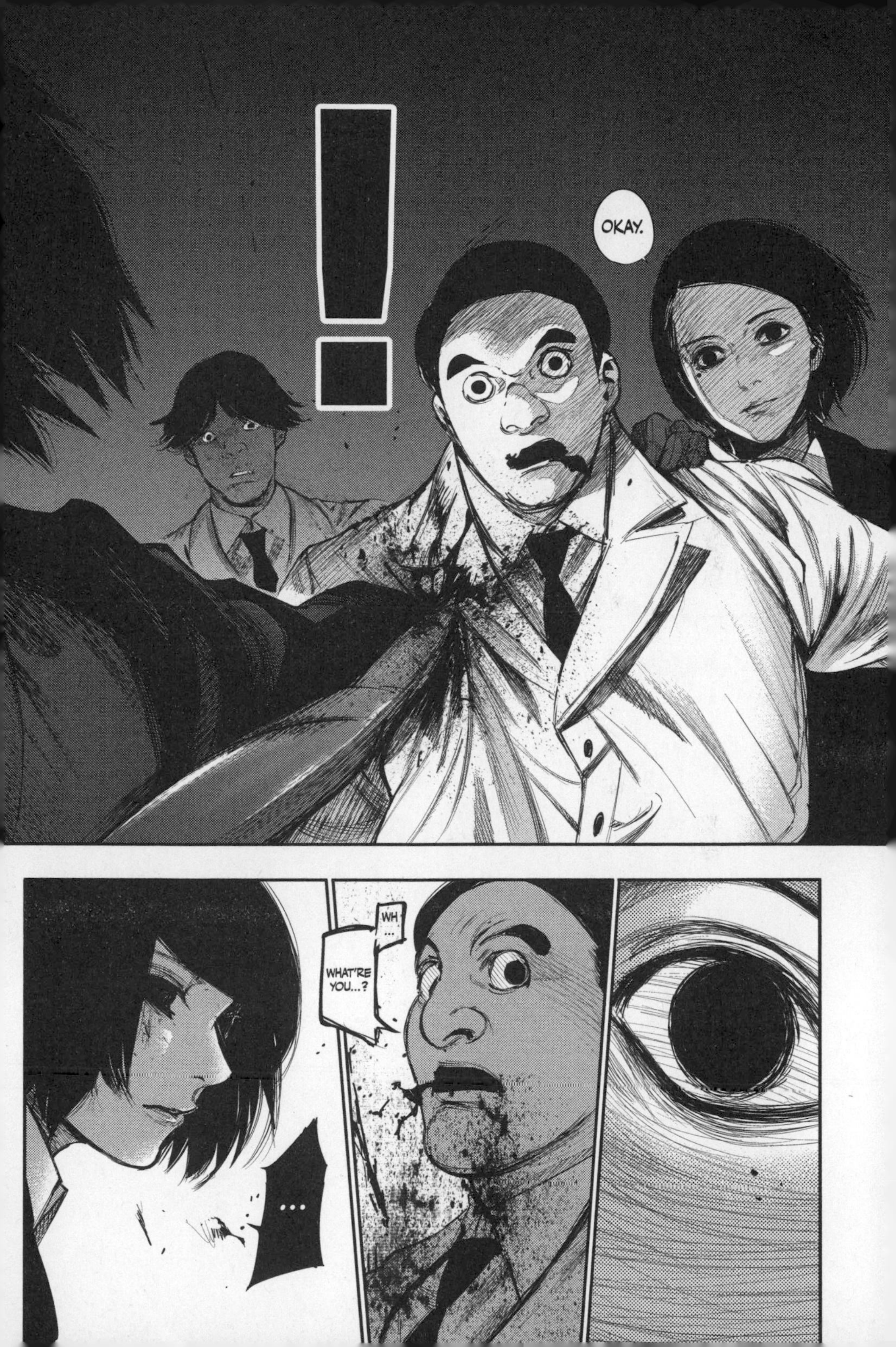
OKAY.
!
WH...
WHAT'RE YOU...?
...

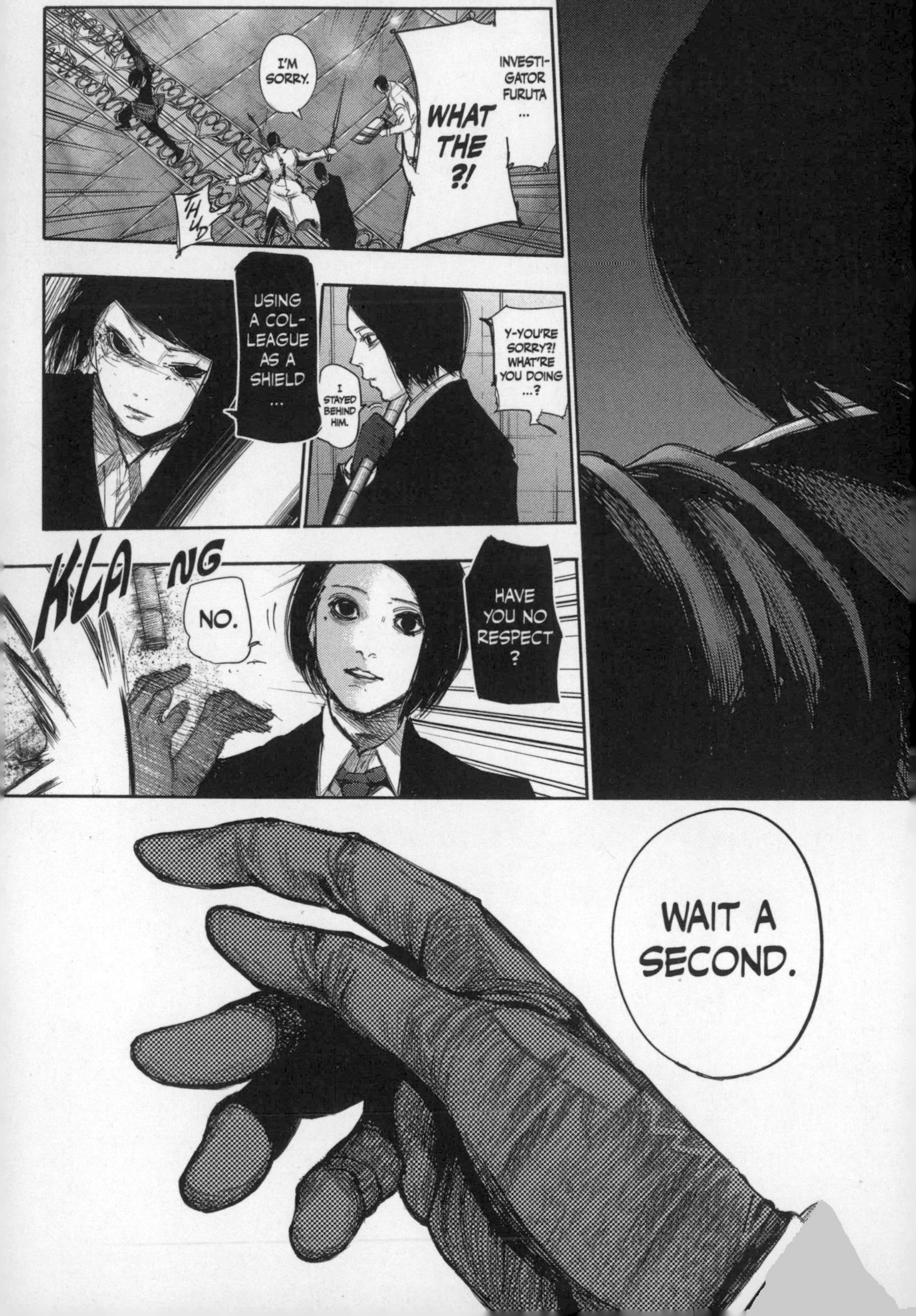
INVESTI-
GATOR
FURUTA
...
WHAT
THE
?!
I'M
SORRY.
THUD
Y-YOU'RE
SORRY?!
WHAT'RE
YOU DOING
...?
I
STAYED
BEHIND
HIM.
USING
A COL-
LEAGUE
AS A
SHIELD
...
HAVE
YOU NO
RESPECT
?
NO.
KLANG
WAIT A
SECOND.

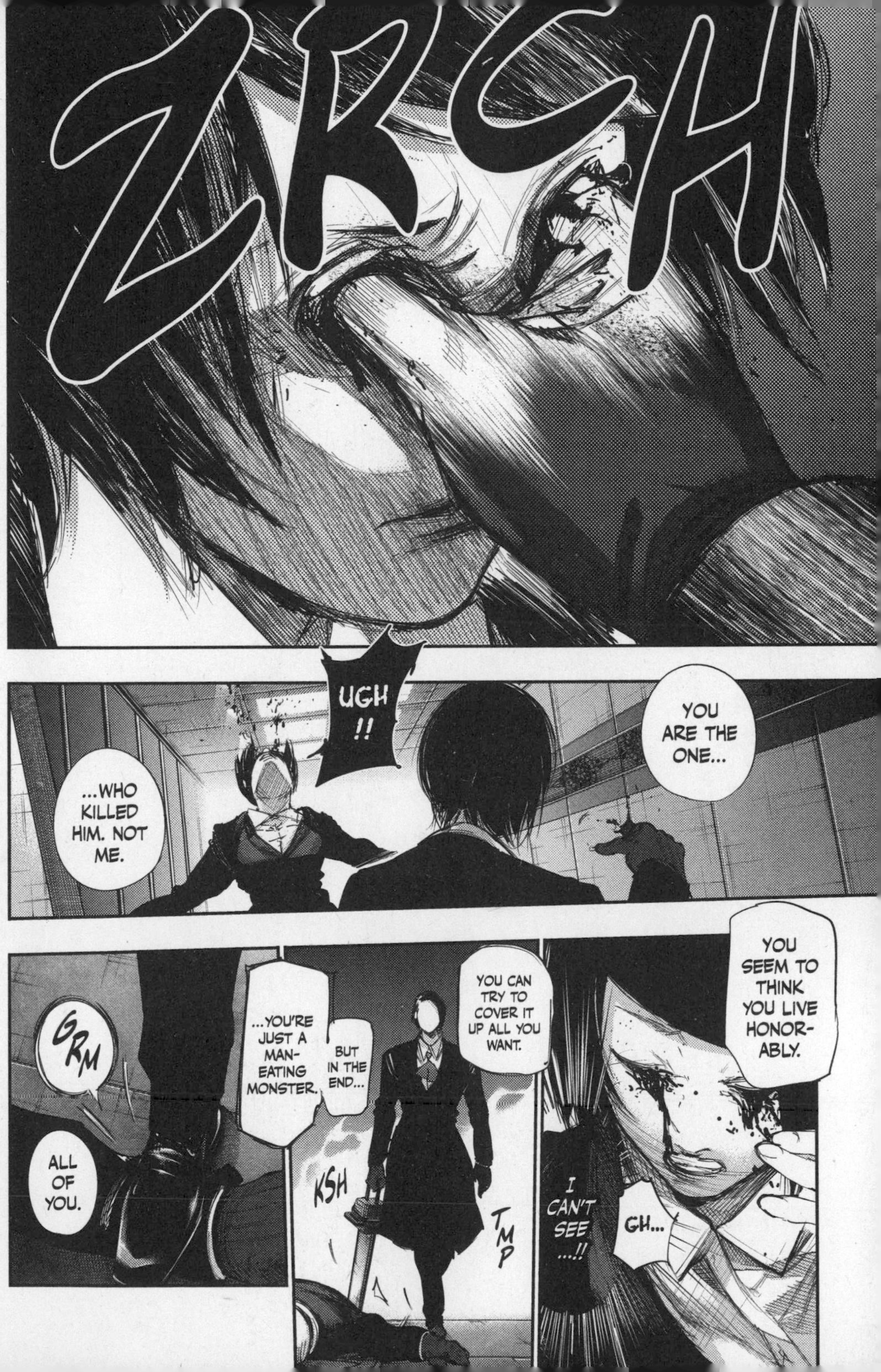
ZRCH
YOU ARE THE ONE...
UGH !!
...WHO KILLED HIM. NOT ME.
YOU SEEM TO THINK YOU LIVE HONOR-ABLY.
GH...
I CAN'T SEE ...!!
YOU CAN TRY TO COVER IT UP ALL YOU WANT.
BUT IN THE END...
...YOU'RE JUST A MAN-EATING MONSTER.
TMP
KSH
GRM
ALL OF YOU.

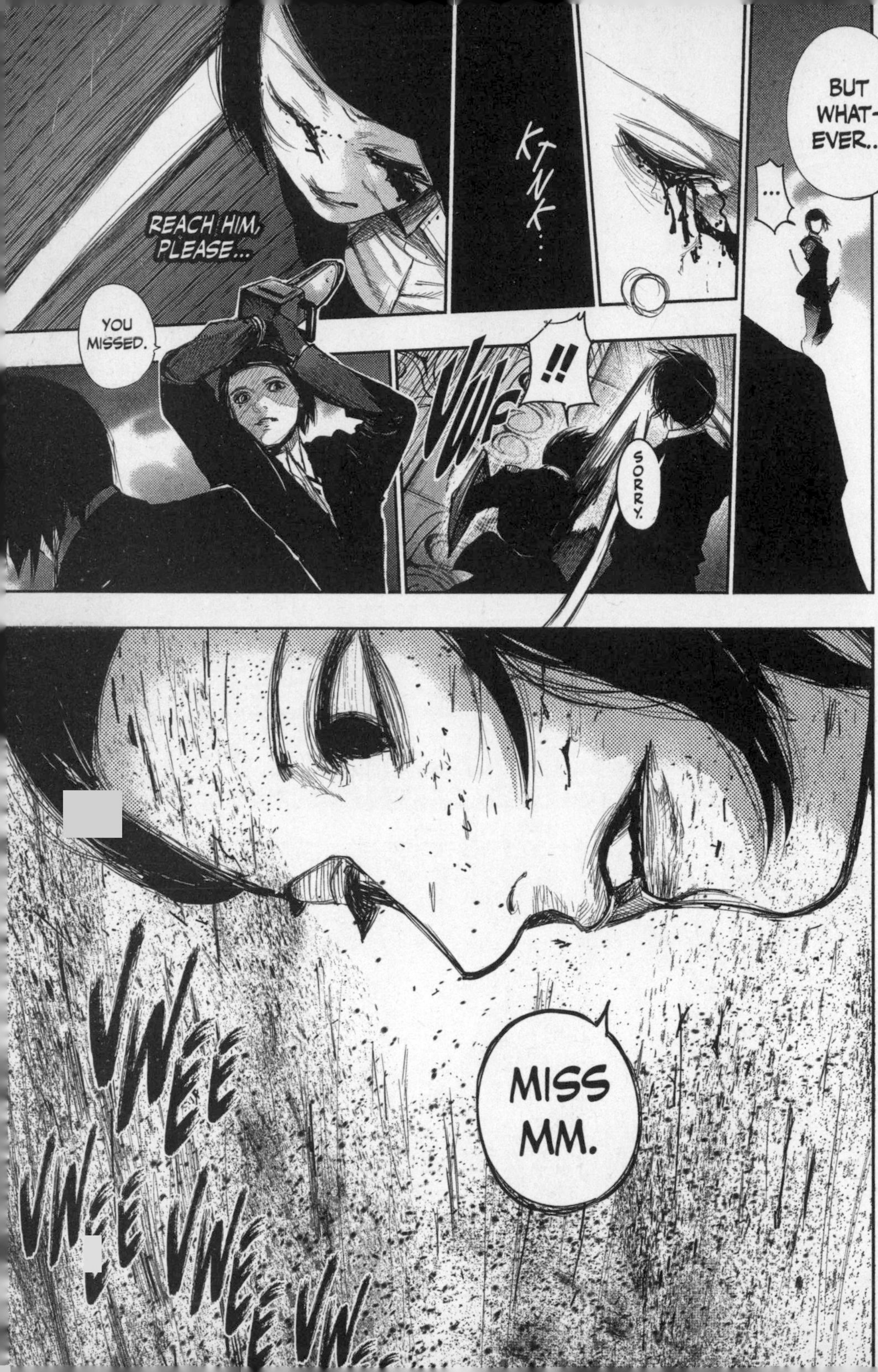

BUT WHAT-EVER...
...
KTINK...
REACH HIM, PLEASE...
!!
VWF
SORRY.
YOU MISSED.
MISS MM.
VWEE VWEE VWEE VWEE VW

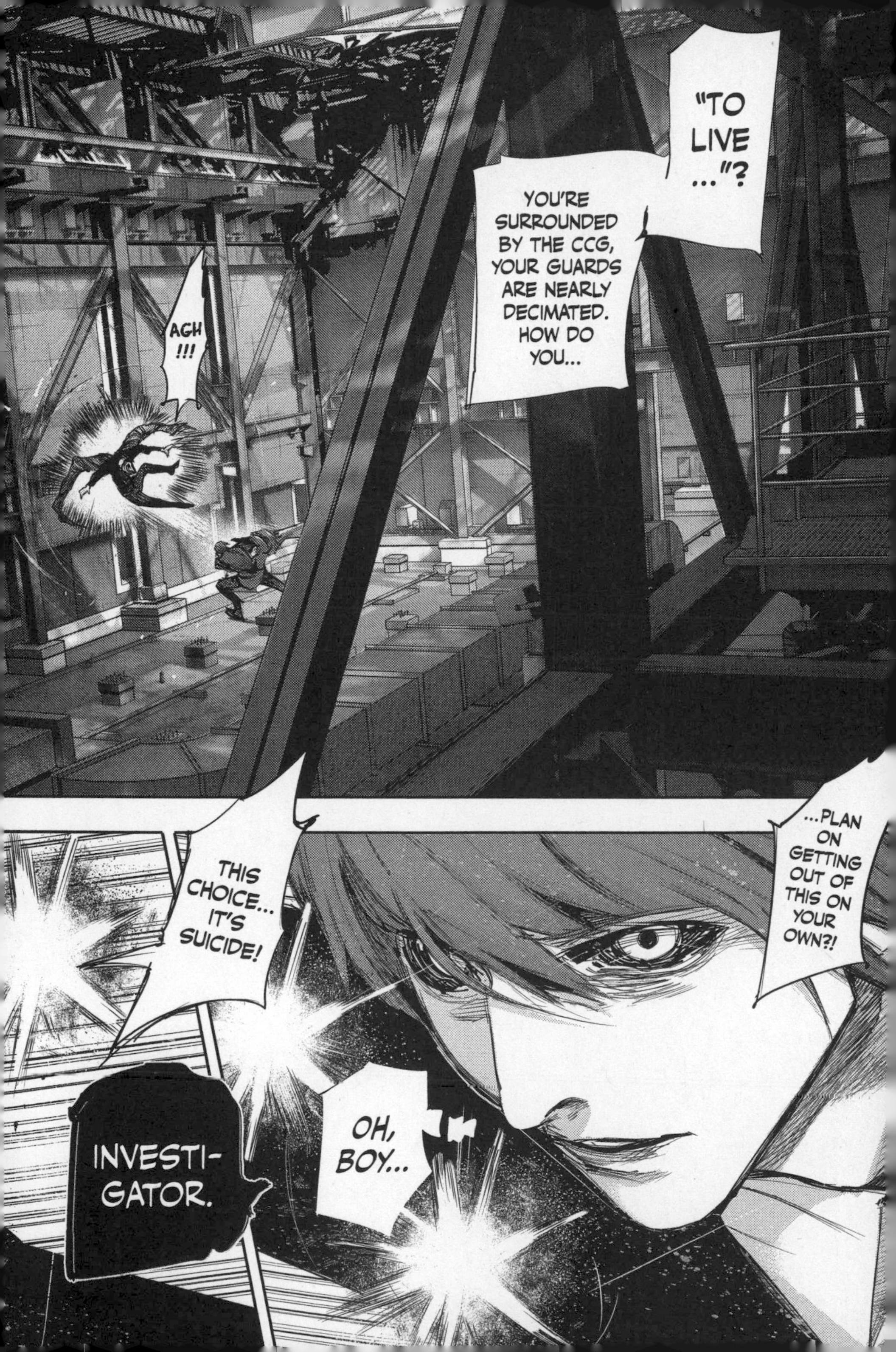
"TO LIVE ..."?
YOU'RE SURROUNDED BY THE CCG, YOUR GUARDS ARE NEARLY DECIMATED. HOW DO YOU...
AGH !!!
...PLAN ON GETTING OUT OF THIS ON YOUR OWN?!
THIS CHOICE... IT'S SUICIDE!
OH, BOY...
INVESTI-GATOR.

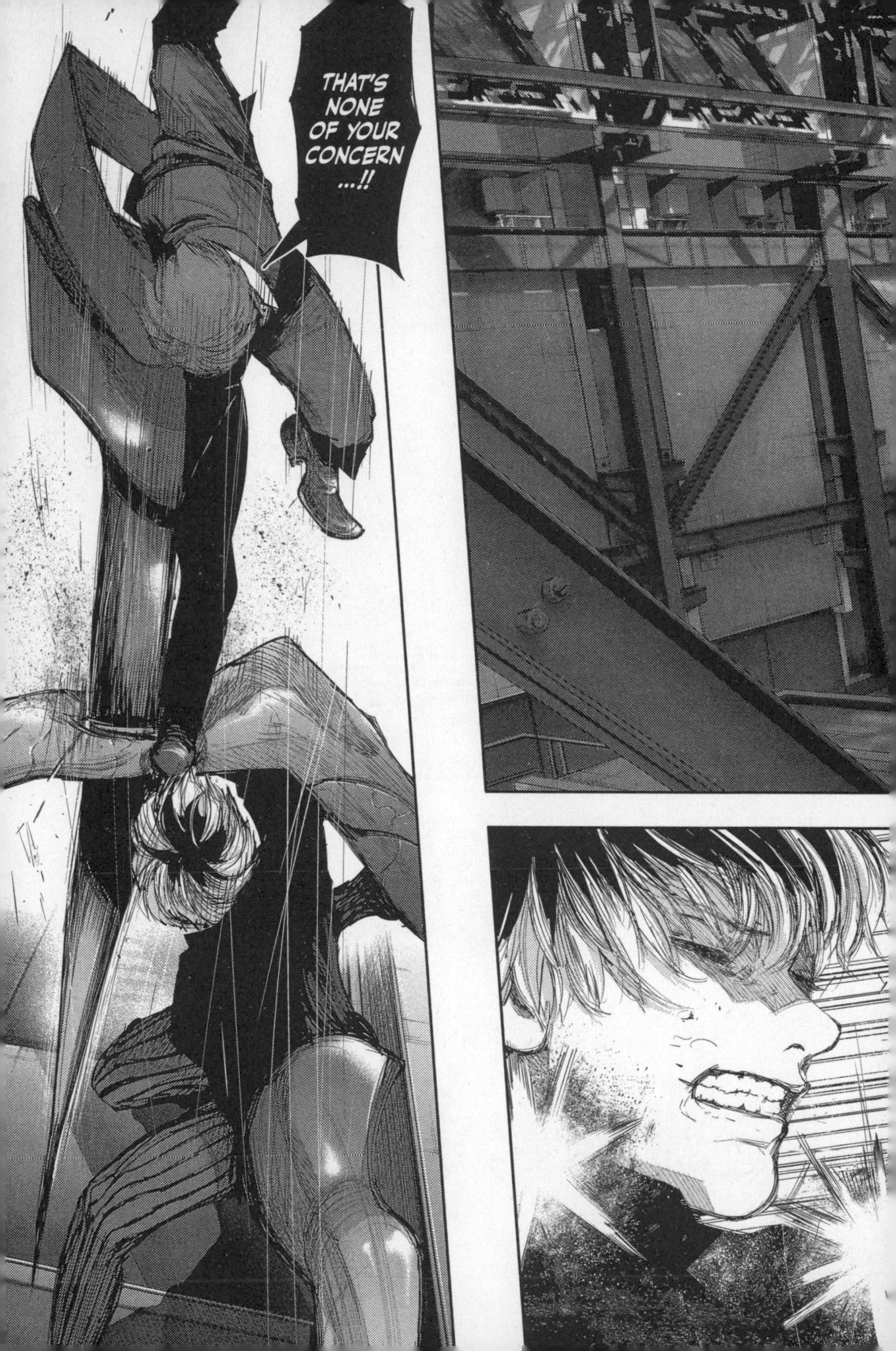
THAT'S NONE OF YOUR CONCERN ...!!

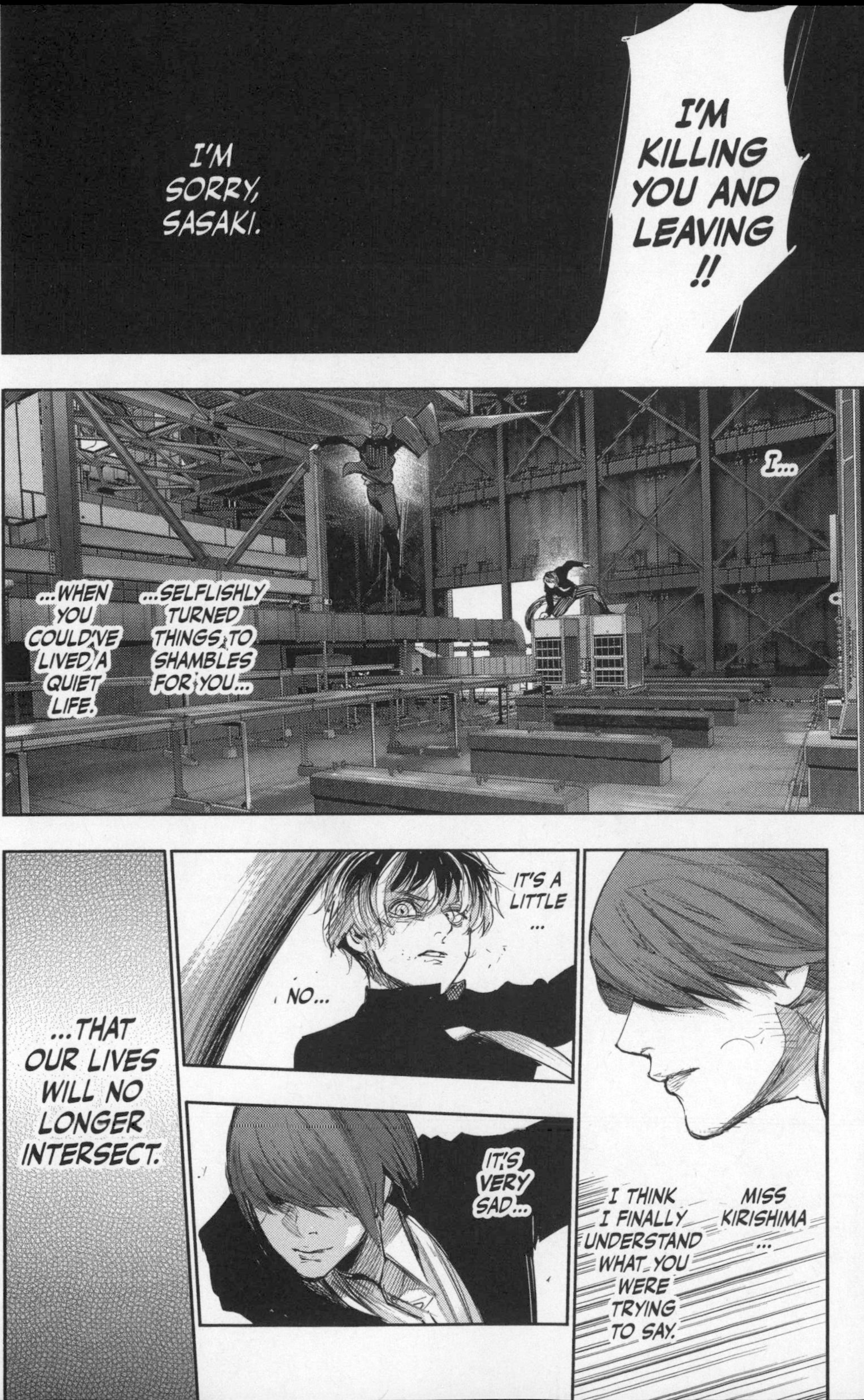
I'M KILLING YOU AND LEAVING !!
I'M SORRY, SASAKI.
I...
...SELFLISHLY TURNED THINGS TO SHAMBLES FOR YOU...
...WHEN YOU COULD'VE LIVED A QUIET LIFE.
MISS KIRISHIMA...
I THINK I FINALLY UNDERSTAND WHAT YOU WERE TRYING TO SAY.
IT'S A LITTLE ...
NO...
IT'S VERY SAD...
...THAT OUR LIVES WILL NO LONGER INTERSECT.

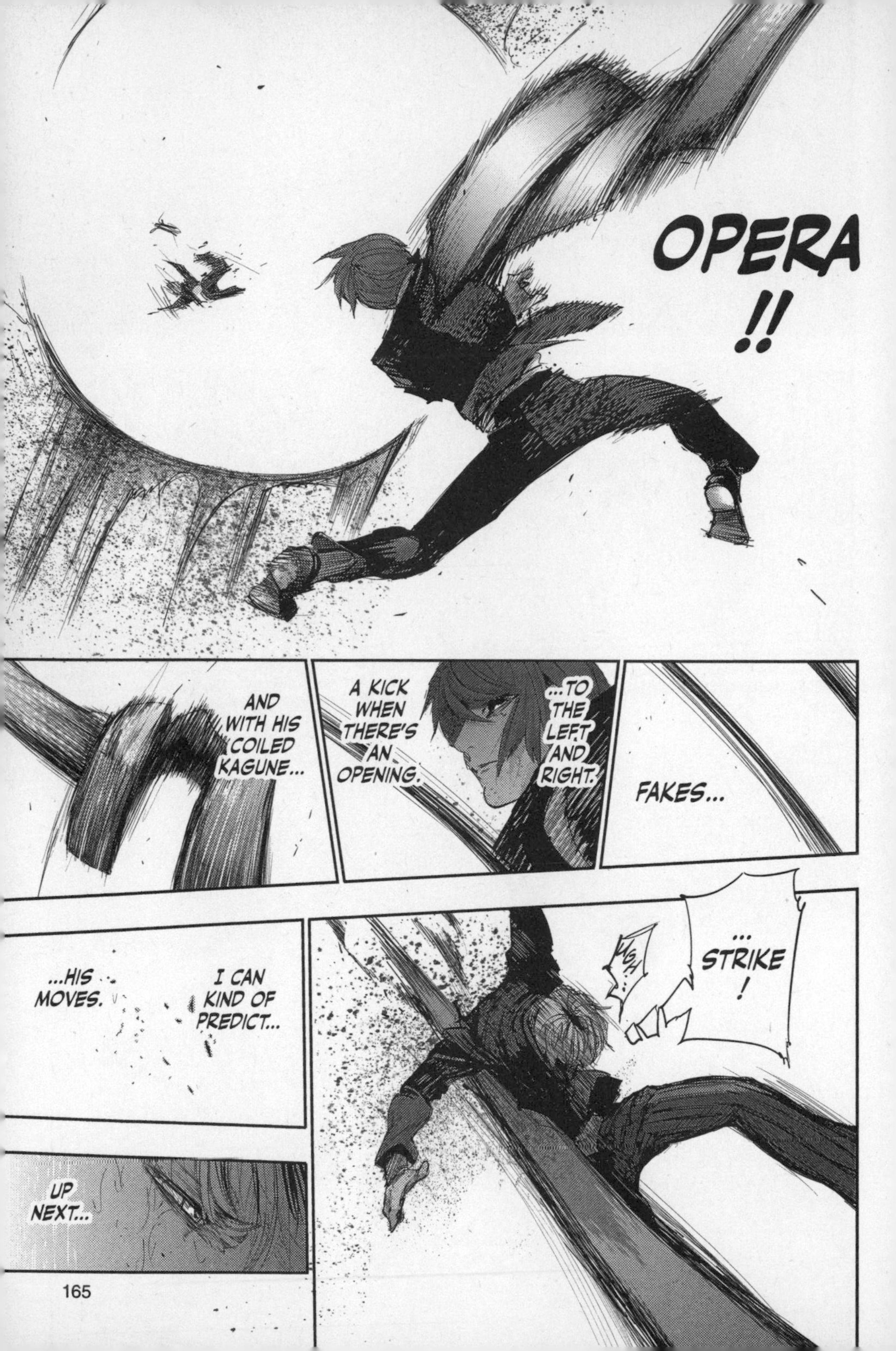
OPERA !!
FAKES...
...TO THE LEFT AND RIGHT.
A KICK WHEN THERE'S AN OPENING.
AND WITH HIS COILED KAGUNE...
...STRIKE!
I CAN KIND OF PREDICT...
...HIS MOVES.
UP NEXT...

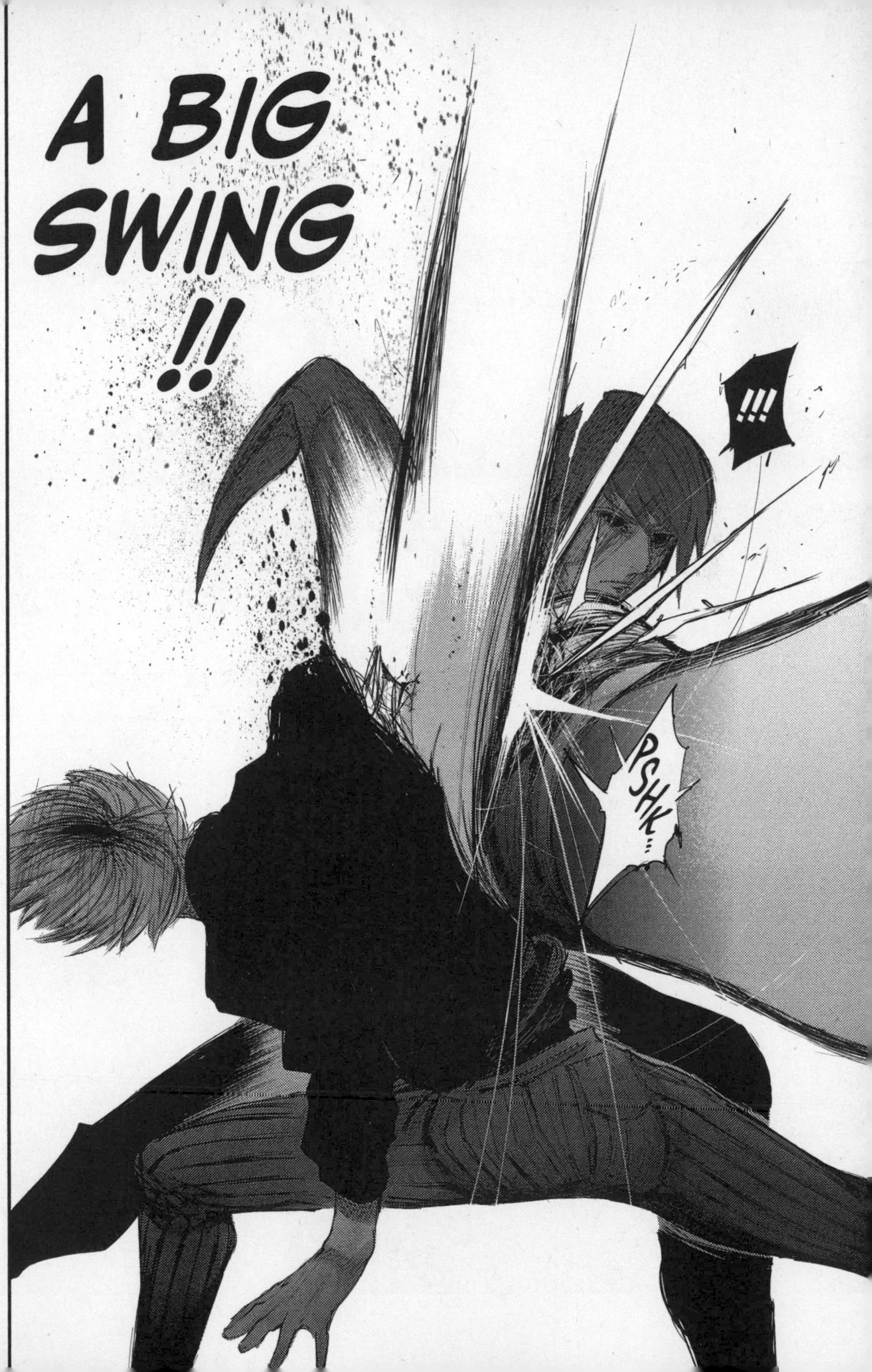
!!!
PSHK...
A BIG SWING!!

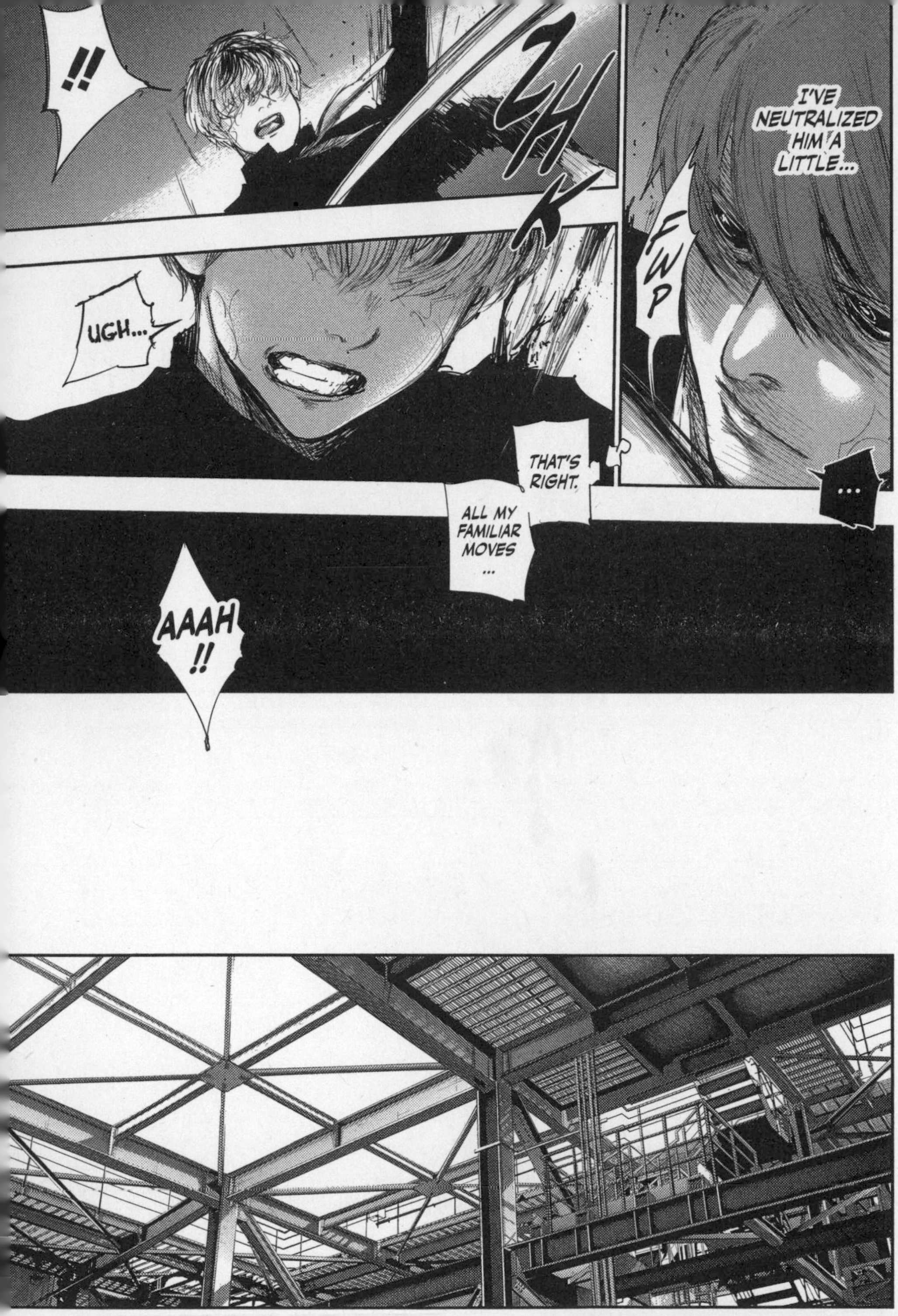
I'VE NEUTRALIZED HIM A LITTLE...
FWP
...
!!
ZHK
UGH...
THAT'S RIGHT.
ALL MY FAMILIAR MOVES ...
AAAH!!

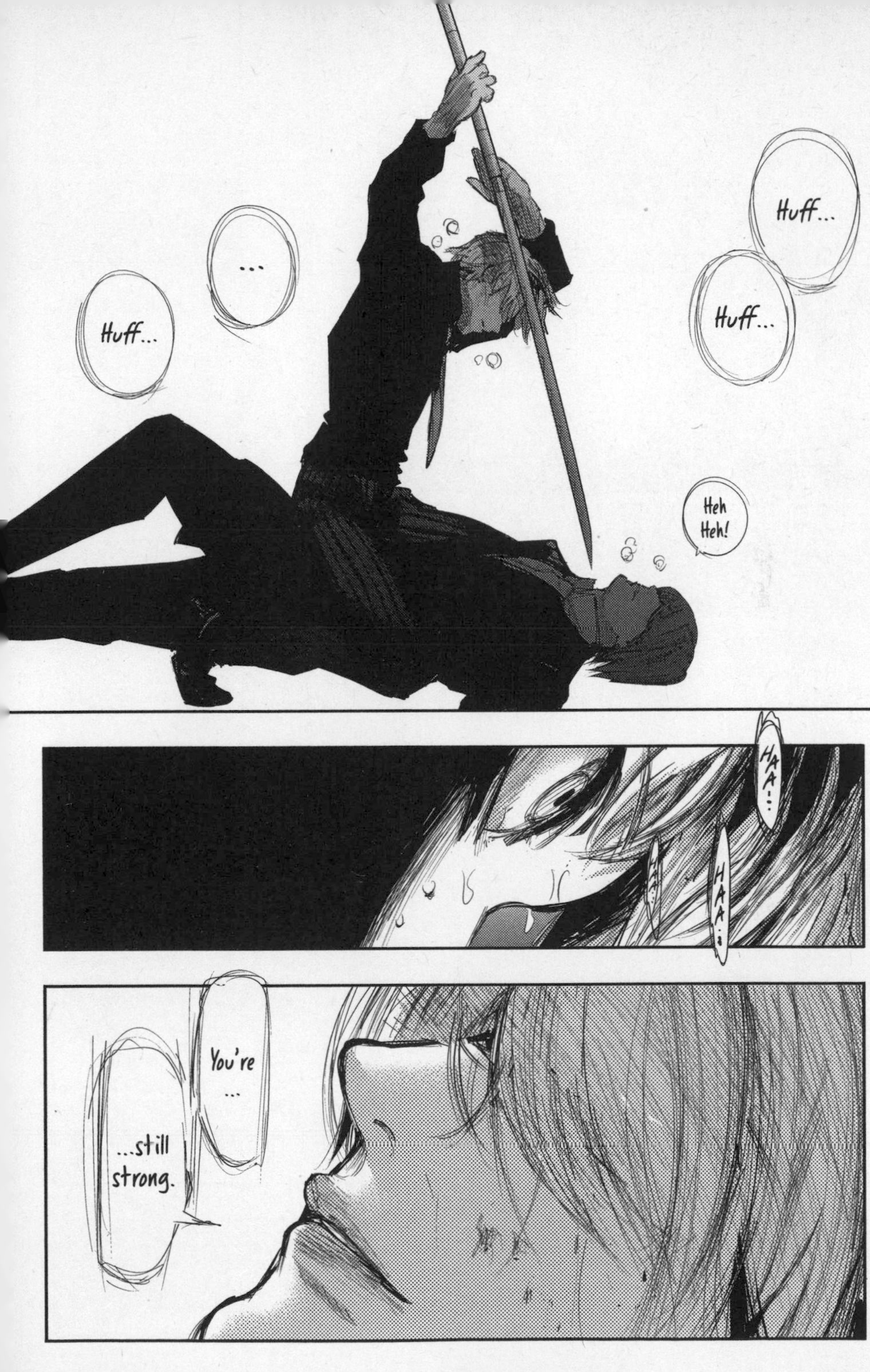
Huff...
Huff...
Heh Heh!
...
Huff...
HAA...
HAA...
You're ...
...still strong.

...
STING
STING
STING
STING
STING
STING
STING
STING
A...
WHAT'S THE MATTER, HAISE SASAKI ...?
KILL ME.
Huff ...
Huff ...
Huff ...
AARGH...
Huff ...
LL ME DON'T KILL ME
ON'T KILL ME DON'T
LL ME DON'T KILL ME
DON'T KILL ME DON'T
LL ME DON'T KILL ME
DON'T KILL ME DON'T
LL ME DON'T KILL ME DON'T
ME DON'T KILL ME DON'T
HOW!!!!!
"CHOOSE" "CHOOSE"
HOW...?
...

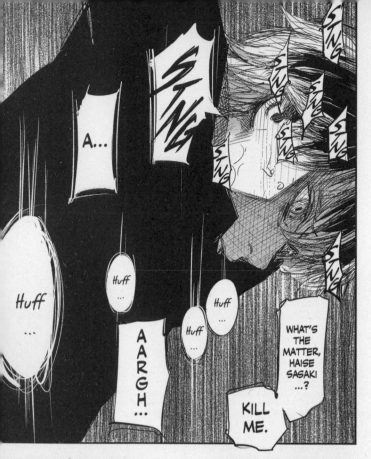

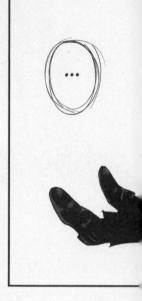

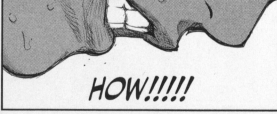

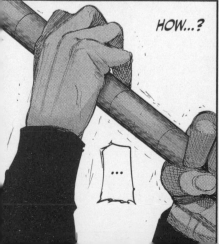

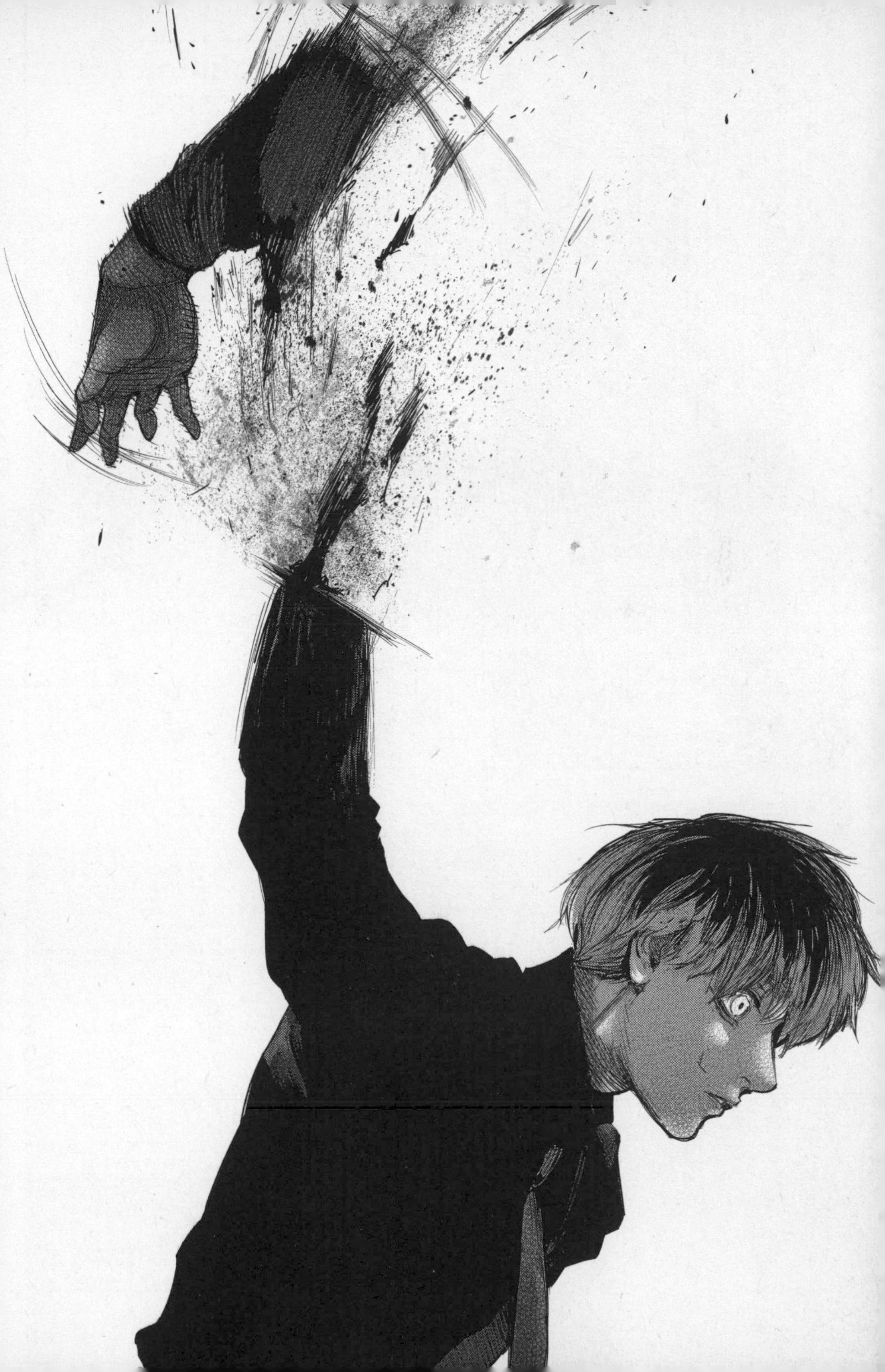

Resolution :51

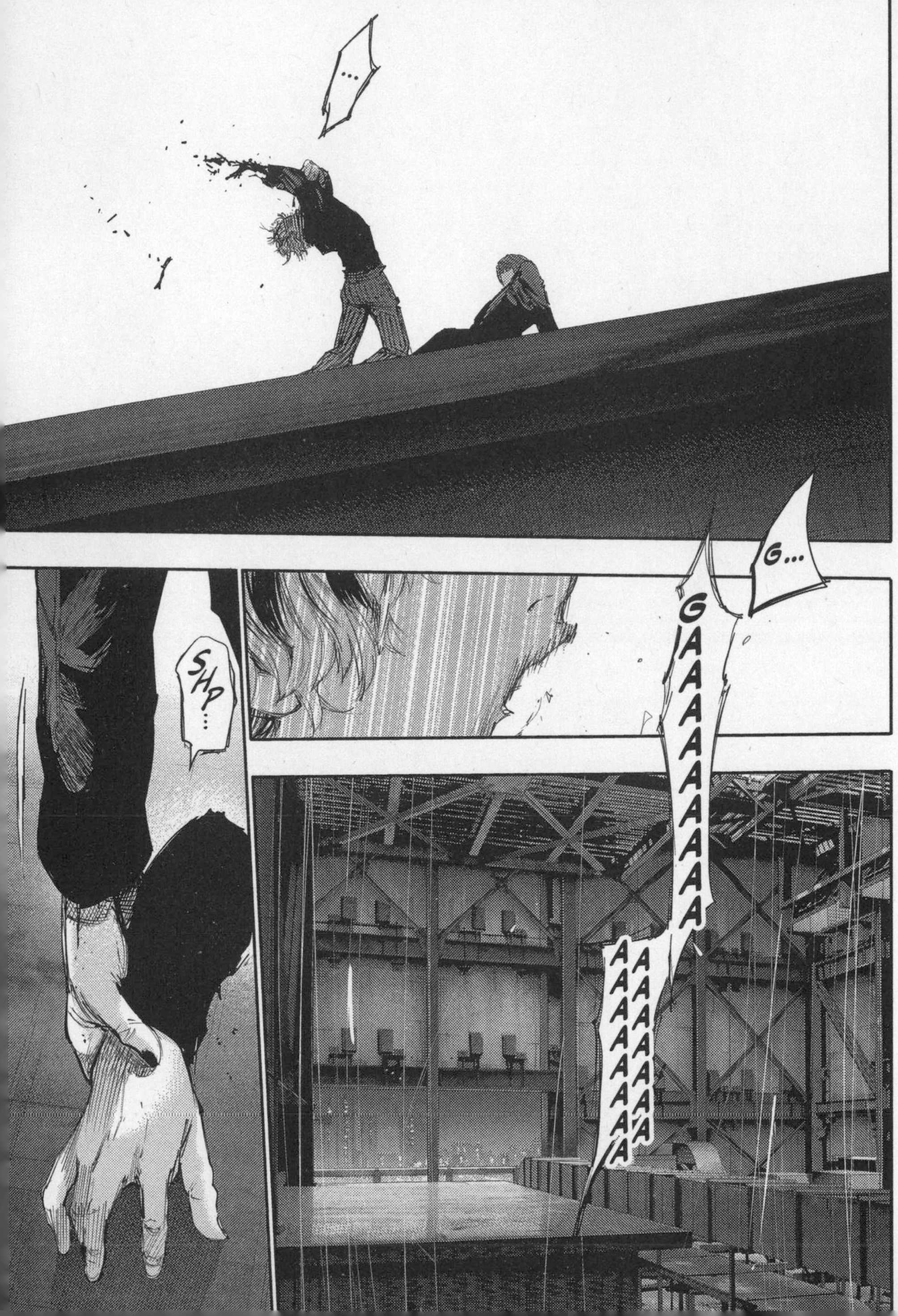
...
G...
GAAAAAAAAAAAAAAAAAAAAAAAA
SHP...

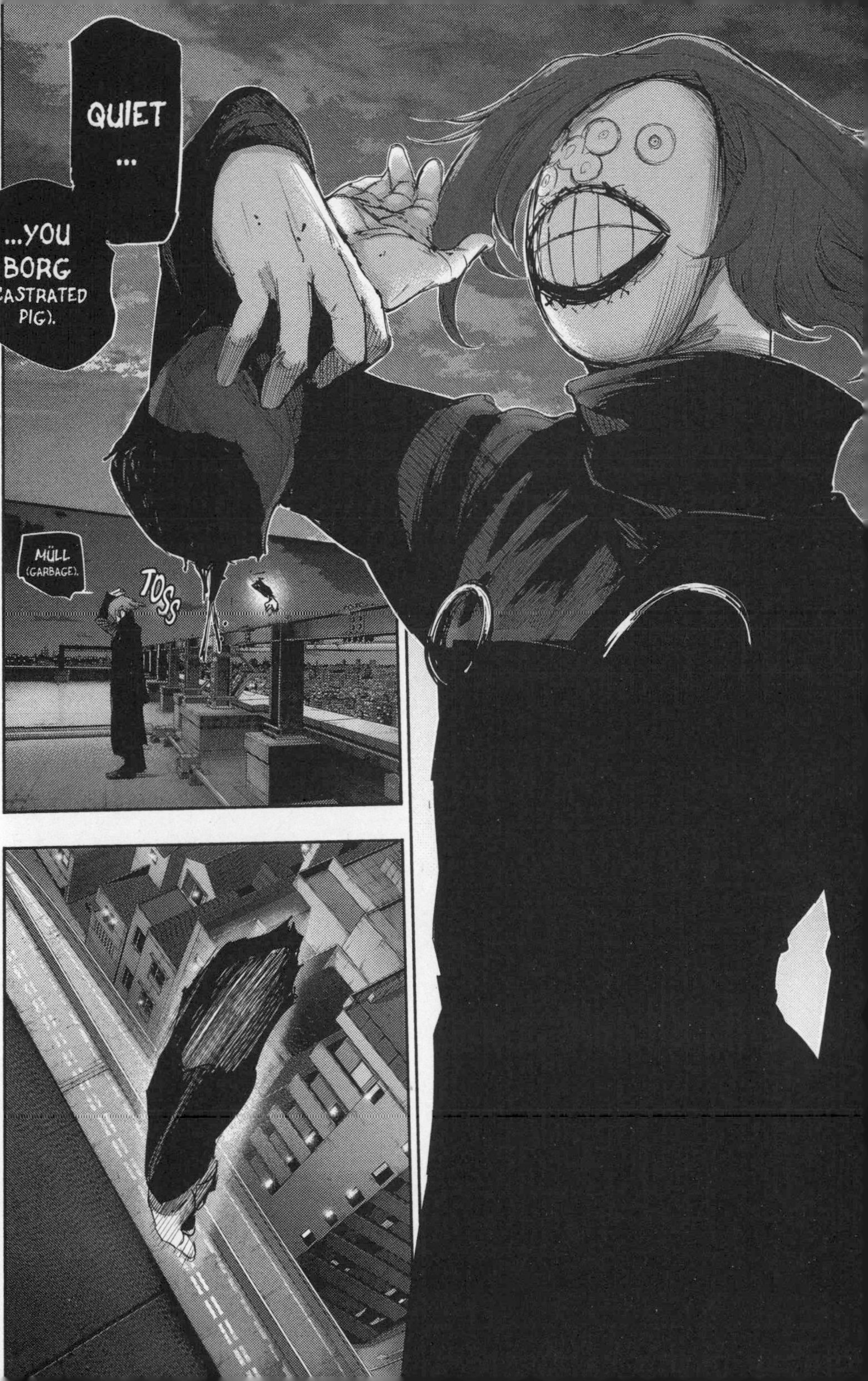
QUIET ...
...YOU BORG (CASTRATED PIG).
TOSS
MÜLL (GARBAGE).

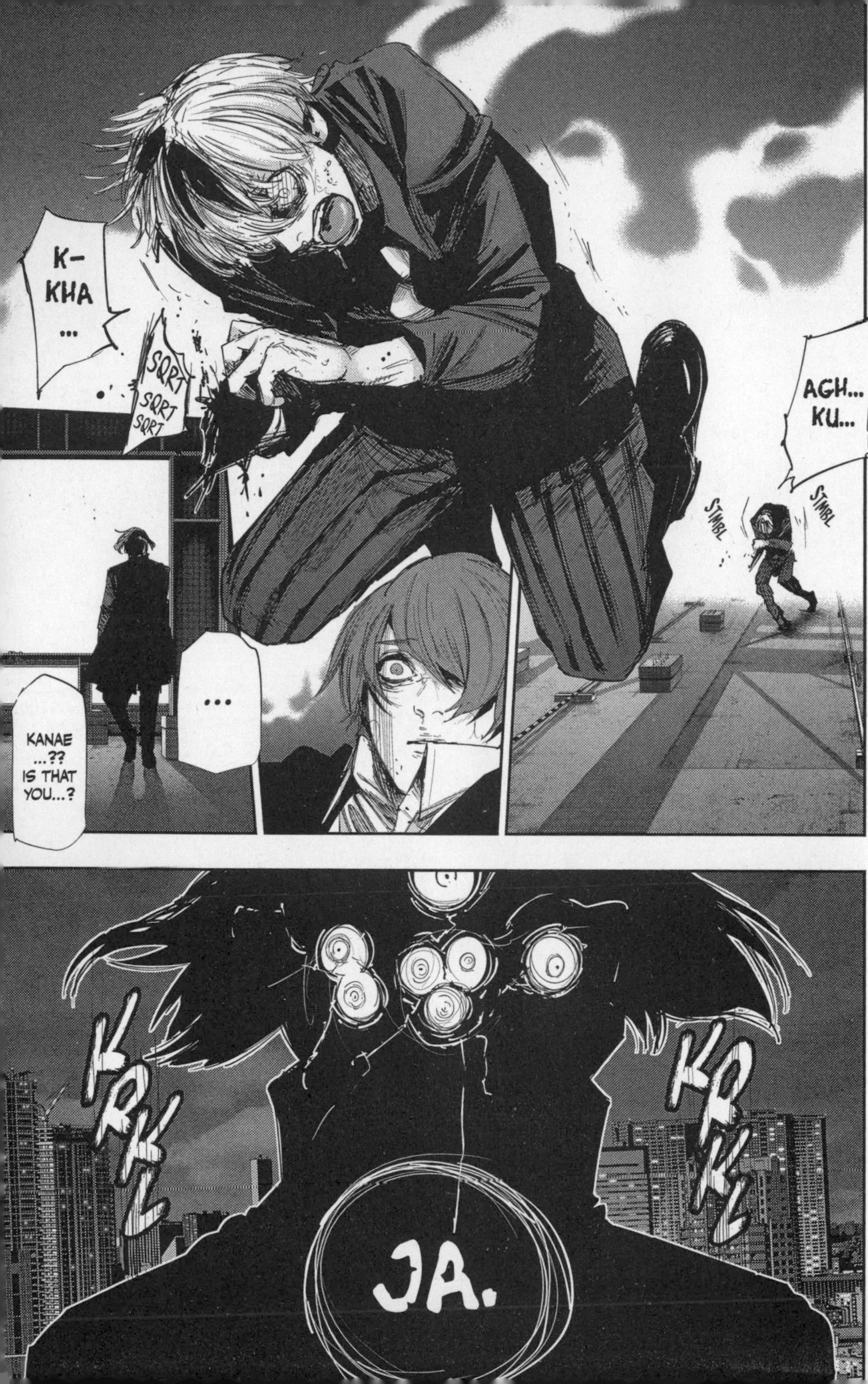
K- KHA ...
SQRT SQRT SQRT
AGH... KU...
STMBL
STMBL
...
KANAE ...?? IS THAT YOU...?
KRKL
KRKL
JA.

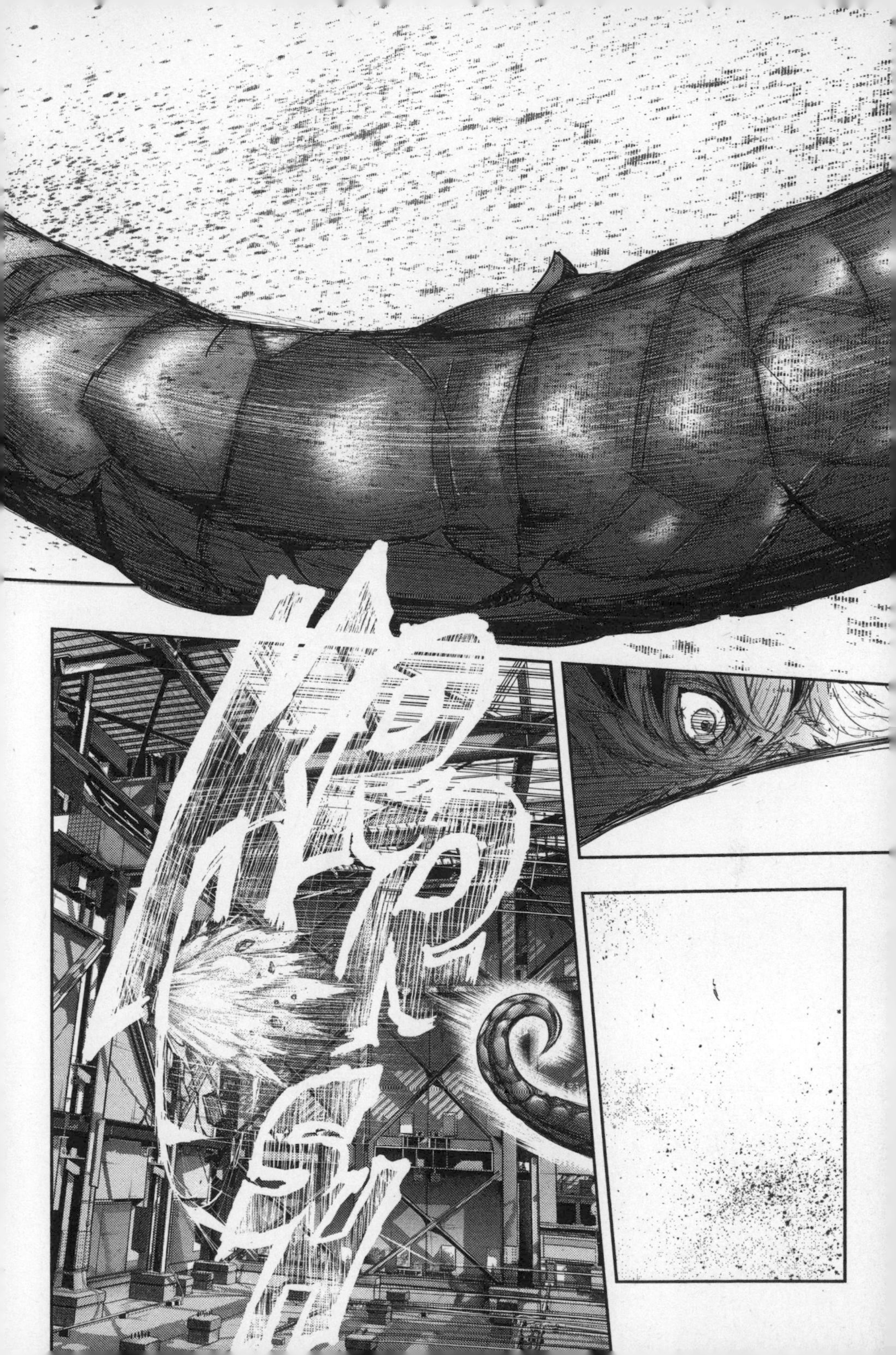

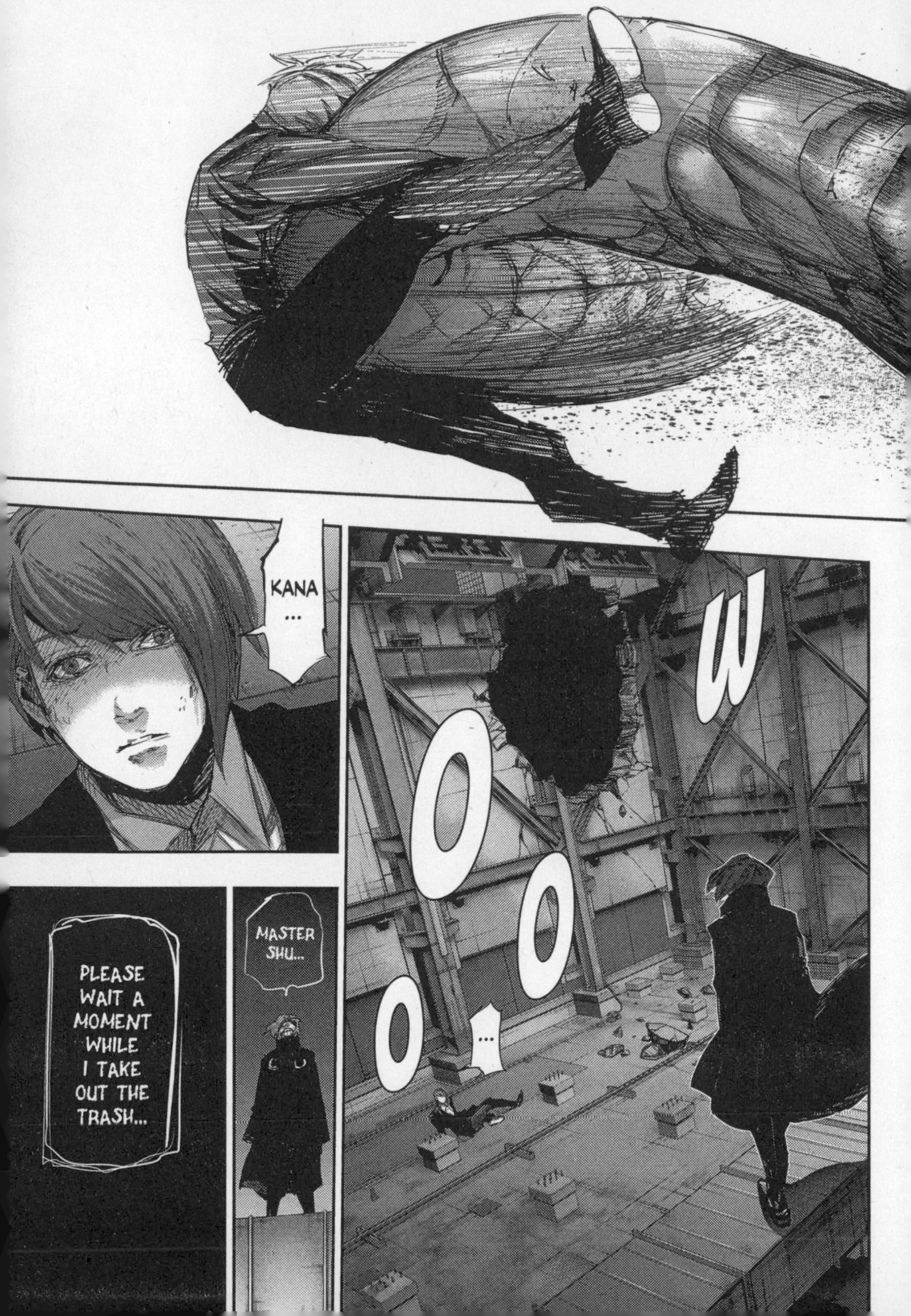
WOOOO
...
KANA ...
MASTER SHU...
PLEASE WAIT A MOMENT WHILE I TAKE OUT THE TRASH...

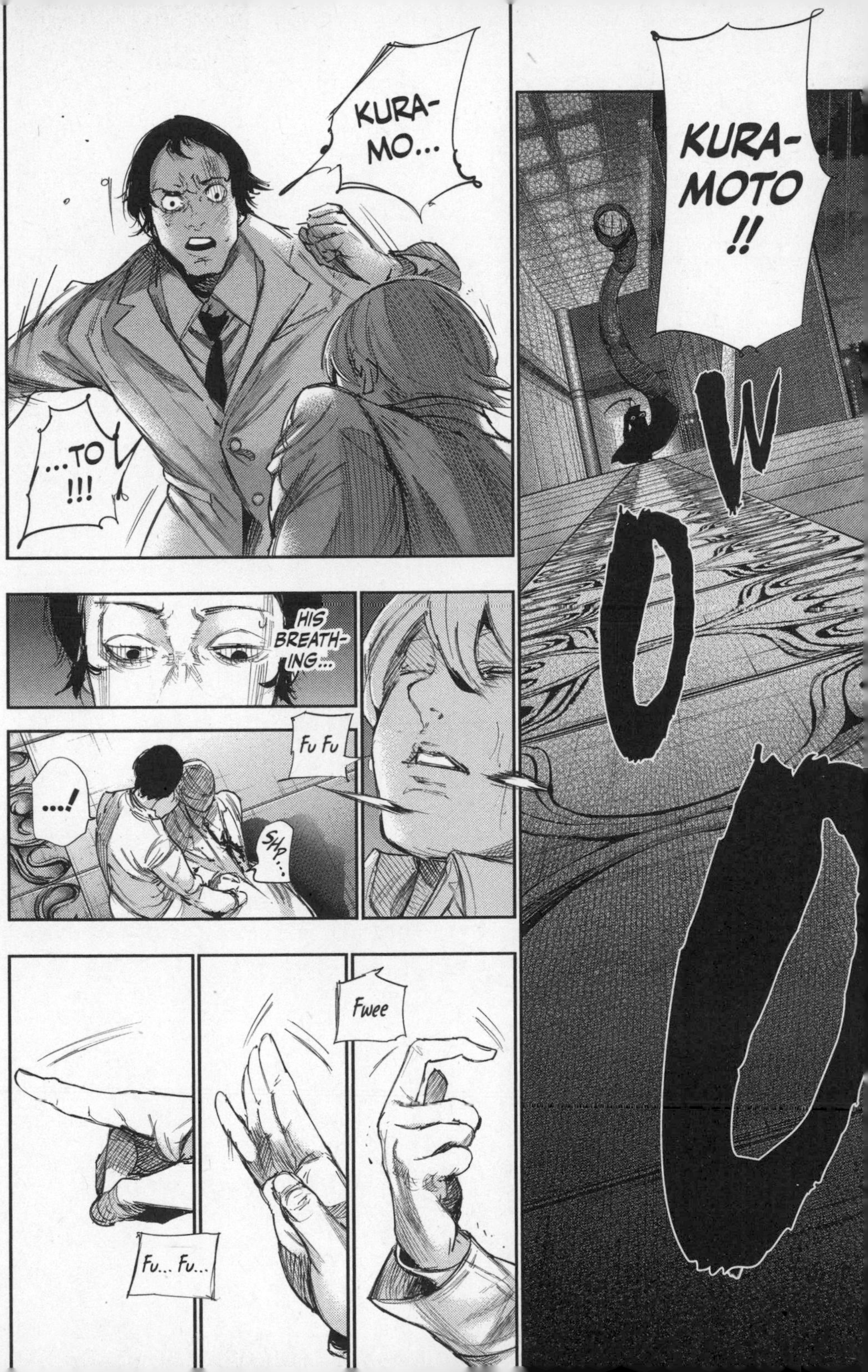
KURA-MOTO !!
WOO
KURA-MO...
...TO !!!
HIS BREATH-ING...
Fu Fu
...!
Shp...
Fwee
Fu... Fu...

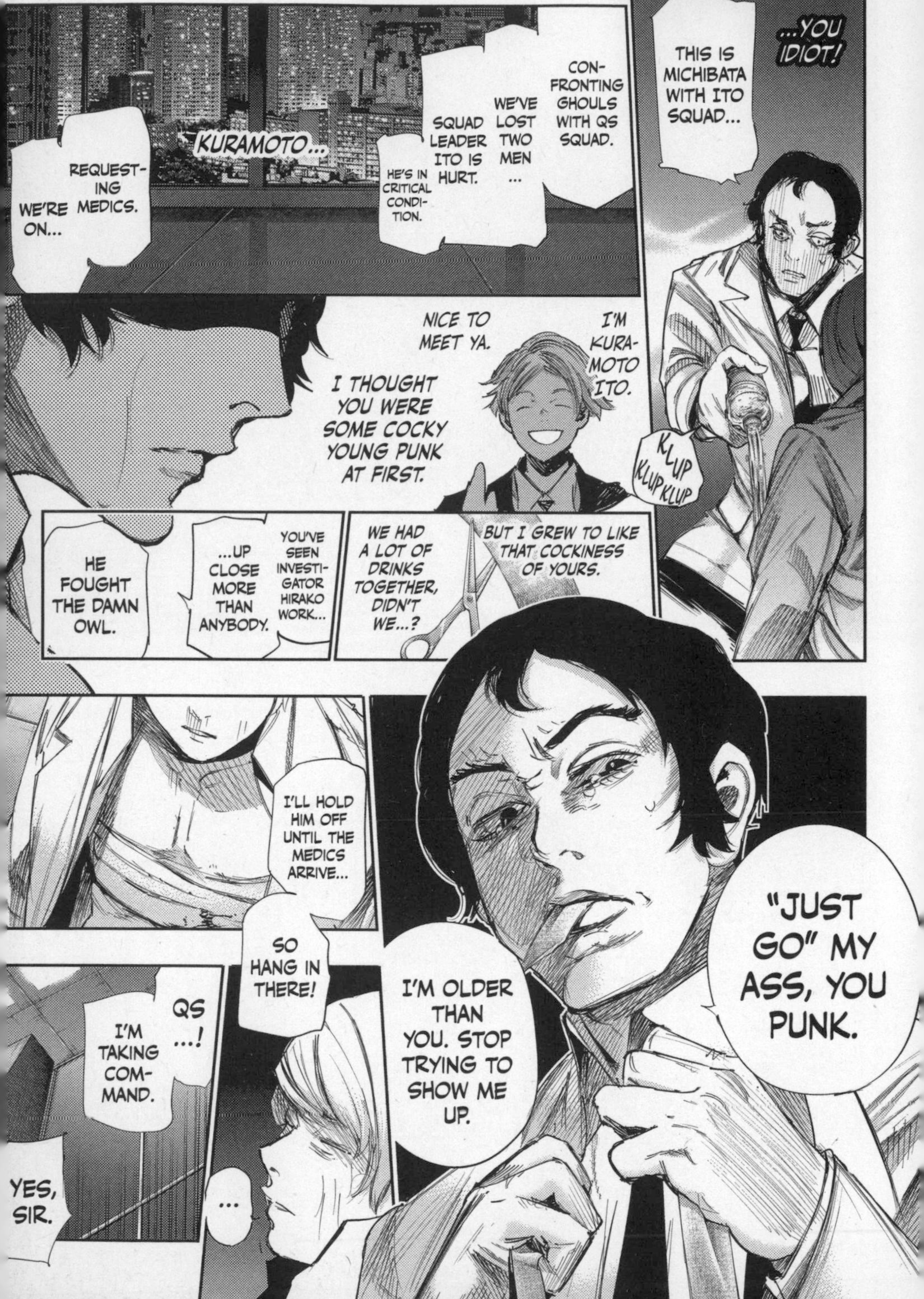
...YOU IDIOT!
THIS IS MICHIBATA WITH ITO SQUAD...
KLUP KLUP KLUP
CON-FRONTING GHOULS WITH QS SQUAD.
WE'VE LOST TWO MEN ...
SQUAD LEADER ITO IS HURT.
HE'S IN CRITICAL CONDI-TION.
KURAMOTO...
REQUEST-ING MEDICS.
WE'RE ON...
I'M KURA-MOTO ITO.
NICE TO MEET YA.
I THOUGHT YOU WERE SOME COCKY YOUNG PUNK AT FIRST.
BUT I GREW TO LIKE THAT COCKINESS OF YOURS.
WE HAD A LOT OF DRINKS TOGETHER, DIDN'T WE...?
YOU'VE SEEN INVESTI-GATOR HIRAKO WORK...
...UP CLOSE MORE THAN ANYBODY.
HE FOUGHT THE DAMN OWL.
"JUST GO" MY ASS, YOU PUNK.
I'M OLDER THAN YOU. STOP TRYING TO SHOW ME UP.
I'LL HOLD HIM OFF UNTIL THE MEDICS ARRIVE...
SO HANG IN THERE!
QS ...!
I'M TAKING COM-MAND.
...
YES, SIR.

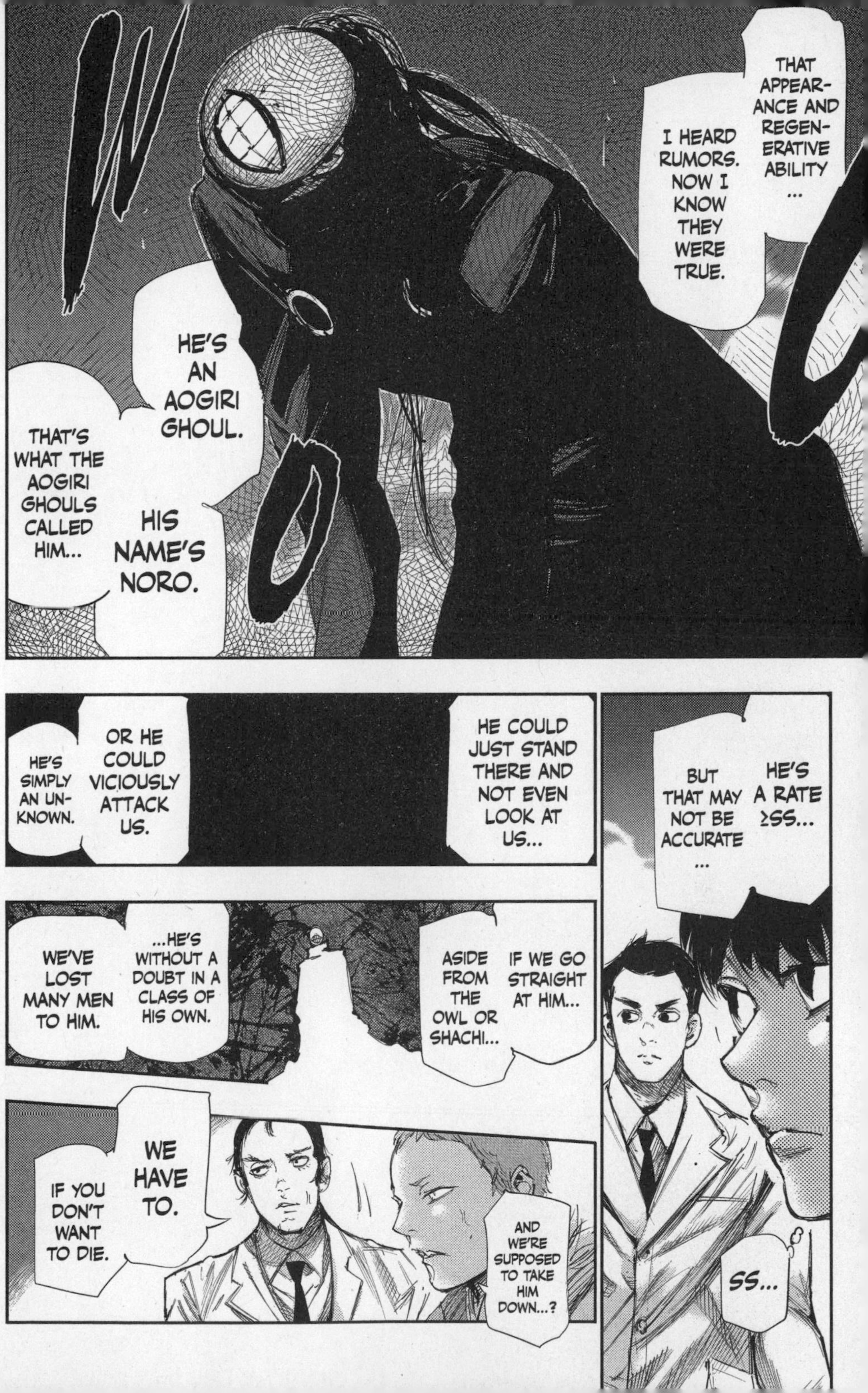

THAT APPEARANCE AND REGENERATIVE ABILITY...
I HEARD RUMORS. NOW I KNOW THEY WERE TRUE.
HE'S AN AOGIRI GHOUL.
HIS NAME'S NORO.
THAT'S WHAT THE AOGIRI GHOULS CALLED HIM...
HE'S A RATE ≥SS...
BUT THAT MAY NOT BE ACCURATE...
SS...
HE COULD JUST STAND THERE AND NOT EVEN LOOK AT US...
OR HE COULD VICIOUSLY ATTACK US.
HE'S SIMPLY AN UNKNOWN.
IF WE GO STRAIGHT AT HIM...
ASIDE FROM THE OWL OR SHACHI...
...HE'S WITHOUT A DOUBT IN A CLASS OF HIS OWN.
WE'VE LOST MANY MEN TO HIM.
AND WE'RE SUPPOSED TO TAKE HIM DOWN...?
WE HAVE TO.
IF YOU DON'T WANT TO DIE.

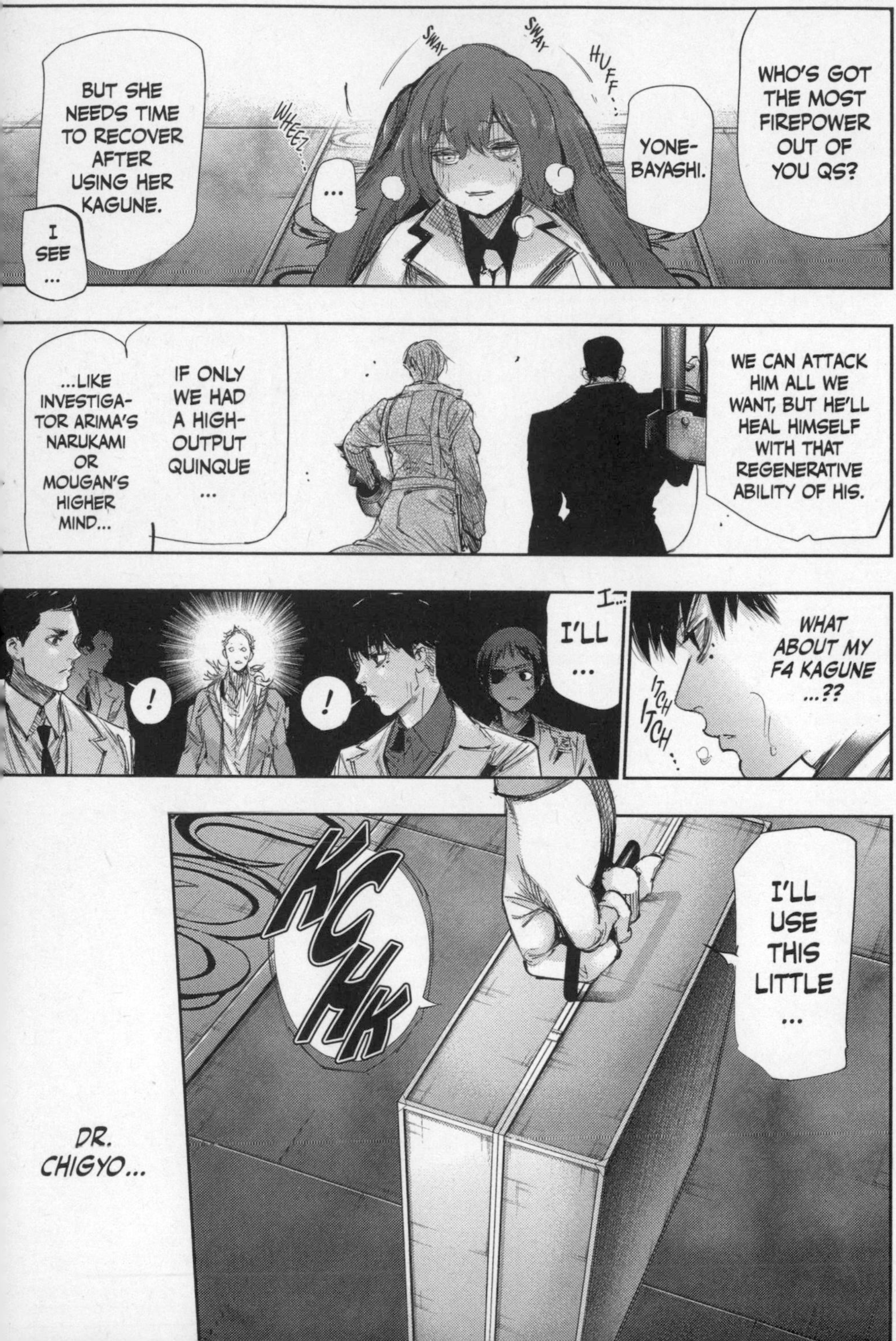
WHO'S GOT THE MOST FIREPOWER OUT OF YOU QS?
SWAY
SWAY
HUFF...
YONE-BAYASHI.
WHEEZ...
...
BUT SHE NEEDS TIME TO RECOVER AFTER USING HER KAGUNE.
I SEE...
WE CAN ATTACK HIM ALL WE WANT, BUT HE'LL HEAL HIMSELF WITH THAT REGENERATIVE ABILITY OF HIS.
IF ONLY WE HAD A HIGH-OUTPUT QUINQUE...
...LIKE INVESTIGATOR ARIMA'S NARUKAMI OR MOUGAN'S HIGHER MIND...
WHAT ABOUT MY F4 KAGUNE...??
ITCH ITCH...
I...
I'LL...
!
!
I'LL USE THIS LITTLE...
KCHK
DR. CHIGYO...

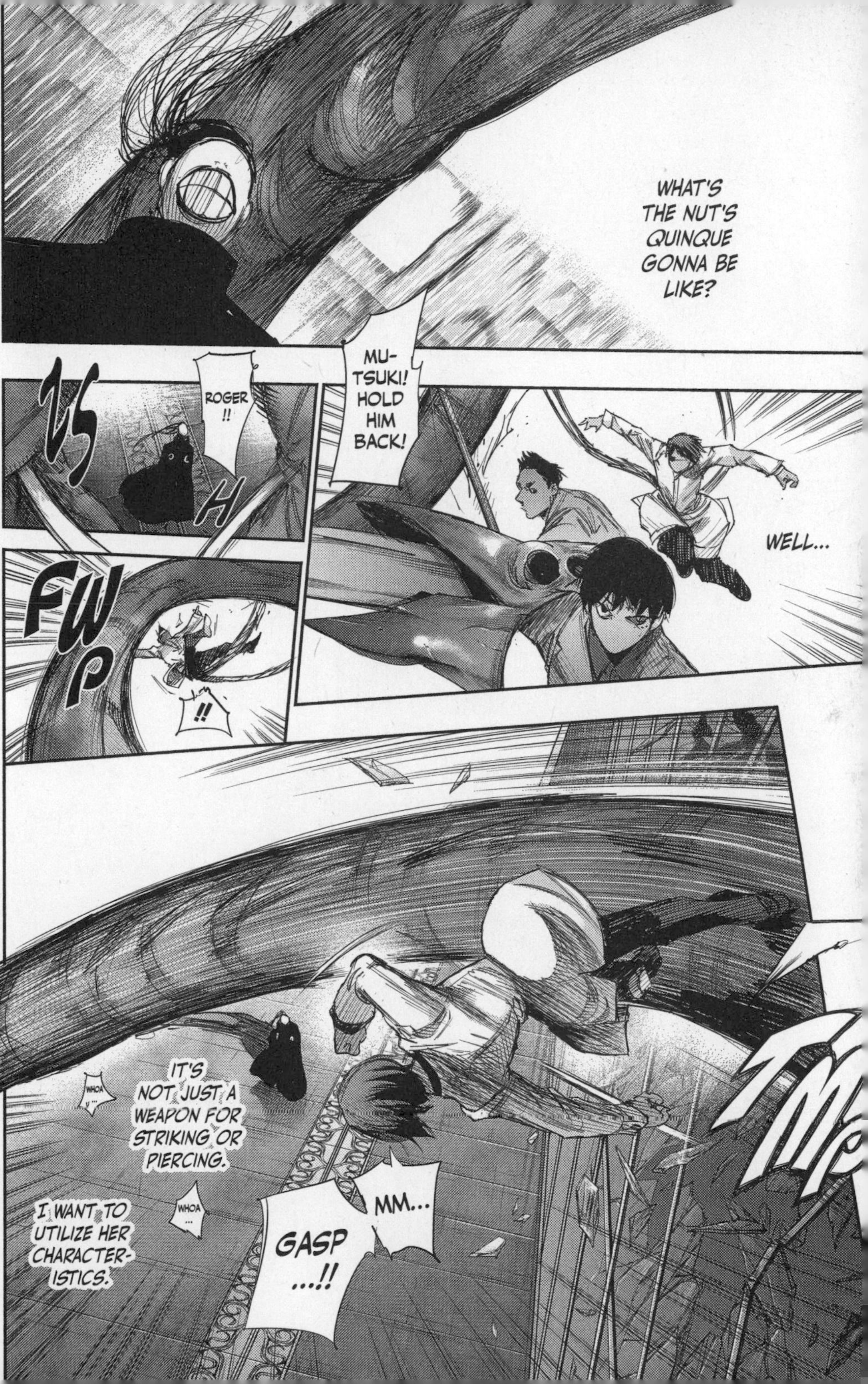
WHAT'S THE NUT'S QUINQUE GONNA BE LIKE?
MU-TSUKI! HOLD HIM BACK!
WELL...
ROGER !!
FWP
!!
IT'S NOT JUST A WEAPON FOR STRIKING OR PIERCING.
WHOA...
I WANT TO UTILIZE HER CHARACTER-ISTICS.
MM...
GASP ...!!
WHOA ...

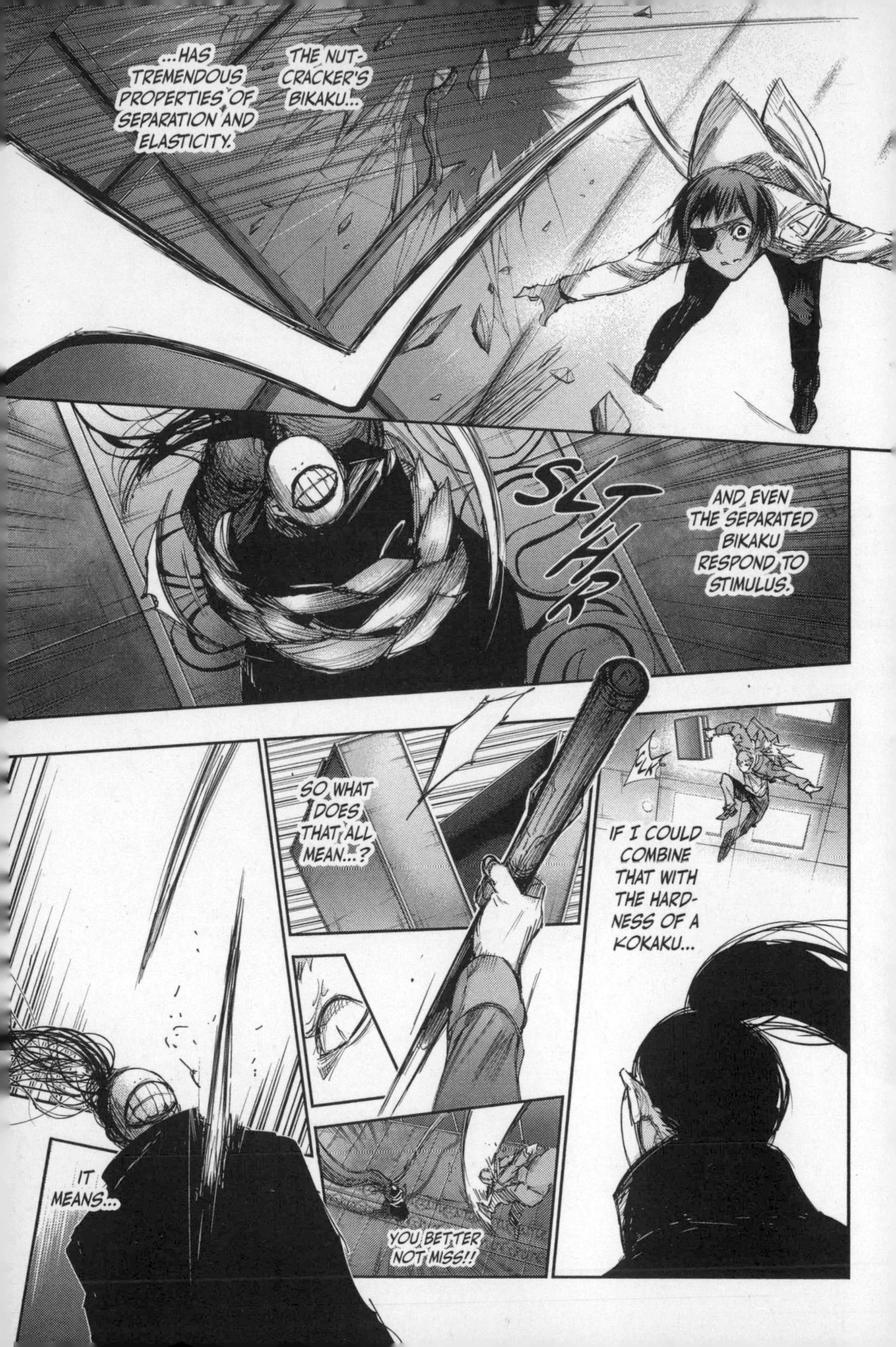
THE NUT-CRACKER'S BIKAKU...
...HAS TREMENDOUS PROPERTIES OF SEPARATION AND ELASTICITY.
AND EVEN THE SEPARATED BIKAKU RESPOND TO STIMULUS.
SLTHR
CLK
IF I COULD COMBINE THAT WITH THE HARD-NESS OF A KOKAKU...
SO WHAT DOES THAT ALL MEAN...?
YOU BETTER NOT MISS!!
IT MEANS...

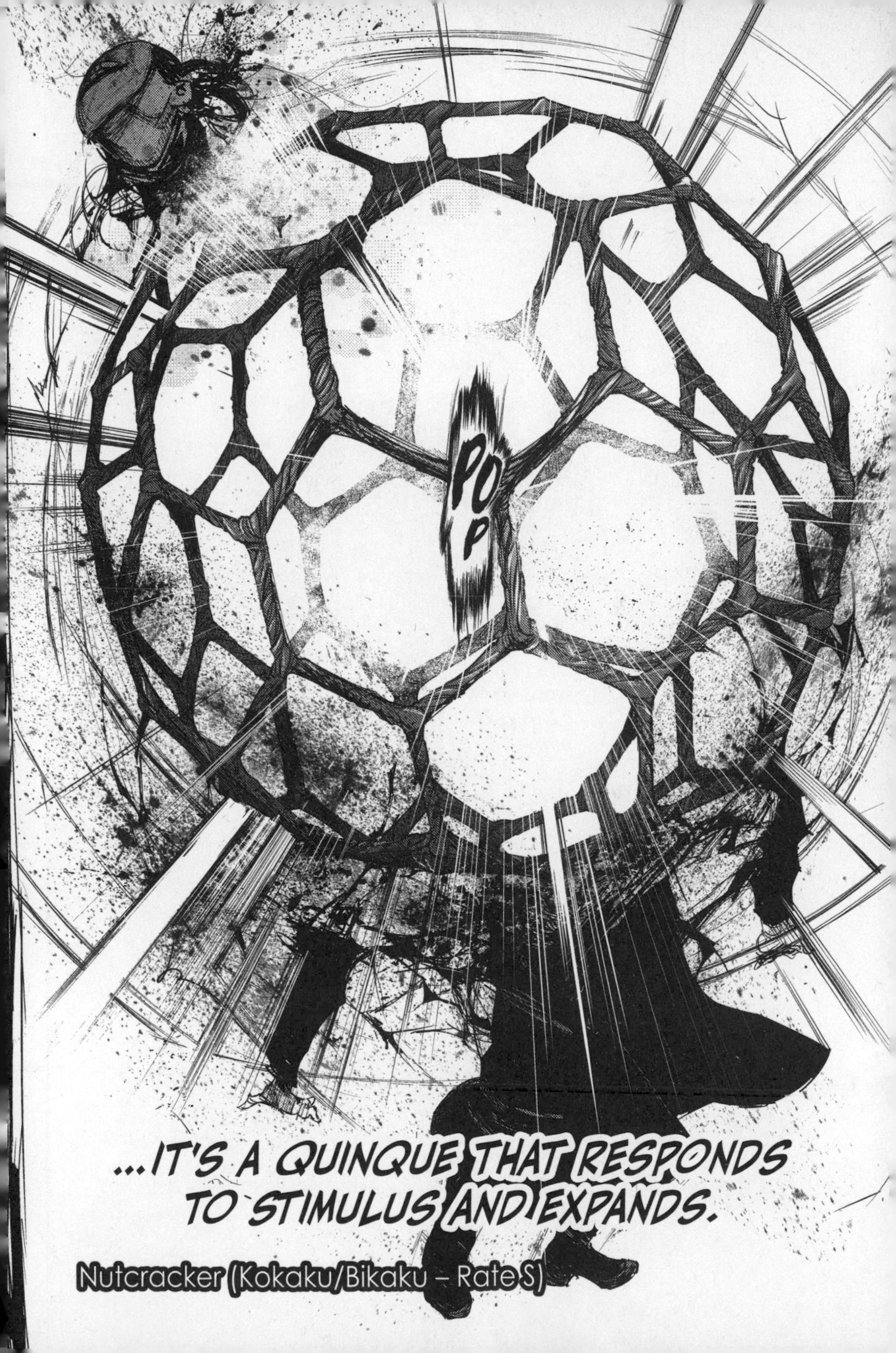
POP
...IT'S A QUINQUE THAT RESPONDS TO STIMULUS AND EXPANDS.
Nutcracker (Kokaku/Bikaku – Rate S)

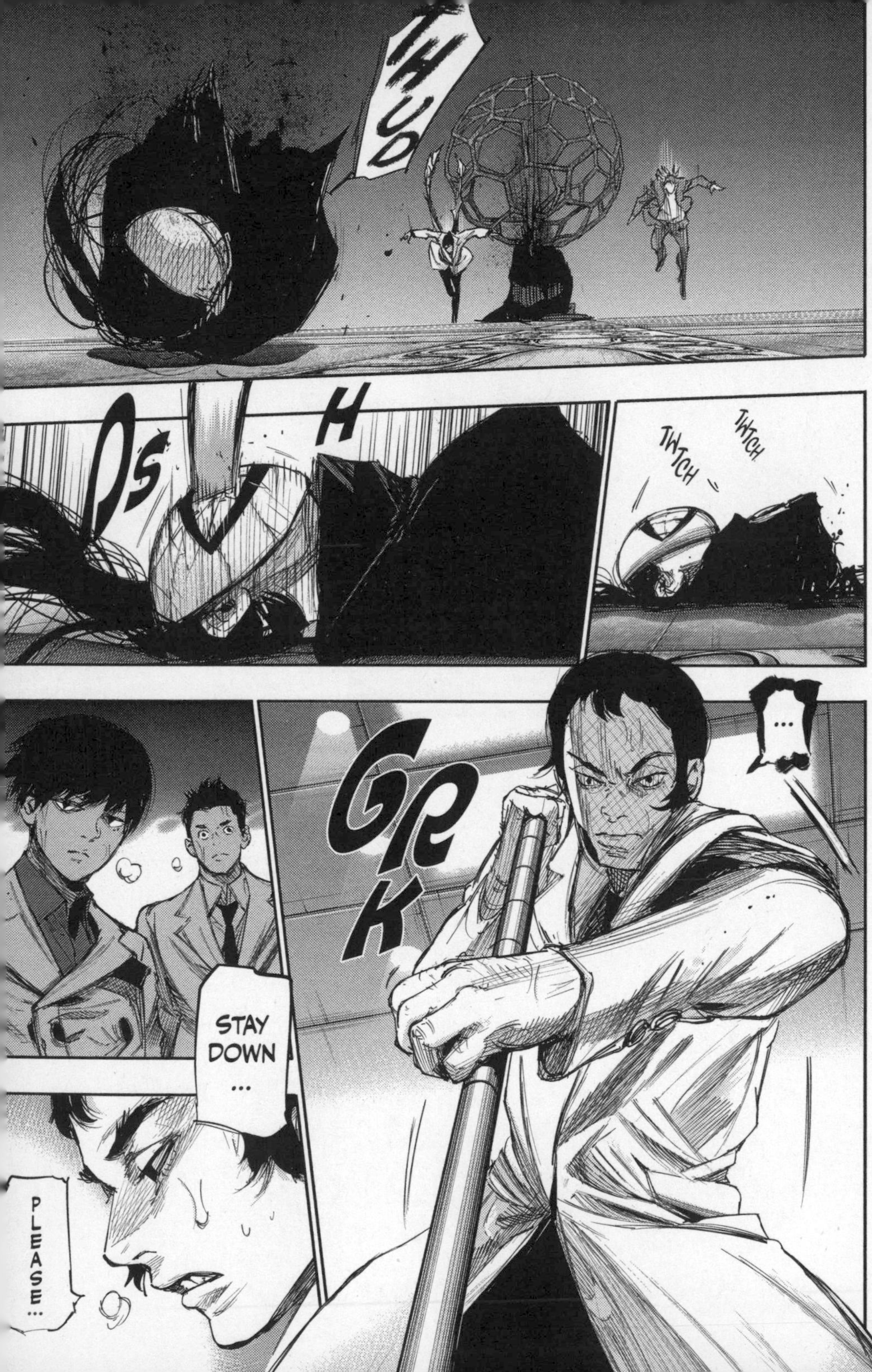
THUD
TWITCH TWITCH
PSH
...
GRK
STAY DOWN ...
PLEASE...

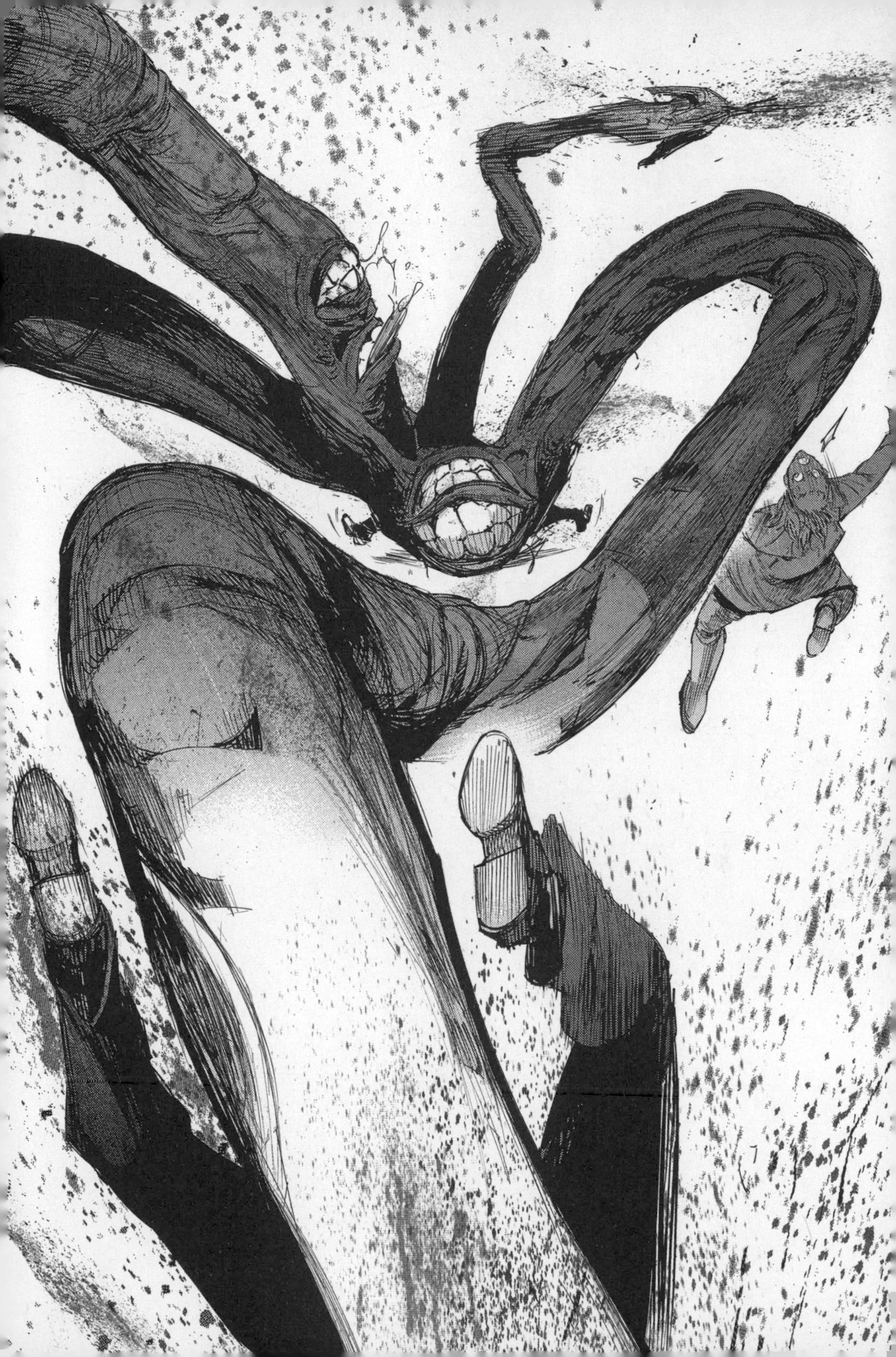

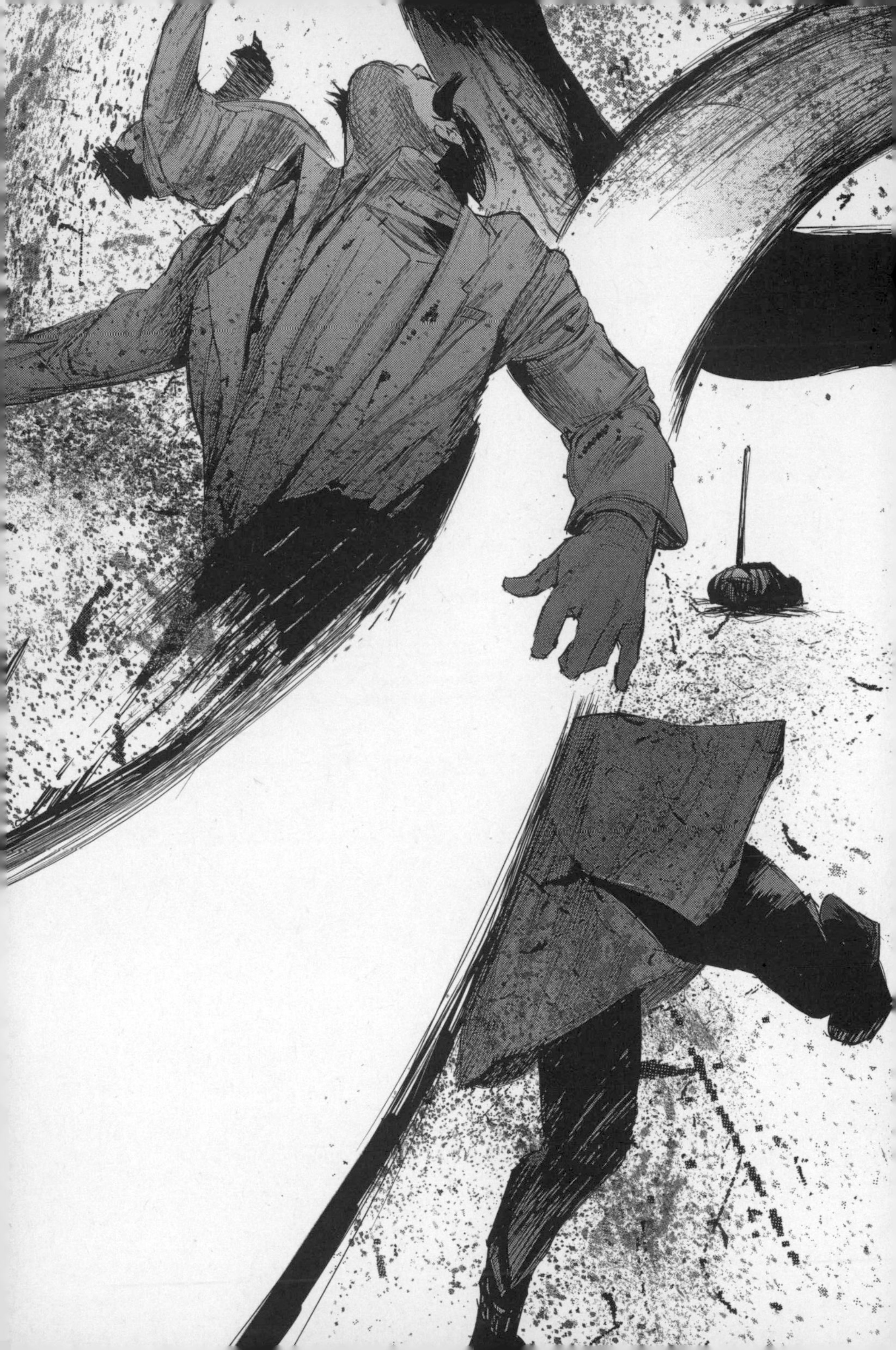

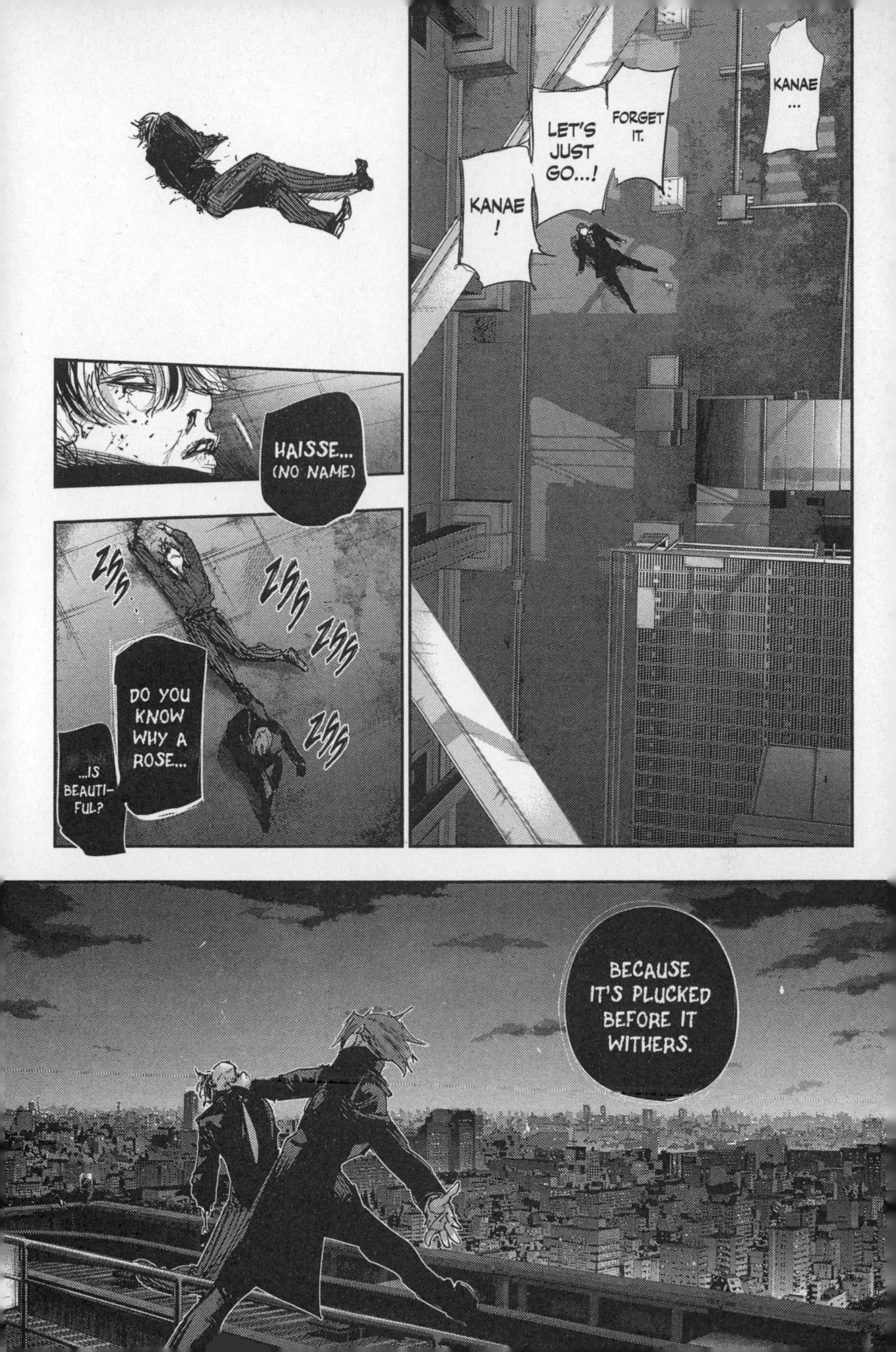
KANAE...
FORGET IT.
LET'S JUST GO...!
KANAE!
HAISSE... (NO NAME)
DO YOU KNOW WHY A ROSE...
...IS BEAUTIFUL?
BECAUSE IT'S PLUCKED BEFORE IT WITHERS.

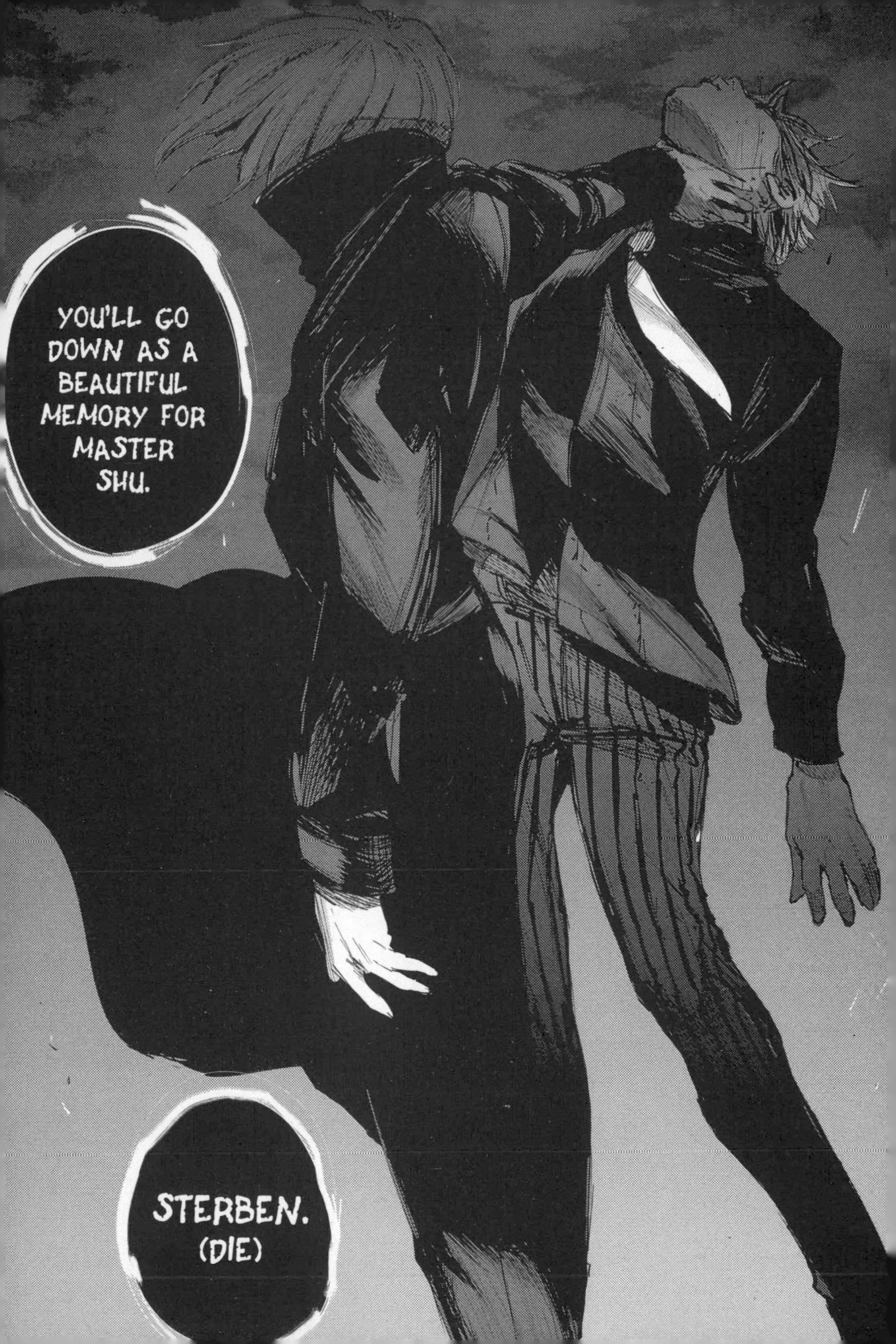
YOU'LL GO DOWN AS A BEAUTIFUL MEMORY FOR MASTER SHU.
STERBEN. (DIE)

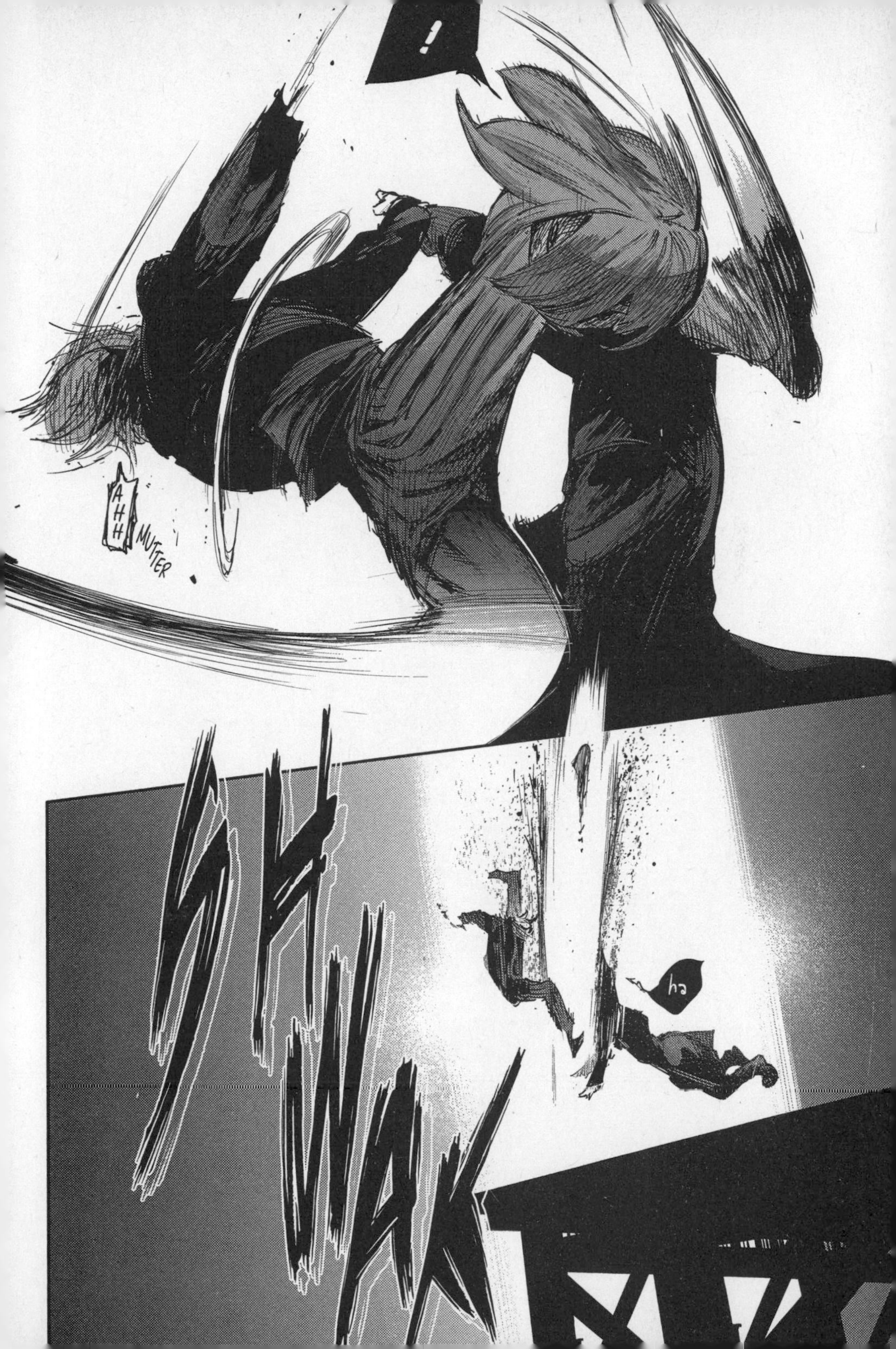
!
AHH
MUTTER
SHUNK
eh

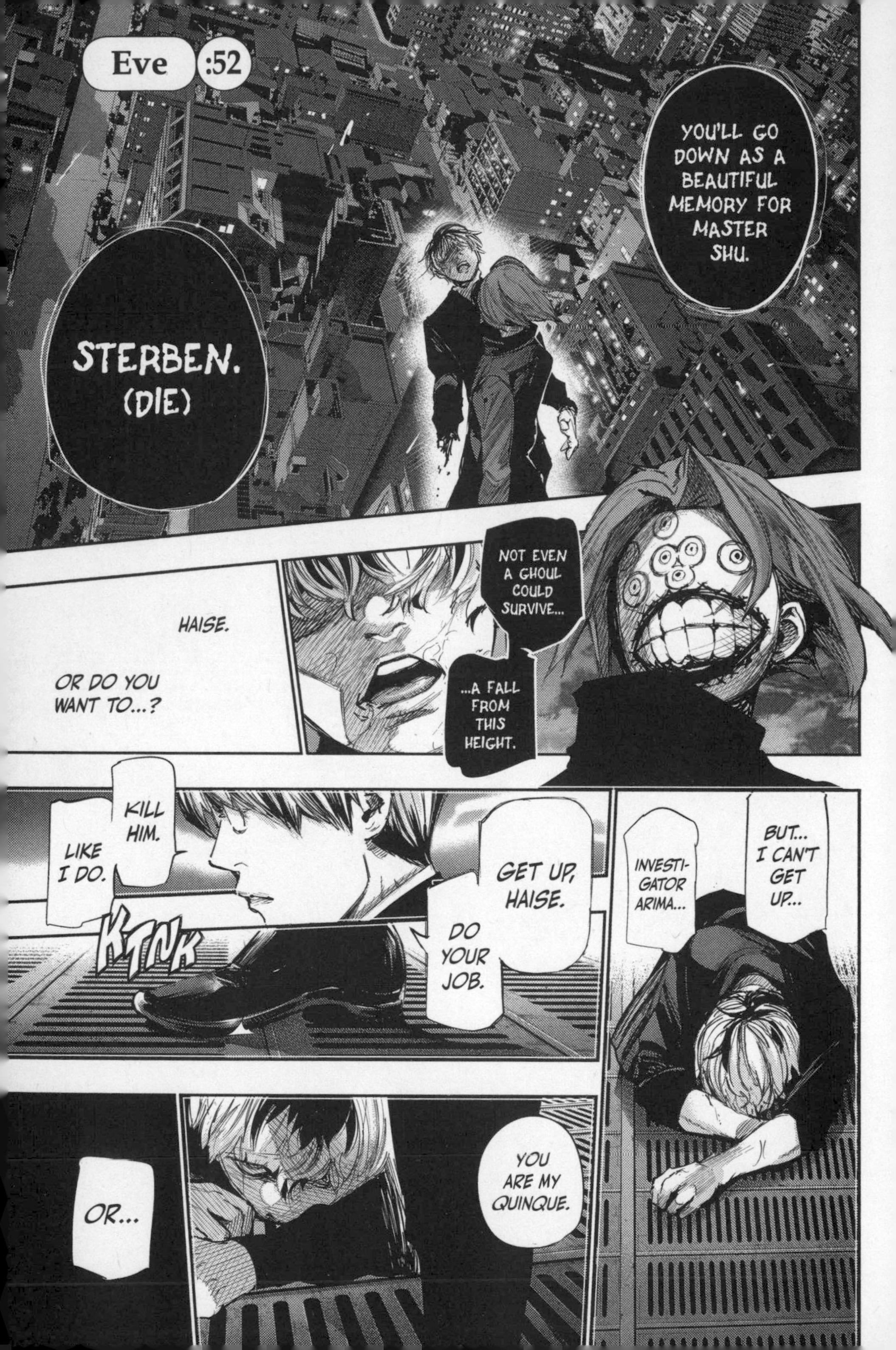
Eve :52
YOU'LL GO DOWN AS A BEAUTIFUL MEMORY FOR MASTER SHU.
STERBEN. (DIE)
NOT EVEN A GHOUL COULD SURVIVE...
...A FALL FROM THIS HEIGHT.
HAISE.
OR DO YOU WANT TO...?
BUT... I CAN'T GET UP...
INVESTIGATOR ARIMA...
GET UP, HAISE.
DO YOUR JOB.
KILL HIM.
LIKE I DO.
KTNK
YOU ARE MY QUINQUE.
OR...

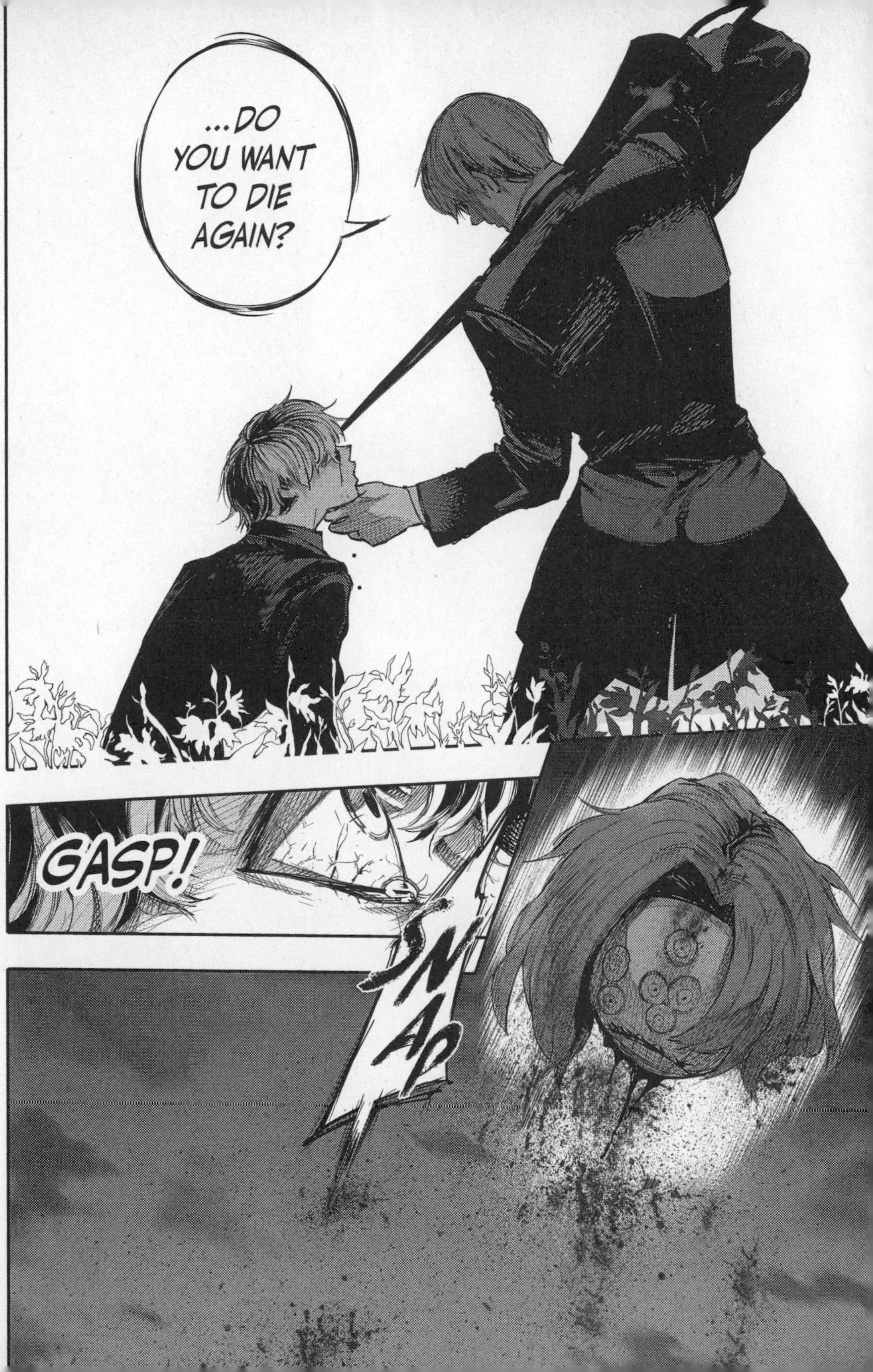
...DO YOU WANT TO DIE AGAIN?
GASP!
SNAP

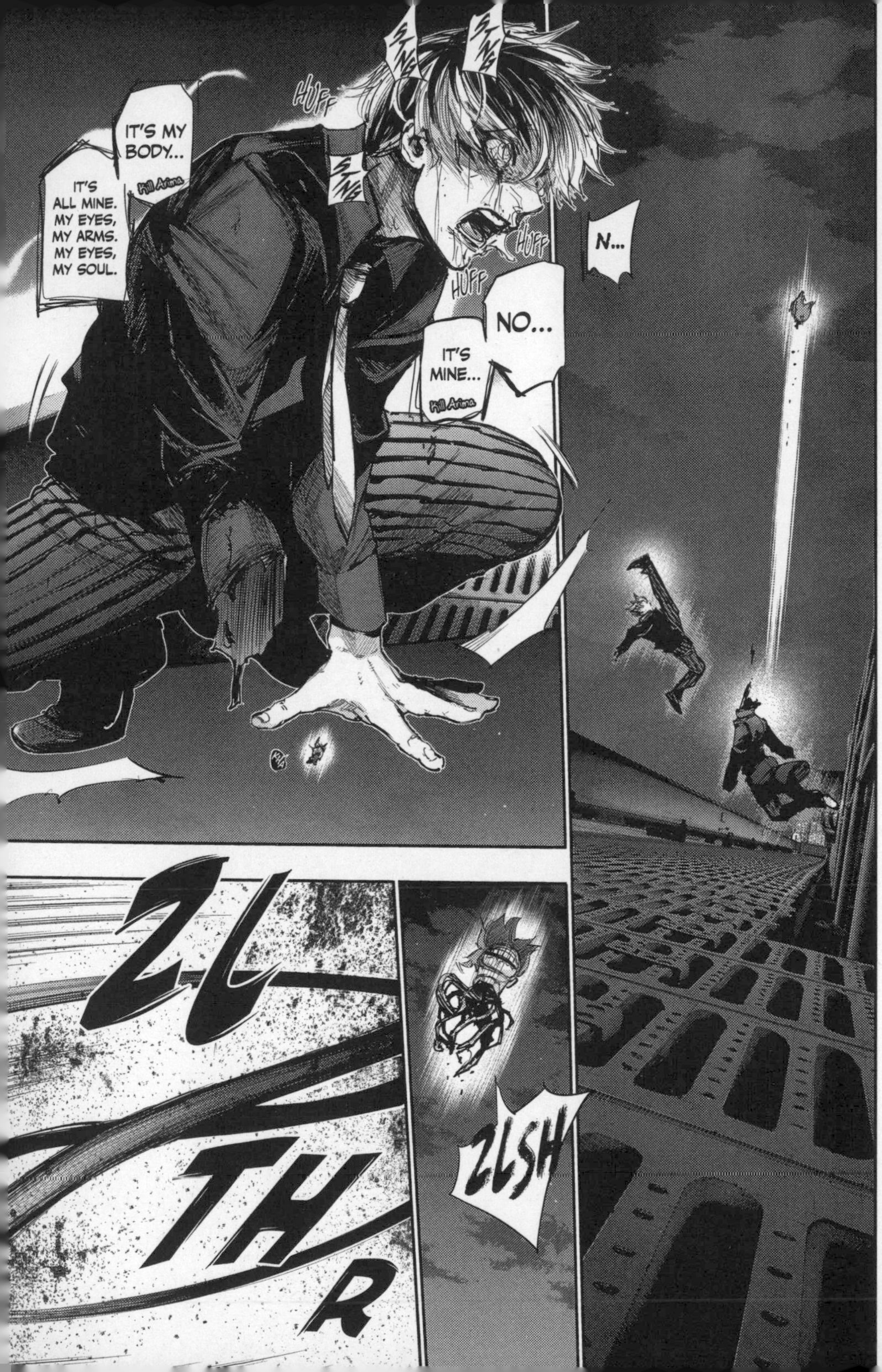
N...
STING
STING
STING
HUFF
HUFF
HUFF
NO...
IT'S MINE...
Kill Arima
IT'S MY BODY...
Kill Arima
IT'S ALL MINE. MY EYES, MY ARMS. MY EYES, MY SOUL.
ZLSH
ZU
THR

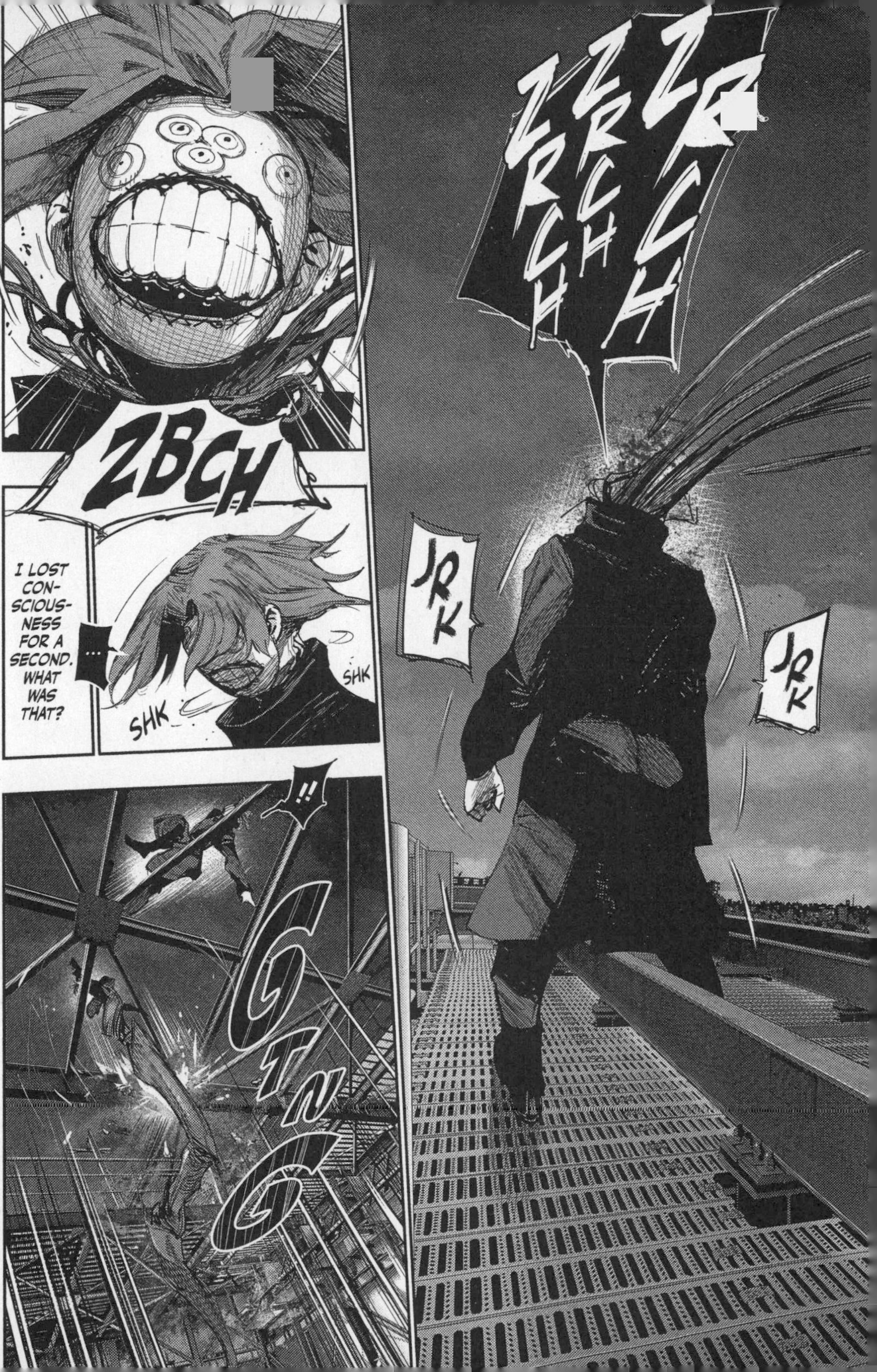
ZRRCH
ZRRCH
ZRRCH
JRK
JRK
ZBCH
...
SHK
SHK
I LOST CON- SCIOUS- NESS FOR A SECOND. WHAT WAS THAT?
!!
GTNG

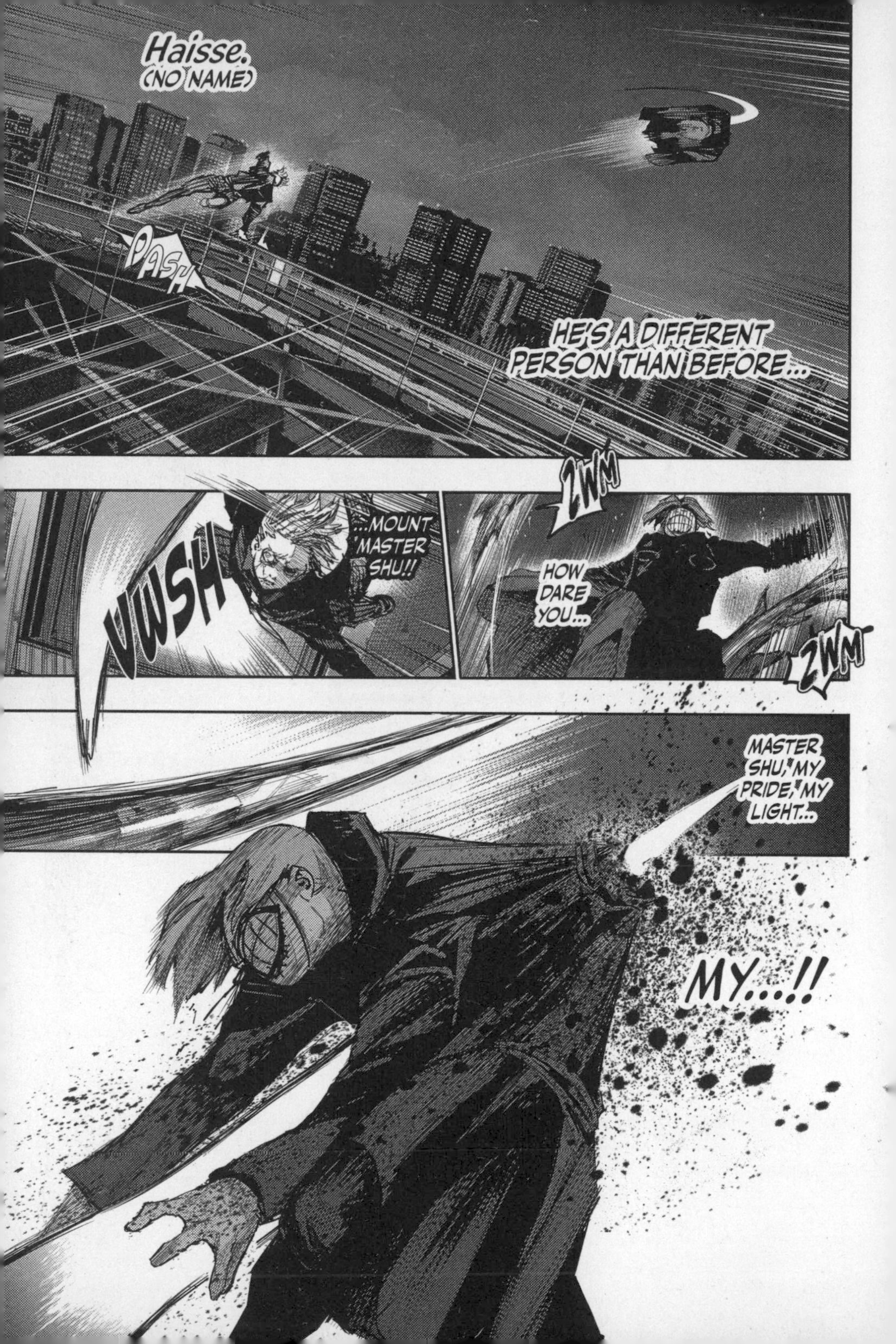
Haisse.
(NO NAME)
PASH
HE'S A DIFFERENT PERSON THAN BEFORE...
ZWM
HOW DARE YOU...
ZWM
...MOUNT MASTER SHU!!
VWSH
MASTER SHU, MY PRIDE, MY LIGHT...
MY...!!

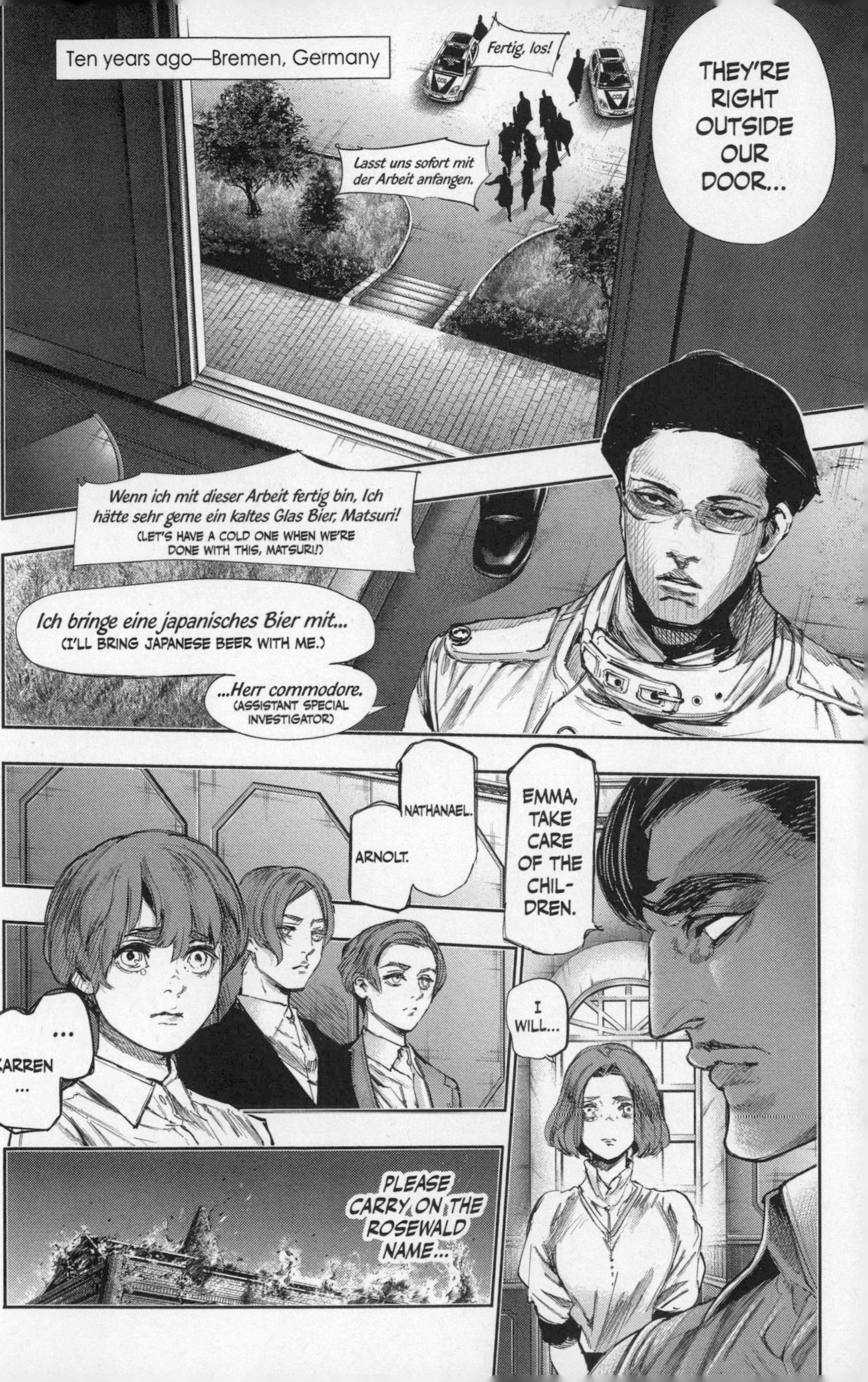

THEY'RE RIGHT OUTSIDE OUR DOOR...
Fertig, los!
Ten years ago—Bremen, Germany
Lasst uns sofort mit der Arbeit anfangen.
Wenn ich mit dieser Arbeit fertig bin, Ich hätte sehr gerne ein kaltes Glas Bier, Matsuri!
(LET'S HAVE A COLD ONE WHEN WE'RE DONE WITH THIS, MATSURI!)
Ich bringe eine japanisches Bier mit...
(I'LL BRING JAPANESE BEER WITH ME.)
...Herr commodore.
(ASSISTANT SPECIAL INVESTIGATOR)
EMMA, TAKE CARE OF THE CHIL-DREN.
NATHANAEL.
ARNOLT.
I WILL...
...
KARREN ...
PLEASE CARRY ON THE ROSEWALD NAME...

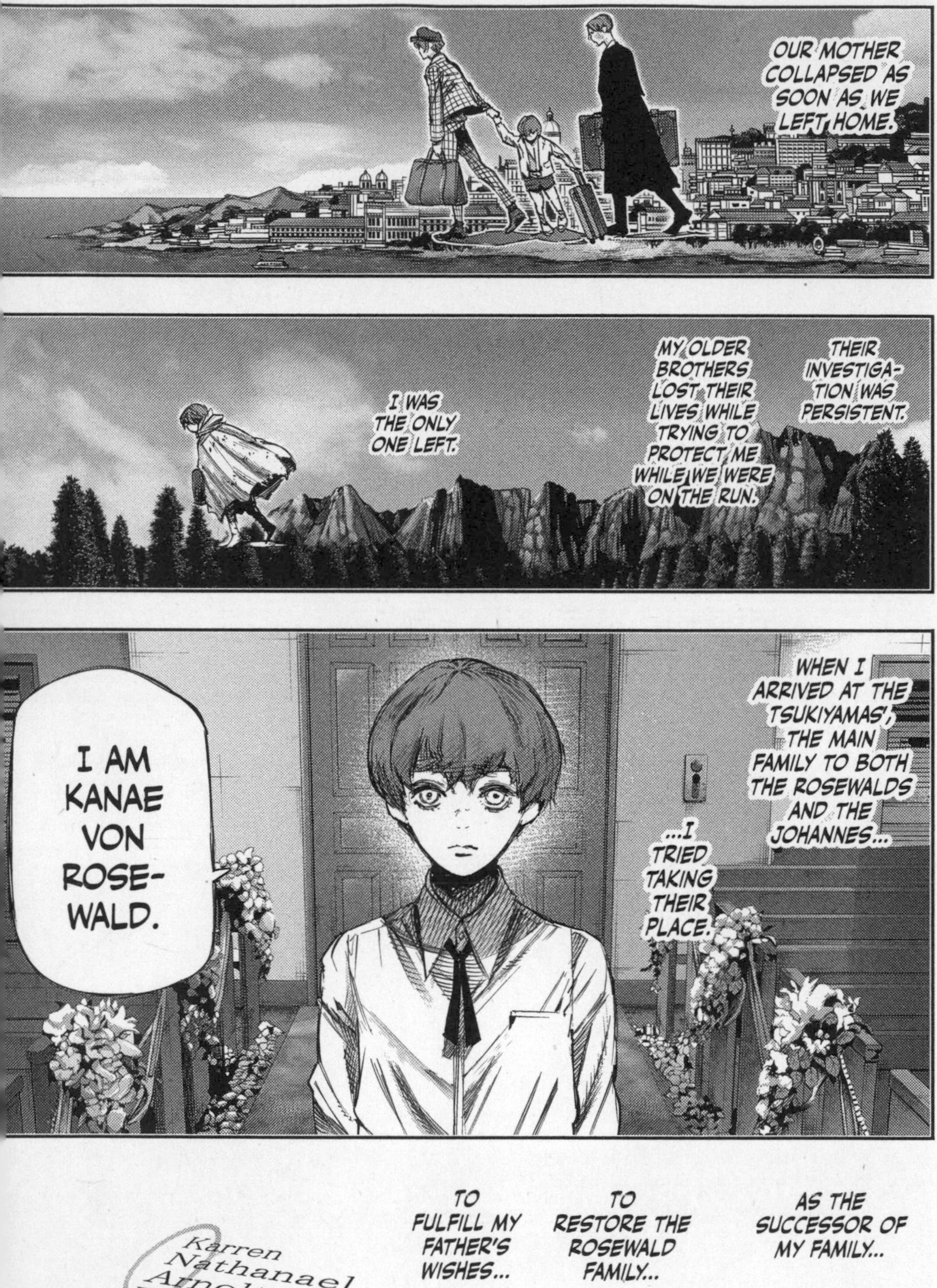
OUR MOTHER COLLAPSED AS SOON AS WE LEFT HOME.
THEIR INVESTIGA-TION WAS PERSISTENT.
MY OLDER BROTHERS LOST THEIR LIVES WHILE TRYING TO PROTECT ME WHILE WE WERE ON THE RUN.
I WAS THE ONLY ONE LEFT.
WHEN I ARRIVED AT THE TSUKIYAMAS', THE MAIN FAMILY TO BOTH THE ROSEWALDS AND THE JOHANNES...
...I TRIED TAKING THEIR PLACE.
I AM KANAE VON ROSE-WALD.
AS THE SUCCESSOR OF MY FAMILY...
TO RESTORE THE ROSEWALD FAMILY...
TO FULFILL MY FATHER'S WISHES...
Karren
Nathanael
Arnolt
Emma

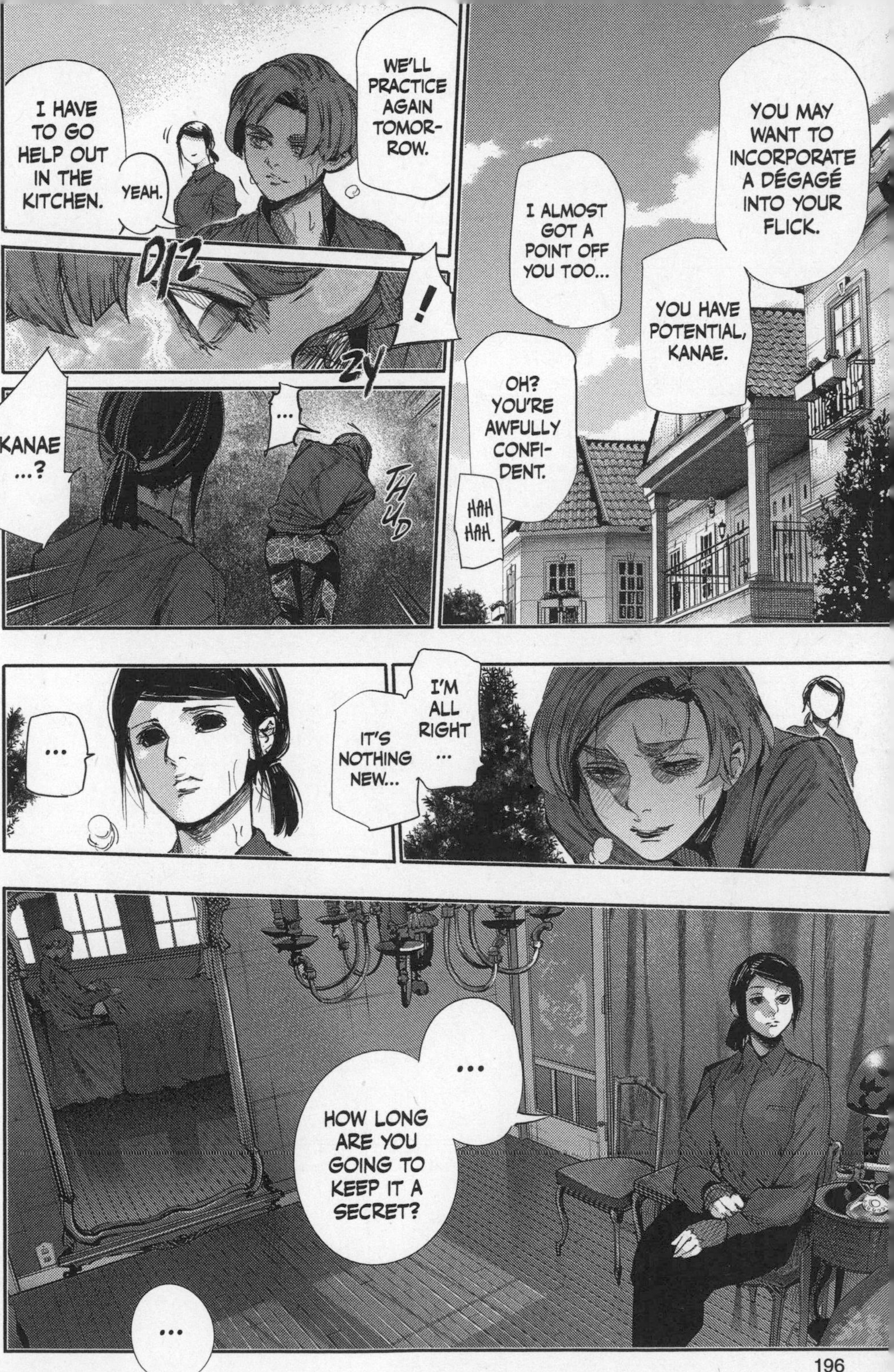
YOU MAY WANT TO INCORPORATE A DÉGAGÉ INTO YOUR FLICK.
I ALMOST GOT A POINT OFF YOU TOO...
YOU HAVE POTENTIAL, KANAE.
OH? YOU'RE AWFULLY CONFI-DENT.
HAH HAH.
WE'LL PRACTICE AGAIN TOMOR-ROW.
YEAH.
I HAVE TO GO HELP OUT IN THE KITCHEN.
DIZ
!
ZY
...
THUD
KANAE ...?
I'M ALL RIGHT ...
IT'S NOTHING NEW...
...
...
HOW LONG ARE YOU GOING TO KEEP IT A SECRET?
...

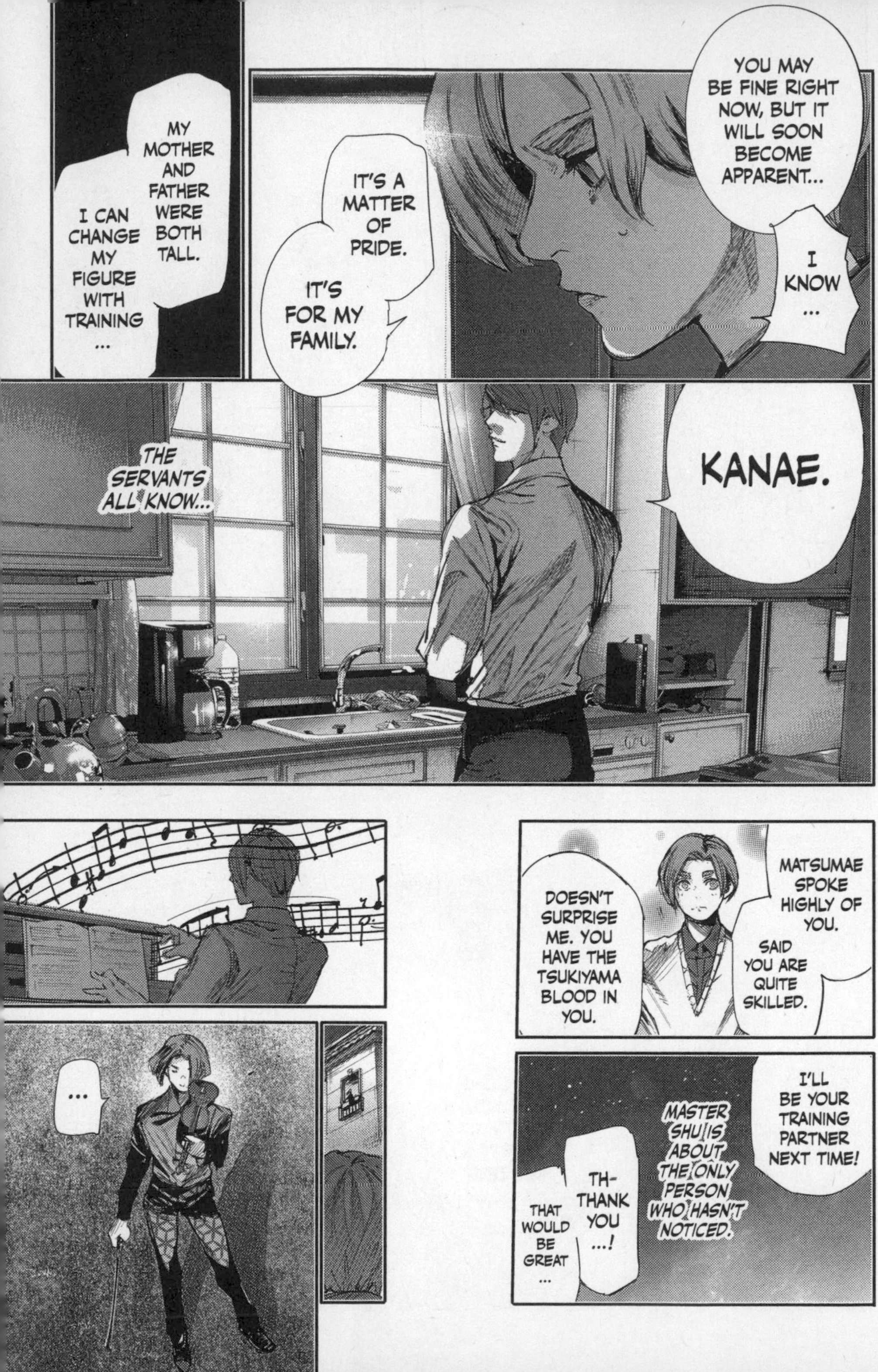

YOU MAY BE FINE RIGHT NOW, BUT IT WILL SOON BECOME APPARENT...
I KNOW ...
IT'S A MATTER OF PRIDE.
IT'S FOR MY FAMILY.
MY MOTHER AND FATHER WERE BOTH TALL.
I CAN CHANGE MY FIGURE WITH TRAINING ...
KANAE.
THE SERVANTS ALL KNOW...
MATSUMAE SPOKE HIGHLY OF YOU.
SAID YOU ARE QUITE SKILLED.
DOESN'T SURPRISE ME. YOU HAVE THE TSUKIYAMA BLOOD IN YOU.
I'LL BE YOUR TRAINING PARTNER NEXT TIME!
MASTER SHU IS ABOUT THE ONLY PERSON WHO HASN'T NOTICED.
TH-THANK YOU ...!
THAT WOULD BE GREAT ...
...

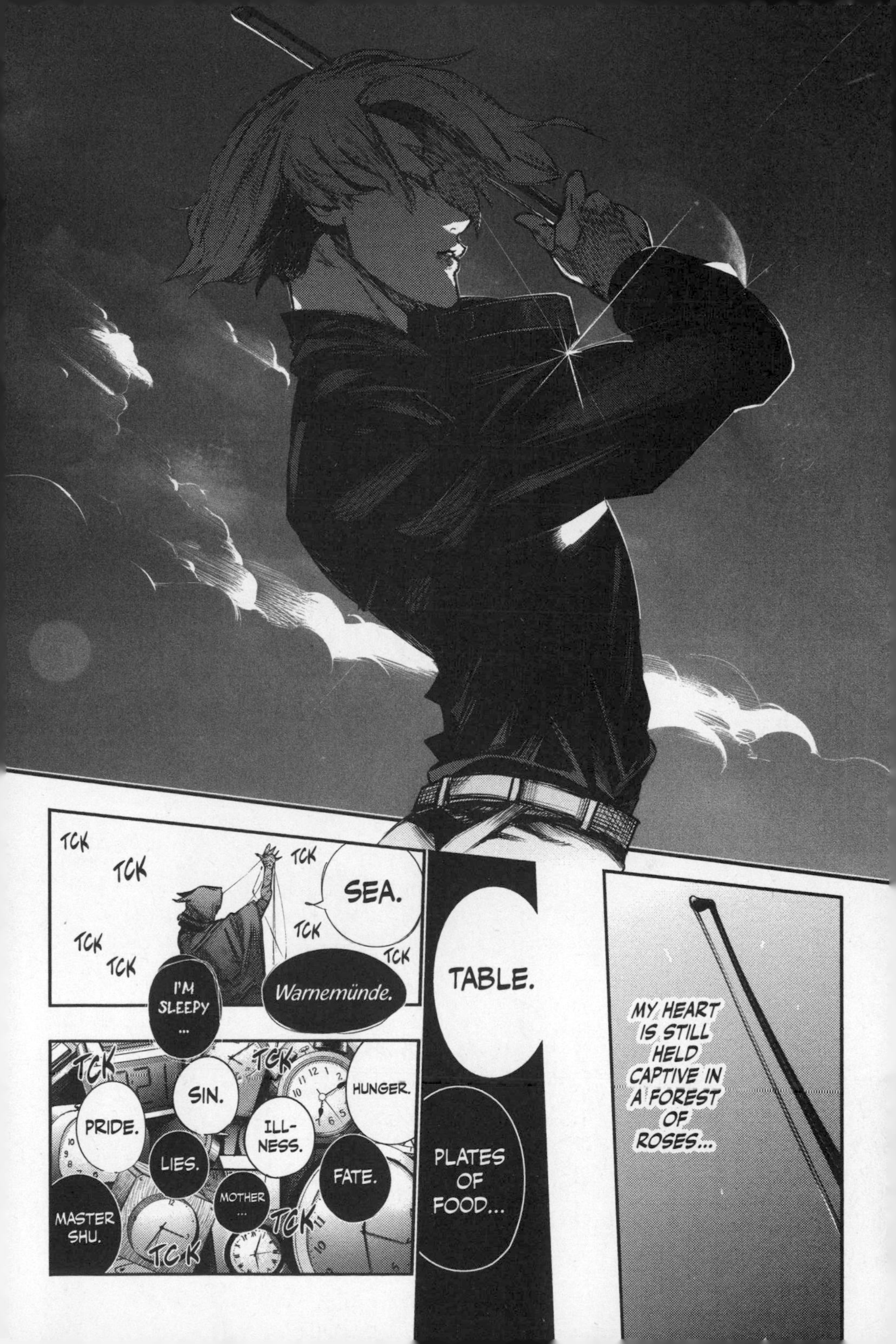
MY HEART IS STILL HELD CAPTIVE IN A FOREST OF ROSES...
TABLE.
PLATES OF FOOD...
TCK
SEA.
TCK
TCK
Warnemünde.
TCK
TCK
TCK
TCK
I'M SLEEPY ...
TCK
TCK
HUNGER.
SIN.
ILL-NESS.
PRIDE.
FATE.
LIES.
MOTHER ...
TCK
MASTER SHU.
TCK

MASTER SHU...

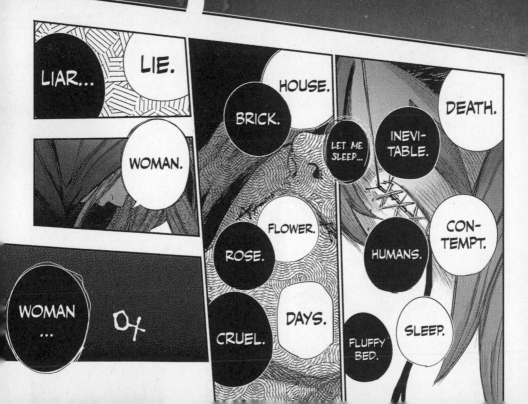

LIAR...

LIE.

WOMAN.

WOMAN...

Oy

HOUSE.

BRICK.

LET ME SLEEP...

FLOWER.

ROSE.

DAYS.

CRUEL.

DEATH.

INEVITABLE.

CONTEMPT.

HUMANS.

FLUFFY BED.

SLEEP.

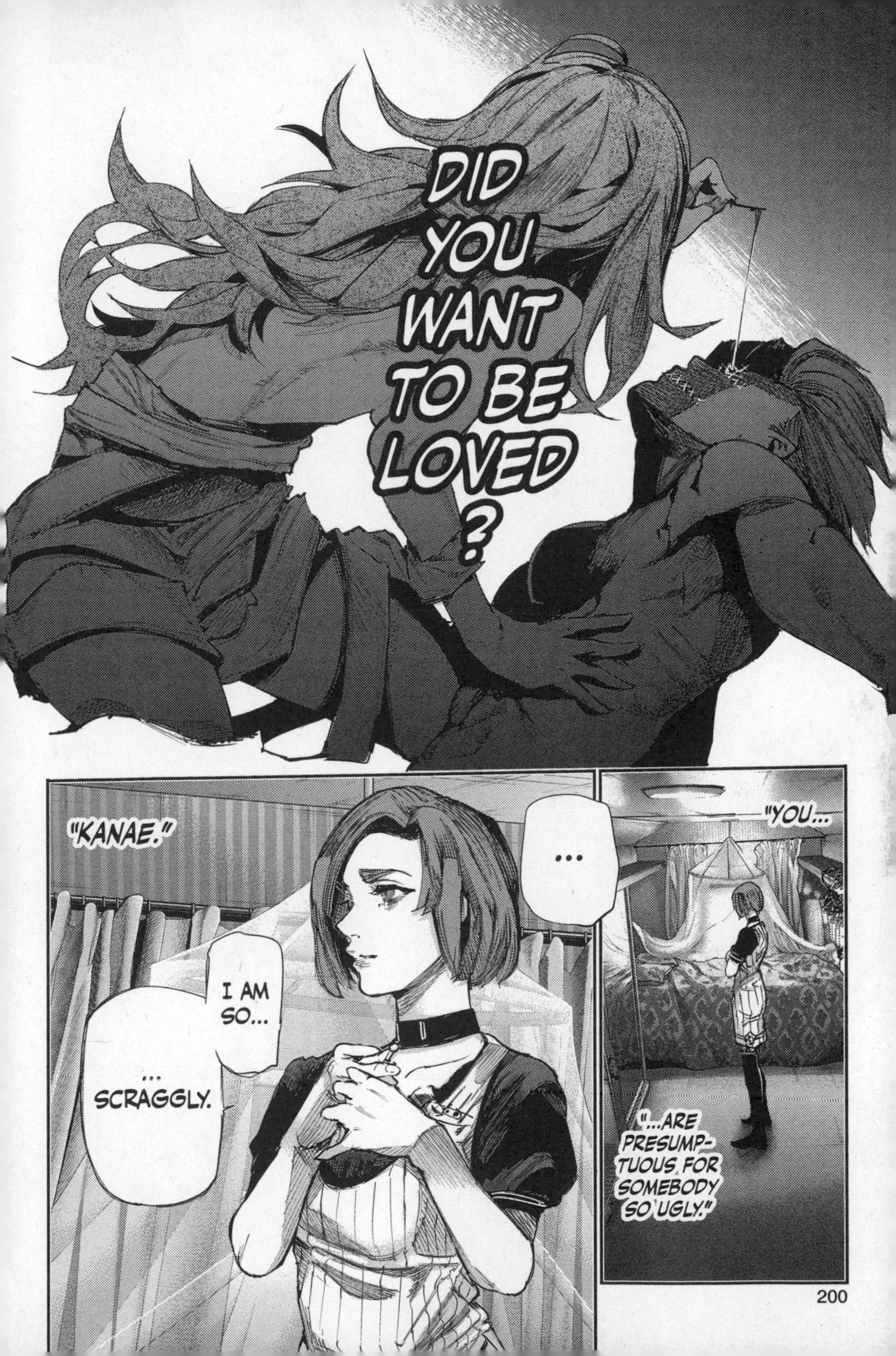
DID YOU WANT TO BE LOVED?
"YOU...
"...ARE PRESUMP-TUOUS FOR SOMEBODY SO UGLY."
...
"KANAE."
I AM SO...
... SCRAGGLY.

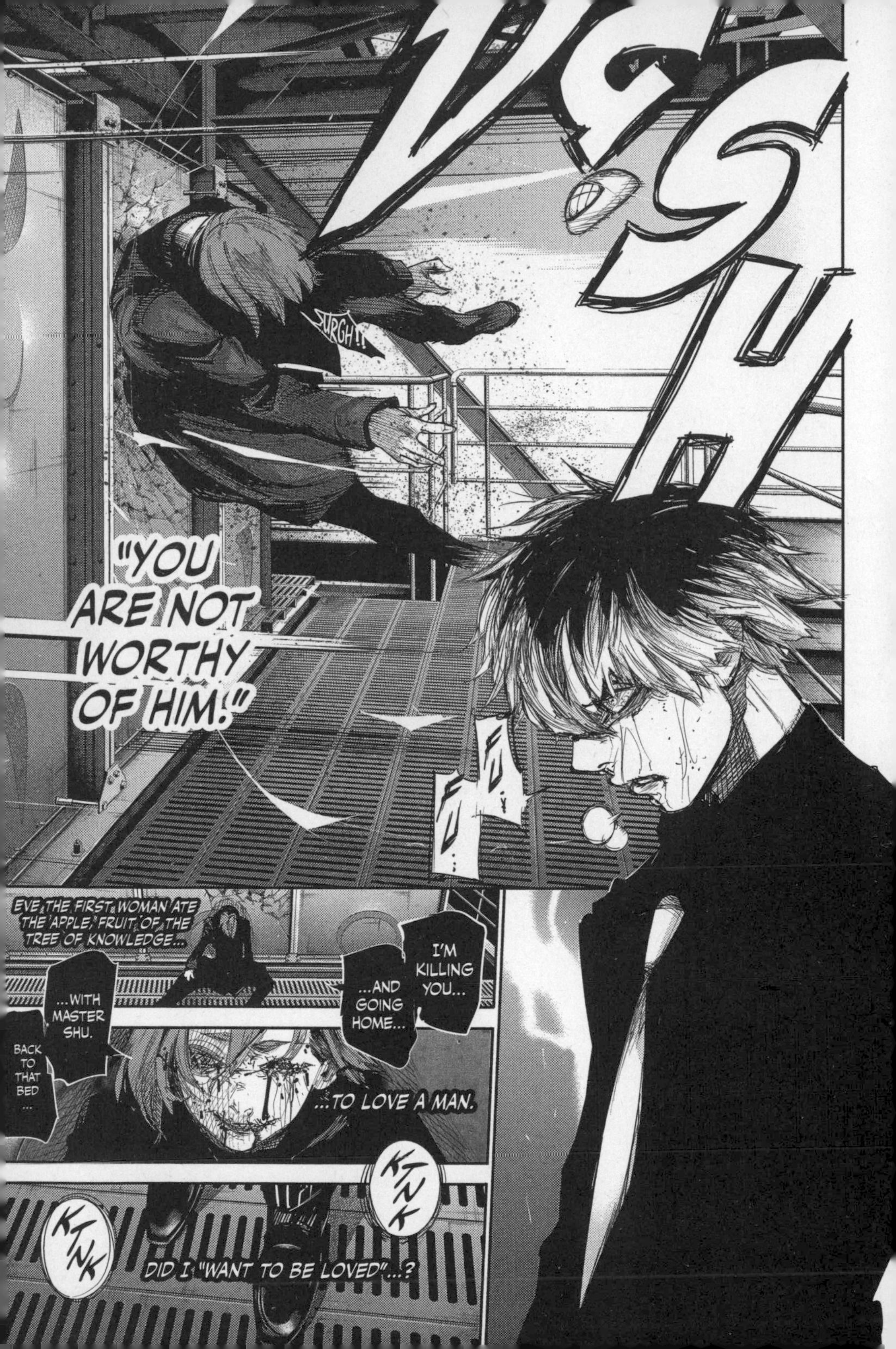
URGH!!
"YOU ARE NOT WORTHY OF HIM!"
I'M KILLING YOU...
...AND GOING HOME...
EVE THE FIRST WOMAN ATE THE APPLE, FRUIT OF THE TREE OF KNOWLEDGE...
...WITH MASTER SHU.
BACK TO THAT BED...
...TO LOVE A MAN.
KTNK
KTNK
DID I "WANT TO BE LOVED"...?

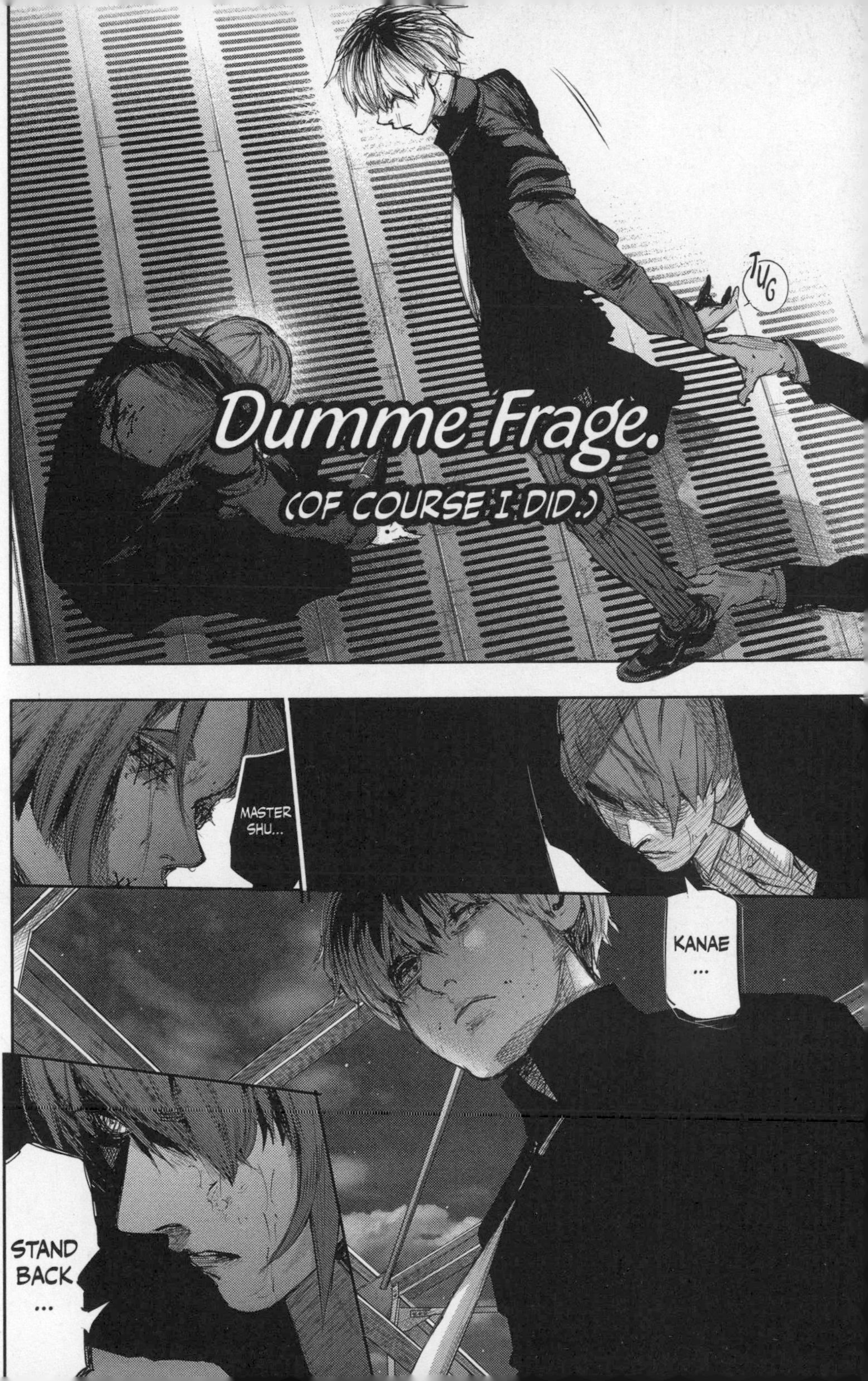
TUG
Dumme Frage.
(OF COURSE I DID.)
MASTER SHU...
KANAE ...
STAND BACK ...

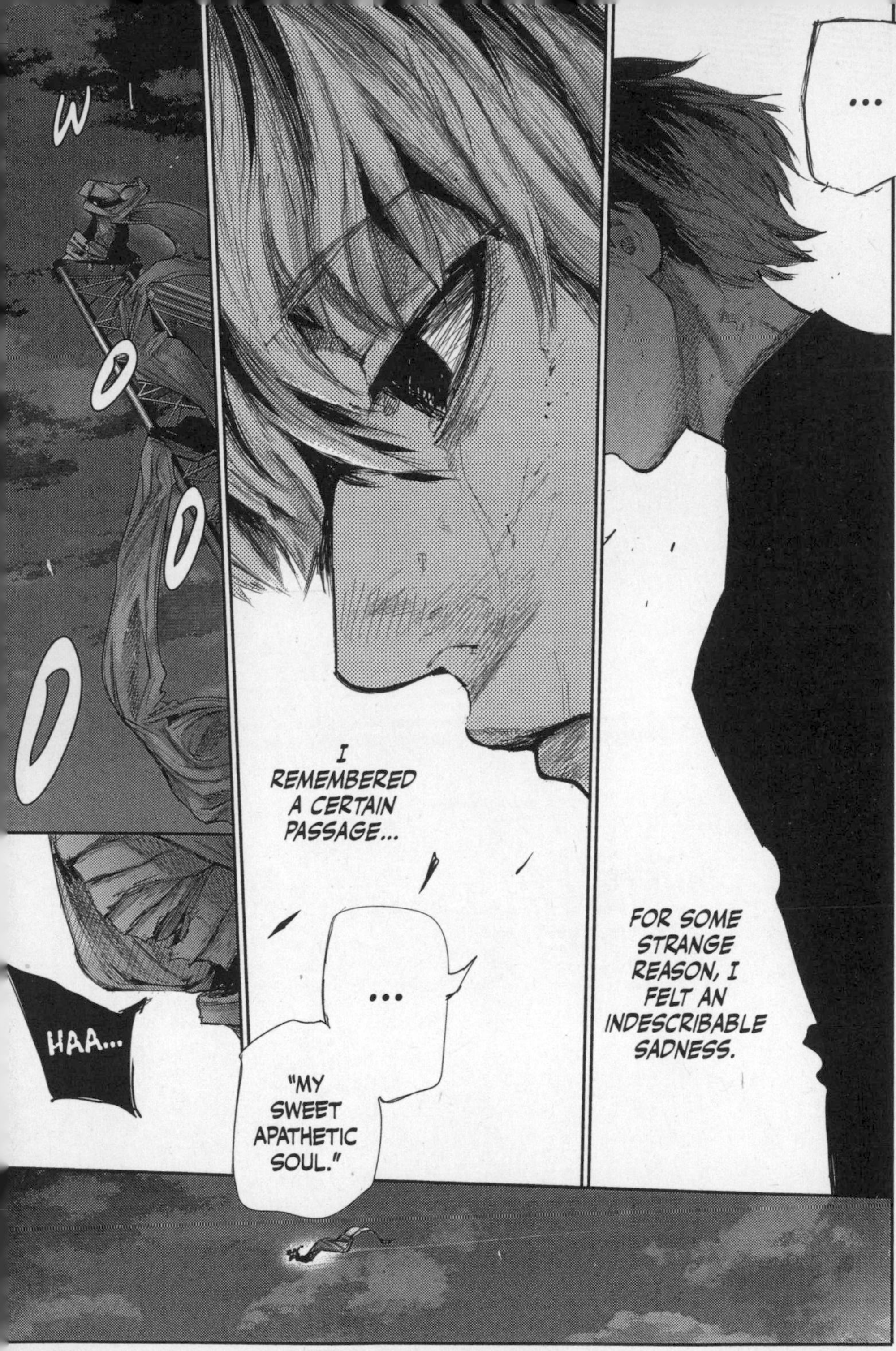
...
FOR SOME STRANGE REASON, I FELT AN INDESCRIBABLE SADNESS.
I REMEMBERED A CERTAIN PASSAGE...
...
"MY SWEET APATHETIC SOUL."
WOOO
HAA...

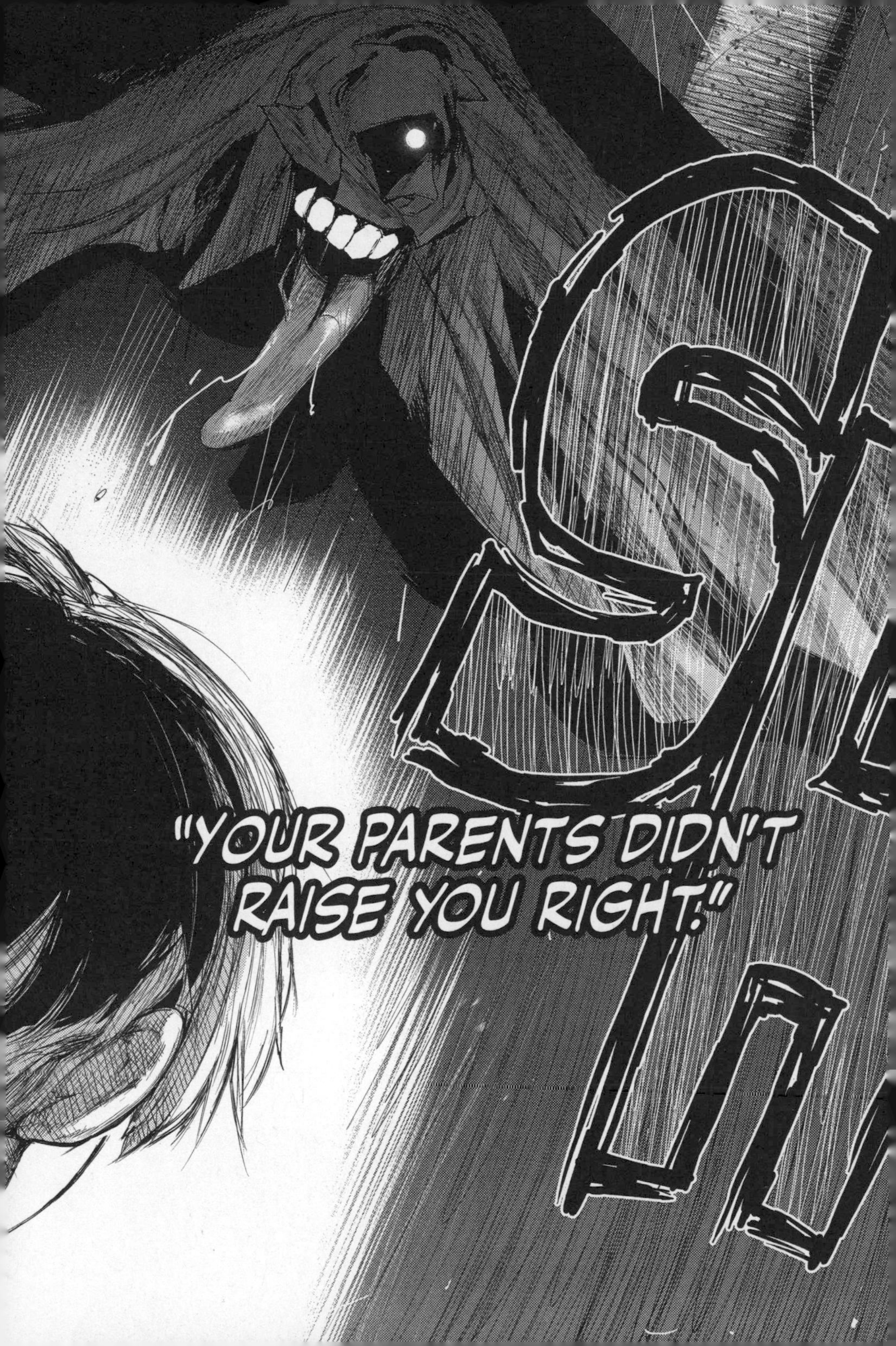
"YOUR PARENTS DIDN'T RAISE YOU RIGHT."

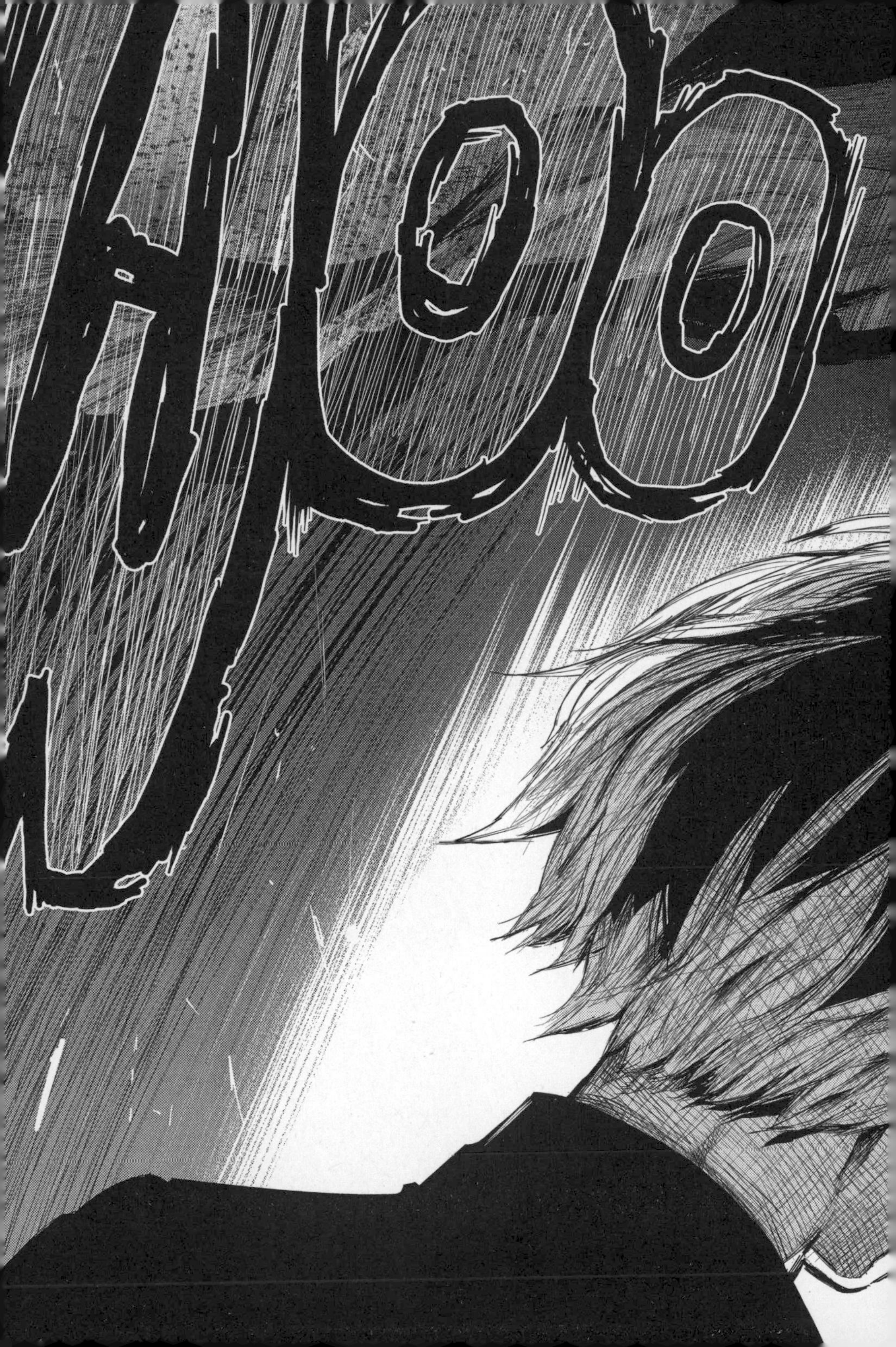

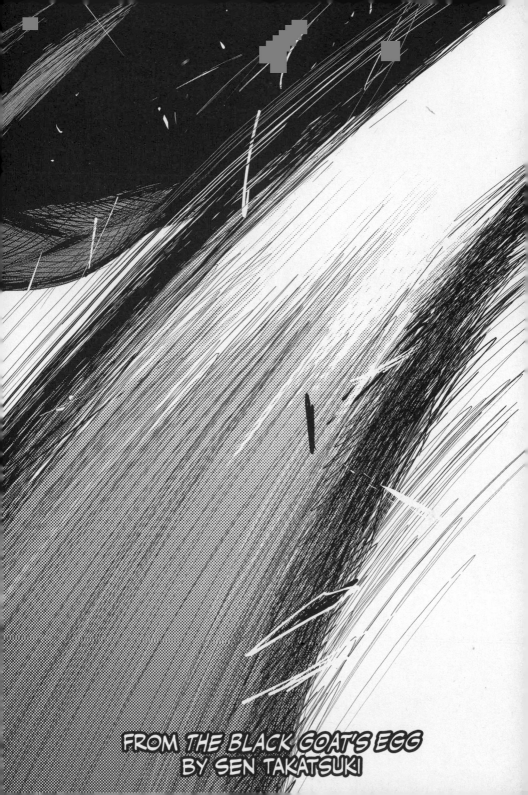

FROM *THE BLACK GOAT'S EGG*
BY SEN TAKATSUKI

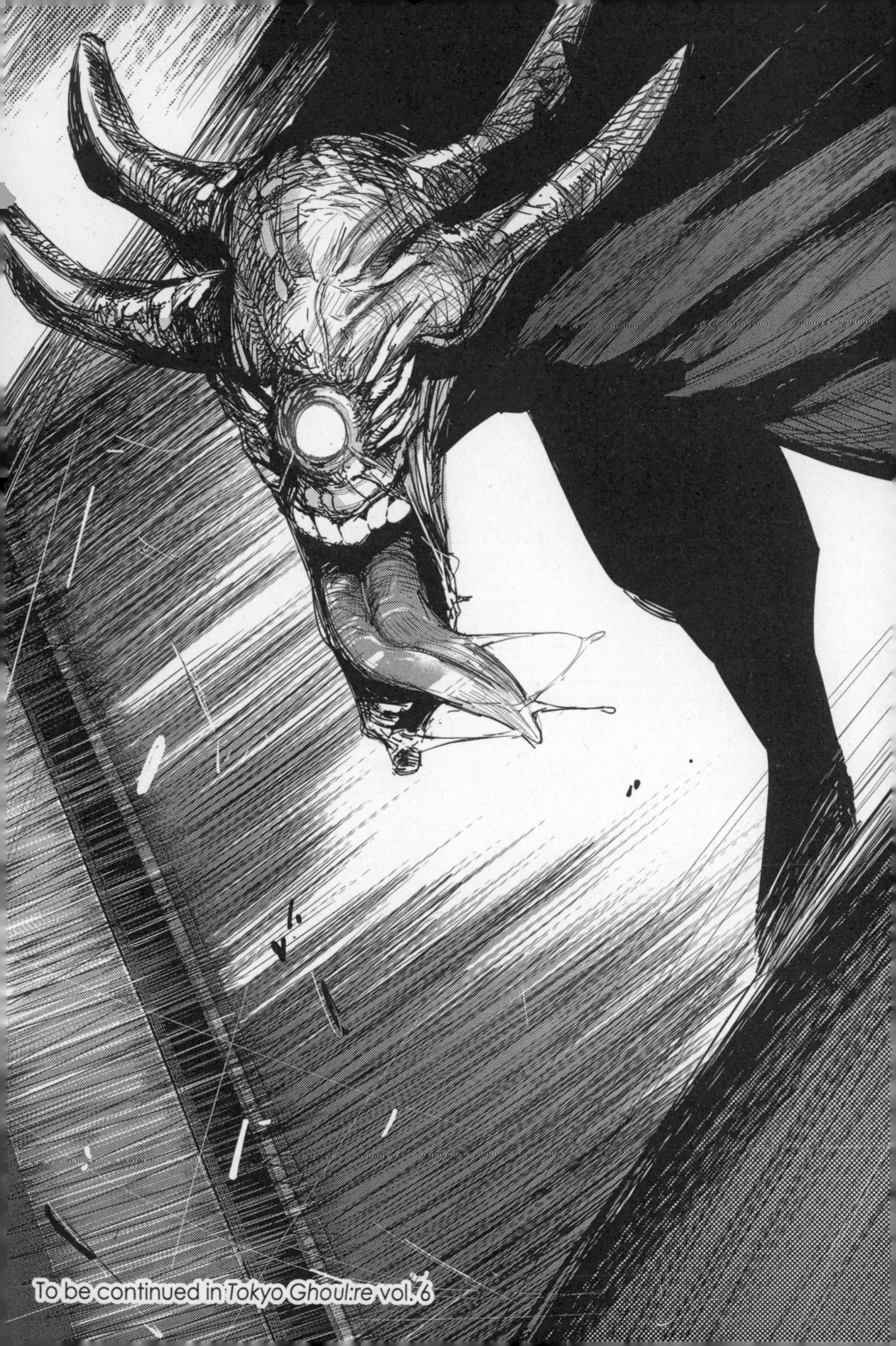
To be continued in *Tokyo Ghoul:re* vol. 6

And now for some bonus manga

These were palindromes in the original Japanese.
Can you come up with an English palindrome
to go with each panel?

Vzz
Seriously, Kijima?

EVERY-BODY DOES WHAT I SAY.
Really...
Ui says being a "Special Investigator" is special.

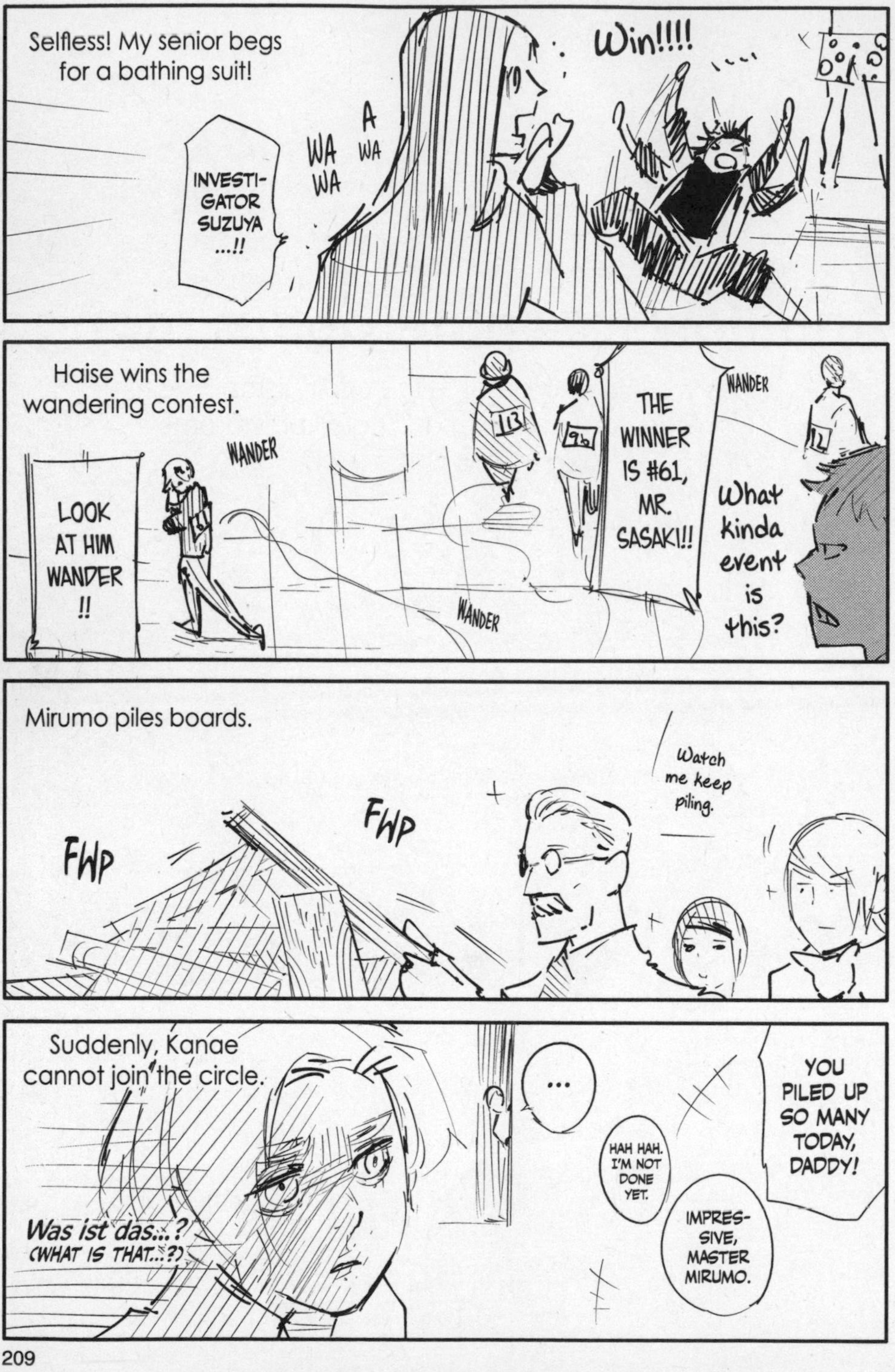

Win!!!!
...
A WA WA WA
INVESTIGATOR SUZUYA ...!!
Selfless! My senior begs for a bathing suit!
WANDER
THE WINNER IS #61, MR. SASAKI!!
What kinda event is this?
WANDER
Haise wins the wandering contest.
LOOK AT HIM WANDER !!
WANDER
Watch me keep piling.
FWP
Mirumo piles boards.
FWP
YOU PILED UP SO MANY TODAY, DADDY!
...
HAH HAH. I'M NOT DONE YET.
IMPRESSIVE, MASTER MIRUMO.
Suddenly, Kanae cannot join the circle.
Was ist das...?
(WHAT IS THAT...?)

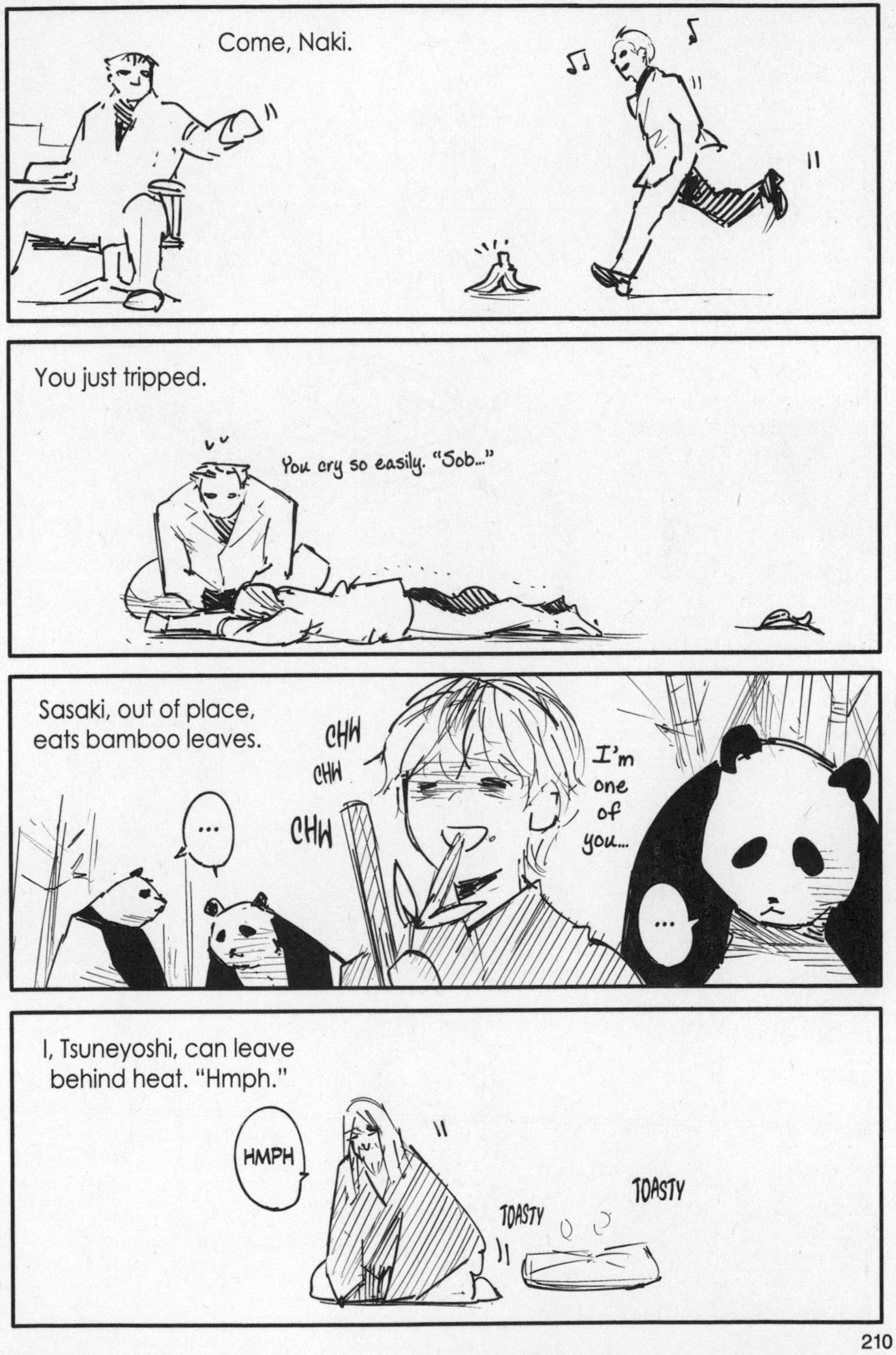
Come, Naki.
You just tripped.
You cry so easily. "Sob..."
Sasaki, out of place, eats bamboo leaves.
I'm one of you...
...
CHW
CHW
CHW
...
I, Tsuneyoshi, can leave behind heat. "Hmph."
TOASTY
TOASTY
HMPH

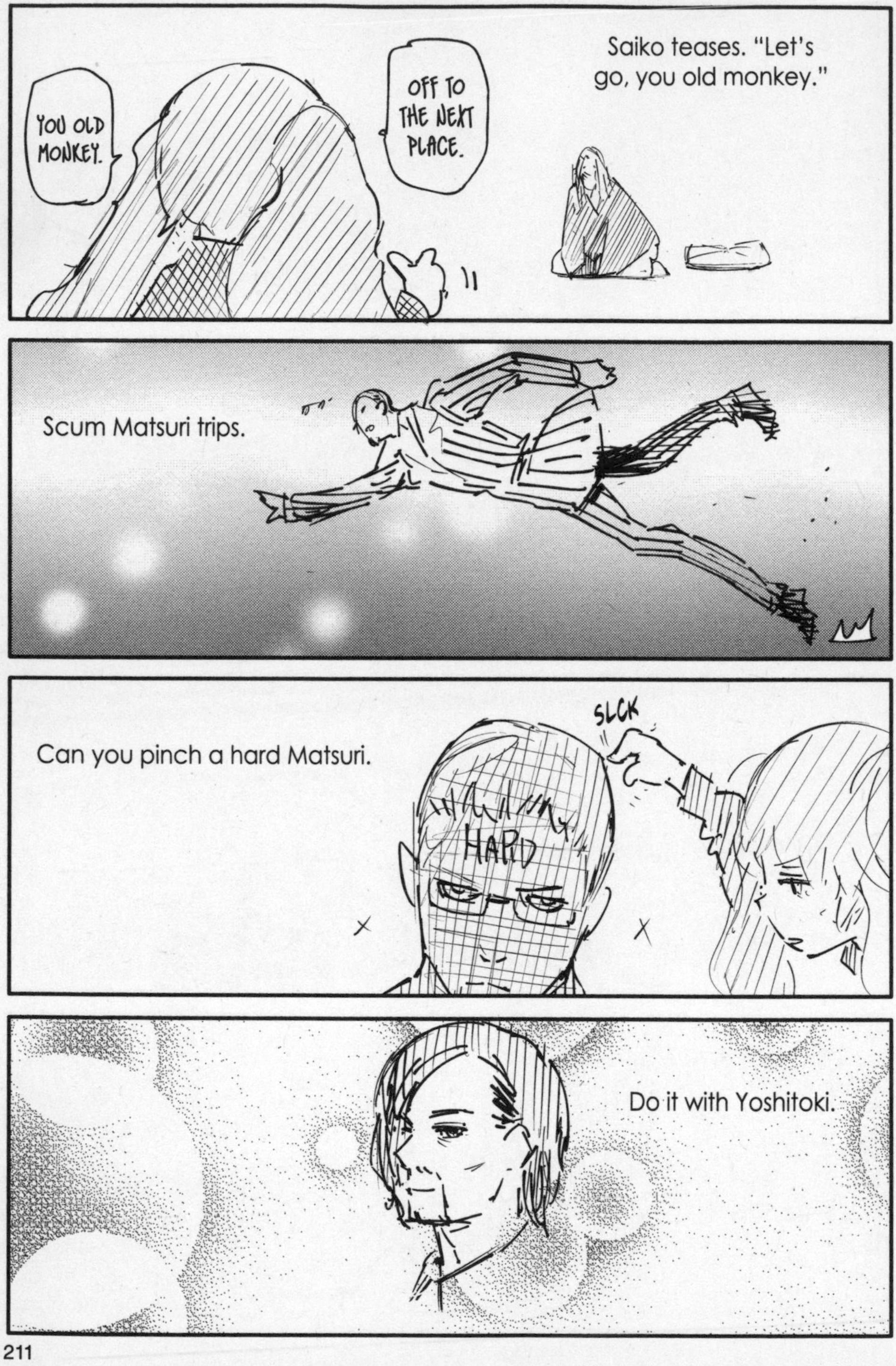
Saiko teases. "Let's go, you old monkey."
OFF TO THE NEXT PLACE.
YOU OLD MONKEY.
Scum Matsuri trips.
SLCK
Can you pinch a hard Matsuri.
HARD
Do it with Yoshitoki.

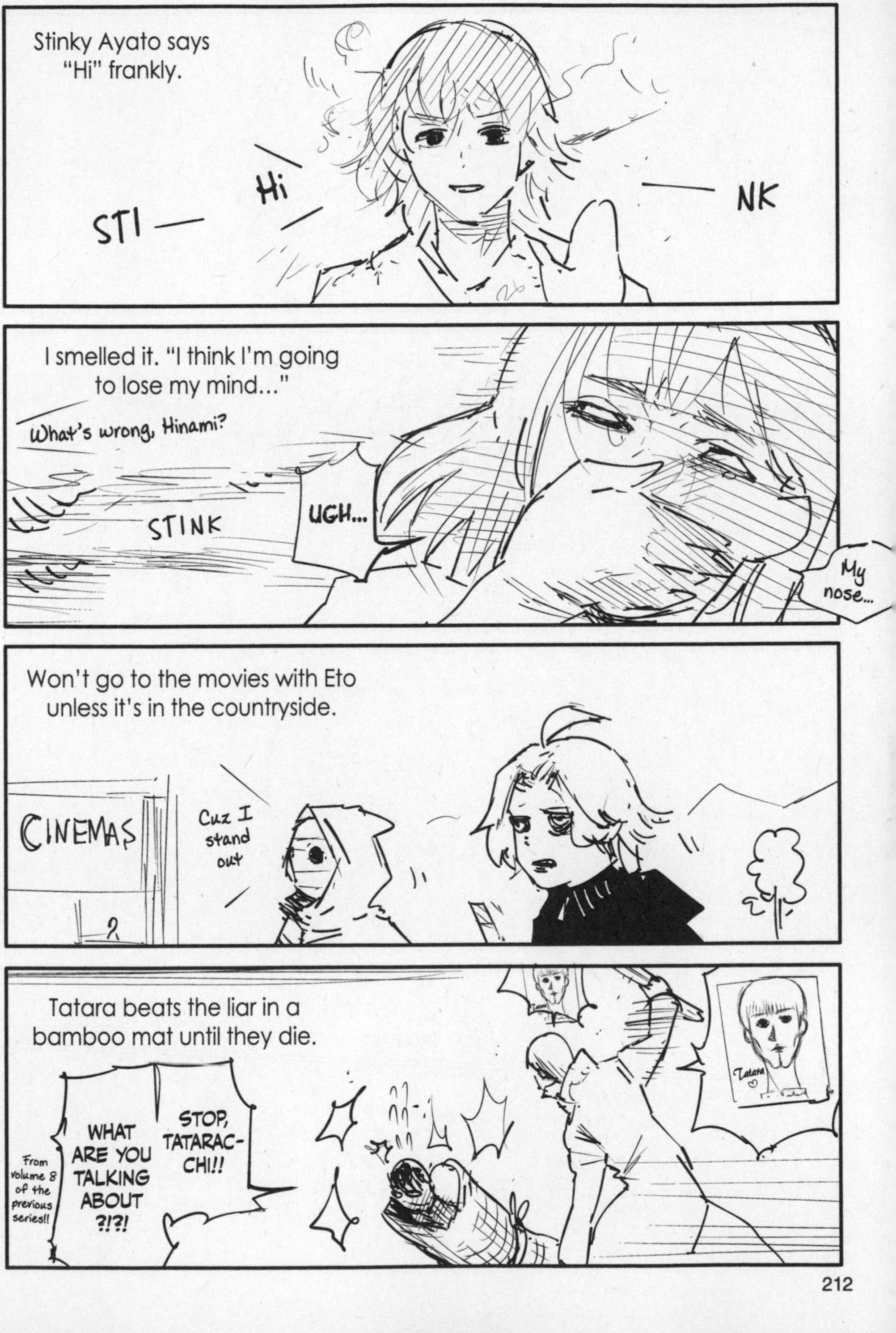

Stinky Ayato says "Hi" frankly.
NK
Hi
STI
I smelled it. "I think I'm going to lose my mind..."
My nose...
UGH...
What's wrong, Hinami?
STINK
Won't go to the movies with Eto unless it's in the countryside.
Cuz I stand out
CINEMAS
Tatara beats the liar in a bamboo mat until they die.
Tatara
STOP, TATARAC-CHI!!
WHAT ARE YOU TALKING ABOUT ?!?!
From volume 8 of the previous series!!

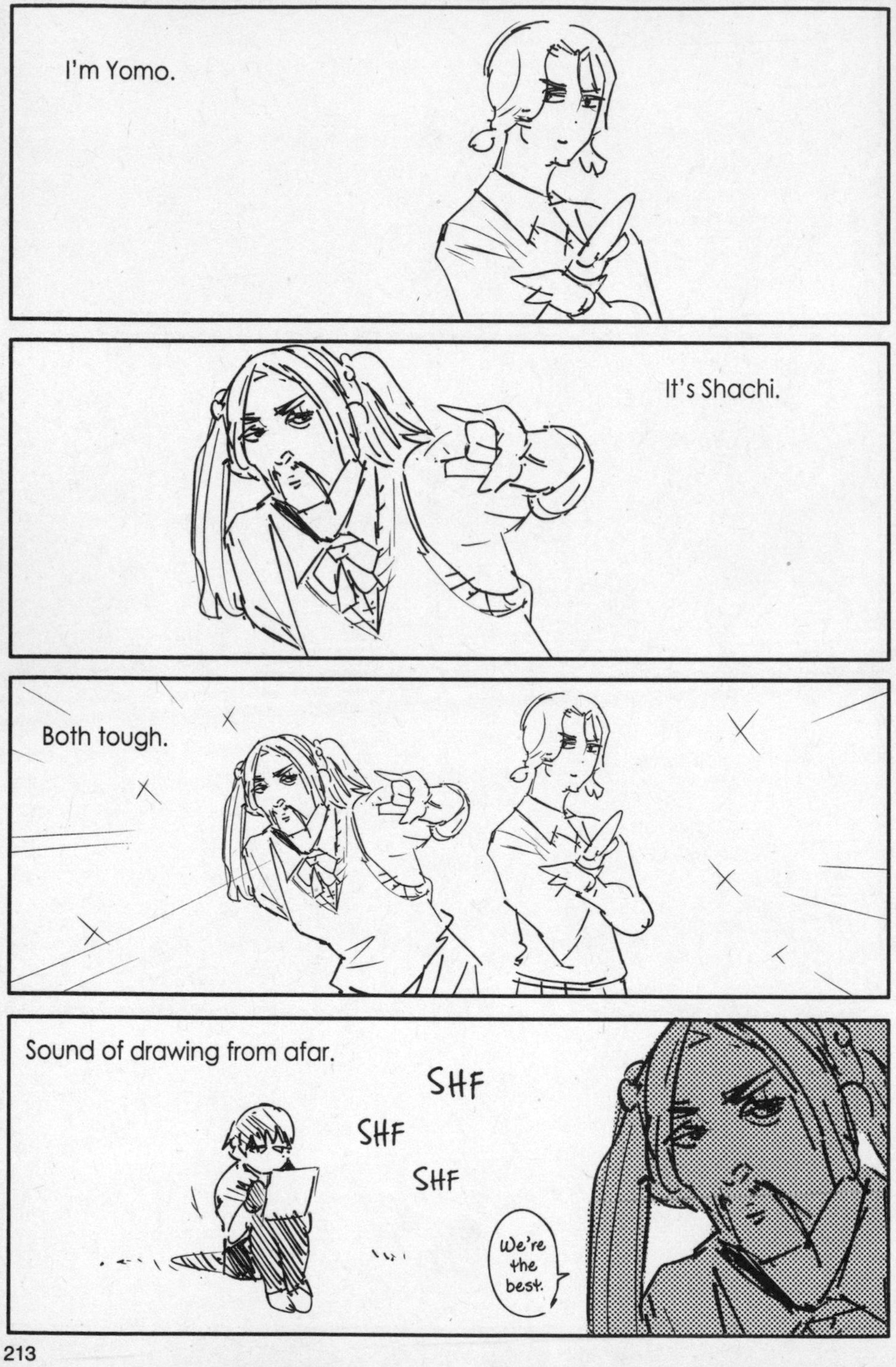
I'm Yomo.
It's Shachi.
Both tough.
Sound of drawing from afar.
SHF
SHF
SHF
We're the best.
...

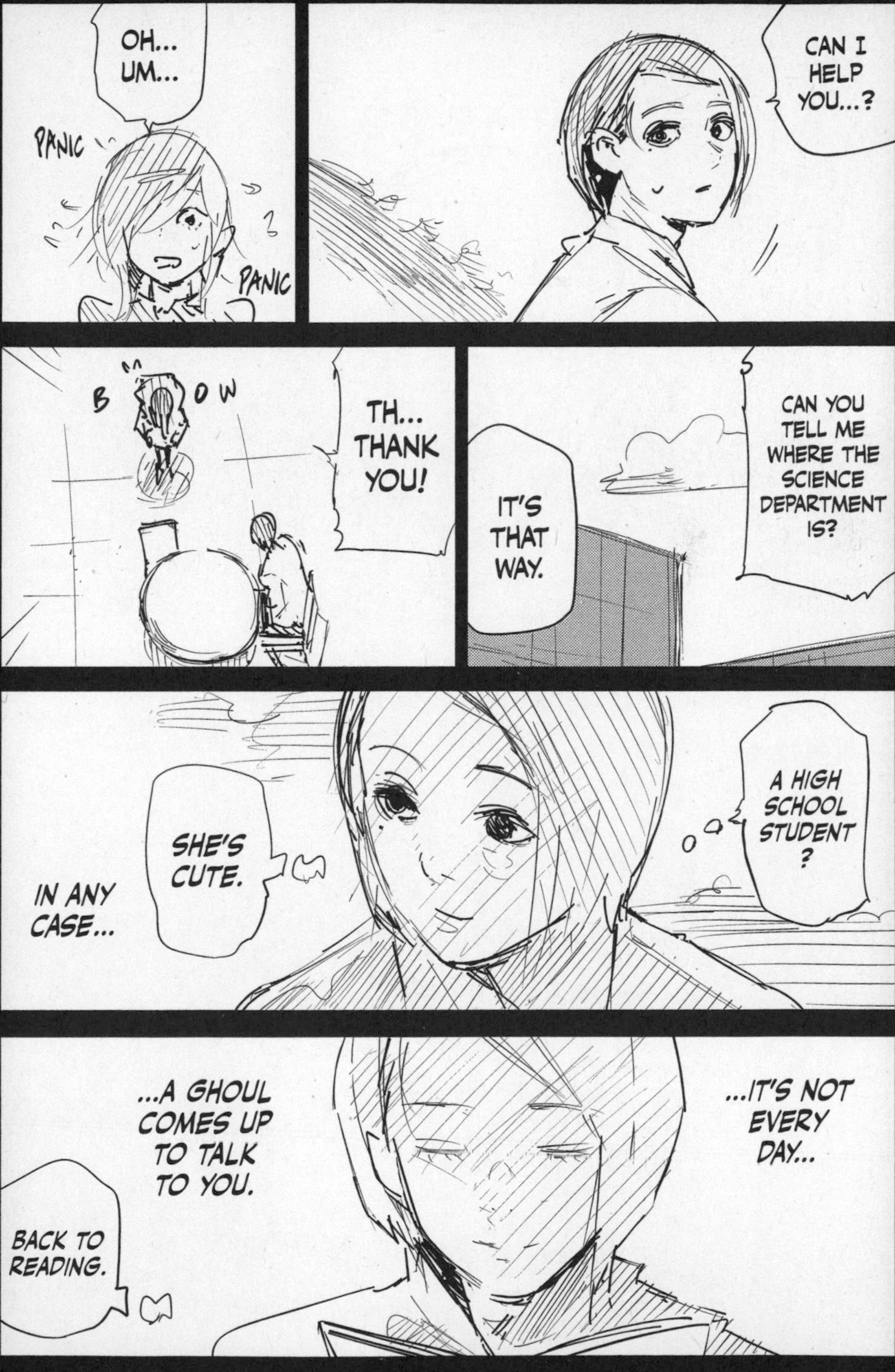
CAN I HELP YOU...?
OH... UM...
PANIC
PANIC
CAN YOU TELL ME WHERE THE SCIENCE DEPARTMENT IS?
IT'S THAT WAY.
TH... THANK YOU!
BOW
A HIGH SCHOOL STUDENT ?
SHE'S CUTE.
IN ANY CASE...
...IT'S NOT EVERY DAY...
...A GHOUL COMES UP TO TALK TO YOU.
BACK TO READING.

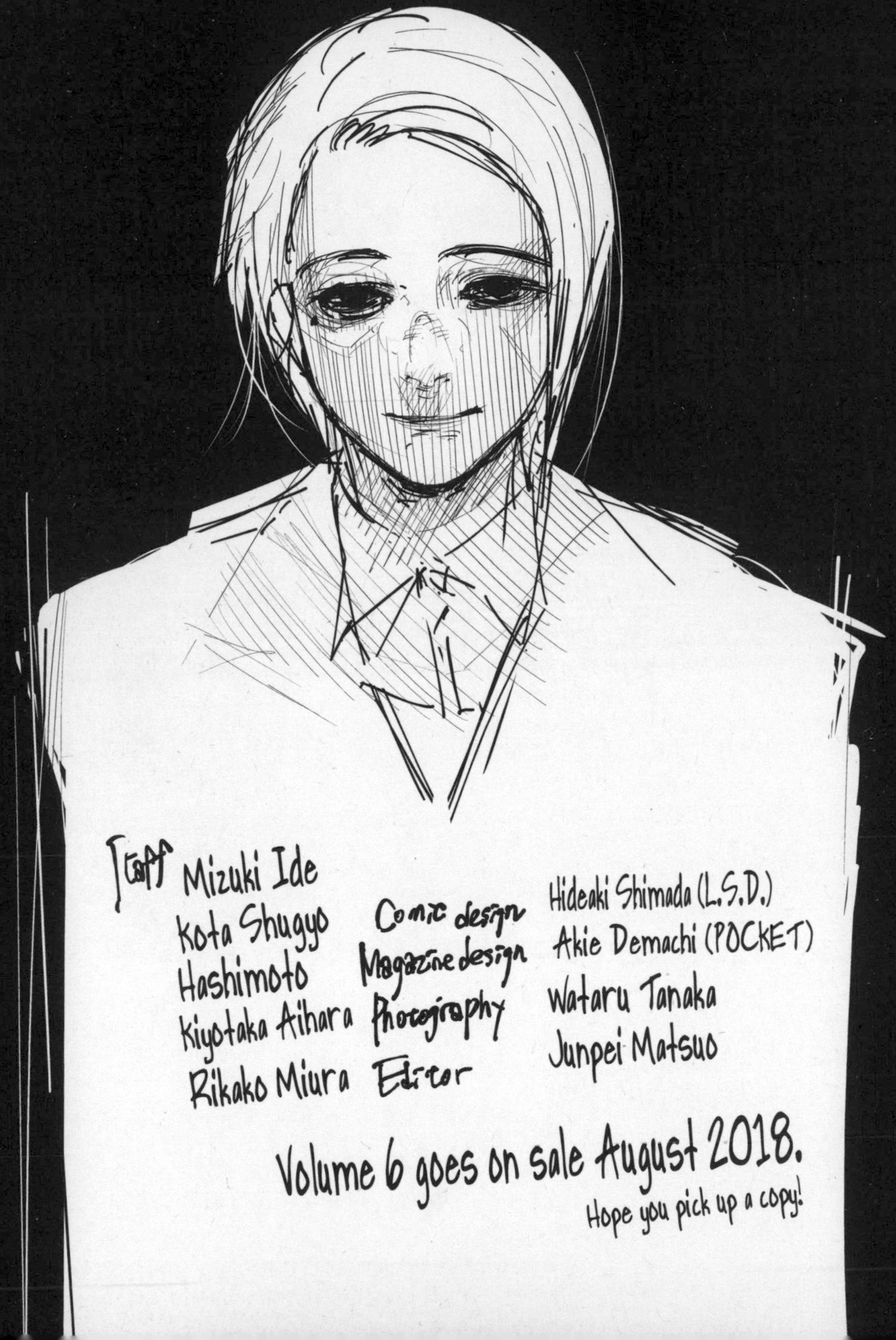

Staff
Mizuki Ide
Kota Shugyo
Hashimoto
Kiyotaka Aihara
Rikako Miura
Comic design Hideaki Shimada (L.S.D.)
Magazine design Akie Demachi (POCKET)
Photography Wataru Tanaka
Editor Junpei Matsuo
Volume 6 goes on sale August 2018.
Hope you pick up a copy!

hOUL:re

Ryukitsu Badge

Special badge awarded to investigators for outstanding achievement. The CCG's highest-ranking official, the General Chairman, conducts the presentation ceremony.

It is the highest honor an investigator can receive.

TOKYO G

Kijima Squad

(Squad Leader)

- **Shiki Kijima**
  キジマ 式 （きじま しき）

  Special Investigator (Class 53)
  Former interrogator at Cochlea

  - Age: 43 (DOB 12/16) ♂ • Blood type: A • Height/weight: 157cm/66kg
  - Quinque: Rotten Follow (Rinkaku – Rate/S) A chainsaw-type Quinque made from the Kakuho of Jail's (a Ghoul Kijima was pursuing) older brother. Tetoro (Kokaku – Rate/S) Allows users to freeze opponents.
  - Honors: None in particular
  - Hobbies: Dismantling Ghouls, crossword puzzles, tap dancing

- **Nimura Furuta**
  旧多 二福 （ふるた にむら）

  Rank 1 Investigator

  - Age: Unknown (DOB 2/29) ♂ • Blood type: AB • Height/weight: 175cm/66kg
  - Quinque: Tsunagi (custom) (Bikaku – Rate/C)
  - Honors: None in particular
  - Hobbies: None in particular

GHOUL:re

SUI ISHIDA is the author
of the immensely popular
Tokyo Ghoul and several
Tokyo Ghoul one-shots,
including one that won
second place in the *Weekly
Young Jump* 113th Grand
Prix award in 2010. *Tokyo
Ghoul:re* is the sequel to
Tokyo Ghoul.

Story and art by
SUI ISHIDA

TOKYO GHOUL:RE © 2014 by Sui Ishida
All rights reserved.
First published in Japan in 2014 by SHUEISHA Inc., Tokyo.
English translation rights arranged by SHUEISHA Inc.

Translation Joe Yamazaki
Touch-Up Art & Lettering Vanessa Satone
Design Shawn Carrico
Editor Pancha Diaz

The stories, characters and incidents mentioned in this publication are entirely fictional.

Printed in the U.S.A.

Published by VIZ Media, LLC
P.O. Box 77010
San Francisco, CA 94107

10 9 8 7 6 5 4 3 2 1
First printing, June 2018

viz.com

VIZ SIGNATURE
vizsignature.com

PARENTAL ADVISORY
TOKYO GHOUL: RE is rated T+ for Older Teen and is recommended for ages 16 and up. This volume contains violence and gore.

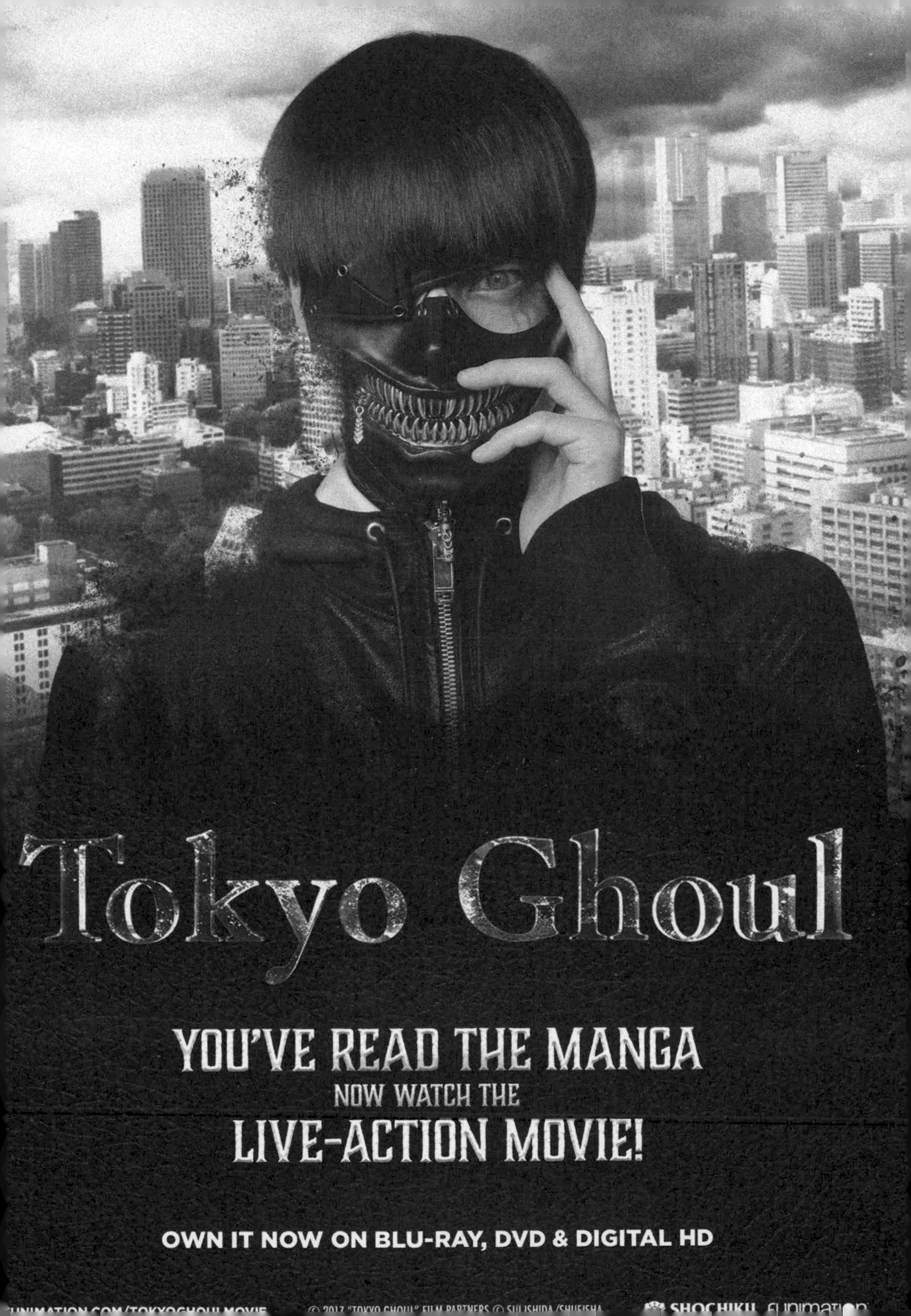
Tokyo Ghoul
YOU'VE READ THE MANGA
NOW WATCH THE
LIVE-ACTION MOVIE!
OWN IT NOW ON BLU-RAY, DVD & DIGITAL HD
© 2017 "TOKYO GHOUL" FILM PARTNERS © SUI ISHIDA/SHUEISHA
SHOCHIKU

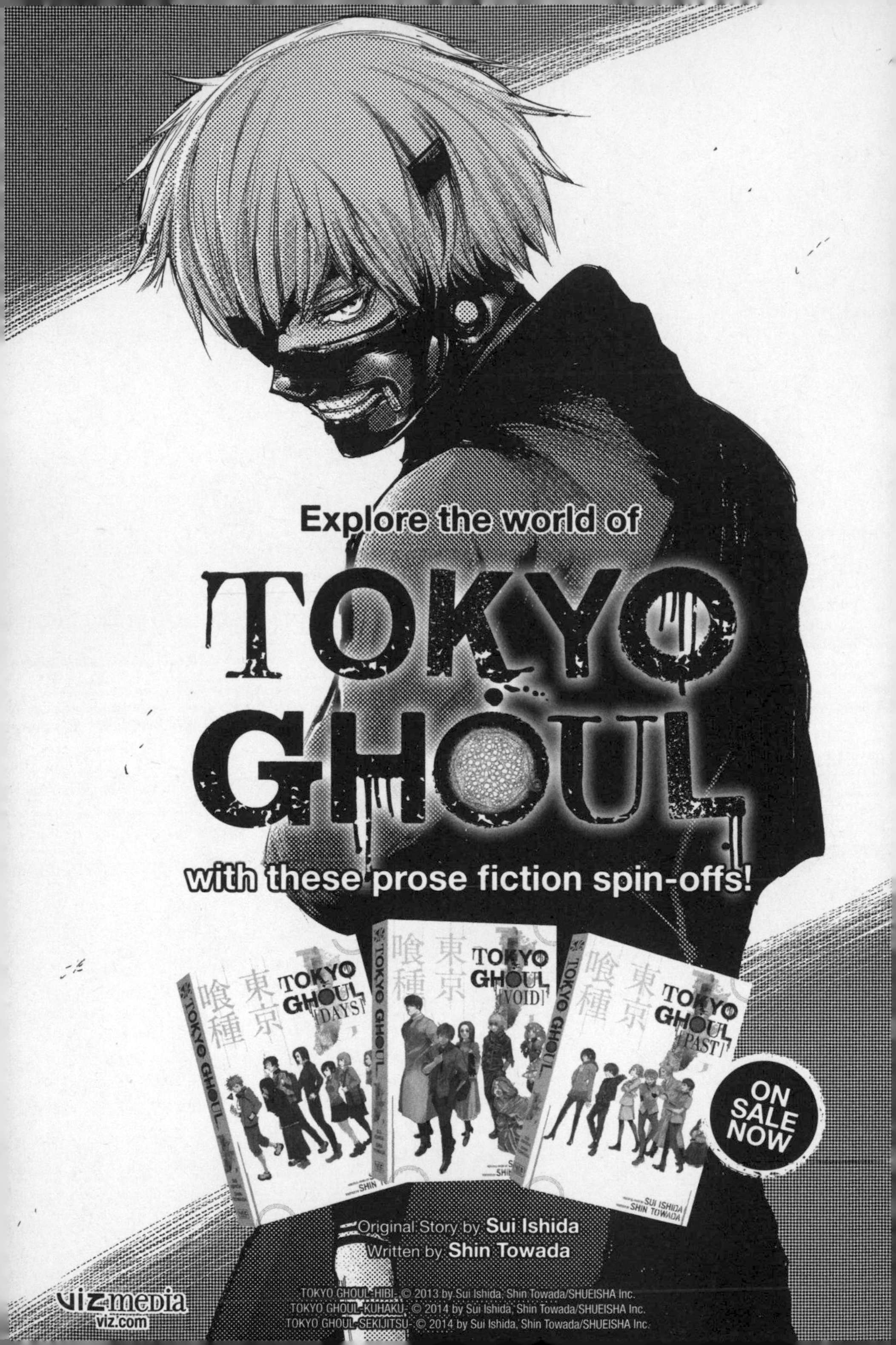
Explore the world of
TOKYO GHOUL
with these prose fiction spin-offs!
東京喰種
TOKYO GHOUL [DAYS]
TOKYO GHOUL [VOID]
TOKYO GHOUL [PAST]
ON SALE NOW
Original Story by Sui Ishida
Written by Shin Towada
VIZ media
viz.com
TOKYO GHOUL-HIBI- © 2013 by Sui Ishida, Shin Towada/SHUEISHA Inc.
TOKYO GHOUL-KUHAKU- © 2014 by Sui Ishida, Shin Towada/SHUEISHA Inc.
TOKYO GHOUL-SEKIJITSU- © 2014 by Sui Ishida, Shin Towada/SHUEISHA Inc.

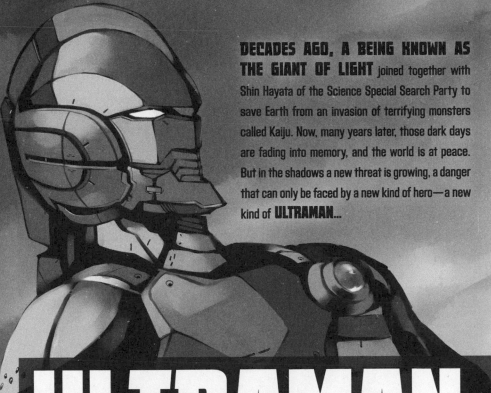

DECADES AGO, A BEING KNOWN AS THE GIANT OF LIGHT joined together with Shin Hayata of the Science Special Search Party to save Earth from an invasion of terrifying monsters called Kaiju. Now, many years later, those dark days are fading into memory, and the world is at peace. But in the shadows a new threat is growing, a danger that can only be faced by a new kind of hero—a new kind of ULTRAMAN...

ULTRAMAN

STORY & ART BY
EIICHI SHIMIZU
TOMOHIRO SHIMOGUCHI

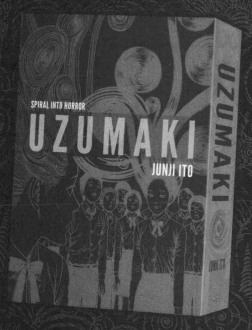

TOKYO GHOUL:re

This is the last page.
TOKYO GHOUL:re reads right to left.

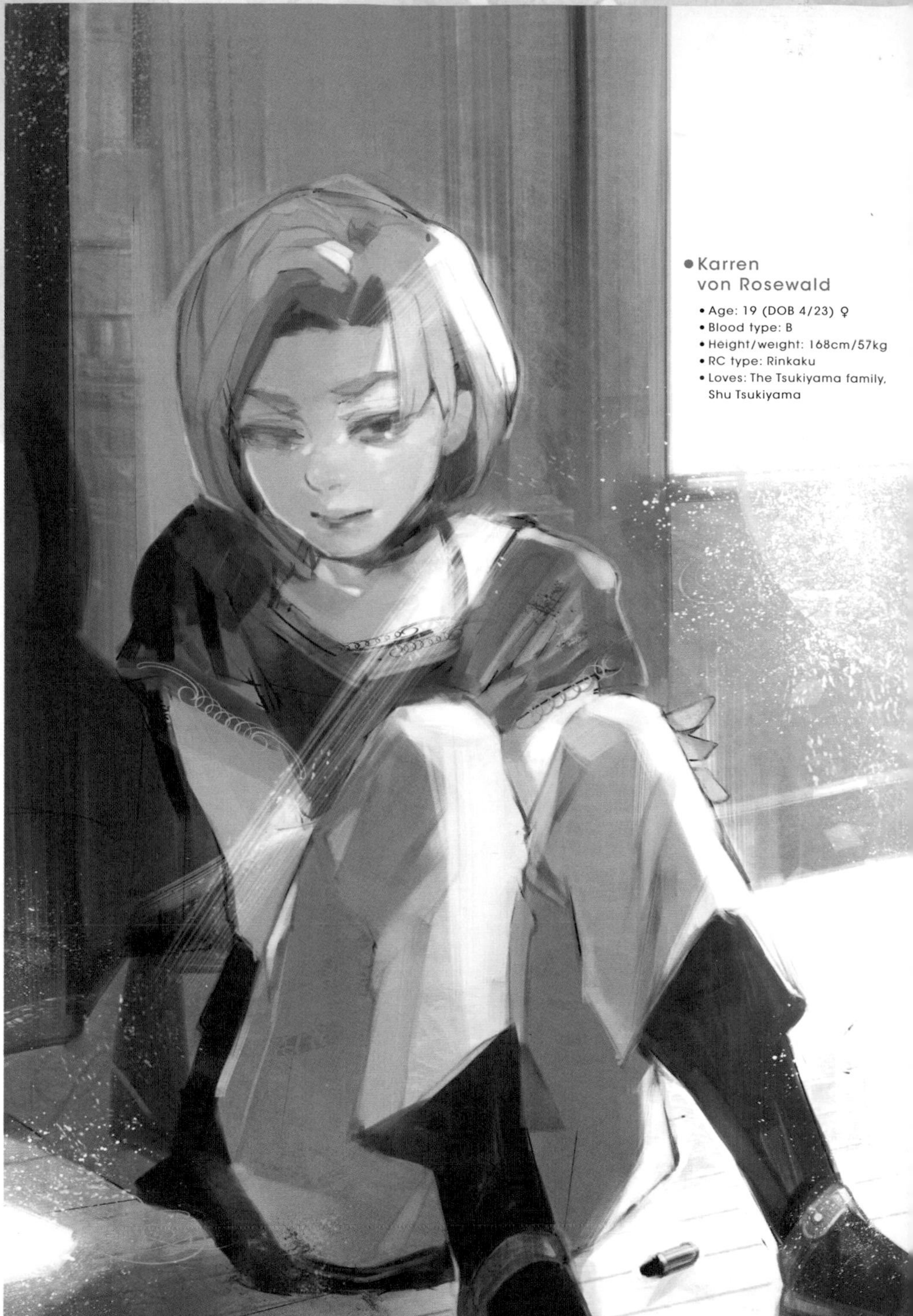

● Karren von Rosewald

- Age: 19 (DOB 4/23) ♀
- Blood type: B
- Height/weight: 168cm/57kg
- RC type: Rinkaku
- Loves: The Tsukiyama family, Shu Tsukiyama

"I saw the **Reaper**.

He was beautiful."

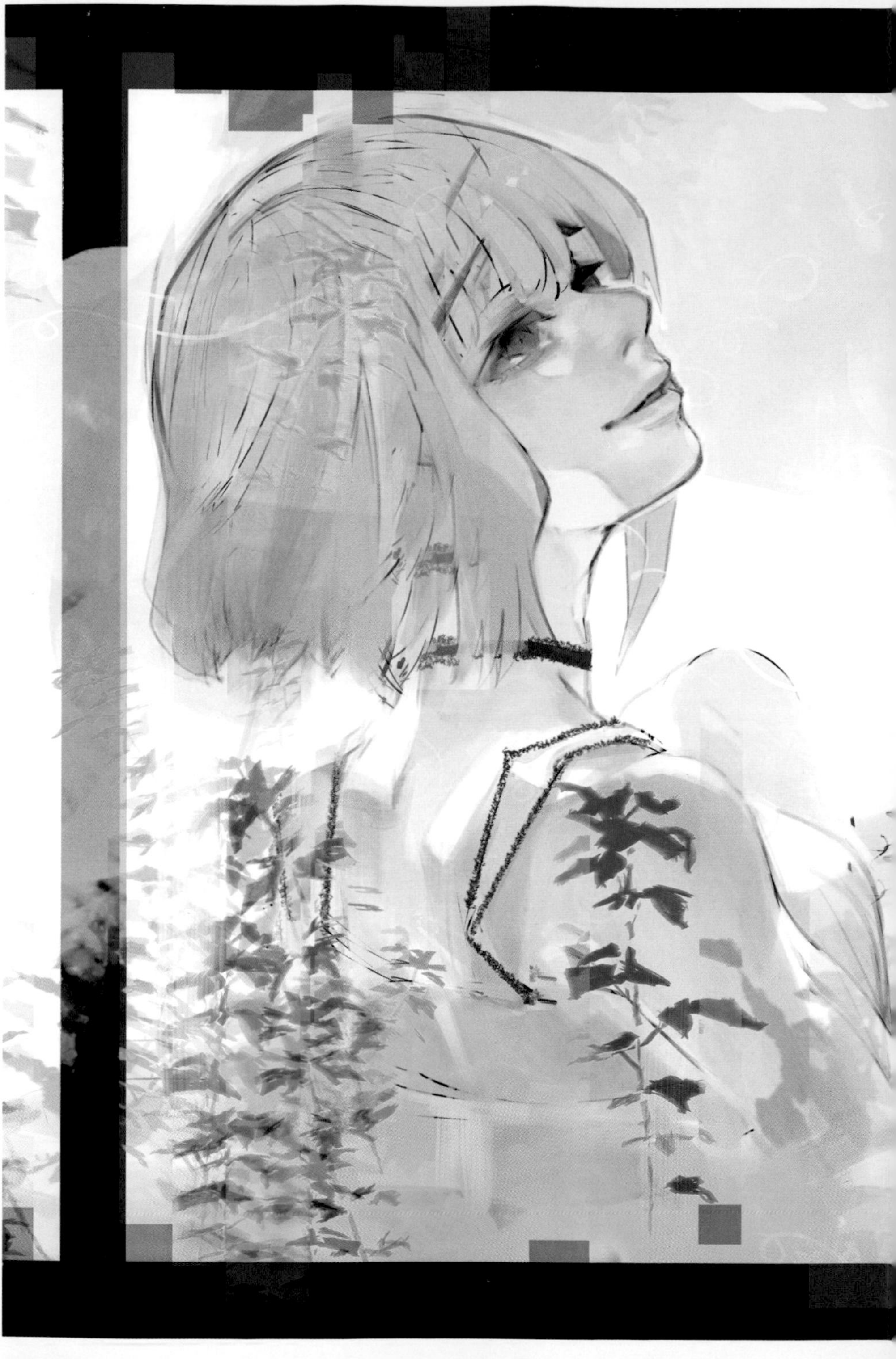

*

Three melted heads, like mortar in a blender.

Miracles have seen better days. It lies on cold concrete.

Killed.
I killed them.
Did I kill them?

The eyes open like genitals, as if to say hello.

The heads speak to me in my mother's voice.

"You."
"You."
"You."

"You."
"What made you think you were loved?"
"You are so ugly."

"Ugh…"

The kind abuse repeated in the box.
The sky flickered like a signal.

Before I knew it, nine thorns leaped from my thoracic cavity.
My diaphragm trembled as if it were about to cry.

(My body!)

Now utterly confused, I began climbing the steel tower.
The rail I touched rusted black.

(I am made of poison!)
(No, that woman is poison.)

(Climb, climb.)

(It's not enough to die for.)
(Climb. Higher, higher!)

*

The entrails of those already gone stretched toward heavens from the top of the tower.

The entrails entwined like a rope.
I desperately tried to pull it in.

Mush, mush, mush.

The knot was almost at the sun.

My beloved tower of corpses.
I climbed higher as I climaxed each time I held the rope. I couldn't see the ground anymore.

The tower began to shake.
It whispered in my mother's voice.

"Automatic failure of happiness, intangible infant."

(Oh)

"My sweet apathetic soul."

"Your parents didn't raise you right."

And died.